Writing Home

ALAN BENNETT

faber and faber

First published in 1994
by Faber and Faber Limited
3 Queen Square London WC1N 3AU
Revised edition first published in 1997
This paperback edition first published in 1998

Photoset by Parker Typesetting Service, Leicester
Printed and bound in Great Britain by Mackays of Chatham PLC,
Chatham, Kent

A CIP record for this book
is available from the British Library

ISBN 0–571–19667–5

Contents

List of Illustrations

The drawing on page 84 showing the removal of Miss Shepherd's van is by David Gentleman.

Introduction

In a Manner of Speaking

This book brings together the talks, diaries and occasional journalism that I have written over the last twenty years or so, mostly for the BBC or the *London Review of Books*. I have called the book *Writing Home*, though there is plenty here that has nothing to do with home and some of it, looked back on, that seems not to have much to do with me.

Most of the journalism was grudgingly undertaken, in particular the book reviews, which were teased out of me (in both senses) by my friend Mary-Kay Wilmers, the present editor of the *London Review of Books*. There are writers, I'm told, who dash off these occasional pieces with ease and pleasure before turning back, reinvigorated, to the job in hand. Not me, I'm afraid. Book reviewing is not my element, demanding a breadth of reading and reference that I generally do not have and which writing plays seldom requires; the result is I find myself either covering up or showing off, while at the same time opting to write in what I imagine to be a metropolitan mode.

That I should admit to having a choice in the way I write isn't an advertisement for versatility so much as an anxiety about sincerity, and it takes me back to a not quite primal scene of my youth.

I was born and brought up in Leeds, where my father was a butcher. As a boy, I sometimes went out on the bike delivering orders to customers, one of whom was a Mrs Fletcher. Mrs

Fletcher had a daughter, Valerie, who went away to school then to London, where she got a job with a publishing firm. She did well in the firm, becoming assistant to one of the directors, whom, though he was much older than she was, she eventually married. The firm was Faber and Faber, and the director was T. S. Eliot. So there was a time when I thought my only connection with the literary world would be that I had once delivered meat to T. S. Eliot's mother-in-law.

A few years later, when my dad had sold the shop but we were still living in Leeds, my mother came in one day and said, 'I ran into Mrs Fletcher down the road. She wasn't with Mr Fletcher; she was with another feller – tall, elderly, very refined-looking. She introduced me, and we passed the time of day.' And it wasn't until some time later that I realized that, without it being one of the most momentous encounters in western literature, my mother had met T. S. Eliot. I tried to explain to her the significance of the great poet, but without much success, *The Waste Land* not figuring very largely in Mam's scheme of things.

'The thing is,' I said finally, 'he won the Nobel Prize.'

'Well,' she said, with that unerring grasp of inessentials which is the prerogative of mothers, 'I'm not surprised. It was a beautiful overcoat.'

I can imagine that meeting: Mam smiling desperately, as she and Dad always did when they were out of their depth; nodding a good deal, too, so as not to have to speak; and, if she has to contribute, trying to 'speak properly', though without 'putting it on' – 'putting it on' being one of the (several) charges Dad had against my mother's sisters, Auntie Kathleen and Auntie Myra, both of whom nursed pretensions to refinement and who never knew, in Dad's words, 'when to keep their traps shut'. It would have taken more than T. S. Eliot to silence them.

Having said goodbye to Mrs Fletcher and the refined gentleman (whoever he was), Mam would have come away wishing she 'had a bit more off' – i.e. more confidence – and regretting that she and Dad hadn't been educated, believing as they always did that education was a passport to social ease and that had they been able to 'stop on at school' everything would have been different.

It wouldn't, of course: it was class and temperament, not want of education, that held their tongues; 'stopping on at school' might have loosened them a little but it never entirely loosened mine, and I stopped on at school one way or another until I was twenty-eight. Thirty years on, this book still shows traces of speech difficulties they passed on to me. What am I doing in book reviews, for instance, but trying to 'speak properly'? What is writing sketches if not 'putting it on'? 'Just be yourself,' my parents would say, ignoring the fact that this was something they themselves seldom managed to be, at any rate in company. Funny and voluble on their own, the slightest social pressure sent them into smiling, nodding silence. But it was different for me, they thought. I was educated; I could be myself; I had a self it was not embarrassing to be.

So I see this awkward encounter with Mr Eliot as a kind of parable, a prefiguring of how, when I did eventually start to write, it should be in two different voices, metropolitan ('speaking properly') and provincial ('being yourself'), and that if one takes T. S. Eliot to represent Art, Culture and Literature (all of them very much in the upper case) and my mother to represent life (resolutely in the lower case), then what happened at the end of Shire Oak Street that morning nearly forty years ago went on happening when I started to write plays and is still happening between the covers of this book.

It wasn't that I had any particular affection for the works of T. S. Eliot. I had seen, though not entirely understood, *The Cocktail Party* when it came to the Leeds Grand Theatre on its provincial tour, and also *Murder in the Cathedral* done at a local church. I had even read *Notes Towards a Definition of Culture*, but only because I was soon to try for a Cambridge scholarship and it seemed the kind of thing one was expected to read. And just as one read what one was expected to read, so, when I started very haltingly to write, I wrote what one was expected to write: not, that is, about life, in my case the life of a northern town – provincial, dull and at that time, the late 1950s, largely unwritten about – but the life that I had read about in books or seen at Saturday matinées at the Grand Theatre – metropolitan, literary and middle-class. Admittedly these first efforts only took the form of sketches and parodies which I performed at concerts in my college at Oxford, but they led in 1960 to my collaboration in the revue *Beyond the Fringe*.

Whether *Beyond the Fringe* was satire was much debated at the time. It scarcely mattered, as there was no debate about how funny it was, though I had a sneaking feeling that some of my contributions were less so and more earnest than the rest. After a spell in the West End the show went to America in 1962, where, despite opening in New York during the week of the Cuban Missile Crisis, it was a great success. Towards the end of 1963 it was decided to revamp it, and, with the addition of some new sketches, the show went into a second edition. It was perhaps the earnestness coming out, and also because I had been away from home for more than a year, that made me decide for the first time to try to speak and write in a voice that was my own, rather than putting one on. I was going to be myself.

What I chose to do was a monologue about death, and in particular death and its supposedly comic aspects in the North of England. Now in 1963 death was not the subject of lively interest it has since become, and even today it's hardly big on Broadway. This was also death as met with in Morecambe and Blackpool, neither of them settings which an American audience could be expected to know about or want to. I performed the sketch nightly for six months to the embarrassment of my colleagues and the stunned silence of the audience, and when the revue ended it was nearly ten years before I ventured to write about the North of England again. So much for 'being myself'. The first round had gone to T. S. Eliot.

And he won the second round too, because when I wrote my first stage play, *Forty Years On* (1968), it had much more to do with art than life, wasn't life at all in fact but the product (and it's not to disparage it to say it's also the waste product) of years of reading memoirs of literary life, tales of novelists' schooldays and the period between the wars. Or, as a character in a later play puts it, somewhat over-elaborately, as he describes a bookshelf:

Horizon, the parish magazine, *Scrutiny*, the school chronicle, all the nice distinctions, careful cross-bearings and distances on the pedometer. Relief maps of anxiety, the contours of small depressions. Get Well cards and invites to funerals. Notes under the general heading of amelioration. Deaths in vicarages and (Little) Venice. Bottles of Jordan water and basinfuls of the warm South. School and the trenches, good talk and good wine and the never-ending siege of the country house. Messages from an unvisited island.

(*The Old Country*)

Set in a public school, part play and part revue, *Forty Years On* had nothing to do with any world that I'd known outside books, let alone with 'being myself'. An elegy for the passing of a traditional England, the play is constructed round a series of literary parodies, which in retrospect I can see were a form of apprenticeship, as indeed had been some of the sketches in *Beyond the Fringe*. Art comes out of art; it begins with imitation, often in the form of parody, and it's in the process of imitating the voices of others that one comes to learn the sound of one's own. This is the theory anyway. With me it hasn't quite worked out like that, the fissure between provincial and metropolitan persisting, T. S. Eliot and my mother shaking but never joining hands.

For a while after *Forty Years On* I kept the voice I had acquired for the stage and the voice I had been born with for television; my first TV plays, *A Day Out* (1972) and *Sunset Across the Bay* (1974), were both set in the North, as have been many others since. This neat division didn't persist all that long, but though I've written several TV plays 'speaking properly' (e.g. *An Englishman Abroad* and *102 Boulevard Haussmann*) I've still only managed one Northern play for the stage (*Enjoy*) and that was hardly a success, as mystifying to a West End audience as the northern way of death had been on Broadway. Sometimes I envy the power of my contemporary, the poet Tony Harrison, who has one defiant Leeds voice to which he subjugates everything he writes. But he had to suffer for his voice at school as I never did, and so sets more store by it (nor, I imagine, did his mother ever meet T. S. Eliot). Not that having two voices is much of a problem, more a worry about consistency – and even that seldom surfaces nowadays, except on occasions like this when I try to make sense of what I have written.

It could all, I suppose, be less ponderously put in terms of wearing this hat or that, except that hats are supposed to give you confidence, not make you uneasy. Speaking is more of a trial than writing, particularly speaking on the radio, and several of the pieces printed here began as radio talks. I tried to lose my northern accent at one period, then reacquired it, and now don't know where I am, sometimes saying my 'a's long, sometimes short, and 'u's a continuing threat, words like 'butcher' and names like 'Cutbush' always lying in ambush. Anyone who ventures south of the Trent is likely to contract an incurable disease of the vowels; it's a disease to which for some reason weather forecasters are particularly prone, and lecturers in sociology.

Some of these pieces have been hard to classify. *Dinner at Noon* is as much reminiscence as it is record, so that puts it among the recollections. I'm sure the address to the Prayer Book Society belongs under 'Books', but what does one call 'Tit for Tatti' or 'Going Round'? Skits, I suppose, though I don't like the word; humour, though I don't like that very much either — too close to the BBC's 'light-hearted look at'. These are the pieces I'm most unsure about and the ones most likely to have dated but for completeness's sake I've included them under 'Stocking Fillers', just glad that I don't feel tempted to write like that any more. I know there are repetitions, but I've made no attempt to eradicate them lest I be left with a literary doily. I think it was Kenneth (not the Chancellor of the Exchequer) Clark who said that most of us have only a few pennies to rattle about in our tins (though he had more, in every sense, than most).

I would like to thank Jean McNicol of the *London Review of Books*, who has edited much of this material. As I've said, many of the pieces would not have been written but for the persistence of Mary-Kay Wilmers and the staff of the *London Review*. The LRB has been in existence now for fifteen years, and it seems to me (and not just because I occasionally contribute to it) the liveliest, most serious and also the most radical literary periodical we have. I would have liked the LRB to have published this volume, as it did the original version of *The Lady in the Van*. That proved not to be possible, but I hope this book will at least bring the paper to the notice of a wider readership.

This revised edition of *Writing Home* includes some additional material: extracts from my diaries for 1993, 1994 and 1995 and some previously overlooked entries from 1986, all again from the *London Review of Books*; there is also an account of the making of the film *The Madness of King George* and two memorial addresses, one delivered at the dedication of a window to A. E. Housman in Westminster Abbey, the other at a service for Peter Cook in Hampstead Parish Church. This latter address was done from what the *Dictionary of National Biography* always refers to as 'personal knowledge'; the Housman piece was not done from personal knowledge at all, though the presentation of the window fell to Enoch Powell, who did know Housman, having been his pupil, and who confirmed that the poet's small talk was largely confined to food.

I note in the new diary material a continuation of that mild depression which has persisted for over sixteen years now, coterminous with the life of a seedy and increasingly discredited administration. In a previously unpublished entry for 11 May 1986 I mention a local doctor in Settle whose prompt action at the time of Chernobyl probably safeguarded the future health of the children of the neighbourhood. Unlike mid-Wales and Cumbria, our area of Craven was not thought to be a heavy fallout area; at any rate we were not told so. It was only six or nine months later that it was revealed that Craven had been a fall-out black spot and that Whitehall had kept it quiet. It was a repetition, admittedly on a smaller scale, of the cover-up after the Windscale nuclear accident in 1957 (see page 336). This confirms me in my view, set out in the introduction to *An Englishman Abroad*, that the damage done out of conviction by self-confessed traitors like Burgess and Blunt does not compare with the far greater injuries done to this country by politicians and higher civil servants out of cowardice, self-advancement and a need to save their own skins. The last sixteen years has seen a good deal of that.

I was both surprised and gratified by the success of this book when it was first published in October 1994 though there were, of course, drawbacks. It is standard form nowadays that, bringing out a book, one has to go on a promotional tour. That autumn I was escorted round a good many bookshops in the provinces signing copies of *Writing Home*, these public signing sessions invariably followed by an even longer stint doing what is called 'signing stock'. One was seldom allowed to sign stock in the shop, presumably because the public would be outraged at the speed and indifference with which one did it. Instead I was taken into a back room where, unfeeling and unobserved, I could polish off four hundred copies an hour.

Waterstone's don't seem to have many back rooms so I usually ended up signing stock in the staff room. Bath, Cambridge, Manchester, Leeds . . . these staff rooms are the same: one goes in and there is a nylon shirt hanging up to dry, some socks over the radiator, half a pizza three days old and a bicycle wheel.

I was following round the Australian novelist Peter Carey. He was more Calvinist in his approach than I was, so when fans asked him if he would sign their book 'To Mum and Dad' he refused on the semantically quite proper grounds that they weren't *his* Mum and Dad. Lacking his Antipodean grit I put down whatever the purchasers wanted; since they'd paid £17.50 I felt they were entitled to it.

Still, readers do ask one to write some very peculiar things in their books. One youth said, 'Could you put "To Christine. I'm sorry about last night and it won't happen again!"' This I dutifully did and then had to sign it 'Alan Bennett'. If I'm ever deemed worthy of a biography I'd like to see what Andrew Motion or Humphrey Carpenter will make of that.

Alan Bennett

Past and Present

===

The Treachery of Books

‘What you want to be’, Mam said to my brother and me, ‘is gentlemen farmers. They earn up to £10 a week.’ This was in Leeds some time in the early years of the war, when my father, a butcher at Armley Lodge Road Co-op, was getting £6 a week and they thought themselves not badly off. So it's not the modesty of my mother's aspirations that seems surprising now but the direction. Why gentlemen farmers? And the answer, of course, was books.

We had, it's true, had some experience of a farm. I was five when the war started, and Monday 4 September 1939 should have been my first day at school; but that was not to be. I wish I could record our family as gathered anxiously round the wireless, as most were at eleven o'clock that Sunday morning, but I already knew at the age of five that I belonged to a family that without being in the least bit remarkable or eccentric yet managed never to be quite like other families. If we had been, my brother and I would have been evacuated with all the other children the week before, but Mam and Dad hadn't been able to face it. So, not quite partaking in the national mood and, as ever, unbrushed by the wings of history, Mr Chamberlain's broadcast found us on a tram going down Tong Road into Leeds. Fearing the worst, my parents had told my brother and me that we were all going out into the country that day and we were to have a picnic – something I had hitherto only come across in books. So

3

on that fateful Sunday morning what was occupying my mind was the imminent conjunction of life with literature; that I should remember nothing of the most momentous event in the twentieth century because of the prospect of an experience found in books was, I see now, a melancholy portent.

Nor was the lesson that life was not going to live up to literature slow in coming, since the much-longed-for picnic wasn't eaten as picnics were in books, on a snowy tablecloth set in a field by a stream, but was taken on a form in the bus station at Vicar Lane, where we waited half that day for any bus that would take us out of the supposedly doomed city.

Early that afternoon a bus came, bound for Pateley Bridge, the other side of Harrogate. Somewhere along the way and quite at random the four of us got off and our small odyssey was ended. It was a village called Wilsill, in Nidderdale. There were a few houses, a shop, a school and a church and, though we were miles from any town, even here the stream had been dammed to make a static water tank in readiness for the firefighters and the expected bombs. Opposite the bus-stop was a farm. My father was a shy man and, though I'm sure there were many larger acts of bravery being done elsewhere that day, to knock at the door of the farm and ask some unknown people to take us in still seems to me to be heroic. Their name was Weatherhead and they did take us in and without question, as people were being taken in all over England that first week of the war.

That night Dad took the bus back to Leeds, my mother weeping as if he were returning to the front, and there at Wilsill we stayed – but for how long? My brother, then aged eight, says it was three weeks; to me, three years younger, it seemed months; but, weeks or months, very happy it was until, once it became plain nothing was going to happen for a while, we went back home, leaving Byril Farm (which is now, alas, not a farm and has carriage lamps) standing out in my mind as the one episode in my childhood that lived up to the story-books.

I had read quite a few story-books by this time, as I had learned to read quite early by dint, it seemed to me, of staring over my brother's shoulder at the comic he was reading until suddenly it made sense. Though I liked reading (and showed off at it), it was soon borne in upon me that the world of books was only distantly related to the world in which I lived. The families I read about were not like our family (no family ever quite was). These families had dogs and gardens and lived in country towns equipped with thatched cottages and mill-streams, where the children had adventures, saved lives, caught villains, and found treasure before coming home, tired but happy, to eat sumptuous teas off chequered tablecloths in low-beamed parlours presided over by comfortable pipe-smoking fathers and gentle aproned mothers, who were invariably referred to as Mummy and Daddy.

In an effort to bring this fabulous world closer to my own, more threadbare, existence, I tried as a first step substituting 'Mummy' and 'Daddy' for my usual 'Mam' and 'Dad', but was pretty sharply discouraged. My father was hot on anything smacking of social pretension; there had even been an argument at the font because my aunties had wanted my brother given two Christian names instead of plain one.

Had it been only stories that didn't measure up to the world it wouldn't have been so bad. But it wasn't only fiction that was fiction. Fact too was fiction, as textbooks seemed to bear no more relation to the real world than did the story-books. At school or in my *Boy's Book of the Universe* I read of the minor wonders of nature – the sticklebacks that haunted the most ordinary pond, the newts and toads said to lurk under every stone, and the dragonflies that flitted over the dappled surface. Not, so far as I could see, in Leeds. There were owls in hollow trees, so the nature books said, but I saw no owls – and hollow trees were in pretty short supply too. The only department where nature actually lined up with the text was frog-spawn. Even in Leeds there was that, jamjars of which I duly fetched home to stand beside great wilting bunches of bluebells on the backyard window-sill. But the tadpoles never seemed to graduate to the full-blown frogs the literature predicted, invariably giving up the ghost as soon as they reached the two-legged stage when, unbeknownst to Mam, they would have to be flushed secretly down the lav.

It was the same when we went on holiday. If the books were to be believed, every seashore was littered with starfish and delicately whorled shells, seahorses in every rockpool and crabs the like of which I had seen only in Macfisheries' window. Certainly I never came across them at Morecambe, nor any of the other advertised treasures of the seashore. There was only a vast, untenanted stretch of mud and somewhere beyond it the sea, invisible, unpaddleable and strewn with rolls of barbed wire to discourage any parachutist undiscerning enough to choose to land there.

These evidences of war and the general shortage of treats and toys made me somehow blame the shortcomings of the natural world on the current hostilities. I don't recall seeing a magnolia tree in blossom until I was fifteen or so, and when I did I found myself thinking 'Well, they probably didn't have them during the war.' And so it was with shells and starfish and all the rest of Nature's delights: she had put these small treasures into storage for the duration, along with signposts, neon lights and the slot machines for Five Boys chocolate that stood, invariably empty, on every railway platform.

This sense of deprivation, fully developed by the time I was seven or eight, sometimes came down to particular words. I had read in many stories, beginning I suppose with *Babes in the Wood*, how the childish hero and heroine, lost in the forest, had nevertheless spent a cosy night bedded down on *pine needles*. I had never come across these delightfully accommodating features and wondered where they were to be found. Could one come across them in Leeds? It was not short of parks after all – Gott's Park, Roundhay Park – surely one of them would have pine needles.

And then there was *sward*, a word that was always cropping up in *Robin Hood*. It was what tournaments and duels were invariably fought on. But what was sward? 'Grass,' said my teacher, Miss Timpson, shortly; but I knew it couldn't be. Grass was the wiry, sooty stuff that covered the Rec in Moorfield Road where we played at night after school. That was not sward. So once, hearing of some woods in Bramley, a few miles from where we lived, I went off on the trail of sward, maybe hoping to come across pine needles in the process. I trailed out past the rhubarb fields at Hill Top, over Stanningley Road then down into the valley that runs up from Kirkstall Abbey. But all I found were the same mouldy old trees and stringy grass that we had at Armley. Pine needles, sward, starfish and sticklebacks – they were what you read about in books.

Books are where the gentlemen farmers must have come from too, from Winifred Holtby's *South Riding* perhaps, or something by Phyllis Bentley, both novelists my mother favoured – local celebrities (as much later was John Braine), writers who had escaped the mill or the mine and made good, the making good invariably taking the form of going Down South. These books, and those my brother and I read, would be borrowed from Armley Library at the bottom of Wesley Road, a grand turn-of-the-century building with a marble staircase and stained-glass swing doors.

The Junior Library was in a room of its own, and an institution more intended to discourage children from reading could not have been designed. It was presided over by a fierce

7

British Legion commissionaire, a relic of the Boer War, who, with his medals and walrus moustache was the image of Hindenburg as pictured on the German stamps in my brother's album. The books were uniformly bound in stout black or maroon covers, so whether they were Henty, Captain Marryat or (my favourite) Hugh Lofting, they looked a pretty unenticing read.

In contrast the Adults' Library was a bright and cheerful place, where Dad would be looking for something funny by Stephen Leacock or what he called 'a good tale', and Mam would be in Non-Fiction seeking her particular brand of genteel escape – sagas of couples who had thrown up everything to start a smallholding (gentlemen farmers in the making) or women like Monica Dickens who had struck out on their own. A particular favourite was William Holt, whose *I Haven't Unpacked* was one of the few books Mam ever bought, and again it was escape – the story of someone brought up, as she had been, in a mill town but who had bought a horse and gone off on his travels.

This theme of escape, very strong in Wells and Priestley, tantalized my parents for much of their lives. Dreams of leaving I suppose they had, and I now share them, feeling myself as nailed to my table as ever my Dad was to his shop counter. They never did escape quite, though they made a shot at it just once when, towards the end of the war, my father gave up his job at the Co-op, answered an advert in the *Meat Trades Journal* and got a job working for a private butcher in Guildford. And in Guildford for a year we lived. Down South. And there were thatched cottages and mill-streams and children who called their parents 'Mummy' and 'Daddy' – the world I had read about in my books, and the world Mam and Dad had read about in theirs.

But, thatched cottages or no thatched cottages, they were not

8

happy, and one miserable December night in 1945 the four of us got off the train at Holbeck and trailed disconsolately back to my grandma's house and reality. It was another lesson that you should not believe what you read in books.

From time to time after this my mother's hands would be covered in terrible eczema, the joints cracked open, the skin sealing away. 'My hands have broken out again,' she would say, and put it down to the wrong soap. But it was as if she was now caged in and this the only 'breaking out' she was capable of.

The few books we owned were largely reference books, bought by subscription through magazines: *Enquire Within, What Everybody Wants to Know* and, with its illustrations of a specimen man and woman (minus private parts and pubic hair), *Everybody's Home Doctor*. No book, whether from the library or otherwise, was ever on view. Anthony Powell's 'Books do furnish a room' was not my mother's way of thinking. 'Books untidy a room' more like, or, as she would have said, 'Books upset.' So if there were any books being read they would be kept out of sight, generally in the cabinet that had once held a wind-up gramophone, bought when they were first married and setting up house.

This undercover attitude to books persisted long after I had grown up and had accumulated books of my own. I worked in the spare room, though it was never dignified as such and just known as the junk room. That was where the books were kept now, and there among the broken lampshades and bits of old carpet and hemmed in by the sewing-machine and the family suitcases I would set up a table and work. To begin with it was for my degree, then it was research in medieval history, and finally writing proper. But to my mother it was all the same: to her my life had not changed since I was fourteen and doing School Certificate, so degree, research or writing plays was always called 'your swotting'.

9

As a young man my father had some literary ambitions, going in for competitions in magazines such as *Tit-Bits* and even sending in little paragraphs and being paid. By the forties his efforts were concentrated on one competition, Bullets, a feature of the magazine *John Bull*, the point of which was to come up with a telling phrase on a given topic, the phrase to be witty, ironic or ambiguous – in effect a verbal cartoon. Once he had regularly won small prizes, but though he went on plugging away during the war, and until the magazine folded in the late forties, he won only a few pounds.

I couldn't get the hang of Bullets or see the point or the humour of the entries that won; they seemed like Tommy Handley's jokes – everybody said they were funny, but they never made you laugh. If I missed *John Bull* when it closed down it was for its cover paintings, in particular the landscapes of Rowland Hilder – idyllic downland farms, beech trees against a winter sky – or the townscapes of deaf and dumb artist A. R. Thomson, as English as Norman Rockwell was American.

In later life my father was often ill and this started him reading again, only now his taste was much more eclectic and he would try any book he found on my shelves. Knowing nothing of reputation and just judging a book by whether he could 'get into it' or not, he lapped up Evelyn Waugh and Graham Greene, revelled in Nancy Mitford, but couldn't take (at opposite extremes) Buchan or E. F. Benson; Orwell he just about managed ('though there's not much of a tale to it'), and he liked Gavin Maxwell and especially Wilfred Thesiger. When he came to the episode in *Ring of Bright Water* where a Scots road-mender casually kills one of Maxwell's pet otters with a spade he burst out, 'Why, the bad sod!'

This phrase had a literary history and was something of a family joke. As a child Dad had been taken to the Grand Theatre to see *Uncle Tom's Cabin* and in the scene in which Uncle Tom was being flogged by the overseer, Simon Legree, a woman sitting next to Dad in the gallery shouted out, 'You bad sod!' The actor playing Simon Legree stopped, looked up at the gallery, leered, and then laid it on twice as hard.

Towards the end of his life I had so taken it for granted that our taste in reading coincided that I forgot how shy and fastidious my father was and how far his world still was from mine. Though there may have been a priggish element of 'I think you are now ready for this' about it, I did think that when I gave him Philip Roth's *Portnoy's Complaint* he would find it as funny as I did. Always anxious to talk about what he had read, on my next visit home he never mentioned it, and I later found it back on the shelf, the jacket marking the twenty pages or so that he had got through before deciding it was pornography and not something for him, and by implication not something for me, though nothing was ever said. It was a miscalculation that mortifies me to this day.

My mother was more broadminded and might have found *Portnoy's Complaint* quite funny, but Dad's literary renaissance never infected her, and for years her reading was largely confined to *Woman's Own* and in particular to the column written by Beverley Nichols, of whom she was a great fan. But seeing the Brontës frequently referred to in the *Yorkshire Evening Post* she began to persuade herself she had read them or perhaps would like to – maybe because (another escape story) if they hadn't got away from their surroundings they had at any rate transcended them. So on a bleak February day in the late forties she and I took the Keighley bus to Haworth to see the famous parsonage. Not so famous then, Haworth was still happily unaware of its potential as a tourist trap, its situation on the frontiers of *Last of the Summer Wine* country far in the future. The place must have had some charm, but it looked to me like any other grim mill town and all I could think as we toiled up that long hill was that it must be even more dismal on a Sunday.

We were the only visitors to the parsonage that day, and it was as dark and damp as it must have been when the famous trio lived there. Ramshackle and unrenovated, it was, even for 1948, a decidedly eccentric museum, looked after by a lady who, if not actually a contemporary of the Brontës, seemed their sister in suffering. Objects around the house were only haphazardly labelled: the sofa on which Emily died, for instance, just had pinned to it a yellowing piece of paper that said starkly, 'Sofa Emily died on'. Mam was horrified. The fireplace wanted blackleading and the curtains were a disgrace. 'Too busy writing their books to keep the place up to scratch,' was her comment.

Though this was long before the tasteful pall of heritage was laid across the past, the parsonage can have survived in this Victorian state only a few years longer. Had it been kept as it was then, it would today be in a museum itself, a museum of museums perhaps. It would certainly be more interesting and characteristic than the branch of Laura Ashley the parsonage is nowadays, though there's not much doubt which Mam would have preferred.

My parents always felt that had they been educated their lives and indeed their characters would have been different. They imagined books would make them less shy and (always an ambition) able to 'mix'. Quiet and never particularly gregarious, they cherished a lifelong longing to 'branch out', with books somehow the key to it. This unsatisfied dream they have bequeathed to me, so that without any conscious intention I find I am often including in plays or films what is essentially the same scene: someone is standing at a bookcase; it may be a boy with no education, not daring to choose a book, or a wife anxious to share in the literary world of men; it can be Joe Orton looking at Kenneth Halliwell's bookcase and despairing of ever catching up, or even Coral Browne, idly turning over the pages of Guy Burgess's books while being quizzed about Cyril Connolly, whom she does not know. One way or another they are all standing in for my parents and sharing their uncertainty about books. As for me, while I'm not baffled by books, I can't see how anyone can love them ('He loved books'). I can't see how anyone can 'love literature'. What does that mean? Of course, one advantage of being a gentleman farmer is that you seldom have to grapple with such questions.

Leeds Trams

There was a point during the Second World War when my father took up the double bass. To recall the trams of my boyhood is to be reminded particularly of that time.

It is around 1942 and we are living in the house my parents bought when they got married, 12 Halliday Place in Upper Armley. The Hallidays are handily situated for two tram routes, and if we are going into town, rather than to Grandma's in Wortley, the quickest way is to take a number 14. This means a walk across Ridge Road, down past the back of Christ Church (and Miss Marsden's the confectioner's) to Stanningley Road. Stanningley Road is already a dual carriageway because the tram tracks running down the middle of the road are pebbled and enclosed by railings, so splitting what little traffic there is into lanes. The Stanningley trams are generally somewhat superior to those on other routes, more upholstered, and when the more modern streamlined variety comes in after the war, it is more likely to be found on this route than elsewhere. But the drawback with the Stanningley Road trams is that they come down from Bramley or even Rodley, and are always pretty crowded, so more often than not we go for the other route, the number 16, which means walking up Moorfield Road to Charleycake Park and Whingate Junction.

This being the terminus, the tram is empty and as likely as not waiting, or, if we've just missed one, the next will already be in sight, swaying up Whingate. We wait as the driver swings outside and with a great twang hauls over the bogey ready for the journey back, while upstairs the conductor strolls down the aisle, reversing the seats before winding back the indicator on the front. The driver and conductor then get off and have their break sat on the form by the tram-stop, the driver generally older and more solid than the conductor (or, I suppose, the conductress, though I don't recall conductresses coming in until after the war).

Dad is a smoker, so we troop upstairs rather than going 'inside', the word a reminder of the time when upstairs was also outside. On some trams in 1942 it still is, because in these early years of the war a few open-ended trams have been brought back into service. We wedge ourselves in the front corner to be exposed to the wind and weather, an unexpected treat, and also an antidote to the travel sickness from which both my brother and I suffer, though I realize now that this must have been due as much to all the smoking that went on as to the motion of the tram itself. Neither of us ever actually is sick, but it's not uncommon and somewhere on the tram is a bin of sand just in case.

So the four of us – Mam, Dad, my brother and me – are ensconced on the tram sailing down Tong Road into town or, if we are going to see Grandma, who lives in the Gilpins, we will get off halfway at Fourteenth Avenue.

Around 1942, though, we come into the double-bass period, when some of our tram journeys become fraught with embarrassment. Dad is a good amateur violinist, largely self-taught, so taking up the double bass isn't such a big step. He practises in the front room, which is never used for anything else, and, I suppose because the bass never has the tune, it sounds terrible; he sounds as if he's sawing (which he also does, actually, as one of his other hobbies is fretwork). Though the instrument is large the repertoire is small, except in one area: swing. Until now Dad has never had much time for swing, or popular music generally; his idea of a good time is to turn on the Home Service and play along with the hymns on *Sunday Half Hour*, or (more tentatively) with the light classics that are the staple of Albert Sandler and his Palm Court Orchestra. But now, with Dad in the grip of this new craze, Mam, my brother and I are made to gather round the wireless, tuned these days to the Light Programme, so that we can listen to dance-band music.

'Listen, Mam. Do you hear the beat? That's the bass. That'll be me.'

Dad has joined a part-time dance band. Even at eight years old I know that this is not a very good idea and just another of his crazes (the fretwork, the home-made beer) – schemes Dad has thought up to make a bit of money. So now we are walking up Moorfield Road to get the tram again, only this time to go and watch Dad play in his band somewhere in Wortley, and our carefree family of four has been joined by a fifth, a huge and threatening cuckoo, the double bass.

Knowing what is to happen, the family make no attempt to go upstairs, but scuttle inside while Dad begins to negotiate with the conductor. The conductor spends a lot of his time in the little cubby-hole under the winding metal stairs. There's often a radiator here that he perches on, and it's also where the bell-pull hangs, in those days untouchable by passengers, though it's often no fancier than a knotted leather thong. In his cubby-hole the conductor keeps a tin box with his spare tickets and other impedimenta which at the end of the journey he will carry down to the other end of the tram. The niche that protects the conductor from the passengers is also just about big enough to protect the double bass, but when Dad suggests this there is invariably an argument, which he never wins, the clincher generally coming when the conductor points out that strictly speaking 'that thing' isn't allowed on the tram at all. So while we sit inside and pretend he isn't with us, Dad stands on the platform grasping the bass by the neck as if he's about to give a solo. He gets in the way of the conductor, he gets in the way of the people getting on and off, and, always a mild man, it must have been more embarrassing for him than it ever was for us.

Happily this dance-band phase, like the fretwork and the herb beer, doesn't last long. He gets bored with the fretwork, the herb beer regularly explodes in the larder, and the double bass is eventually advertised in the Miscellaneous column of the *Evening Post* and we can go back to sitting on the top deck again.

After the war we move to Far Headingley, where Dad, having worked all his life for the Co-op, now has a shop of his own just below the tram-sheds opposite St Chad's. We live over the shop, so I sleep and wake to the sound of trams: trams getting up speed for the hill before Weetwood Lane, trams spinning down from West Park, trams shunted around in the sheds in the middle of the night, the scraping of wheels, the clanging of the bell.

It is not just the passage of time that makes me invest the trams of those days with such pleasure. To be on a tram sailing down Headingley Lane on a fine evening lifted the heart at the time just as it does in memory. I went to school by tram, the fare a halfpenny from St Chad's to the Ring Road. A group of us at the Modern School scorned school dinners and came home for lunch, catching the tram from another terminus at West Park. We were all keen on music and went every Saturday to hear the Yorkshire Symphony Orchestra in the Town Hall, and it was on a tram at West Park that another sixth-former, 'Fanny' Fielder, sang to me the opening bars of Brahms's Second Piano Concerto, which I'd never heard and which the YSO was playing that coming Saturday. Trams came into that too, because after the concert many of the musicians went home by tram (though none with a double bass), sitting there, rather shabby and ordinary and often with tab ends in their mouths, worlds away from the Delius, Walton and Brahms which they had been playing. It was a first lesson to me that art doesn't have much to do with appearances, and that ordinary middle-aged men in raincoats can be instruments of the sublime.

Odd details about trams come back to me now, like the slatted platforms, brown with dust, that were slung underneath either end, like some urban cowcatcher; or the little niche in the glass of the window on the seat facing the top of the stairs so that you could slide it open and hang out; and how convivial trams were, the seats reversible so that if you chose you could make up a four whenever you wanted.

How they work was always a mystery. As a child I had difficulty in understanding that the turning motion the driver made with the handle was what drove the tram, it seeming more like mixing than driving. And then there was the imposing demeanour of the ticket inspectors, invested with a spurious grandeur on a par with the one-armed man who showed you to your seat in Schofield's Café, or the manager of the Cottage Road cinema in his dinner-jacket, or gents' outfitters in general.

I don't recall anyone ever collecting tram numbers, but the route numbers had a certain mystique, the even numbers slightly superior to the odd, which tended to belong to trams going to Gipton, Harehills, or Belle Isle, parts of Leeds where I'd never ventured. And Kirkstall will always be 4, just as Lawnswood is 1.

Buses have never inspired the same affection – too comfortable and cushioned to have a moral dimension. Trams were bare and bony, transport reduced to its basic elements, and they had a song to sing, which buses never did. I was away at university when they started to phase them out, Leeds as always in too much of a hurry to get to the future, and so doing the wrong thing. I knew at the time that it was a mistake, just as Beeching was a mistake, and that life was starting to get nastier. If trams ever come back, though, they should come back not as curiosities, nor, God help us, as part of the heritage, but as a cheap and sensible way of getting from point A to point B, and with a bit of poetry thrown in.

Not History at All . . .

When Brian Harrison invited me to take part in this seminar,* I warned him that I knew little about university theatre and that, a magisterial overview not being forthcoming, the most you were likely to get would be an exercise in licensed name-dropping. Even in that I find I was over-optimistic. I recall few names that became names – the broadcaster Russell Harty, the director Patrick Garland, and then I'm done. It hardly adds up to a generation. So if I confine myself to what is really a memoir of my somewhat atypical career outside university theatre it's not because I believe that this was the most significant thing going on at the time, just that I so seldom ventured out of my college that I didn't have much notion of what was happening outside at all.

The years after the war had seen a great flowering of talent in the theatre in Oxford. The backlog of ex-service under-graduates who came up then included some, like film director John Schlesinger, who were veterans of that ENSA concert party Peter Nichols has written about in *Privates on Parade*. There was sterner stuff in directors in the making like Lindsay Anderson and Ronald Eyre, and even management was represented in the infant impresario Michael Codron. Leading the rout and easily the most colourful figure, in clothes which

* On 'The History of the University since 1945', held at Nuffield College, Oxford, in 1986.

20

in those days started fights but now would scarcely lift an eyebrow, was Kenneth Tynan. By 1954 these were long gone, but most undergraduates still came up, as I did, after two years' national service.

I imagine the point may have come up in earlier sessions of this seminar, but the abolition of national service later in the fifties must have made an incalculable difference to the university in all sorts of ways. I speak only for myself. Although when I came up I was two years older than most undergraduates are now, and was here in all for some eight years, it took me all that time to hit upon what I wanted to do. I found my niche eventually, but if I'd come here straight from school I should probably still be looking.

My college, Exeter, was in 1954 a fairly modest, not to say undistinguished establishment. Which was precisely why I'd chosen it, as I'd stand a better chance there, I reasoned, than at socially more exalted foundations such as Trinity, which I think was in the same group. My mother had actually suggested I try Balliol. (She mispronounced the name, of course, but I'm not sure I didn't at that time.) My mother's idea of a university owed less to Cardinal Newman than it did to Beverley Nichols, of whose weekly column in the *Woman's Own* she was a great fan. Beverley had been to Balliol, my mother said, so why not me? There were plenty of reasons, the chief one being that it was so academically tip-top. It was also quite ugly. At seventeen I was a bit of an architectural snob. I was coming to Oxford hell-bent on going through a process I suppose I thought of as 'blossoming', and I saw as an essential ingredient in the blossoming process a nice period background. Exeter's strong artistic suit was its connection with Morris and Burne-Jones, but the Pre-Raphaelites weren't quite back in fashion by 1954 so even in this department I thought it no great shakes. Still it did have its picturesque corners, though not enough to attract the more fastidious and discerning applicants, who would, I hoped, be winnowed out by the glories of Magdalen or St John's, thus leaving the field open to dowdy and devious creatures like myself.

One jokes about these options now but they were no joke then, and it all had to be decided at home – the wireless off, the kitchen table cleared and wiped (no more certain way of being rejected, I thought, than jam on the entrance form). In the mystifying permutations of choice my parents stood by helpless; they scarcely knew what a university was, let alone the status of its component parts. The irony, of course, was that when I finally landed up at Exeter I found that in my callow assessment of college form I had not been unique. Others had reasoned in the same way, with the result that Exeter was far harder to get into than anywhere else.

In 1954 Exeter was an inward-looking college. Few of its members figured in the wider life of the university, and it had a close-knit family atmosphere. This should have meant that in-college societies were that much more vigorous, but this certainly wasn't true of drama. So far as I recall, Exeter's dramatic society was in abeyance the whole of my time as an undergraduate. This was no doubt a relief to the college. Dons have always been dubious about drama. Though rowing, and indeed running, can scarcely be said to hone the mind, they have always been looked on more favourably than the stage. Acting is somehow thought to rot both mind and character. Whereas it would be inconceivable to stop someone rowing or running in their final year, it was (and perhaps still is) quite common to forbid him or her to act.

None of which – acting, rowing, or running – bothered me much, as I wasn't inclined to do any of them. I had carried over from national service (and in this I'm sure I wasn't alone) a suspicion of volunteering, of joining, indeed of conspicuous activity of any sort. So I became a member of no clubs; no cards decorated my mantelpiece; no societies met in my rooms. It was all very dull and, apart from the fact that I had to share a set with someone who had been in the same barrack room for much of my national service and whom I loathed and who loathed me, I was quite happy.

In the army one of my friends was Michael Frayn, subsequently the novelist and playwright. He was now at Cambridge, and his attitude was the opposite of mine. In the first week of his first term he was writing for *Varsity*, had enrolled with the Footlights, and had taken to university life with a large, unselfconscious splash. In those days we used to correspond, and whereas my letters accuse him of 'selling out', his letters to me, slightly more sensibly, urge me to pull my socks up. On one point in particular we differed absolutely and this was college life. Whereas I was happy to settle down in the cosy, undemanding atmosphere of the Exeter Junior Common Room, Frayn regarded his college, Emmanuel, as little more than an address – and not a very smart one at that. And since Exeter was to me all that I wanted in the way of a club, this was another reason for not joining any others. There was certainly no thought of joining either OUDS or the Experimental Theatre Club, both somehow sounding wrong: OUDS the plump, self-assured, good-mannered theatre of the Establishment; ETC the opposite – seedy, plaintive, out at the elbows. What there was not, of course, was anything like the Cambridge Footlights, with a tradition of revue and comedy-writing. I'm sure if there had been I would have failed to join that too.

So it was with a certain sense of already having thrown in the towel that I settled down to college life. The JCR in Exeter at that time was more central to the life of the college than in other colleges I visited. At the heart of it was the institution of the Suggestions Book. As a repository of actual suggestions, the

Suggestions Book was useless, but it served besides as a college newspaper, a diary, a forum for discussion, and a space in which those who were so inclined could attempt to amuse and even paddle in the direction of literature. The result was a volume (in time a succession of volumes) that was parochial, silly and obscene, but to me, and possibly to others, of a particular value. A family atmosphere, a captive audience and a set of shared references are good conditions in which to learn to write, and I think it was through my contributions to the JCR Suggestions Book that I first realized I could make people laugh and liked doing it.

At the end of each term the JCR held a smoking-concert. These smokers were really just a dramatized version of the Suggestions Book: vulgar, private, silly – all the things my literary friends abhorred. They were uproarious drunken affairs, confined to members of the college and in the direct line of those camp concerts POWs spent their time acting in when they weren't busy tunnelling under the foundations. One regular feature was a Queen's Christmas Broadcast; very tame it would seem now, but in those pre-satirical days, when HMQ's annual pronouncement was treated with hushed reverence, the very idea of it seemed sacrilegiously funny. And it was for one of these smoking-concerts that I wrote a cod Anglican sermon, something I found no problem doing as I'd sat through so many in my youth. It took me half an hour to put together, and, since it later figured in (indeed earned me my place in) *Beyond the Fringe*, it was undoubtedly the most profitable half-hour I've ever spent. At the same time, having written it I had no sense that a corner had been turned.

I had always been a late starter, so, friendly though the atmosphere was, I didn't pluck up courage to take part even in these JCR smokers until my third year, by which time my days at the university seemed numbered. However, after I'd taken my degree I found myself able to stay on as a postgraduate, doing research on Richard II. I also began to teach a little, first for Magdalen and then for Exeter. I had some sense, I think, that making people laugh was not a proper activity for a post-graduate and that I ought somehow to be acquiring more dignity; except that by now I was being asked to perform in other colleges and do cabaret for dances and Commem Balls, and was sometimes even paid. The situation was more delicate because I was supervised in my research by the medieval historian Bruce McFarlane. McFarlane was a man of great austerity and singleness of mind. He was shy, very kind, and the most impressive teacher, and in some ways the most impressive man, I have ever come across. One could go and chat to him without seemingly ever touching on the subject of one's research and come away convinced that studying one's tiny slip of a subject (mine was Richard II's retinue from 1388 to 1399) was the only thing in the world worth doing. He knew a little of my cabaret performances, but they were never referred to. Around this time I recorded some sketches for BBC radio, and told him when they were due to be broadcast; 'I listened,' was all he ever said.

By this time I had been at Oxford some five years, and it was plain to me, if I did not quite admit it to myself, that I was not going to make a don. To begin with I had no memory to speak of, and the notes of my research proliferated without ever congealing into anything approaching a thesis. As for teaching, I could never find sufficient comments to fill the necessary hour, and nor could my pupils. If I ventured on argument I was soon floored, and the tutorials ended in awkward silence. Eventually I took to putting the clock on before my pupils arrived, so there was less time to fill.

Deliverance came in the summer of 1959. In that year the Oxford Theatre Group first put on a revue on the fringe at the

Edinburgh Festival. Feeling immensely old and foolish at twenty-five, I nervously auditioned for the writer and director Stanley Daniels. He was an American, also a postgraduate, who appeared (so much for my qualms) at least forty, with no dignity at all nor seeming to want any. I see his name nowadays in the credits as one of the producers of the excellent American TV series *Taxi*. We performed at the Cranston Street Hall in Edinburgh, where in the same hall the previous year the Oxford Theatre Group had premièred Willis Hall's *The Long, the Short and the Tall* and where another première a few years later was Tom Stoppard's *Rosencrantz and Guildenstern are Dead*. In any account of university theatre the OTG should figure largely. Our contribution in 1959 was called *Better Late*. It was a great success, to the extent that the official Festival took note and the following year decided to put on a revue of its own, inviting Peter Cook and Jonathan Miller from Cambridge and Dudley Moore and myself from Oxford to write and perform it. This we did firstly in Edinburgh in 1960 and subsequently in the West End. Though Dudley had been an organ scholar at Magdalen and we had even appeared on the same bill, I don't think we had ever met until the first script conference for *Beyond the Fringe*.

While I was writing this I was puzzled why, when I'd performed so little at university and not been an avid playgoer, I yet remembered Oxford as a place of theatrical excitement. I think it was that I somehow regarded the nightly experience of dining in hall as a kind of theatre, a theatre in which the undergraduates were the audience and the actors were the dons. At Exeter they entered – *climbed* almost – on to the stage from the mysterious backstage of the Senior Common Room, a room dimly remembered from one's scholarship interview and not seen again until three years later, when one entered it before one's Schools Dinner. Fanciful perhaps to compare the bang of the block for grace with the knocks that signal the rise of the curtain at the Comédie-Française, but there was, as there is in every college, a regular repertory company enlivened at weekends and on guest nights by visitors and the occasional star. Auden I remember seeing once, hearing that quacking voice without recognizing the face, which in the mid-fifties had just begun to go under the harrow. Richard Burton was there one night, Dennis Healey, Harold Wilson – hardly fabled names but still names one had read in the papers, creatures from a world elsewhere. Nowadays dining arrangements at Exeter are different. The undergraduates are halfway through their meal when High Table comes in, so they don't have this sense of a nightly performance that I had – and feel it faintly ridiculous to have had.

When I moved to Magdalen, as the most junior of junior lecturers, it was rather different. Whereas Exeter was still in the era of the proscenium arch with the dons entering stage left in single file, at Magdalen it was altogether more dramatic and the choreography more fluid. There the fellows made a swift dash around the cloisters before entering in a crowd through the body of the hall, streaming through the standing assembly and up to High Table as if directed by Ariane Mnouchkine or some fashionable young man from the RSC. At Magdalen too the visitors were grander and the regular repertory company more distinguished: C. S. Lewis, Gilbert Ryle, A. J. P. Taylor, daunting neighbours at dinner, my memories of those meals as vivid and painful as any embarrassment that happened to me subsequently on the stage. The first or second time I dined there I sat down and, as I pushed in my chair, caught the sleeves of my BA gown under the legs. Despite the fact that my movements were thus severely restricted I was too shy to get up and free them. It was a particularly delicious dinner that night, but I saw little of it. The scouts kept lowering dishes towards me but hovered tantalizingly out of reach of my pinioned arms. As I thus appeared to wave away dish after dish my neighbour leaned over solicitously and said, 'You know, if you're a vegetarian, they'll do you something special.'

Much of the time I was at Magdalen I was playing in *Beyond The Fringe* in London and commuting to Oxford three days a week in order to teach. Or not to teach, because I wasn't getting any better at it, though the celebrity of the revue to some degree compensated my pupils for the shortcomings of the tuition. This period came to an end in 1962, when the show went to Broadway, thus putting an end to my dwindling hopes of being a historian. The rest, one might say pompously, is history. Except that in my case the opposite was true. What it had been was history. What it was to be was not history at all.

Uncle Clarence

Once we have located the cemetery, the grave itself is not hard to find, one of a row of headstones just inside the gate and backing on to a railway. Flanders in April and it is, not inappropriately, raining, clogging our shoes the famous mud. The stone gives the date of his death, 21 October 1917, but not his age. He was twenty.

He was always twenty all through my childhood, because of the photograph on the piano at my grandmother's house in Leeds. He was her only son. He sits in his uniform and puttees in Mr Lonnergan's studio down Woodsley Road. Lonnergan's, a classy place that does you a good likeness. Less classy but still doing a good likeness, Mr Lonnergan takes pictures of my brother and me in 1944 in the closing stages of the next war. An artier study this, two boys aged twelve and nine emerge from a shadowy background to look unsmiling at Mr Lonnergan under his cloth. My brother is in his Morley Grammar School blazer, his hand resting unselfconsciously on my grey-flannelled shoulder. In his picture Uncle Clarence is on embarkation leave from the King's Royal Rifles. In 1944 we too are going away, though not to certain death, only 'Down South' to fulfil a dream of my father's. He has answered an advert in the *Meat Trades Journal* and, having worked twenty-five years for the Co-op, is now going to manage a family butcher's in Guildford. Uncle Clarence never comes back but we are back within the

graph still standing on the piano on its lace doily,
s has been put beside it.

no itself does not belong to Grandma. She gives it
om at 7 Gilpin Place for her sister-in-law, Aunt Eveline.
Au Eveline has never married and has beautiful handwriting.
Her name is on all the music in the piano stool, and in her time
she accompanied the silent films at the Electric Cinema,
Bradford. Come the talkies, she turns housekeeper and now
looks after a Mr Wilson, sometime chairman of the Bradford
Dyers' Association, who is a widower with a fancy woman,
whom Aunt Eveline dislikes because she has dyed hair and is not
Aunt Eveline. On Sundays there are musical evenings in the
front room at Gilpin Place. The children are warned to keep
back as a shovelful of burning coals from the kitchen range is
carried smoking through the house to light the fire in the
sitting-room before we sit down to high tea in the kitchen. After
tea, the sitting-room still smelling of smoke, Aunt Eveline
arranges herself on the piano stool and with my father on the
violin ('Now then, Walter, what shall we give them?') kicks off
with a selection from *Glamorous Night*. Then, having played
themselves in, they accompany Uncle George, my father's
brother, in some songs. Uncle George is a bricklayer and has a
fine voice and a face as red as his bricks. He sings 'Bless This
House' and 'Where'er You Walk', and sometimes Grandma has
a little cry. These occasions go on until about 1950, when
Grandma dies.

Grandma, whose name is Mary Ann Peel, has three
daughters, Kathleen, Lemira and my mother, Lilian. Clarence
is the eldest child, and the only son. Whenever he is talked of it
is always 'Our Clarence' or, to my brother and me, 'Your Uncle
Clarence'. But he is only our would-be uncle, an uncle-who-
might-have-been, not like my father's brothers, uncles of flesh
and blood, two of them veterans of the same war and very much

alive. We are his nephews by prolepsis and he our posthumous uncle, protected even in death by the convention that children do not refer to relatives by anything so naked as their name.

When Uncle Clarence's name comes up it is generally in connection with the undisputed nobility of his character. What is disputed is which of the sisters resembles him most. It is accepted in our wing of the family that this role belongs to my mother, who certainly looks most like him. The prettiest of the three, she marries early and does not get on with the other two, who marry late. Clarence, later to become a silly-ass kind of name, a name out of farce and, like Albert, never revamped, remains in our family the name of a saint. If my mother is asked about Uncle Clarence the reply is always 'He was a love. He was a grand fellow.' What job he did in the few years given to him to have a job, whether he had a dog or a bike or a girlfriend, none of this I know or bother to ask, and with both my aunties dead there is no one now who does know. My mother lives, but she does not remember she had a brother, or even what 'a brother' is. When asked, she still says, 'He was a grand fellow.' She says the same now about my father. I am a grand fellow too. In these her flat, unmemoried days she would probably say the same about Adolf Hitler.

In the front room at Gilpin Place is an elaborate dresser, with mirrors and alcoves and fretwork shelves. Stripped of its warm chestnut varnish, it will have gone up in the world now, moved from Leeds 12 to Leeds 16 to grace the modish kitchen of a polytechnic lecturer or a designer at Yorkshire TV. In my time this dresser is laden with ornaments housing Grandma's hoard of silver paper, and the drawers are stuffed with bundles of seaside postcards: Sunset across the Bay, Morecambe; The Illuminations, Blackpool; The Bandstand, Lytham St Annes. Glossy, deckle-edged cards in rich purples and browns. To my brother and me, who have never seen fairy lights along the prom or the sands without tank traps and barbed wire, they are what the world was like Before the War. We take the cards and steam off any Edward VII or George V stamps to use as (pretty mediocre) swaps. Among the picture postcards are photographs on stiffer card: Grandma on outings with the ladies' bowling club, striding along some promenade in a long, laughing line, big ladies in cloche hats and black duster coats on trips to Bangor or Dunoon.

The cupboard in the dresser has more mysterious artefacts: old scent sprays, cigar-cutters, some candle-snuffers and a pile of ten-inch 78s in torn brown-paper covers. One is 'I Lift up My Finger and I Say Tweet Tweet, Hush Hush, Now Now, Come Come'. I find some needles in the cupboard and play it on the wind-up gramophone in its red Rexine cover. In theory the dresser is out of bounds and I can only look in it if my brother is out playing with his pals or swimming at Armley Baths and Grandma and I are alone in the house. This is generally on a Saturday afternoon. She dozes in front of the kitchen fire while I investigate the cupboard in the front room. 'Rooting' she calls it. From time to time she wakes up. 'What are you doing in there?' I say nothing. 'Are you rooting? Give over.'

In the first year of the war there is a tin of biscuits in the dresser. The biscuits have long since gone but the legend of them remains, and I always think if I can get to the very back of the cupboard there will be another tin that has been forgotten. There are plenty of other tins. When I ask what's in them my grandmother always gives the same answer: 'Chums.' It is a joke which never fails to amuse her. But before I know that chums are friends they are something mysterious, sweet and secret, that one should not look for because forbidden.

Whereas the kitchen cupboard is dedicated to use, with the old familiar cutlery, threadbare tablecloths, and knives that years of sharpening have brought to the width of skewers, the front-room cupboard houses stuff that never gets used, often in sets: the set of trifle glasses with the green stems, the set of cake knives won at a whist drive, besides all the items no well-run household should be without (grapefruit knives, a cheese-slice) but which are never actually required. It is a museum, this cupboard, to a theory of domestic economy. But it is also a shrine. For somewhere among the packets of doilies and cake frills, the EPNS salad-servers, the packets of spills in violent colours, the whist scoring-cards and the enema in its black box, somewhere among all this is the box with Uncle Clarence's Victory medal, 'which', the citation says, 'would have been conferred on C7/044 Pte C. E. Peel, had he lived'. The letter is dated Winchester, 10 May 1921. 'In forwarding the Decoration I am commanded by the King to assure you of His Majesty's high appreciation of the services rendered.' Even as a small child rooting for biscuits, I can see that His Majesty's high appreciation didn't amount to much.

Besides, what His Majesty's high appreciation didn't run to – could not be expected to run to – was that Uncle Clarence had been ruptured. So, while everyone who died in this war died needlessly, Uncle Clarence died more needlessly than most. My mother always says he should not have gone at all. I do not quite know what 'being ruptured' means. Some shame attaches to it, I know, because Mr Dixon, who takes Standard 5 at Armley National, where I go to school, is ruptured and all the boys think it is a joke. Mr Dixon is the first male teacher I have come up against. He is short and fat and said to wear a truss. What a truss is I don't know either, but I think of it as a device to stop your balls popping out. I find it difficult to connect – still less reconcile – someone as noble as Uncle Clarence and a condition that is both shameful and comical and affects such as Mr Dixon, and maybe I pity Uncle Clarence less for his early death than for his earlier rupture. Though, as my mother says, the one should

33

have prevented the other, because in that condition he could not enlist. With the risk attaching to any surgical operation at that time, he was under no obligation to have the rupture treated, so for a year or two the matter was left and he went on living at home with his sisters. But in the third year of the war he found himself jeered at in the street, taunted by girls from the munitions works, and so he went into St James's, had the operation, and in due course joined up. And here he sits in the photograph, just three months before his death, a whole man again.

In the photograph he is wearing puttees. At what point private soldiers ceased to wear these long bandages wrapped round their legs I don't know. It is certainly gaiters by 1939, 'anklets webbing khaki, pairs two' when I am called up in 1952. But the puttee survives (along with many of the attitudes that go with it) in that stagnant military backwater the Army Cadet Corps. No school I ever attend runs to one, but in the short time we are in Guildford my brother is a pupil at the grammar school there and in a uniform identical to that of Uncle Clarence goes on manoeuvres at Pirbright. I watch him as he winds off these muddy brown bandages to find his legs ridged like those of the common house fly, pictured one thousand times life-size in the *Children's Encyclopedia*.

I never remember anyone mentioning Uncle Clarence's grave. There is no photograph of that in the dresser, only a picture of the war-memorial tablet in St Mary of Bethany, Tong Road. If he has a grave, no one visits it. My grandmother never goes abroad, nor do my parents for that matter, and, though they think of themselves as women of the world, Aunty Kathleen and Aunty Myra only take to globe-trotting late in life. So, knowing only that he had died at Ypres in 1917, in March 1986 I write to the War Graves Commission at Maidenhead, curious to know if he is just a name on a monument or whether he enjoys the luxury of a burial place. It turns out to be more than one and less than the other. For the records say that, though he is commemorated by a special memorial in Larchwood (Railway Cuttings) Cemetery and is thought to lie within that cemetery, the exact location of his body is lost. So now it is a wet Friday morning and we have come over on the hovercraft and are driving through Saint-Omer and north to Zillebeke, a village south-east of Ypres, or since we have now crossed the Belgian frontier, Ieper.

The guidebook says there were three battles at Ypres. The first, in 1914, ended in stalemate and marked the beginning of trench warfare. The second, in 1915, saw the first use of gas. The *Blue Guide* calls 'Passchendaele', the third battle, in 1917, 'tragic and barren', as if that distinguished it from the previous two. The ground gained or lost in each case amounted to a few kilometres. The dead, not noted in the *Blue Guide*, amounted to a quarter of a million.

So now the cemeteries are everywhere, some one hundred and seventy in this salient alone, neat and regular, with their gates and walls and entrances like Roman camps, much neater and more orderly than the suburbs and factory farms they now find themselves among, as if the dead are here to garrison the living, with the countryside not caring, though the place-names aren't hazed over at all, and each location is immaculately signposted. The cemeteries are so thick on the ground that we can't find Larchwood and eventually end up down a cul-de-sac at Hill 60, the slight vantage point south of the town that changed hands many times during the fighting. Now it's a bare, muddy common with a stone telling its history and a memorial to the dead left entombed in its burrows. There is a car park and a home-made museum-cum-café with vases made out of shell cases and a pin-table. Bungalows back on to the common, with garden sheds. One has a car-port and a Peugeot in the drive.

Rustic wooden seats denote this desolate place a picnic area, though nothing much grows, grass the permanent casualty, the ground as brown and bare as an end-of-the-season goalmouth. Was it for this the clay grew tall, for the plastic flowers in the picture windows, the fishman with his van, and a boy riding over the ancient humps of trenches on his BMX bike? Well, yes, I suppose it was.

Unable still to find our cemetery, we give it up and drive back into Ypres and eat a waffle in a chocolate shop, where plump businessmen dally with the proprietress while choosing pralines for the weekend. They go back to the office, tiny boxes of chocolates dangling from one finger, while we drive out on the Menin Road in the rain. Eventually we spot the tip of a cross across a sloping field. There is a railway and there are trees which may be larches and here is the signpost, broken off by a tractor and lying in the ditch.

The cemetery is over a crossing on the far side of a single-track railway. There is a gate, a long finger of lawn alongside the railway, another gate and the burial-ground proper: Uncle Clarence's stone, the stone which is not his grave, is in a row backing on to the railway.

Known to be buried in this cemetery

C7/044

Rifleman C. E. Peel.

King's Royal Rifle Corps.

21 October 1917

†

Their Glory Shall not be Blotted Out.

To one side is a Gunner Hucklesby of the Royal Field Artillery, to the other a Private Oliver of the Hampshires. It is like seeing who is in the next bed in a barrack room. Many of the

names are from Leeds: a Pte Smallwood, a Pte Seed from
Kirkstall Road, some with family details, some not. Uncle
Clarence's not. A Second-Lieutenant Broderick from Farnley,
at thirty-five a bit old for the war, like Waugh's Crouchback,
another Uncle. Sergeant Fortune, a character out of Hardy. Pte
Ruckledge of the Wellingtons, Pte Leaversedge of the York-
shires: rugged names, which, had their owners been spared, one
feels the years might have smoothed out to end up Rutledge and
Liversedge. Many Canadians 'known only to God'.

The low walls are sharp and new-looking, unblurred by
creeper. There is no lichen on the gravestones, the dead seeming
not to have fertilized the ground so much as sterilized it. This is
April and too soon to mow, yet the grass is neat and shorn.
Standard at the entrance to each graveyard is a small cupboard
in the wall, the door of bronze. In it is lodged the register of
graves in this and adjacent cemeteries. Larchwood is a modest
example, with only some three hundred graves. The register
begins by describing the history of the place: 'On the NE side of
the railway line to Menin, between the hamlets of Verbranden-
molen and Zwarvelden was a small plantation of larches, and a
cemetery was made at the north end of this wood. It was begun
in April 1915 and used by troops holding this sector until April
1918.' The tone is simple, almost epic. It might be a translation
from Livy, the troops any troops in any war. There is a plan of
the graves, drawn up like an order of battle, these soldiers laid in
the earth still in military formation, with the graves set in files
and groups and at slight angles to one another, as if they were
companies waiting for some last advance. All face east, the
direction of the enemy and only incidentally of God.

I sit in the little brick pavilion looking at this register. The
book is neat (so much is neat now when nothing was neat then);
it is unfingermarked, not even dog-eared. It might be drawn
from the Bodleian Library, not from a cupboard in a wall in the

middle of a field. Of course if this foreign field were forever England the bronze door would long since have been wrenched off, the gates nicked, 'Skins' and 'Chelsea' sprayed over all. The notion of a register so freely available would in England seem ingenuous nonsense. I sit there, wondering about this, never knowing if our barbarism denotes vigour or decay. Across the hedgeless fields are the rebuilt towers of Ypres, looking, behind a line of willows, oddly like Oxford. At which point, with a heavy symbolism that in a film would elicit a sophisticated groan, a Mirage jet scorches low over the fields.

For all the dead who lie here and the filthy, futile deaths they died, it is still hard to suppress a twinge of imperial pride, partly to be put down to the design of these silent cities: the work of Blomfield, Baker and Lutyens, the last architects of Empire. The other feeling, less ambiguous here than it would be in a cemetery of the Second War, is anger. Nobody could say now why these men died. The phrase 'Their glory shall not be blotted out' was a contribution by Kipling, who served on the War Graves Commission. This is the Friday after President Reagan's Libyan venture, and to assert that there is anything under the sun that will not be blotted out seems quite hopeful. We instinctively think of the conflict between East and West on the model of the Second War, the one with a purpose. The instructive parallel is with the First.

Dinner at Noon

I have had unfortunate experiences in hotels. I was once invited to Claridge's by the late John Huston in order to discuss a script he had sent me. The screenplay was bulky (that was what he wanted to discuss) and looked like a small parcel. Seeing it and (I suppose) me, the commissionaire insisted I use the tradesman's entrance.

On another occasion, during the run of *Beyond the Fringe* in New York, Dudley Moore and I took refuge from a storm in the Hotel Pierre, where we were spotted by an assistant manager. Saying that there had been a spate of thefts from rooms recently, he asked us to leave. A small argument ensued, in the course of which an old man and his wife stumped past, whereupon the assistant manager left off abusing us in order to bow. It was Stravinsky. We were then thrown out. I have never set foot in the Pierre since, fearing I might still be taken for a petty thief. Dudley Moore, I imagine, goes in there with impunity; the assistant manager may even bow to him now while throwing somebody else out. Me still, possibly.

Dinner at Noon was a documentary about the Crown Hotel, Harrogate, which Jonathan Stedall and I made for the BBC TV series 'Byline' in April 1988. Up to that time I had never embarked on a TV programme without carefully scripting it first, but this was obviously neither possible nor appropriate when making a documentary, particularly a 'fly-on-the-wall'

39

exercise such as this was intended to be. I was accordingly a little apprehensive.

The film was also meant to illustrate some of the work of the American sociologist Erving Goffman.* Goffman's first field study was in a hotel in the Shetlands, and much of the research he did there was incorporated into his pioneering book *The Presentation of Self in Everyday Life*, though other insights gleaned at this eccentric and sometimes hilarious establishment crop up in all his books.

In the era of *Fawlty Towers* it might seem folly to try to say anything more on the subject of the roles of staff and guests in a hotel, and certainly it became plain in the first two days of filming that a respectable sociological study of hotel life would take much longer than the ten days we were scheduled to film. The early material we shot was also pretty stilted and banal, and I became even more apprehensive about the end result. Documentary film-makers, of course, must often find themselves in this predicament, but it was new to me, and so, feeling slightly panic-stricken, I scribbled some autobiographical notes which I could deliver either straight to camera or as a commentary over footage of the various functions and goings-on in the hotel.

Thus the finished film ended up having not much to do with Goffman and a lot more to do with me; it certainly wasn't the film we set out to make, but this must often be the case with documentaries, and even with feature films. I hadn't intended *Dinner at Noon* to be as personal or as revealing as it turned out to be – or perhaps the intention had been at the back of my mind and this was just a roundabout way of getting there.

What follows is a transcript of the documentary, with notes to indicate who is speaking and where. Though the voice is only one element in the spoken word and a transcript wants both gesture and inflection, I've made no attempt to supplement the

* See pages 475–88.

dialogue, clean it up, or make it more coherent and grammatical. This occasionally makes it hard to read, but it's a reminder that one cannot overstate the untidiness of human speech or reproduce it accurately on the page.

———

(*A hotel bedroom.*)

I was conceived in a strange bedroom.
My birthday, like my brother's, is in May, and, though three years separate us, we were both born on the same date. Counting back the months, I realize we must both have been conceived during the old August Bank Holiday, in a boarding-house bedroom in Morecambe, or Flamborough, or Filey – oilcloth on the floor, jug and basin on the wash-hand stand, the bathroom on the next landing. Nowhere like this, anyway, a bedroom in the Crown Hotel, Harrogate.

(*An hotel corridor. A young boy walks past a chambermaid.*)

That said, though, I might be expected to feel at home in rented accommodation, but for years nowhere filled me with the same unease as did a hotel.

(*Opening titles.*)

Town of teashops, a nice run-out from Leeds – Harrogate, where hotels abound and always have.

(*Reception desk.*)
    RECEPTIONIST: Crown Hotel, good morning. Can I help you? I'll put you through.

(*Dining-room: breakfast.*)

Once, visitors came to take the waters; now it's a 'Leisure
Break' or a conference, a mecca for the businessman.
Nowadays I like hotels, at any rate in small doses; they're a
setting where you see people trying to behave, which is always
more interesting than them just behaving. When people are on
their best behaviour they aren't always at their best. But I
wasn't always so relaxed. For years, hotels and restaurants were
for me theatres of humiliation, and the business of eating in
public every bit as fraught with risk and shame as taking one's
clothes off.

What it was – when I was little my parents didn't have much
money, and when we went into cafés the drill was for my Mam
and Dad to order a pot of tea for two, and maybe a token cake,
and my brother and me would be given sips of tea from their
cup, while under the table my mother unwrapped a parcel of
bread and butter that she'd brought from home, and she
smuggled pieces to my brother and me, which we had to eat
while the waitress wasn't looking.

(*Lobby. A chambermaid polishes the revolving doors.*)

The fear of discovery, exposure and ignominious expulsion
stayed with me well into my twenties, and memories of that and
similar embarrassments come back whenever I stay in a hotel.
Not that this is an intimidating establishment at all: it's
comfortable and straightforward and caters for what the
marketing men call 'a good social mix'. I hope that's what the
film's about – not class, which I don't like, but classes, types,
which I do; and a hotel like this is a good place to see them.

(*Lobby.*)

Behaviour's a bit muted, but that's part of the setting. The
foyers of American hotels are like station concourses or airport
lounges, they're really part of the street, so you don't expect

people to behave in any particular way. Here, with the sofas and the fire, we're still visibly related to the hall of the country house, and people try to behave accordingly. For some, of course, this isn't too big a jump.

> (*A sporty young couple reading* Country Life.)
> HE: . . . boring. Is yours boring?
> SHE: Mine's riveting.
> HE: Mine's thoroughly dull.
> SHE: That's what they're for.
>   Oh, look at that! Isn't it gorgeous?
> HE: . . . country houses round here, going to lots of the people moving out of London – sell their three-bedroomed flat in Notting Hill and buy a huge country mansion . . .

> (*An elderly couple, he studying the racing page.*)
> HE: . . . the Thirsty Farmer.
> SHE: The what?
> HE: Thirsty Farmer . . . Oh – Rattling Jack.
> SHE: That would be a good one. That's sure to be all right.

I've never been able to get worked up about class and its distinctions, but then I've never felt the conventional three-tier account of social divisions has much to do with the case. What class are these?
My parents would have called them a grand couple.

> SHE: Is it sweet enough for you? Sweet enough for you?
> HE: Yes. It never worries me.

My mother's scheme of things admitted to much finer distinctions than were allowed by the sociologists. She'd talk about people being 'better-class', 'well-off', 'nicely spoken', 'refined', 'educated', 'genuine', 'ordinary' and – the ultimate condemnation – 'common'.

(*The elderly couple are still poring over the racing page.*)

HE: I wonder if I could trust you.

SHE: What, to pick one?

HE: No. Very Special Lady.

SHE: Oh well, well I am at the moment, aren't I? I don't know how long you'll keep me that way, but . . .

HE: Oh we'll have a bit of fun while we're here.

SHE: Your pencil's upside down.

(*Reception desk.*)

RECEPTIONIST: Can I book you a paper for the morning, or a morning call?

GUEST: *Daily Telegraph*, and what about a morning call?

RECEPTIONIST: Right.

GUEST: I get up at half past five normally.

PORTER: The lift's round the corner. Shall I take your bag for you?

Right, this way.

(*Upstairs corridor.*)

I always carry my bags myself – avoids the tip. It's not the money: like catching the barman's eye, it's a skill I've never mastered; but then my parents graduated from boarding-houses to hotels when I was in my teens and at my most thin-skinned.

PORTER: This way.

Hope the weather's going to perk up a bit for you. Here we are then.

GUEST: It's been lovely for the last couple of days.

PORTER: That's right.

(*Bedroom.*)

Arriving at the hotel, like leaving it, was fraught with anxiety: there was always the question of 'the tip'.

Dad would probably have his shilling ready before he'd even signed the register, and when the porter had shown them up to their room would give it to him, as often as not misjudging the moment, not waiting till his final departure but slipping it to him while he was still demonstrating what facilities the room had to offer – the commodious wardrobe, the luxurious bathroom – so the tip came as an unwelcome interruption.

Once the potentially dangerous procedure of arrival had been got through, the luggage fetched up, the porter endowed with his shilling, and the door finally closed, my parents' apprehension gave way to huge relief – it was as if they'd bluffed their way into the enemy camp, and relief gave way to giggles as they explored the delights of the place.

'Come look in here, Dad. It's a spanking place – there's umpteen towels.'

(A boy runs down the staircase.)

Every family has a secret, and the secret is that it's not like other families.

(A maid cleans a bathroom.)

In a new refinement of gentility, the maids these days plait the ends of the toilet roll. It's a good job they didn't do this when I was a child or I'd have imagined this was standard practice throughout the land, our family's toilet roll unique in its ragged and inconsequent termination.

This was long before the days of trouser presses and hair-dryers, and even kettles in the rooms came in just too late for my parents. That would have been the ultimate, though. With a kettle and the wherewithal to make some tea, they could have fetched some stuff in from outside, been free of the terrors of the

dining-room, and never needed to stir out of the room at all.
When we stayed in boarding-houses we didn't actually board
but took our own food: screws of tea, packets of sugar and
corned beef cushioned by shirts and socks and bathing-
costumes, all packed in a bulging cardboard box, cat's-cradled
in string and fetched on the train from Leeds. So when we were
on holiday there was no romance to the food: we ate exactly what
we did at home. Come six o'clock, while the rest of the clientele
at The Waverley or The Clarendon or The Claremont would be
wiring into 'a little bit of plaice' or the 'bit of something tasty'
which the landlady had provided, the Bennett family would be
having their usual slice of cold brisket and a tomato. It was home
from home.

> (*Reception desk.*)
> GUEST: Can we just register, please?

> (*Lobby.*)
> GUEST: And she's lovely legs, beautiful legs and lovely
> face, hips like that, she shows you, you know; it's just
> like a leg of pork.

So, what's on the agenda for today, then?

> (*Hotel notice-board: 'Dr Barnardo's Fashion Show'.*
> *Ballroom: two girls practise modelling.*)

Although these are amateurs, fashion shows seem brisker than
they once were. Gone the languid elegance of Barbara Goalen
– not even a name to Janet and Tina, cavorting on the cat-walk.

> (*Grosvenor Room.*)
> ANDY: . . . because York has this lovely sewage problem
> that we all know so much about, and in fact Tracy's . . .
> Tracy's got more to spend on sewage than you have,
> Mike.

TRACY: Well, they wouldn't have delivered any toilet rolls as yet.

What is new in hotels is the meetings. In the Grosvenor Room the manageresses of some roadside eateries are being grilled by Andy, the local representative.
Tracy has sewage problems, which Andy will want to talk her through before reporting back to District, where he will be grilled in his turn – another meeting.

ANDY: OK, because the budgets are out but they're not out in computer form at the moment, so, in order to help you . . .

(*A table of customers' complaints on the blackboard. Top of the list (with 0) is Thirsk. Bottom (with 9) is Rainton North.*)

Steer clear of Rainton North seems to be the message. Discerning diners go to Thirsk.

ANDY: It doesn't need an awful lot doing to it, so consequently he's paying the money for other restaurants to benefit . . .
Yes, but then eventually there'll come a time when Tracy needs special maintenance – probably on drainage – in which case she doesn't pay for the drainage, you see, it comes back . . .

(*Melbourne Room.*)
LECTURER: Of these volunteers, at least one half – and it can be more if you can do this – are going to be what we call 'starters'; that is, they have not been using hormonal contraceptives in the previous two months.

In the Melbourne Room the doctors wrestle with birth control.

And the topic is not confined to the Melbourne Room either. In the lobby begins a muted saga from the same department.

(*Lobby.*)

GENTEEL WOMAN: . . . she wouldn't tell me where it was she thought he might be, and I said, 'You just pass this message on to him and tell him that' – I've a bit of experience because I've gone through this – I said, 'that you can't be haemorrhaging like that.' He says, 'You've got a very good friend, Mrs Birmingham.' So that was nice, wasn't it?

FRIEND: That's her about the . . . wasn't it?

GENTEEL WOMAN: And he said, 'I'm glad she did.' He was going to leave it while Monday.

Anyway, he's coming now so he's made a fourth. And, you see, the receptionist – you don't listen to these receptionists. I mean, they're . . . always so . . . I don't know.

The coffee's not very hot.

(*Lobby.*)

My parents liked this side of hotel life, and they would have liked this kind of hotel: weddings, dinner dances, functions galore. Not that there'd ever be anything in which they'd dream of participating, only there'd be more to see, more types, more going off. They'd station themselves on the sofa and watch what went on, other people leading their lives, and envying the accomplishment with which they led them. And, without realizing it, my mother would make up stories about people: 'You see that woman over there? I think she's the owner of the hotel, and that fellow with her must be her nephew.' And when the woman came in next day by herself she'd say, 'Oh, I see the owner's here. She must have quarrelled with her nephew,' forgetting it was all invention in the first place.

> GUEST: Did you have a slice?
> GUEST: Yes. Thanks very much.

(*Montpelier Room.*)
> PRESIDENT: . . . the responsibility for private-sector housing . . . health and safety, noise and air-pollution control and caravan sites. Quite an impressive list.

(*Applause.*)
> CHAIRMAN: Mr Mayor, Mr President, thank you for those kind words, and, friends, today I feel very proud to stand before you all as Chairman of the General Council of the Institution of Environmental Health Officers. To have that honour this year is the highlight so far of my professional career, and today for me is perhaps the ultimate memory that I shall hold for the remainder of my life, for today, Mr Mayor, there is that ultimate recognition from the two organizations that I hold dear, the Institution and Harrogate Borough Council, both of which have had such an important influence on my personal and professional life.

(*Lobby. Children arriving for a party.*)

While in the Montpelier Room the apotheosis of a sanitary inspector reaches its tail-end, some chic little five-year-olds head for another function in the Brontë Room.

> RECEPTIONIST: How old are you?
> CHILD: Five already.
> RECEPTIONIST: Five already? . . .

There must be Brontë Rooms all over Yorkshire – venues for discos and parades of beachwear, demonstrations of fire-fighting equipment and new lines in toiletries, all brought under the grim umbrella of those three ailing and unconvivial sisters. Today it's jelly and a conjuror.

(*Children shouting as the door of the Brontë Room opens.*)

More treats, an outing, the old people slowly trek towards the Grosvenor Room.

> (*Corridor.*)
> HELPER: Are you following?
> OLD MAN: By the right, quick march.

> (*Grosvenor Room.*)
> OLD MAN: We've been here though once before, haven't we, Anne?
> OLD LADY: Thank you, love. Can I have the plate?
> HELPER: Would you like me to put jam on your scone for you?
> Do you want me to put the jam on for you?
> OLD LADY: No, it's all right.

One more tea in a lifetime of teas. They'll have had teas all over in their time. Tea in Hitchen's in Leeds and Brown Muff's in Bradford. Teas in Betty's and Marshall & Snelgrove. Teas when they were courting; teas after they got married. Tea now.

> OLD LADY: It'll never come back.
> OLD MAN: Well, they're trying their best to do so, you know. That's what it is.

I like ladies like Mrs Baker and Miss Wood – and don't think of them as old people. Just as Paris is geared to thirty-five-year-old career women, so is the North to women like these. In London they'd be displaced and fearful; here, accomplished pianists and stylish ballroom dancers, they still help rule the roost.

OLD MAN: Well, we'll be having another meal at 5.30.
I thought we were just having a drink of tea now,
but . . .

OLD LADY: There's no need to know . . .

OLD MAN: I don't, I'm not used to this sort of thing.
What's that?

HELPER: Just chocolate.

OLD LADY: Just chocolate. I'll have a wee chocolate . . .
No, thank you, that's quite enough – that's a record for
me anyway.
I love anything chocolatey. Thank you.

OLD MAN: . . . have something like that in all the songs,
you know. We think they're old songs, but that's what I
remember about . . .

OLD LADY: Harrogate. I used to come in my youth to
Harrogate, to the Majestic and – what do you call the
one that's closed now – the Grand . . .

HELPER: The Grand Hotel.

OLD LADY: . . . and dance there a lot. It was lovely.

OLD MAN: . . . remind me I did a sword dance in the
Albert Hall in a wee kilt when I was twelve years of age
as a Scout – a Caledonian, you know. A sword dance,
with crossed swords. Aye, Ged, you can do that when
you're twelve, but you daren't do it when you're
fourteen.

OLD LADY: I've been here when I was twelve.

OLD MAN: It's a funny thing this puberty business when
you think of it, isn't it?

(*Music. The Crown Bar.*)

Puberty long since behind them, the nicely-off members of the
Boston Spa Tennis Club have said farewell to embarrassment
and are whooping it up at their annual disco. Never having

been able to dance, watching it generally fills me with envy and melancholy; but all this disco does is to convince me of the ultimate charms of the Zimmer frame.

(*Exterior of hotel. Night.*)
RECEPTIONIST: Reception, can I help you?
Yes, you can have both English and Continental in your room, if you just put the card that's on your bed, if you put it on the door, and the night porter will pick it up in the night for you and then we'll have your breakfast there in the morning. All right?

(*Dining-room.*)

The pound is twitching this morning, the radio says, but it doesn't seem to be upsetting the business appetite. Breakfast as a meal never occurred in our house, and with our motto of 'Let's pretend we're like everyone else' this was another fact we concealed from the outside world. We imagined that every family except us sat down together to a cooked breakfast – an assumption a hotel seems to confirm.
It lives on as a myth in television commercials, but I can't think anybody's taken in. Still, it's the business of hotels to be one step behind the times – hotels, like colonies, keeping up a way of life that is already outmoded.

(*A chambermaid in the corridor.*)

Beverley goes hoover hoover outside the day's first meeting – this time a meeting about how to hold meetings.

(*Melbourne Room.*)
LECTURER: The discipline of the meeting is very important, and I'm sure that most of you have had an enormous amount of experience when thinking of some of the meetings that you've had and . . . that lack

of discipline has caused a considerable waste of time. The person has got to have the ability to be able to present himself, he's got to be competent and present the . . . the company.

OK, any more . . . any more questions?

(*Lobby*.)

Meanwhile, the lobby swarms with amateur gardeners off to the Harrogate Flower Show. Hobbies were another thing our family never managed. Dad played the violin and Mam went through a lampshade-making phase, but nothing ever got them in its teeth, not like these nice, gentle people; they are fanatics. 'In the context of ground cover, dare one mention the humble myosotis?', and off go the gardeners to the flower show. Lucky them!

(*Melbourne Room*.)

LECTURER: . . . may well be the same people who
    supervise the doing of the work . . .

But no truants among the businessmen, who have another lesson before playtime.

LECTURER: An owner who starts his own company may
    well clear his dining-room table in the evening and do
    this part – and to a great extent this as well. In all sorts
    of ways companies operate in different means. As we
    get bigger, of course, we have establishments, we have
    departments, we may even have office blocks of people
    who are doing that.

Oddly touching I find these middle-aged schoolboys – still wanting to learn, still convinced they can do it better, wives left at home, whom they'll go up and phone later to tell them how well their group did in the test.

53

LECTURER: . . . and in fact what we ought to be doing is
   dead simple – just keep taking pound notes from
   people and keep them smiling as you do it. It's as
   simple as that.

(*Brontë Bar.*)
TOASTMASTER: Hello sir, Mr Mayor.
   Hello, Lady Mayoress. How are you?
MAYORESS: Fine, thank you.
GUEST: Good. Drinks are here, are they?

The Flower Show Committee are having drinks in the Brontë
Bar, flowers flushing out a lot of what my mother would call
'the better class'.

GUEST: . . . awful conditions, and the winds come straight
   off Ilkley Moor . . .
GUEST: And all I say is a lot of things grow jolly well on it.
GUEST: But you do grow everything?
GUEST: I usually come on the second day; I always think
   it's rather a nice day to come.
GUEST: Yes.
GUEST: . . . that's what I've been saying: let's walk
   today . . .
GUEST: Did you?
GUEST: Yes I did.
GUEST: I'm so glad, because you can do the Valley
   Gardens, which are lovely, and then have a Pinewood
   walk, then come to our seventy acres.
GUEST: Have a cup of tea or something and there you
   are . . .
GUEST: Yes.
GUEST: No, I liked Australia better than New Zealand
   simply because New Zealand's more like Europe . . .

My parents never went to – still less gave – a cocktail party. The education they always regretted not having would have had cocktails on the syllabus, and small talk, and the ability to converse, and the necessary accomplishment of saying things one doesn't mean.

GUEST: . . . yesterday we thought, 'Oh gosh, we're in for an absolute soaking.'
GUEST: I know – pouring at home when we came up . . .
GUEST: Our timing was pretty good . . .
GUEST: I say he could . . .
GUEST: Hello, Max. How are you?
GUEST: Very well, thanks.
GUEST: Good.
GUEST: Do you know the Mayoress?
GUEST: No, we haven't been introduced yet.

(*Lobby.*)

The real solvent of class distinction is a proper measure of self-esteem, a kind of unselfconsciousness. Some people are at ease with themselves so the world is at ease with them. My parents thought this kind of ease was produced by education: 'Your Dad and me can't mix; we've not been educated.' They didn't see that what disqualified them was temperament, just as, though educated up to the hilt, it disqualifies me. What keeps us in our place is embarrassment.

GUEST: Mind you, it's getting to the stage where it takes a bit more out of you every year, doesn't it?
GUEST: That's right.

(*Ballroom.*)

Not that there's much embarrassment in the ballroom, where the road hauliers' wives are also having a do. Less refined these ladies – some of them (dare one say?) a little common – but jollier by a long chalk. What do they talk about? Youth? Trysts in long-gone transport cafés, marriages that began in lay-bys, or even in a long tailback on the M6?

How at seventeen and soaked to the skin, one stood for hours at the Wakefield turn-off when suddenly Mr Right, ferrying a load of minced morsels from Rochdale to Penzance, slowed his juggernaut to a halt beside her and now they've got a fleet of six and a son at catering college and she's having her lunch in Harrogate?

(*Brontë Room.*)

The Mayor of Harrogate has collared the Brontë Room this lunch-time to entertain his fellow mayors. The party includes a French delegation and the Mayor of Harrogate's twin town, Luchon.

FRENCH MAYOR: (*A long speech in French.*)
LADY GUEST: Ye–es.
FRENCH MAYOR: (*More French.*)
LADY GUEST: . . . that's right, yes. (*Laughs.*)
FRENCH MAYOR: (*Still more French.*)
LADY GUEST: Well, I'm very glad you came.

Oh! Charlotte and Emily – nothing has changed. A Mr Heathcliff is calling you from a Haworth call-box and wishes you to pay for the call.

(*Lobby. Guests arriving for a wedding reception.*)

Mr and Mrs M. C. Dakin request the pleasure of your company on the occasion of the marriage of their daughter Susan Margaret with Dr Robert Frederick Logan at St John the Divine Parish Church, Menston, on Saturday 23 April 1988 at 4 p.m. and afterwards at the Crown Hotel, Harrogate.

(Champagne poured into two glass slippers.)

The slippers are a bit of tradition invented by the hotel. 'Do you want the slippers and champagne? People seem to like them. It's a little touch that we do – makes it a bit classier.' Do they go in the dishwasher now, the slippers – difficult, one would have thought, to get a tea towel into the toes.

(Corridor, outside the ladies' loo.)

GUEST: Yours is round the corner.

(Lobby.)

RECEPTIONIST: What sort of accommodation do you require?
Twin-bedded room, and is it for anything special at all or . . . oh that's lovely. I can offer you – we actually do extra special-occasions Leisure Break weekend that weekend, which is £173 . . .

The end of a Leisure Break for one couple, but for some it was once all leisure.

UPPER–CLASS MAN: I never see a hotel like this but I see my father walking about, smoking a cigar with a glass of whisky in his hand.

UPPER–CLASS WOMAN: Oh yes.

UPPER–CLASS MAN: The ruination of our home.

UPPER–CLASS WOMAN: Some memories never die, do they?

UPPER–CLASS MAN: No.

(Another part of the lobby.)

TIMID WOMAN: Do you want to . . . All right, do you want any jam?

HER MOTHER: No.

57

TIMID WOMAN: Eat it, don't leave it.

HER MOTHER: Well, I can't eat it all . . .

TIMID WOMAN: Oh you mustn't leave it.

HER MOTHER: I can't eat it all . . .

UPPER-CLASS MAN: Is it possible to have scones and butter and jam and a pot of tea, and toast. Is that possible?

WAITRESS: Yes.

UPPER-CLASS MAN: Scones and butter and jam, and some nice toast.

WAITRESS: White or brown bread?

WOMAN SMOKING: This used to be all in one before they put the bar there . . .

WAITRESS: White or brown bread?

WOMAN SMOKING: And this hotel – I've seen this altered quite a lot. I was in here one morning having coffee and there was Lord Hailsham in, and he came across and shook hands with me.

(*Dining-room. Hotel pianist playing.*)

When we were at home we always had our dinner at lunch-time. For my parents, anything that came after that was never more than a snack. But when I was at university and they came to see me, we'd go into the hotel dining-room at night and the waiter would present the menu, and my Mam would say the dread words, 'Do you do a poached egg on toast?' and we'd slink from the dining-room, the only family in England not to have its dinner at night.

GUEST: Yes, I'll have a small piece – very tiny.

'Would you like the wine list?' the waiter would ask. 'Not really,' Dad would say, and one had to be quick in order to stop Mam explaining about his duodenal ulcer. Mind you, what wine was there that would go with spaghetti on toast? 'Which is really all we want at this time in the evening. Mr Bennett has to watch his tummy.'

> WAITRESS: Potatoes?
> DINER: Yes please, I'm a growing lad, you know.
> WAITRESS: Yes.

As I grew older and came to delight in these eccentricities and ceased to be embarrassed by them, my parents still struggled to fulfil what they imagined were my aspirations for them. 'We've found an alcoholic drink that we like,' my mother said. 'It's called Bitter Lemon.' Of course by this time my aspirations for them had changed anyway. Now I wanted them to stay the same as they'd been when I was a child. It didn't matter any more.

Once, when I had a play on in the West End, they came to a matinée and I took them afterwards to the Savoy Grill, where there was no set menu and it was all à la carte. They appreciated this. 'Oh it's a grand place,' my mother told my brother. 'You can have anything you want. Well, you can have poached egg on toast, which is what we want.'

> GIRL REP: I can't wait, I can't wait . . . I've got into the
> swing of doing speeches now.
> But when you've to follow you it's a bit hard.

These are TV-rental reps, and, reluctant though I am to admit it, I can see that with their conferences and camaraderie and their leisurewear it's business people like this who are banishing class from hotels and elsewhere.

The snobbish bit of me regrets this, but it's a small regret. If you want a poached egg, you can have a poached egg, and there's no nonsense about ties or even jeans. This is what they put on after a day at the office, so this is what they put on here.

They're at home in hotels; they're at home everywhere. I envy them.

> (*Lounge Bar.*)
> BUSINESSMAN: . . . was on an innovator, so I have innovated in the areas which I've worked and my intention is to be the person who makes it very profitable and to enlarge the turnover by at least twice.
> ANOTHER BUSINESSMAN: . . . next two years.
> BUSINESSMAN: . . . what I want to do is understand whether the people in the roles I have are doing the job they're supposed to be doing professionally, and, if it's not, to gauge the cost that I will incur to change those people who are very professional.

> (*Lobby.*)

I suppose one of the purposes of coming to this hotel in Harrogate was an evangelical one: I wanted to find people who were as awkward as I used to be in these surroundings and show them it didn't matter. Only I didn't find them, and besides, quite sensibly, everybody seems to know it doesn't matter. I wanted to revive or relocate some of the embarrassments or awkwardnesses I felt when I was younger. I didn't. I'm older, the world has changed, and maybe it's the businessmen who've changed it. Class isn't what it was; or nowadays perhaps people's embarrassments are differently located.

> LADY HAVING TEA: . . . perhaps go to . . . Wouldn't that be nice? We could just get across the road and sit on the seat and look at the shops, you know. I thought that would be rather nice. What do you think?
> HER FRIEND: Yes.
> LADY HAVING TEA: There's a most revolting smell. Can't you smell it?

HER FRIEND: I can now.

LADY HAVING TEA: Ooh, it's horrible.

(*Brontë Bar.*)

ITALIAN BARTENDER: And today lunch where are you going?

SMOKING WOMAN: Today for lunch I'm going home.

BARTENDER: Usual Sunday lunch?

SMOKING WOMAN: No.

BARTENDER: No?

SMOKING WOMAN: I've got a little piece of steak – ever so common – with chips and peas.

(*Lobby.*)

RECEPTIONIST: Thank you very much. Thank you. Goodbye.

That was going to be it. I came back to London after the filming had finished by train, and as it was the weekend I paid the £3 supplement and went First Class. I was sitting there when the ticket collector came round. He looked at my ticket. 'Oh, you don't belong in here,' he said. 'These are proper First Class people – the £3 supplement are further down. Come on – out.'

(*Credits over sound collage of conversations.*)

TIMID WOMAN: Eat it, don't leave it.

HER MOTHER: Well, I can't eat it all . . .

TIMID WOMAN: Oh you mustn't leave it . . .

ANDY . . . eventually there'll come a time when Tracy needs special maintenance – probably on drainage . . .

HELPER: Would you like me to put jam on your scone?

LECTURER: . . . they have not been using hormonal contraceptives . . .

GARDENER: . . . that's what I've been saying: let's walk today . . .

ANOTHER GARDENER: Did you?

ENVIRONMENTAL HEALTH OFFICER: Today I feel very proud to stand before you . . .

OLD MAN: It's a funny thing this puberty business when you think of it, isn't it?

LECTURER: . . . just keep taking pound notes from people and keep them smiling as you do it.

OLD LADY: I used to come in my youth to Harrogate . . .

RECEPTIONIST: Crown Hotel, good morning. Can I help you?

Russell Harty, 1934–1988

━━━━

'I don't seem to be able to get started,' Russell wrote to me in 1966. He was a lecturer at a training college in Derby and at the age of thirty-two had just made his first foray into television, a catastrophic appearance as a contestant on Granada's *Criss Cross Quiz*. The only question he got right was about Catherine of Braganza. It was such a public humiliation that Myrtle, his mother, refused to speak to him, treating him, as he said in the same letter, 'like Ena Sharples treated the now late Vera Lomax'.

When he did get started, of course, there was no stopping him, and it was soon hard to recall a time when he had not been on television, though it was the capacity for provocative half-truths and outrageous overstatement that stood him in such good stead as a schoolmaster which now fitted him for a career on the small screen.

To me and his other close friends his career in radio and television was almost incidental. It furnished him with more stories, the cast of them more glamorous and distinguished and the attendant disasters and humiliations more public, but he never really altered from the undergraduate who had rooms on the same staircase as I did thirty-four years ago at Exeter College, Oxford.

He had learned then, by the age of twenty, a lesson it took me half a lifetime to learn, namely that there was nothing that could not be said and no one to whom one could not say it. He knew instinctively that everybody was the same (which is not to say they are not different), and he assumed instinctively that if a thought had occurred to him then it must have occurred to someone else. So by the time he got to Oxford he had long since shed youth's stiff, necessary armour, and the television personality who, in the last year of his life, introduced himself to a slightly mystified Pope wasn't very different from the undergraduate who invited Vivien Leigh round for drinks. 'You can't do that,' I would protest. 'Why not?' said this youth off Blackburn market. 'They can only say no.' And if one had to point to the quality that distinguished Russell throughout his life it would be *cheek*.

While cheek is not quite a virtue, still it belongs in the other ranks of courage, so that even when he embarrassed you, you had to admire him for it – and, of course, laugh. It came out in the silliest things. He was one of the first people I knew who drove. It was the family car – opulent, vulgar, the emblem of successful greengrocery – and driving through Leeds or Manchester and seeing an old lady waiting at a bus-stop he would pip his horn and wave. She would instinctively wave back and, as we drove on, one would see her gazing after us, wondering who among her scant acquaintance had a large cream-coloured Jaguar. 'Brought a bit of interest into her life,' he would say, and that was as far as he got towards a philosophy: he understood that most people are prisoners in their lives and want releasing, even if it's only for a wave at a bus-stop.

He spent his life fleeing boredom, and he had no real goal beyond that. He had various romantic notions of himself, it's true – the country squire, for instance, though he was never particularly rustic; the solitary writer, though he hated being alone. Half an hour at his desk and he'd be on the phone saying 'Is the patch of wall you're staring at any more interesting than the one I'm staring at?'

'Private faces in public places', says Auden, 'Are wiser and nicer/Than public faces in private places.' For his friends he was naturally a private face, but for the public he seemed a private face too, and one that had strayed on to the screen seemingly untouched by expertise. That was why, though it infuriated his critics, the public liked him and took him to their hearts as they never did more polished performers. And yes he fumbled, and yes one wished he would reach for the right word rather than the next but two, and yes his delivery could be as tortured as his mother's was answering the telephone, but it didn't matter. That was part of his ordinariness and part of his style.

Still, television magnifies some personalities, but Russell it diminished, and people watching him saw only a fraction of the man. He once had to do a promotion for British goods in Bahrein. Flown there on Concorde with a party that included a beauty queen and a town crier, they sat down to a lunch of roast beef and Yorkshire pudding in a temperature of 110 in the shade. They all got on very well, except that after Russell had stood up and done his bit and sat down the town crier leaned over and said, 'I'll tell you something. You're better off than on.' And of course he was.

One laughed more helplessly with him than with anyone else I know, but so much of his humour – immediate and throwaway and born out of disaster and humiliation – is hard to recapture. The worst meal I ever had in my life was with him, and, ironically, in France. After the soup he pushed his plate back. 'Well, that soup might be a big event in a day in the life of Ivan Denisovitch but it didn't do much for me.' International figures had a habit of intruding on the domestic scene. 'I think', he'd say, popping in another violet cream, 'the only person who must be more depressed than I am at this moment is Benazir Bhutto.' He took no interest in current affairs except insofar as they intruded on his immediate concerns. 'I think the pace of glasnost is too hectic. The next thing you know we shall have Mr Gorbachev on *Blankety Blank*.'

'I'm fed up with Agewatch and Childwatch. I'm thinking of founding a society against potential suicide called Wristwatch.'

Some random thoughts:

He loved Italy, hated Greece.

He liked families and was an *ami de maison* in half a dozen households.

He was uncensorious of himself and of other people.

He knew that there are no rules.

He never kept people in compartments, introducing and mixing one layer of his friends with another. If somebody new came into his life he expected his old friends to budge up and make room for them. Which, Russell being Russell, they generally did. And he would do the same for them.

He was unashamedly self-interested. He switched on Dennis Potter's *The Singing Detective* at the point where the naked Michael Gambon is having his psoriasis anointed by a nurse. In order to stop himself getting excited, Gambon recites a list of the most boring television programmes he can think of. Russell waited with bated breath long enough to make sure he wasn't on the list, and then switched off.

He would telephone in the morning to find out whether you were free for supper that evening, promising to call back later to confirm. When he didn't, you knew he'd had a Better Offer. This principle of the Better Offer was respected, though complained of, by all his friends.

If you did manage a meal, a couple of hours would do it. 'I'm bored now,' he would say.

'But he's so silly,' pompous people would tell you, not understanding that that was why one loved him, that to be silly is not to be foolish.

The fourteen-year-old boy who had thought it worthwhile confiding in his diary that Princess Margaret had a slight cold remained all his life a sucker for royalty, and unashamed of it. A couple of years ago he arranged for the Princess of Wales to visit Settle and Giggleswick. At the end of the visit the Princess offered him a lift back to London in the royal plane. Notwithstanding he had to get into the plane with a plastic bag over his head to evade the attentions of the press, he accepted with alacrity. They had both of them got on very well and made each other laugh, and now spent a happy hour chatting as they flew south. Arrived at Northolt they said goodbye, the Princess sped off to Windsor while Russell flung himself into a taxi and rushed to Heathrow and a plane back. He hadn't wanted a lift at all, but just couldn't resist the offer. It was sheer cheek.

The spell of royalty persisted to the end. The last time I saw him I had gone up to Leeds for some function and met there Professor Losowsky, the head of the team that fought so long for his life at St James's Hospital. At that time prospects were quite hopeful, and the professor told me how patient Russell had been under weeks of wearisome treatment, unable to speak, fed intravenously, rest impossible. 'I have', said the professor, 'great admiration for his qualities of character'. Now this set me back, because it was taken for granted by all his friends that Russell had no qualities of character at all. How else could he have been such good company? But I went up to the hospital prepared for a change, expecting, in Larkin's phrase, to see a new man when I'd quite liked the old.

I need not have worried. I found him festooned with wires and equipment, a tracheotomy tube in his throat, monitored, ventilated. But underneath all this he had a message he wanted to convey. The nurse, who had got used to lip-reading him, thought it was something about sherry. Russell shook his head and closed his eyes in that familiar gesture of impatience, learned from Annie Walker in *Coronation Street*. We tried again, and he began to get agitated. Fearful of a relapse, the nurse thought we'd better find out what this vital message was, so she laboriously disconnected Russell from his machine, took out the tracheotomy tube, and pressed a pad over his throat so we could hear his faint voice and the essential words. They were: 'Ned Sherrin had supper with Princess Margaret last week and she asked how I was. Twice.' It was a triumph for the strength of weak character.

Russell never made any secret of his homosexuality even in those unliberated days when he was an undergraduate. He didn't look on it as an affliction, but he was never one for a crusade either. He just got on with it. He had never read Proust, but he had somehow taken a short cut across the allotments and arrived at the same conclusions. His funniest stories were always of the absurdities of sex and the ludicrous situations it had led him into, and if he was never short of friends it was because his partners knew that there would always be laughs, sharing a joke something rarer than sharing a bed.

In the succession of his friends he was happier than most people, certainly during the last five or six years of his life in his friendship with Jamie O'Neill, but with the gutter press systematically trawling public life for sexual indiscretion he knew he was in a delicate position. So when in March last year the *News of the World* set him up, then broke to an unstartled public the shocking news, Russell thought his career was over. One longed for him to say 'So what?', but here, not surprisingly, with his livelihood at stake, his cheek failed him. He expected the BBC not to renew his contract and that offers of work elsewhere would be bound to dwindle.

In fact this did not happen, and he began to work harder than he had ever worked before. So convinced was he that there would soon be no more, he accepted every offer that came his way. Thus at the same time he was making his television series *The Grand Tour* for the BBC, he was doing a weekly TV programme for BBC NorthWest and presenting *Start the Week* on radio, besides doing a weekly column for the *Sunday Times*. In addition to all this he had to write the book of his television series. On the surface it seemed things had never been better. But his first instinct had been right. The gutter press had finished him because they had panicked him into working so hard that by the time he was stricken with hepatitis he was an exhausted man.

And it went on. Reporters intermittently infested his home village for more than a year, bribing local children for information about his life, even (there is terrible comedy in it) trying to bribe the local vicar. Now as he fought for his life in St James's Hospital one newspaper took a flat opposite and had a camera with a long lens trained on the window of his ward – the nurses would point it out to you when you visited him. A reporter posing as a junior doctor smuggled himself into the ward and demanded to see his notes, and every lunch-time journalists took the hospital porters over the road to the pub to try to bribe them into taking a photo of him. One saw at that time in the tireless and unremitting efforts of the team at St James's the best of which we are capable, and in the equally tireless, though rather better rewarded, efforts of the journalists the worst.

As the days went on their fury mounted, and one had to sympathize. Russell, with his usual lack of consideration, was dying of the wrong disease. Even worse, for a time it seemed he wasn't dying at all and looked boringly likely to recover. The final touch, however, came on television, when Russell was actually on his deathbed, and the woman who had written the original story in the *News of the World* could not be restrained from retelling the tale of her journalistic triumph. Some of you may think that these kind of recriminations are out of place at a memorial service, and certain it is that Russell would not have approved of them. Had he recovered he would have gone on going to Mr Murdoch and Mr Maxwell's parties and doing his column for a Murdoch newspaper. The world was like that. Or at least England is like that.

There was one more joke before he died. Many of you will know Russell's secretary and personal assistant of many years, Pat Heald. Pat maintained some order in his frenzied life; no one understood him better, and the efficiency – clairvoyance almost – with which she anticipated his requirements and outflanked his changes of mind never ceased to gratify and also to infuriate him. He did not like to think he was known so well. On the day before he died I rang his oldest friends, Hugh and Joan Stalker, to find out what the situation was, but they were already at his bedside. The person who answered the phone told me that in a last desperate gamble the team at St James's were going to try a liver transplant. 'But', she went on, 'there's some confusion. The hospital hasn't been able to find a liver, but apparently Pat Heald has managed to put her hands on one.' It wasn't true, quite, but for both of them it would have been a wonderful apotheosis.

But it was the last joke, and the first that he was never going to be able to share.

God bless him.

Innes Lloyd, 1925–1991

My telephone went one morning in 1972. Never having written a television film before, I'd cobbled some scenes together about a group of cyclists before the First World War who go on a day out to Fountains Abbey from Hebden Bridge. Then just embarking on his film career, Stephen Frears had hawked it round the BBC with no success and I'd stopped thinking about it and got on with something else until that morning when the phone went. The voice was lazy, genial and utterly untinged by art. 'I gather the Head of Plays has turned it down. Well, that seems a pretty good recommendation to me. The report says it doesn't really go anywhere. Well, it goes to Fountains Abbey and back, and I think that's quite far enough.'

Thereafter we did nearly a score of films and plays together – the last one this summer, in the final months of Innes's life.

To begin with I was surprised how well we got on. The sort of character he seemed to be – conservative, clubbable, at ease with himself and the world – often makes me uneasy and aware of my own social inadequacies. It was only gradually that I came to appreciate how tolerant he was, and gentle, and lacking in any respect for the forms of things.

His appearance too was deceptive. Though it was the navy that Innes had served in, he always looked to me vaguely military: one could imagine him a slightly eccentric colonel in the North Africa campaign, swanning about the desert in

An Address given at St James's, Piccadilly, 19 November 1991 battledress top, cravat and a pair of old corduroy trousers. Instead of that it was the fifth floor of TV Centre. But maybe it was a sense of just having missed his time that made him in so much of his work celebrate heroes – Orde Wingate, Donald Campbell, Amy Johnson, Bomber Harris and the troops at Arnhem.

It was a side of him that my stuff didn't cater for – to say the least – but with which Innes was in his element. Stephen Frears had been drawn to him because Innes had come to Drama via Outside Broadcasting and so had no particular aesthetic or political axe to grind. And indeed, shivering in a bitter spring on the Yorkshire wolds or on the sands at Morecambe, my first films with Innes just seemed to be Outside Broadcasting carried on by other means.

Though I knew him for twenty years, I have found it hard to write about him. This is not the place to catalogue someone's faults, but the odd shortcoming or two does make things easier. With Innes I find it hard to name one. In all the time we worked together I cannot remember him even once getting cross. I mentioned this to John Schlesinger, who's something of a connoisseur in this department, but he could only recall one occasion. It was when we were filming *An Englishman Abroad* and had one short afternoon to do, I think, four set-ups at Lobb's, the smart bootmakers in St James's. For some reason the scenes hadn't been rehearsed, and time that should have been spent setting up the shot had to be taken up rehearsing the actors. This apparently made Innes annoyed with John, but his bad temper must soon have blown over because it never got as far as me. All I remember of that afternoon was Innes sidling up to me and telling me to take a good look at the solitary customer in the shop, who, amid all the fret and upset of filming, was waiting impatiently for his shoes. He was a tall and elegant black gentleman with a silver-topped cane who treated our frenzied activity with obvious disdain. Innes whispered that the cobblers downstairs had warned the make-up department to keep out of this gentleman's way lest he eat them. 'That's a deplorable thing to say,' I said. 'I agree,' said Innes. 'Except that it's true. It's the ex-Emperor Bokassa.'

There is always a temptation on occasions such as this to talk less about the dead than about oneself, to see their lives as refracted through one's own, so that even as one celebrates a life one appropriates it. This is hard to avoid with Innes because we didn't mix socially. I think I went to his house once, and I'm not sure that he ever came to mine. Then when we did work together he made himself so totally available to me and to the job in hand that he might not have had any other life at all. And so every couple of years on average I'd have a play to do and I would send him the script, and the familiar process would begin again. It was like putting on the same pair of worn and comfortable shoes – suede shoes probably, as there was a hint of raffishness about him: shoes that had been kept for you between whiles ready for another stroll together. And it was a stroll. You knew you would have a good time, that there would be a lot of laughs, and that the drama would be confined to the script, not to the filming of it. Or, if there were dramas behind the scenes, behind the scenes they would stay; you would know nothing about it, because that was his responsibility not yours.

It was perhaps a stratagem, a useful fiction we both conspired in, but it was usual to pretend that we were engaged in a conspiracy to smuggle whatever production we were doing past the bureaucracy, which was never as keen on having it as we were on doing it. This was frequently no more than the truth, and however successful Innes's productions were they were seldom the favoured ones, still less the flagship – which only added to his satisfaction when they were eventually well received. I'm not sure if this was a stratagem he practised with his other writers, but it always worked with me.

Certainly we were always pretty far down the line when production money was handed out, however good our track record. Hence the Moscow scenes in *An Englishman Abroad* had to be filmed in Dundee, which turned out to be a blessing, and the Paris scenes in *102 Boulevard Haussmann* were filmed in Perth, which was . . . well, less so. Other productions with foreign settings somehow wangled weeks of exotic location filming even when they largely consisted of interiors, but that we never managed it was a joke, never a grumble. I always put it down to Innes being too nice, not a wheeler–dealer, and so a small price to pay. And besides he loved a studio and, though he enjoyed a production jaunt, he was never happier than when he was in the gallery at TC3 or on the stage at Ealing, where we were this last summer, Innes sitting beside the camera with his stick between his knees still with all his fun and zest, surveying the gallery at Buckingham Palace.

He was of course by this time desperately ill, but, just as he never passed on his worries about the production, so he would not burden you with problems he did not think were yours, dismissing his operation after Christmas as 'just a spot of plumbing. Nothing to worry about.' When Coral Browne had been ill during *An Englishman Abroad* she too had been very brave without, as must often be the temptation, letting you know she was being 'brave' about it. And so it was with Innes – no indication in his talk or his demeanour of the burden he was carrying, and no hint that there was anything else he would rather be doing at this moment in his life than the film. He even wondered about future projects, one on the Orgreave Riots with Don Shaw, and he asked me whether I thought there was a film to be made of A. J. P. Taylor's letters to his Hungarian wife. 'A lot of it takes place in Budapest,' said Innes, 'so at least we might get to Aberdeen.'

Some odd thoughts about him:

In all the years we worked together he never once told me what my viewing figures were or even mentioned them; to have done so would have been a concession to a view of television for which he had no time.

Though conservative by temperament, he hated Mrs Thatcher, 'Do you see what she's done now?' the initial topic at many a production meeting. That apart, his strongest condemnation of anyone was 'Bloody man' or 'Frightful person'.

Unstinting in his appreciation of others, he was pleased if you liked one of his productions but rarely complained if it had been badly received – just got on with the next job in hand.

For many years he shared a suite of offices on the fifth floor with a producer of a more radical stamp, Kenith Trodd. It was an unlikely pairing, and Trodd's doings often filled Innes with childlike amazement, but for all their disparity they were closer to each other than they were to many of their colleagues. 'He's all right is old Trodd,' Innes would say, one enthusiast recognizing another. And because he was laconic and unassuming – laid-back would be the current phrase – it wasn't immediately obvious that an enthusiast was what Innes was – and, though cast in a different mould, as much an enthusiast as that other BBC Welshman, Huw Wheldon.

He always had his priorities right. When things went wrong he was more concerned that no one should be hurt or treated unfairly than that his own reputation should be kept intact. On one film of mine, through no fault of his own, the director lost his nerve. We got behind, deadlines began to loom and the production to fall apart. In all this Innes's first concern was that this young man should recover his nerve and suffer no damage, and, though eventually another director had to take over, Innes straightaway made plans that once the opportunity arose the young man would get another production in less exacting circumstances.

Innes pretended to be an amateur while in truth being the supreme professional. It's a very English approach, and his preferences were very English. But he went his own way, and there are many writers besides myself who count themselves lucky that that way coincided with theirs – Don Shaw, Reg Gadney, Roger Milner, Andrew Davies, Richard Gordon, Robin Chapman, Michael Palin all have cause to be grateful to him. The greatest compliment he paid you was that he trusted you. He let you go your own way even though that might be well off the beaten track. I can't believe that Proust was quite his cup of tea, and it is surely only in remembering this lovely man that you would ever find Kafka even in the same sentence as Bomber Harris.

We all of us, I suppose, add up to, come down to, a jumble of attitudes, and Innes's, a code if not quite a creed, has taken something of a battering in recent years, both in the country and in the Corporation. It was no accident that he should have detested Mrs Thatcher to the comic extent that he did, because she stood for a single-mindedness, a want of magnanimity and an exclusiveness that challenged all the variety of qualities and attributes Innes celebrated in his work. They were, I suppose, the qualities of the old BBC, and in retrospect one can see how fitting it was that it should have been Innes who produced Roger Milner's play about Reith.

Liberal, magnanimous, indifferent to criticism, Innes Lloyd was in the best sense old-fashioned. But, tolerant, various, prodigal, fearless and passionate, his standards are – or were – those of the BBC he served so faithfully for twenty-six years, and to see those values fought for, reinstated and celebrated again would be the best memorial to this steadfast, gentle, generous man.

Peter Cook, 1937–1995

It is thirty-five years, almost to the day, since I first set eyes on
Peter, at lunch in a restaurant, I think on Goodge Street, with
Dudley Moore and Jonathan Miller, the meeting arranged by
John Bassett, whose idea it was that we should all work together
writing the review that turned into *Beyond the Fringe*.

Having already written while still an undergraduate a large
slice of the two West End shows *Pieces of Eight* and *One Over the
Eight*, Peter was quite prosperous and it showed. He dressed out
of Sportique, an establishment – gents' outfitters wouldn't
really describe it – at the west end of Old Compton Street, the
premises I think now occupied by the Café España.

There hadn't really been any men's fashions before 1960 –
most of the people I knew dressed in sports coat and flannels, as
some of us still do – but when I saw Peter he was wearing a
shortie overcoat, a not quite bum-freezer jacket, narrow
trousers, winkle-picker shoes and a silk tie with horizontal bars
across it. But what was most characteristic of him, and which
remained constant throughout his life, regardless of the sometimes quite dramatic changes in his physical appearance, was
that he was carrying, as he always seemed to be carrying, a large
armful of newspapers. He had besides a book on racing form,
and I remember being impressed not merely that this was someone who bet on horses but that here was someone who knew how
to bet on horses, and indeed had an account at a bookmaker's.

An Address given at Hampstead Parish Church on 1 May 1995

But it was the newspapers that were the clue to him. He was nurtured by newspapers, and there's a sense that whatever he wrote or extemporized, which he could at that time with a fluency so effortless as to make us all feel in differing degrees costive, was a kind of mould or fungus that grew out of the literally yards of newsprint that he daily digested. Newspapers mulched his talents, and he remained loyal to them all his life; and when he died they repaid some of that loyalty.

In those days I never saw him reading a book. I think he thought that most books were a con or at any rate a waste of time. He caught the drift of books though, sufficient for his own purposes, namely jokes, picking up enough about Proust, for instance, to know that he suffered from asthma and couldn't breathe very well; he decided in the finish, according to Peter, that if he couldn't do it well he wouldn't do it at all, and so died – this one of the gems from the monologue in *Beyond the Fringe* about the miner who wanted to be a judge but didn't have the Latin. How Proust had managed to work his way into the sketch I can't now remember, because it was less of a sketch than a continuing saga which each night developed new extravagances and surrealist turns, the mine at one point invaded by droves of Proust-lovers, headed by the scantily clad Beryl Jarvis. Why the name Beryl Jarvis should be funny I can't think. But it was and plainly is.

In those days Peter could tap a flow of mad verbal inventiveness that nothing could stem: not nerves, not drink, not embarrassment, not even the very occasional lack of response from the audience. He would sit there in his old raincoat and brown trilby, rocking slightly as he wove his ever more exuberant fantasies, on which, I have to admit, I looked less admiringly then than I do in retrospect. I had the spot in the show immediately following Peter's monologue, which was scheduled to last five minutes or so but would often last for

78

fifteen, when I would be handed an audience so weak from laughter I could do nothing with them.

Slim and elegant in those days, he was also quite vain, sensing instinctively as soon as he came into a room where the mirror was and casting pensive sidelong glances at it while stroking his chin, as if checking up on his own beauty. He also knew which was his best side for photographers.

There were limits to his talents; one or two things he thought he could do well he actually couldn't do for toffee. One was an imitation of Elvis and another was to ad lib Shakespeare. Both were deeply embarrassing, though of course Peter was immune to embarrassment – that was one of his great strengths.

What makes speaking about him a delicate task is that he was intolerant of humbug: detecting it (and quite often mistakenly), he would fly into a huge self-fuelling rage which propelled him into yet more fantasy and even funnier jokes. So it's hard to praise him to his face – even his dead face – that quizzical smile, never very far away, making a mockery of the sincerest sentiments. So he would be surprised, I think, to be praised for his strength of character, but in his later years when some of his talent for exuberant invention deserted him I never heard him complain. It must have been some consolation that the younger generation of comic writers and performers drew inspiration from him, but he never bragged about that either. Nor did he resent that Dudley had gone on to success in Hollywood and he hadn't. The only regret he regularly voiced was that at the house we rented in Fairfield, Connecticut in 1963 he had saved David Frost from drowning.

In later years I saw him quite seldom, though if he'd seen something you'd done on television he'd generally telephone, ostensibly to congratulate you, but actually to congratulate you on having got away with it yet again. There's a scene in *Brideshead Revisited* where Charles Ryder has an exhibition of his worthy but uninspired paintings which is a great success. Then Anthony Blanche turns up, who knows exactly what's what: 'My dear,' he says, 'let us not expose your little imposture before these good, plain people; let us not spoil their moment of pleasure. But we know, you and I, that this is all t-terrible t-tripe.' And sometimes what Peter was telephoning about had been tripe and sometimes it hadn't, but you didn't mind because there's always a bit of you thinks it is anyway, and it was to that part of you that Peter spoke. And since he did it without rancour or envy it was a great relief. I suppose it was partly this that made him in his latter days such an unlikely father-figure for younger performers.

In the press coverage of his death one could detect a certain satisfaction, the feeling being that he had paid some sort of price for his gifts, had died in the way the press prefer funny men to die, like Hancock and Peter Sellers, sad and disappointed. I don't know that that was true, and it certainly wouldn't have found much favour with Peter.

Trying to sum him up in his latter years – the television in the afternoon, the chat shows, the golf in Bermuda – one thinks of one of the stock characters in an old-fashioned Western: Thomas Mitchell, say, in John Ford's *Stagecoach*, the doctor who's always to be found in the saloon and whose allegiance is never quite plain. Seldom sober, he is cleverer than most of the people he associates with, spending his time playing cards with the baddies but taking no sides. Still, when the chips are down, and slightly to his own surprise, he does the right thing. But there is never any suggestion that, having risen to the occasion, he is going to mend his ways in any permanent fashion. He goes on much as ever down the path to self-destruction, knowing that redemption is not for him – and it is this that redeems him.

As for us, his audience, we are comforted by the assurance that there is a truer morality than the demands of convention, that this is a figure from the parables, a publican, a sinner, but never a Pharisee. In him morality is discovered far from its official haunts, the message of a character like Peter's being that a life of complete self-indulgence, if led with the whole heart, may also bring wisdom.

The Lady in the Van

Good nature, or what is often considered as such, is the most selfish of all virtues: it is nine times out of ten mere indolence of disposition.

William Hazlitt, 'On the Knowledge of Character'

(1822)

'I ran into a snake this afternoon,' Miss Shepherd said. 'It was coming up Parkway. It was a long, grey snake – a boa constrictor possibly. It looked poisonous. It was keeping close to the wall and seemed to know its way. I've a feeling it may have been heading for the van.' I was relieved that on this occasion she didn't demand that I ring the police, as she regularly did if anything out of the ordinary occurred. Perhaps this was too out of the ordinary (though it turned out the pet shop in Parkway had been broken into the previous night, so she may have seen a snake). She brought her mug over and I made her a drink, which she took back to the van. 'I thought I'd better tell you,' she said, 'just to be on the safe side. I've had some close shaves with snakes.'

This encounter with the putative boa constrictor was in the summer of 1971, when Miss Shepherd and her van had for some months been at a permanent halt opposite my house in Camden Town. I had first come across her a few years previously, stood by her van, stalled as usual, near the convent at the top of the street. The convent (which was to have a subsequent career as the Japanese School) was a gaunt reformatory-like building that housed a dwindling garrison of aged nuns and was notable for a striking crucifix attached to the wall overlooking the traffic lights. There was something about the position of Christ, pressing himself against the grim pebbledash beneath the barred windows of the convent, that called up visions of the Stalag and the searchlight and which had caused us to dub him 'The Christ of Colditz'. Miss Shepherd, not looking un-crucified herself, was standing by her vehicle in an attitude with which I was to become very familiar, left arm extended with the palm flat against the side of the van indicating ownership, the right arm summoning anyone who was fool enough to take notice of her, on this occasion me. Nearly six foot, she was a commanding figure, and would have been more so had she not been kitted out in greasy raincoat, orange skirt, Ben Hogan golfing-cap and carpet slippers. She would be going on sixty at this time.

She must have prevailed on me to push the van as far as Albany Street, though I recall nothing of the exchange. What I do remember was being overtaken by two policemen in a panda car as I trundled the van across Gloucester Bridge; I thought that, as the van was certainly holding up the traffic, they might have lent a hand. They were wiser than I knew. The other feature of this first run-in with Miss Shepherd was her driving technique. Scarcely had I put my shoulder to the back of the van, an old Bedford, than a long arm was stretched elegantly out of the driver's window to indicate in textbook fashion that she (or rather I) was moving off. A few yards further on, as we were about to turn into Albany Street, the arm emerged again, twirling elaborately in the air to indicate that we were branching left, the movement done with such boneless grace that this section of the Highway Code might have been choreographed by Petipa with Ulanova at the wheel. Her 'I am coming to a halt' was less poised, as she had plainly not expected me to give up pushing and shouted angrily back that it was the other end of Albany Street she wanted, a mile further on. But I had had enough by this time and left her there, with no thanks for my trouble. Far from it. She even climbed out of the van and came running after me, shouting that I had no business abandoning her, so that passers-by looked at me as if I had done some injury to this pathetic scarecrow. 'Some people!' I suppose I thought, feeling foolish that I'd been taken for a ride (or taken her for one) and cross that I'd fared worse than if I'd never lifted a finger, these mixed feelings to be the invariable aftermath of any transaction involving Miss Shepherd. One seldom was able to do her a good turn without some thoughts of strangulation.

It must have been a year or so after this, and so some time in the late sixties, that the van first appeared in Gloucester Crescent. In those days the street was still a bit of a mixture. Its large semi-detached villas had originally been built to house the Victorian middle class, then it had gone down in the world, and, though it had never entirely decayed, many of the villas degenerated into rooming-houses and so were among the earliest candidates for what is now called 'gentrification' but which was then called 'knocking through'. Young professional couples, many of them in journalism or television, bought up the houses, converted them and (an invariable feature of such conversions) knocked the basement rooms together to form a large kitchen/dining-room. In the mid-sixties I wrote a BBC TV series, *Life in NW1*, based on one such family, the Stringalongs,* whom Mark Boxer then took over to people a cartoon strip in the *Listener*, and who kept cropping up in his drawings for the rest of his life. What made the social set-up funny was the disparity between the style in which the new arrivals found themselves able to live and their progressive opinions: guilt, put simply, which today's gentrifiers are said famously not to feel (or 'not to have a problem about'). We did have a problem, though I'm not sure we were any better for it. There was a gap between our social position and our social

* See page 598.

obligations. It was in this gap that Miss Shepherd (in her van) was able to live.

October 1969. When she is not in the van Miss S. spends much of her day sitting on the pavement in Parkway, where she has a pitch outside Williams & Glyn's Bank. She sells tracts, entitled 'True View: Mattering Things', which she writes herself, though this isn't something she will admit. 'I sell them, but so far as the authorship is concerned I'll say they are anonymous and that's as far as I'm prepared to go.' She generally chalks the gist of the current pamphlet on the pavement, though with no attempt at artistry. 'St Francis FLUNG money from him' is today's message, and prospective customers have to step over it to get into the bank. She also makes a few coppers selling pencils. 'A gentleman came the other day and said that the pencil he had bought from me was the best pencil on the market at the present time. It lasted him three months. He'll be back for another one shortly.' D., one of the more conventional neighbours (and not a knocker-through), stops me and says, 'Tell me, is she a *genuine* eccentric?'

April 1970. Today we moved the old lady's van. An obstruction order has been put under the windscreen wiper, stating that it was stationed outside number 63 and is a danger to public health. This order, Miss S. insists, is a statutory order: 'And statutory means standing – in this case standing outside number 63 – so, if the van is moved on, the order will be invalid.' Nobody ventures to argue with this, but she can't decide whether her next pitch should be outside number 61 or further on. Eventually she decides there is 'a nice space' outside 62 and plumps for that. My neighbour Nick Tomalin and I heave away at the back of the van, but while she is gracefully indicating that she is moving off (for all of the fifteen feet) the van doesn't budge. 'Have you let the handbrake off?' Nick Tomalin asks. There is a pause. 'I'm just in the process of taking it off.' As we are poised for the move, another Camden Town eccentric materializes, a tall, elderly figure in long overcoat and Homburg hat, with a distinguished grey moustache and in his buttonhole a flag for the Primrose League. He takes off a grubby canary glove and leans a shaking hand against the rear of the van (OLU246), and when we have moved it forward the few statutory feet he puts on his glove again, saying, 'If you should need me I'm just round the corner' (i.e. in Arlington House, the working men's hostel).

I ask Miss S. how long she has had the van. 'Since 1965,' she says, 'though don't spread that around. I got it to put my things in. I came down from St Albans in it, and plan to go back there eventually. I'm just pedalling water at the moment. I've always been in the transport line. Chiefly delivery and chauffeuring. You know,' she says mysteriously – 'renovated army vehicles. And I've got good topography. I always have had. I knew Kensington in the blackout.'

This van (there were to be three others in the course of the next twenty years) was originally brown, but by the time it had reached the Crescent it had been given a coat of yellow. Miss S. was fond of yellow ('It's the papal colour') and was never content to leave her vehicles long in their original trim. Sooner or later she could be seen moving slowly round her immobile home, thoughtfully touching up the rust from a tiny tin of primrose paint, looking, in her long dress and sunhat, much as Vanessa Bell would have looked had she gone in for painting Bedford vans. Miss S. never appreciated the difference between car enamel and ordinary gloss paint, and even this she never bothered to mix. The result was that all her vehicles ended up looking as if they had been given a coat of badly made custard or plastered with scrambled egg. Still, there were few occasions on which one saw Miss Shepherd genuinely happy and one of them was when she was putting paint on. A few years before she died she went in for a Reliant Robin (to put more of her things in). It was actually yellow to start with, but that didn't save it from an additional coat, which she applied as Monet might have done, standing back to judge the effect of each brush-stroke. The Reliant stood outside my gate. It was towed away earlier this year, a scatter of yellow drops on the kerb all that remains to mark its final parking place.

January 1971. Charity in Gloucester Crescent takes refined forms. The publishers next door are bringing out some classical volume and to celebrate the event last night held a Roman dinner. This morning the au pair was to be seen knocking at the window of the van with a plate of Roman remains. But Miss S. is never easy to help. After twelve last night I saw her striding up the Crescent waving her stick and telling someone to be off. Then I heard a retreating middle-class voice say plaintively, 'But I only asked if you were all right.'

June 1971. Scarcely a day passes now without some sort of incident involving the old lady. Yesterday evening around ten a sports car swerves over to her side of the road so that the driver, rich, smart and in his twenties, can lean over and bang on the side of the van, presumably to flush out for his grinning girlfriend the old witch who lives there. I shout at him and he sounds his horn and roars off. Miss S. of course wants the police called, but I can't see the point, and indeed around five this morning I wake to find two policemen at much the same game, idly shining their torches in the windows in the hope that she'll wake up and enliven a dull hour of their beat. Tonight a white car reverses dramatically up the street, screeches to a halt beside the van, and a burly young man jumps out and gives the van a terrific shaking. Assuming (hoping, probably) he would have driven off by the time I get outside, I find he's still there, and ask him what the fuck he thinks he's doing. His response is quite mild. 'What's up with you then?' he asks. 'You still on the telly? You nervous? You're trembling all over.' He then calls me a fucking cunt and drives off. After all that, of course, Miss S. isn't in the van at all, so I end up as usual more furious with her than I am with the lout.

These attacks, I'm sure, disturbed my peace of mind more than they did hers. Living in the way she did, every day must have brought such cruelties. Some of the stallholders in the Inverness Street market used to persecute her with medieval relish – and children too, who both inflict and suffer such casual cruelties themselves. One night two drunks systematically smashed all the windows of the van, the flying glass cutting her face. Furious over any small liberty, she was only mildly disturbed by this. 'They may have had too much to drink by mistake,' she said. 'That does occur through not having eaten, possibly. I don't want a case.' She was far more interested in 'a ginger feller I saw in Parkway in company with Mr Khruschev. Has he disappeared recently?'

But to find such sadism and intolerance so close at hand began actively to depress me, and having to be on the alert for every senseless attack made it impossible to work. There came a day when, after a long succession of such incidents, I suggested that she spend at least the nights in a lean-to at the side of my house. Initially reluctant, as with any change, over the next two years she gradually abandoned the van for the hut.

In giving her sanctuary in my garden and landing myself with a tenancy that went on eventually for fifteen years I was never under any illusion that the impulse was purely charitable. And of course it made me furious that I had been driven to such a pass. But I wanted a quiet life as much as, and possibly more than, she did. In the garden she was at least out of harm's way.

October 1973. I have run a lead out to the lean-to and now regularly have to mend Miss S.'s electric fire, which she keeps fusing by plugging too many appliances into the attachment. I sit on the steps fiddling with the fuse while she squats on her haunches in the hut. 'Aren't you cold? You could come in here. I could light a candle and then it would be a bit warmer. The toad's been in once or twice. He was in here with a slug. I think he may be in love with the slug. I tried to turn it out and it got very disturbed. I thought he was going to go for me.' She complains that there is not enough room in the shed and suggests I get her a tent, which she could then use to store some of her things. 'It would only be three feet high and by rights ought to be erected in a meadow. Then there are these shatterproof greenhouses. Or something could be done with old raincoats possibly.'

March 1974. The council are introducing parking restrictions in the Crescent. Residents' bays have been provided and yellow lines drawn up the rest of the street. To begin with, the workmen are very understanding, painting the yellow line as far as the van, then beginning again on the other side so that technically it is still legally parked. However, a higher official has now stepped in and served a removal order on it, so all this week there has been a great deal of activity as Miss S. transports cargoes of plastic bags across the road, through the garden and into the hut. While professing faith in divine protection for the van, she is prudently clearing out her belongings against its possible removal. A notice she has written declaring the council's action illegal twirls idly under the windscreen wiper.

'The notice was served on a Sunday. I believe you can serve search warrants on a Sunday but nothing else, possibly. I should have the Freedom of the Land for the good articles I've sold on the economy.' She is particularly concerned about the tyres of the van which 'may be miraculous. They've only been pumped up twice since 1964. If I get another vehicle' – and Lady W. is threatening to buy her one – 'I'd like them transferred.'

The old van was towed away in April 1974 and another one provided by Lady W. ('a titled Catholic lady', as Miss S. always referred to her). Happy to run to a new (albeit old) van, Lady W. was understandably not anxious to have it parked outside her front door and eventually, and perhaps by now inevitably, the van and Miss S. ended up in my garden. This van was roadworthy, and Miss S. insisted on being the one to drive it through the gate into the garden, a manoeuvre which once again enabled her to go through her full repertoire of hand signals. Once the van was on site Miss S. applied the handbrake with such determination that, like Excalibur, it could never thereafter be released, rusting so firmly into place that when the van came to be moved ten years later it had to be hoisted over the wall by the council crane.

This van (and its successor, bought in 1983) now occupied a paved area between my front door and the garden gate, the bonnet of the van hard by my front step, its rear door, which Miss S. always used to get in and out of, a few feet from the gate. Callers at the house had to squeeze past the back of the van and come down the side, and while they waited for my door to be opened they would be scrutinized from behind the murky windscreen by Miss Shepherd. If they were unlucky, they would find the rear door open with Miss S. dangling her large white legs over the back. The interior of the van, a midden of old clothes, plastic bags and half-eaten food, was not easy to ignore, but should anyone Miss S. did not know venture to speak to her she would promptly tuck her legs back and wordlessly shut the door. For the first few years of her sojourn in the garden I would try and explain to mystified callers how this situation had arisen, but after a while I ceased to care, and when I didn't mention it nor did anyone else.

At night the impression was haunting. I had run a cable out from the house to give her light and heating, and through the ragged draperies that hung over the windows of the van a visitor would glimpse Miss S.'s spectral figure, often bent over in prayer or lying on her side like an effigy on a tomb, her face resting on one hand, listening to Radio 4. Did she hear any movements she would straightaway switch off the light and wait, like an animal that has been disturbed, until she was sure the coast was clear and could put the light on again. She retired early and would complain if anyone called or left late at night. On one occasion Coral Browne was coming away from the house with her husband, Vincent Price, and they were talking quietly. 'Pipe down,' snapped the voice from the van, 'I'm trying to sleep.' For someone who had brought terror to millions it was an unexpected taste of his own medicine.

December 1974. Miss S. has been explaining to me why the old Bedford (the van not the music-hall) ceased to go, 'possibly'. She had put in some of her home-made petrol, based on a recipe for petrol substitute she read about several years ago in a newspaper. 'It was a spoonful of petrol, a gallon of water and a pinch of something you could get in every High Street. Well, I got it into my head, I don't know why, that it was bicarbonate of soda, only I think I was mistaken. It must be either sodium chloride or sodium nitrate, only I've since been told sodium chloride is salt and the man in Boots wouldn't sell me the other, saying it might cause explosions. Though I think me being an older person he knew I would be more responsible. Though not all old ladies perhaps.'

February 1975. Miss S. rings, and when I open the door she makes a bee-line for the kitchen stairs. 'I'd like to see you. I've called several times. I wonder whether I can use the toilet first.' I say I think this is pushing it a bit. 'I'm not pushing it at all. I just will do the interview better if I can use the toilet first.' Afterwards she sits down in her green mac and purple headscarf, the knuckles of one large mottled hand resting on the clean, scrubbed table and explains how she has devised a method of 'getting on the wireless'. I was to ask the BBC to give me a phone-in programme ('something someone like you could get put on in a jiffy') and then she would ring me up from the house. 'Either that or I could get on *Petticoat Line*. I know a darn sight more on moral matters than most of them. I could sing my song over the telephone. It's a lovely song, called "The End of the World" ' (which is pure *Beyond the Fringe*). 'I won't commit myself to singing it – not at this moment – but I probably would. Some sense should be said and knowledge known. It could all be anonymous. I could be called The Lady Behind the Curtain. Or A Woman of Britain. You could take a *nom-de-plume* view of it.' This idea of The Woman Behind the Curtain has obviously taken her fancy and she begins to expand on it, demonstrating where the curtain could be, her side of it coincidentally taking in the television and the easy chair. She could be behind the curtain, she explains, do her periodic broadcasts, and the rest of the time 'be a guest at the television and take in some civilization. Perhaps there would be gaps filled with nice classical music. I know one: Prelude and "Liebestraum" by Liszt. I believe he was a Catholic priest. It means "love's dream", only not the sexy stuff. It's the love of God and the sanctification of labour and so on, which would recommend it to celibates like you and me, possibly.' Shocked at this tentative bracketing of our conditions, I quickly get rid of her and, though it's a bitter cold night, open the windows wide to get rid of the smell.

The Woman Behind the Curtain remained a favourite project of hers, and in 1976 she wrote to Aiman (*sic*) Andrews: 'Now that *This is Your Life* is ended, having cost too much etc., I might be able to do a bit as The Lady Behind the Curtain. All you need do is put a curtain up to hide me but permit words of sense to come forth in answer to some questions. Sense is needed.' Hygiene was needed too, but possibly in an effort to persuade me about being behind the curtain she brought the subject up herself: 'I'm by nature a very clean person. I have a testimonial for a Clean Room, awarded me some years ago, and my aunt, herself spotless, said I was the cleanest of my mother's children, particularly in the unseen places.' I never fathomed her toilet arrangements. She only once asked me to buy her toilet rolls ('I use them to wipe my face'), but whatever happened in that department I took to be part of some complicated arrangement involving the plastic bags she used to hurl from the van every morning. When she could still manage stairs she did very occasionally use my loo, but I didn't encourage it; it was here, on the threshold of the toilet, that my charity stopped short. Once when I was having some building work done (and was, I suppose, conscious of what the workmen were thinking), I very boldly said there was a smell of urine. 'Well, what can you expect when they're raining bricks down on me all day? And then I think there's a mouse. So that would make a cheesy smell, possibly.'

Miss S.'s daily emergence from the van was highly dramatic. Suddenly and without warning the rear door would be flung open to reveal the tattered draperies that masked the terrible interior. There was a pause, then through the veils would be hurled several bulging plastic sacks. Another pause, before slowly and with great caution one sturdy slippered leg came feeling for the floor before the other followed and one had the first sight of the day's wardrobe. Hats were always a feature: a black railwayman's hat with a long neb worn slightly on the skew so that she looked like a drunken signalman or a French guardsman of the 1880s; there was her Charlie Brown pitcher's hat; and in June 1977 an octagonal straw table-mat, tied on with a chiffon scarf and a bit of cardboard for the peak. She also went in for green eyeshades. Her skirts had a telescopic appearance, as they had often been lengthened many times over by the simple expedient of sewing a strip of extra cloth around the hem, though with no attempt at matching. One skirt was made by sewing several orange dusters together. When she fell foul of authority she put it down to her clothes. Once, late at night, the police rang me from Tunbridge Wells. They had picked her up on the station, thinking her dress was a nightie. She was indignant. 'Does it look like a nightie? You see lots of people wearing dresses like this. I don't think this style can have got to Tunbridge Wells yet.'

Miss S. seldom wore stockings, and alternated between black pumps and brown carpet slippers. Her hands and feet were large, and she was what my grandmother would have called 'a big-boned woman'. She was middle-class and spoke in a middle-class way, though her querulous and often resentful demeanour tended to obscure this; it wasn't a gentle or a genteel voice. Running through her vocabulary was a streak of schoolgirl slang. She wouldn't say she was tired, she was 'all done up'; petrol was 'juice'; and if she wasn't keen on doing something she'd say 'I'm darned if I will.' All her conversation was impregnated with the vocabulary of her peculiar brand of Catholic fanaticism ('the dire importance of justice deeds'). It was the language of the leaflets she wrote, the 'possibly' with which she ended so many of her sentences an echo of the 'Subject to the Roman Catholic Church in her rights etc.' with which she headed every leaflet.

May 1976. I have had some manure delivered for the garden and, since the manure heap is not far from the van, Miss S. is concerned that people passing might think the smell is coming from there. She wants me to put a notice on the gate to the effect that the smell is the manure, not her. I say no, without adding, as I could, that the manure actually smells much nicer.

I am working in the garden when Miss B., the social worker, comes with a boxful of clothes. Miss S. is reluctant to open the van door, as she is listening to *Any Answers*, but eventually she slides on her bottom to the door of the van and examines the clothes. She is unimpressed.

MISS S.: I only asked for one coat.

MISS B.: Well, I brought three just in case you wanted a change.

MISS S.: I haven't got room for three. Besides, I was planning to wash this coat in the near future. That makes four.

MISS B.: This is my old nursing mac.

MISS S.: I have a mac. Besides, green doesn't suit me. Have you got the stick?

MISS B.: No. That's being sent down. It had to be made specially.

MISS S.: Will it be long enough?

MISS B.: Yes. It's a special stick.

MISS S.: I don't want a special stick. I want an ordinary stick. Only longer. Does it have a rubber thing on it?

When Miss B. has gone, Miss S. sits at the door of the van slowly turning over the contents of the box like a chimpanzee, sniffing them and holding them up and muttering to herself.

June 1976. I am sitting on the steps mending my bike when Miss S. emerges for her evening stroll. 'I went to Devon on Saturday,' she said. 'On this frisbee.' I suppose she means freebie, a countrywide concession to pensioners that BR ran last weekend. 'Dawlish I went to. People very nice. The man over the loudspeaker called us Ladies and Gentlemen, and so he should. There was one person shouted, only he wasn't one of us – the son of somebody, I think.' And almost for the first time ever she smiled, and said how they had all been bunched up trying to get into this one carriage, a great crowd, and how she had been hoisted up. 'It would have made a film,' she said. 'I thought of you.' And she stands there in her grimy raincoat, strands of lank grey hair escaping from under her headscarf. I am thankful people had been nice to her, and wonder what the carriage must have been like all that hot afternoon. She then tells me about a programme on Francis Thompson she'd heard on the wireless, how he had tried to become a priest but had felt he had failed in his vocation, and had become a tramp. Then, unusually, she told me a little of her own life, and how she tried to become a nun on two occasions, had undergone instruction as a novice, but was forced to give it up on account of ill-health, and that she had felt for many years that she had failed. But that this was wrong, and it was not a failure. 'If I could have had more modern clothes, longer sleep and better air, possibly, I would have made it.'

'A bit of a spree,' she called her trip to Dawlish. 'My spree.'

June 1977. On this the day of the Jubilee, Miss S. has stuck a paper Union Jack in the cracked back window of the van. It is the only one in the Crescent. Yesterday she was wearing a headscarf and pinned across the front of it a blue Spontex sponge fastened at each side with a large safety pin, the sponge meant to form some kind of peak against the (very watery) sun. It looked like a favour worn by a medieval knight, or a fillet to ward off evil spirits. Still, it was better than last week's effort, an Afrika Korps cap from Lawrence Corner: Miss Shepherd – Desert Fox.

September 1979. Miss S. shows me a photograph she has taken of herself in a cubicle at Waterloo. She is very low in the frame, her mouth pulled down, the photo looking as if it has been taken after death. She is very pleased with it. 'I don't take a good photograph usually. That's the only photograph I've seen looks anything like me.' She wants two copies making of it. I say that it would be easier for her to go back to Waterloo and do two more. No – that would 'take it out of her'. 'I had one taken in France once when I was twenty-one or twenty-two. Had to go into the next village for it. I came out cross-eyed. I saw someone else's photo on their bus-pass and she'd come out looking like a nigger. You don't want to come out like a nigger if you can help it, do you?'

June 1980. Miss S. has gone into her summer rig: a raincoat turned inside out, with brown canvas panels and a large label declaring it the Emerald Weatherproof. This is topped off with a lavender chiffon scarf tied round a sun visor made from an old cornflakes packet. She asks me to do her some shopping. 'I want a small packet of Eno's, some milk and some jelly babies. The jelly babies aren't urgent. Oh and, Mr Bennett, could you get me one of those little bottles of whisky? I believe Bell's is very good. I don't drink it – I just use it to rub on.'

August 1980. I am filming, and Miss S. sees me leaving early each morning and returning late. Tonight her scrawny hand comes out with a letter marked 'Please consider carefully':

An easier way for Mr Bennett to earn could be possibly with my cooperative part. Two young men could follow me in a car, one with a camera to get a funny film like 'Old Mother Riley Joins Up' possibly. If the car stalls they could then push it. Or they could go on the buses with her at a distance. Comedy happens without trying sometimes, or at least an interesting film covering a Senior Citizen's use of the buses can occur. One day to Hounslow, another to Reading or Heathrow. The bus people ought to be pleased, but it might need their permission. Then Mr Bennett could put his feet up more and rake it in, possibly.

October 1980. Miss S. has started hankering after a caravan trailer and has just missed one she saw in *Exchange and Mart*: 'little net curtains all round, three bunks'. 'I wouldn't use them all, except', she says ominously, 'to put things on. Nice little windows – £275. They said it was sold, only they may have thought I was just an old tramp . . . I was thinking of offering to help Mrs Thatcher with the economy. I wouldn't ask any money, as I'm on social security, so it would come cheap for her. I might ask her for some perks, though. Like a caravan. I would write to her but she's away. I know what's required. It's perfectly simple: Justice.'

No political party quite catered to Miss S.'s views, though the National Front came close. She was passionately anti-Communist, and as long ago as 1945 had written a letter to Jesus 'concerning the dreadful situation feared from the Yalta agreement'. The trouble was that her political opinions, while never moderate, were always tempered by her idiosyncratic view of the human physiognomy. Older was invariably wiser, which is fair if debatable, except that with Miss S. taller was wiser too. But height had its drawbacks, and it was perhaps because she was tall herself that she believed a person's height added to their burdens, put them under some strain. Hence, though she was in sympathy with Mr Heath on everything except the Common Market, 'I do think that Mr Wilson, personally, may have seen better in regard to Europe, being on the Opposition bench with less salary and being older, smaller and under less strain.' She was vehemently opposed to the Common Market – the 'common' always underlined when she wrote about it on the pavement, as if it were the sheer vulgarity of the economic union she particularly objected to. Never very lucid in her leaflets, she got especially confused over the EEC. 'Not long ago a soul wrote, or else was considering writing (she cannot recall as to which and it may have been something of either) that she disassociated from the Common Market entry and the injustices feared concerning it, or something like that.' 'Enoch', as she invariably called Mr Powell, had got it right, and she wrote him several letters telling him so, but in the absence of a wholly congenial party she founded her own, the Fidelis Party. 'It will be a party caring for Justice (and as such not needing opposition). Justice in the world today with its gigantic ignorant conduct requires the rule of a Good Dictator, possibly.'

Miss S. never regarded herself as being at the bottom of the social heap. That place was occupied by 'the desperate poor' – i.e. those with no roof over their heads. She herself was 'a cut above those in dire need', and one of her responsibilities in society she saw as interceding for them and for those whose plight she thought Mrs Thatcher had overlooked. Could it be brought to her attention (and she wrote Mrs T. several letters on the subject), alleviation would surely follow.

Occasionally she would write letters to other public figures. In August 1978 it was to the College of Cardinals, then busy electing a Pope. 'Your Eminences. I would like to suggest humbly that an older Pope might be admirable. Height can count towards knowledge too probably.' However this older (and hopefully taller) Pope she was recommending might find the ceremony a bit of a trial, so, ever the expert on headgear, she suggests that 'at the Coronation there could be a not so heavy crown, of light plastic possibly or cardboard for instance.'

February 1981. Miss S. has flu, so I am doing her shopping. I wait every morning by the side window of the van and, with the dark interior and her grimy hand holding back the tattered purple curtain, it is as if I am at the confessional. The chief items this morning are ginger nuts ('very warming') and grape juice. 'I think this is what they must have been drinking at Cana,' she says as I hand her the bottle. 'Jesus wouldn't have wanted them rolling about drunk, and this is non-alcoholic. It wouldn't do for everyone, but in my opinion it's better than champagne.'

October 1981. The curtain is drawn aside this morning and Miss S., still in what I take to be her nightclothes, talks of 'the discernment of spirits' that enabled her to sense an angelic presence near her when she was ill. At an earlier period, when she had her pitch outside the bank, she had sensed a similar angelic presence, and now, having seen his campaign leaflet, who should this turn out to be, 'possibly', but Our Conservative Candidate Mr Pasley-Tyler. She embarks on a long disquisition on her well-worn theme of age in politics. Mrs Thatcher is too young and travels too much. Not like President Reagan. 'You wouldn't catch him making all those U-turns round Australia.'

January 1982. 'Do you see he's been found, that American soldier?' This is Colonel Dozo, kidnapped by the Red Brigade and found after a shoot-out in a flat in Padua. 'Yes, he's been found,' she says triumphantly, 'and I know who found him.' Thinking it unlikely she has an acquaintance in the Italian version of the SAS, I ask whom she means. 'St Anthony of course. The patron saint of lost things. St Anthony of Padua.' 'Well,' I want to say, 'he didn't have far to look.'

May 1982. As I am leaving for Yorkshire, Miss S.'s hand comes out like the Ancient Mariner's: do I know if there are any steps at Leeds Station? 'Why?' I ask warily, thinking she may be having thoughts of camping on my other doorstep. It turns out she just wants somewhere to go for a ride, so I suggest Bristol. 'Yes, I've been to Bristol. On the way back I came through Bath. That looked nice. Some beautifully parked cars.' She then recalls driving her reconditioned army vehicles and taking them up to Derbyshire. 'I did it in the war,' she says. 'Actually I overdid it in the war,' and somehow that is the thin end of the wedge that has landed her up here, yearning for travel on this May morning forty years later.

'Land' is a word Miss S. prefers to 'country'. 'This land . . .' Used in this sense, it's part of the rhetoric if not of madness at any rate of obsession. Jehovah's Witnesses talk of 'this land', and the National Front. Land is country plus destiny – country in the sight of God. Mrs Thatcher talks of 'this land'.

February 1983. A. telephones me in Yorkshire to say that the basement is under three inches of water, the boiler having burst. When told that the basement has been flooded, Miss S.'s only comment is 'What a waste of water.'

April 1983. 'I've been having bad nights,' says Miss S., 'but if I were elected I might have better nights.' She wants me to get her nomination papers so that she can stand for Parliament in the coming election. She would be the Fidelis Party candidate. The party, never very numerous, is now considerably reduced. Once she could count on five votes but now there are only two, one of whom is me, and I don't like to tell her I'm in the SDP. Still, I promise to write to the town hall for nomination papers. 'There's no kitty as yet,' she says, 'and I wouldn't want to do any of the meeting people. I'd be no good at that. The secretaries can do that (you get expenses). But I'd be very good at voting – better than they are, probably.'

May 1983. Miss S. asks me to witness her signature on the nomination form. 'I'm signing,' she says: 'are you witnessing?' She has approached various nuns to be her nominees. 'One sister I know would have signed but I haven't seen her for some years and she's got rather confused in the interim. I don't know what I'll do about leaflets. It would have to be an economy job – I couldn't run to the expense. Maybe I'll just write my manifesto on the pavement; that goes round like wildfire.'

May 1983. Miss S. has received her nomination papers. 'What should I describe myself as?' she asks through the window slit. 'I thought Elderly Spinster, possibly. It also says Title. Well my title is' – and she laughs one of her rare laughs – 'Mrs Shepherd. That's what some people call me out of politeness. And I don't deny it. Mother Teresa always says she's married to God. I could say I was married to the Good Shepherd, and that's what it's to do with, Parliament, looking after the flock. When I'm elected, do you think I shall have to live in Downing Street or could I run things from the van?'

I speak to her later in the day and the nomination business is beginning to get her down. 'Do you know anything about the Act of 1974? It refers to disqualifications under it. Anyway, it's all giving me a headache. I think there may be another election soon after this one, so it'll have been good preparation anyway.'

June 1984. Miss S. has been looking in *Exchange and Mart* again and has answered an advert for a white Morris Minor. 'It's the kind of car I'm used to – or I used to be used to. I feel the need to be mobile.' I raise the matter of a licence and insurance, which she always treats as tiresome formalities. 'What you don't understand is that I am insured. I am insured in heaven.' She claims that since she had been insured in heaven there has not been a scratch on the van. I point out that this is less to do with the celestial insurance than with the fact that the van is parked the whole time in my garden. She concedes that when she was on the road the van did used to get the occasional knock. 'Somebody came up behind me once and scratched the van. I wanted him to pay something – half-a-crown I think it was. He wouldn't.'

October 1984. Some new staircarpet fitted today. Spotting the old carpet being thrown out, Miss S. says it would be just the thing to put on the roof of the van to deaden the sound of rain. This exchange comes just as I am leaving for work, but I say that I do not want the van festooned with bits of old carpet – it looks bad enough as it is. When I come back in the evening I find half the carpet remnants slung over the roof. I ask Miss S. who has put them there, as she can't have done it herself. 'A friend,' she says mysteriously. 'A well-wisher.' Enraged, I pull down a token piece but the majority of it stays put.

April 1985. Miss S. has written to Mrs Thatcher applying for a post in 'the Ministry of Transport advisory, to do with drink and driving and that'. She also shows me the text of a letter she is proposing to send to the Argentinian Embassy on behalf of General Galtieri. 'What he doesn't understand is that Mrs Thatcher isn't the Iron Lady. It's me.'

To Someone in Charge of Argentina. 19 April 1985

Dear Sir,

  I am writing to help mercy towards the poor general who led your forces in the war actually as a person of true knowledge more than might be. I was concerned with Justice, Love and, in a manner of speaking, I was in the war, as it were, shaking hands with your then leader, welcoming him in spirit (it may have been to do with love of Catholic education for Malvinas for instance) greatly meaning kindly negotiators etc. . . . but I fear that he may have thought it was Mrs Thatcher welcoming him in that way and it may hence have unduly influenced him.

Therefore I beg you to have mercy on him indeed. Let him go, reinstate him, if feasible. You may read publicly this letter if you wish to explain mercy etc.

> I remain.
>> Yours truly
>>> A Member of the Fidelis Party
>>> (Servants of Justice)

P.S. Others may have contributed to undue influence also.
P.P.S. Possibly without realizing it.

> Translate into Argentinian if you shd wish.

Sometime in 1980 Miss S. acquired a car, but before she'd managed to have more than a jaunt or two in it ('It's a real goer!') it was stolen and later found stripped and abandoned in the basement of the council flats in Maiden Lane. I went to collect what was left ('though the police may require it for evidence, possibly') and found that even in the short time she'd had the Mini she'd managed to stuff it with the usual quota of plastic bags, kitchen rolls and old blankets, all plentifully doused in talcum powder. When she got a Reliant Robin in 1984 it was much the same, a second wardrobe as much as a second car. Miss Shepherd could afford to splash out on these vehicles because being parked in the garden meant that she had a permanent address, and so qualified for full social security and its various allowances. Since her only outgoings were on food, she was able to put by something and had an account in the Halifax and quite a few savings certificates. Indeed I heard people passing say, 'You know she's a millionaire,' the inference being no one in their right mind would let her live there if she weren't.

Her Reliant saw more action than the Mini, and she would tootle off in it on a Sunday morning, park on Primrose Hill ('The air is better'), and even got as far as Hounslow. More often than not, though, she was happy (and I think she was happy then) just to sit in the Reliant and rev the engine. However, since she generally chose to do this first thing on Sunday morning, it didn't endear her to the neighbours. Besides, what she described as 'a lifetime with motors' had failed to teach her was that revving a car does not charge the battery, so that when it regularly ran down I had to take it out and recharge it, knowing full well this would just mean more revving. ('No,' she insisted, 'I may be going to Cornwall next week, possibly.') This recharging of the battery wasn't really the issue: I was just ashamed to be seen delving under the bonnet of such a joke car.

March 1987. The nuns up the road – or, as Miss S. always refers to them, 'the sisters' – have taken to doing some of her shopping. One of them leaves a bag on the back step of the van this morning. There are the inevitable ginger nuts, and several packets of sanitary towels. I can see these would be difficult articles for her to ask me to get, though to ask a nun to get them would seem quite hard for her too. They form some part of her elaborate toilet arrangements, and are occasionally to be seen laid drying across the soup-encrusted electric ring. As the postman says this morning, 'The smell sometimes knocks you back a bit.'

May 1987. Miss S. wants to spread a blanket over the roof (in addition to the bit of carpet) in order to deaden the sound of the rain. I point out that within a few weeks it will be dank and disgusting. 'No,' she says – 'weather-beaten.'

She has put a Conservative poster in the side window of the

van. The only person who can see it is me.

This morning she was sitting at the open door of the van and as I edge by she chucks out an empty packet of Ariel. The blanket hanging over the pushchair is covered in washing-powder. 'Have you spilt it?' I inquire. 'No,' she says crossly, irritated at having to explain the obvious. 'That's washing-powder. When it rains, the blanket will get washed.' As I work at my table now I can see her bending over the pushchair, picking at bits of soap flakes and redistributing them over the blanket. No rain is at the moment forecast.

June 1987. Miss S. has persuaded the social services to allocate her a wheelchair, though what she's really set her heart on is the electric version.

MISS S.: That boy over the road has one. Why not me?

ME: He can't walk.

MISS S: How does he know? He hasn't tried.

ME: Miss Shepherd, he has spina bifida.

MISS S: Well, I was round-shouldered as a child. That may not be serious now, but it was quite serious then. I've gone through two wars, an infant in the first and not on full rations, in the ambulances in the second, besides being failed by the ATS. Why should old people be disregarded?

Thwarted in her ambition for a powered chair, Miss S. compensated by acquiring (I never found out where from) a second wheelchair ('in case the other conks out, possibly'). The full inventory of her wheeled vehicles now read: one van; one Reliant Robin; two wheelchairs; one folding pushchair; one folding (two-seater) pushchair. Now and again I would thin out the pushchairs by smuggling one on to a skip. She would put down this disappearance to children (never a favourite), and the number would shortly be made up by yet another wheelie from Reg's junk stall. Miss S. never mastered the technique of self-propulsion in the wheelchair because she refused to use the inner handwheel ('I can't be doing with all that silliness'). Instead, she preferred to punt herself along with two walking-sticks, looking in the process rather like a skier on the flat. Eventually I had to remove the handwheel ('The extra weight affects my health').

July 1987. Miss S. (bright-green visor, purple skirt, brown cardigan, turquoise fluorescent ankle socks) punts her way out through the gate in the wheelchair in a complicated manoeuvre which would be much simplified did she just push the chair out, as well she can. A passer-by takes pity on her, and she is whisked down to the market. Except not quite whisked, because the journey is made more difficult than need be by Miss S.'s refusal to take her feet off the ground, so the Good Samaritan finds himself pushing a wheelchair continually slurred and braked by these large, trailing, carpet-slippered feet. Her legs are so thin now the feet are as slack and flat as those of a camel.

Still, there will be one moment to relish on this, as on all these journeys. When she had been pushed back from the market, she will tell (and it is tell: there is never any thanks) whoever is pushing the chair to leave her opposite the gate but on the crown of the road. Then, when she thinks no one is looking, she lifts her feet, pushes herself off, and freewheels the few yards down to the gate. The look on her face is one of pure pleasure.

October 1987. I have been filming abroad. 'When you were in Yugoslavia,' asks Miss S., 'did you come across the Virgin Mary?' 'No,' I say, 'I don't think so.' 'Oh, well, she's appearing there. She's been appearing there every day for several years.' It's as if I've missed the major tourist attraction.

January 1988. I ask Miss S. if it was her birthday yesterday. She agrees guardedly. 'So you're seventy-seven.' 'Yes. How did you know?' 'I saw it once when you filled out the census form.' I give her a bottle of whisky, explaining that it's just to rub on. 'Oh. Thank you.' Pause. 'Mr Bennett. Don't tell anybody.' 'About the whisky?' 'No. About my birthday.' Pause. 'Mr Bennett.' 'Yes?' 'About the whisky either.'

March 1988. 'I've been doing a bit of spring cleaning,' says Miss S., kneeling in front of a Kienholz-like tableau of filth and decay. She says she has been discussing the possibility of a bungalow with the social worker, to which she would be prepared to contribute 'a few hundred or so'. It's possible that the bungalow might be made of asbestos, 'but I could wear a mask. I wouldn't mind that, and of course it would be much better from the fire point of view.' Hands in mittens made from old socks, a sanitary towel drying over the ring, and a glossy leaflet from the Halifax offering 'fabulous investment opportunities'.

April 1988. Miss S. asks me to get Tom M. to take a photograph of her for her new bus-pass. 'That would make a comedy, you know – sitting on a bus and your bus-pass out of date. You could make a fortune out of that with very little work involved, possibly. I was a born tragedian,' she says, 'or a comedian possibly. One or the other anyway. But I didn't realize it at the time. Big feet.' She pushes out her red, unstockinged ankles. 'Big hands.' The fingers stained brown. 'Tall. People trip over me. That's comedy. I wish they didn't, of course. I'd like it easier, but there it is. I'm not suggesting you do it,' she says hastily, feeling perhaps she's come too near self-revelation, 'only it might make people laugh.' All of this is said with a straight face and no hint of a smile, sitting in the wheelchair with her hands pressed between her knees and her baseball cap on.

May 1988. Miss S. sits in her wheelchair in the road, paintpot in hand, dabbing at the bodywork of the Reliant, which she will shortly enter, start, and rev for a contented half-hour before switching off and paddling down the road in her wheelchair. She has been nattering at Tom M. to mend the clutch, but there are conditions. It mustn't be on Sunday, which is the feast of St Peter and St Paul and a day of obligation. Nor can it be the following Sunday apparently, through the Feast of the Assumption falling on the Monday and being transferred back to the previous day. Amid all the chaos of her life and now, I think, more or less incontinent, she trips with fanatical precision through this liturgical minefield.

September 1988. Miss S. has started thinking about a flat again, though not the one the council offered her a few years ago. This time she has her eye on something much closer to home. My home. We had been talking outside, and I left her sitting on the step in the hall while I came back to work. This is often what happens: me sitting at my table, wanting to get on, Miss S. sitting outside rambling. This time she goes on talking about the flat, soliloquizing almost, but knowing that I can hear. 'It need only be a little flat, even a room possibly. Of course, I can't manage stairs, so it would have to be on the ground floor. Though I'd pay to have a lift put in.' (Louder.) 'And the lift wouldn't be wasted. They'd have it for their old age. And they'll have to be thinking about their old age quite soon.' The tone of it is somehow familiar from years ago. Then I realize it's like one of the meant-to-be-overheard soliloquies of Richmal Crompton's William.

Her outfit this morning: orange skirt, made out of three or four large dusters; a striped blue satin jacket; a green headscarf – blue eyeshield topped off by a khaki peaked cap with a skull-and-crossbones badge and Rambo across the peak.

February 1989. Miss S.'s religion is an odd mixture of traditional faith and a belief in the power of positive thinking. This morning, as ever, the Reliant battery is running low and she asks me to fix it. The usual argument takes place:

ME: Well, of course it's run down. It will run down unless you run the car. Revving up doesn't charge it. The wheels have to go round.

MISS S.: Stop talking like that. This car is not the same. There are miracles. There is faith. Negative thoughts don't help. (*She presses the starter again and it coughs weakly.*) There, you see. The devil's heard you. You shouldn't say negative things.

The interior of the van now indescribable.

March 1989. Miss S. sits in the wheelchair trying to open the sneck of the gate with her walking-stick. She tries it with one end, then reverses the stick and tries with the other. Sitting at my table, trying to work, I watch her idly, much as one would watch an ant trying to get round some obstacle. Now she bangs on the gate to attract the attention of a passer-by. Now she is wailing. Banging and wailing. I go out. She stops wailing, and explains she has her washing to do. As I manoeuvre her through the gate, I ask her if she's fit to go. Yes, only she will need help. I explain that I can't push her there. (Why can't I?) No, she doesn't want that. Would I just push her as far as the corner? I do so. Would I just push her a bit further? I explain that I can't take her to the launderette. (And anyway there is no launderette any more, so which launderette is she going to?) Eventually, feeling like Fletcher Christian (only not Christian) abandoning Captain Bligh, I leave her in the wheelchair outside Mary H.'s. Someone will come along. I would be more ashamed if I did not feel, even when she is poorly, that she knows exactly what she's about.

March 1989. There is a thin layer of talcum powder around the back door of the van and odd bits of screwed up tissues smeared with what may or may not be shit, though there is no doubt about the main item of litter, which is a stained incontinence pad. My method of retrieving these items would not be unfamiliar at Sellafield. I don rubber gloves, put each hand inside a plastic bag as an additional protection, then, having swept the faecal artefacts together, gingerly pick them up and put them in the bin. 'Those aren't all my rubbish,' comes a voice from the van. 'Some of them blow in under the gate.'

April 1989. Miss S. has asked me to telephone the social services, and I tell her that a social worker will be calling. 'What time?' 'I don't know. But you're not going to be out. You haven't been out for a week.' 'I might be. Miracles do happen. Besides, she may not be able to talk to me. I may not be at the door end of the van. I might be at the other end.' 'So she can talk to you there.' 'And what if I'm in the middle?'

Miss C. thinks her heart is failing. She calls her Mary. I find this strange, though it is of course her name.

April 1989. A staple of Miss S.'s shopping-list these days is sherbet lemons. I have a stock of them in the house, but she insists I invest in yet more so that a perpetual supply of sherbet lemons may never be in doubt. 'I'm on them now. I don't want to have to go off them.'

I ask her if she would like a cup of coffee. 'Well, I wouldn't want you to go to all that trouble. I'll just have half a cup.'

Towards the end of her life Miss S. was befriended by an ex-nurse who lived locally. She put me in touch with a day centre who agreed to take Miss Shepherd in, give her a bath and a medical examination and even a bed in a single room where she could stay if she wanted. In retrospect I see I should have done something on the same lines years before, except that it was only when age and illness had weakened Miss Shepherd that she would accept such help. Even then it was not easy.

27 April 1989. A red ambulance calls to take Miss S. to the day centre. Miss B. talks to her for a while in the van, gradually coaxing her out and into the wheelchair, shit streaks over her swollen feet, a piece of toilet roll clinging to one scaly ankle. 'And if I don't like it,' she keeps asking, 'can I come back?' I reassure her, but, looking at the inside of the van and trying to cope with the stench, I find it hard to see how she can go on living here much longer. Once she sees the room they are offering her, the bath, the clean sheets, I can't imagine her wanting to come back. And indeed she makes more fuss than usual about locking the van door, which suggests she accepts that she may not be returning. I note how, with none of my distaste, the ambulance driver bends over her as he puts her on the hoist, his careful rearrangement of her greasy clothing, pulling her skirt down over her knees in the interests of modesty. The chair goes on the hoist, and slowly she rises and comes into view above the level of the garden wall and is wheeled into the ambulance. There is a certain distinction about her as she leaves, a Dorothy Hodgkin of vagabonds, a derelict Nobel Prize-winner, the heavy folds of her grimy face set in a kind of resigned satisfaction. She may even be enjoying herself.

When she has gone I walk round the van noting the occasions of our battle: the carpet tiles she managed to smuggle on to the roof, the blanket strapped on to muffle the sound of the rain, the black bags under the van stuffed with her old clothes – sites of skirmishes all of which I'd lost. Now I imagine her bathed and bandaged and cleanly clothed and starting a new life. I even see myself visiting and taking flowers.

This fantasy rapidly fades when around 2.30 Miss S. reappears, washed and in clean clothes, it's true, and with a long pair of white hospital socks over her shrunken legs, but obviously very pleased to be back. She has a telephone number where her new friends can be contacted, and she gives it to me. 'They can be reached', she says, 'any time – even over the holiday. They're on a long-distance bleep.'

As I am leaving for the theatre, she bangs on the door of the van with her stick. I open the door. She is lying wrapped in clean white sheets on a quilt laid over all the accumulated filth and rubbish of the van. She is still worrying that I will have her taken to hospital. I tell her there's no question of it and that she can stay as long as she wants. I close the door, but there is another bang and I reassure her again. Once more I close the door, but she bangs again. 'Mr Bennett.' I have to strain to hear. 'I'm sorry the van's in such a state. I haven't been able to do any spring cleaning.'

28 April. I am working at my table when I see Miss B. arrive with a pile of clean clothes for Miss Shepherd, which must have been washed for her at the day centre yesterday. Miss B. knocks at the door of the van, then opens it, looks inside and – something nobody has ever done before – gets in. It's only a moment before she comes out, and I know what has happened before she rings the bell. We go back to the van where Miss Shepherd is dead, lying on her left side, flesh cold, face gaunt, the neck stretched out as if for the block, and a bee buzzing round her body.

It is a beautiful day, with the garden glittering in the sunshine, strong shadows by the nettles, and bluebells out under the wall, and I remember how in her occasional moments of contemplation she would sit in the wheelchair and gaze at the garden. I am filled with remorse for my harsh conduct towards her, though I know at the same time that it was not harsh. But still I never quite believed or chose to believe she was as ill as she was, and I regret too all the questions I never asked her. Not that she would have answered them. I have a strong impulse to stand at the gate and tell anyone who passes.

Miss B. meanwhile goes off and returns with a nice doctor from St Pancras who seems scarcely out of her teens. She gets into the van, takes the pulse in Miss S.'s outstretched neck, checks her with a stethoscope and, to save an autopsy, certifies death as from heart failure. Then comes the priest to bless her before she is taken to the funeral parlour, and he, too, gets into the van – the third person to do so this morning, and all of them without distaste or ado in what to me seem three small acts of heroism. Stooping over the body, his bright white hair brushing the top of the van, the priest murmurs an inaudible prayer and makes a cross on Miss S.'s hands and head. Then they all go off and I come inside to wait for the undertakers.

I have been sitting at my table for ten minutes before I realize that the undertakers have been here all the time, and that death nowadays comes (or goes) in a grey Ford transit van that is standing outside the gate. There are three undertakers, two young and burly, the third older and more experienced – a sergeant, as it were, and two corporals. They bring out a rough grey-painted coffin, like a prop a conjuror might use, and, making no comment on the surely extraordinary circumstances in which they find it, put a sheet of white plastic bin-liner over the body and manhandle it into their magic box, where it falls with a bit of a thud. Across the road, office workers stroll down from the Piano Factory for their lunch, but nobody stops or even looks much, and the Asian woman who has to wait while the box is carried over the pavement and put in the (other) van doesn't give it a backward glance.

Later I go round to the undertakers to arrange the funeral, and the manager apologizes for their response when I had originally phoned. A woman had answered, saying, 'What exactly is it you want?' Not thinking callers rang undertakers with a great variety of requests, I was nonplussed. Then she said briskly, 'Do you want someone taking away?' The undertaker explains that her seemingly unhelpful manner was because she thought my call wasn't genuine. 'We get so many hoaxes these days. I've often gone round to collect a corpse only to have it open the door.'

9 May. Miss Shepherd's funeral is at Our Lady of Hal, the Catholic church round the corner. The service has been slotted into the ten o'clock mass, so that, in addition to a contingent of neighbours, the congregation includes what I take to be regulars: the fat little man in thick glasses and trainers who hobbles along to the church every day from Arlington House; several nuns, among them the ninety-nine-year-old sister who was in charge when Miss S. was briefly a novice; a woman in a green straw hat like an upturned plant pot who eats toffees throughout; and another lady who plays the harmonium in tan slacks and a tea-cosy wig. The server, a middle-aged man with white hair, doesn't wear a surplice, just ordinary clothes with an open-necked shirt, and, but for knowing all the sacred drill, might have been roped in from the group on the corner outside The Good Mixer. The priest is a young Irish boy with a big, red peasant face and sandy hair, and he, too, stripped of his cream-coloured cassock, could be wielding a pneumatic drill in the roadworks outside. I keep thinking about these characters during the terrible service, and it reinforces what I have always known: that I could never be a Catholic because I'm such a snob, and that the biggest sacrifice Newman made when he turned his back on the C of E was the social one.

Yet kindness abounds. In front of us is a thin old man who knows the service backwards, and seeing we have no prayer books he lays down his own on top of his copy of the *Sun*, goes back up the aisle to fetch us some, and hands them round, all the time saying the responses without faltering. The first hymn is Newman's 'Lead Kindly Light', which I try and sing, while making no attempt at the second hymn, which is 'Kum Ba Ya'. The priest turns out to have a good strong voice, though its tone is more suited to 'Kum Ba Ya' than to Newman and J. B. Dykes. The service itself is wet and wandering, even more so than the current Anglican equivalent, though occasionally one catches in the watered-down language a distant echo of 1662. Now, though, arrives the bit I dread, the celebration of fellowship, which always reminds me of the warm-up Ned Sherrin insisted on inflicting on the studio audience before *Not So Much a Programme*, when everyone had to shake hands with their neighbour. But again the nice man who fetched us the prayer books shames me when he turns round without any fuss or embarrassment and smilingly shakes my hand. Then it is the mass proper, the priest distributing the wafers to the ninety-nine-year-old nun and the lady with the plant pot on her head, as Miss S. lies in her coffin at his elbow. Finally there is another hymn, this one by the (to me) unknown hymnodist Kevin Norton, who's obviously reworked it from his unsuccessful entry for the Eurovision Song Contest; and with the young priest acting as lead singer, and the congregation a rather subdued backing group, Miss Shepherd is carried out.

The neighbours, who are not quite mourners, wait on the

pavement outside as the coffin is hoisted on to the hearse. 'A cut above her previous vehicle,' remarks Colin H.; and comedy persists when the car accompanying the hearse to the cemetery refuses to start. It's a familiar scene, and one which I've played many times, with Miss S. waiting inside her vehicle as well-wishers lift the bonnet, fetch leads and give it a jump start. Except this time she's dead.

Only A. and I and Clare, the ex-nurse who lately befriended Miss S., accompany the body, swept around Hampstead Heath at a less than funereal pace, down Bishop's Avenue and up to the St Pancras Cemetery, green and lush this warm, sunny day. We drive beyond the scattered woods to the furthest edge where stand long lines of new gravestones, mostly in black polished granite. Appropriately, in view of her lifelong love of the car, Miss S. is being buried within sight and sound of the North Circular Road, one carriageway the other side of the hedge, with juggernauts drowning the words of the priest as he commits the body to the earth. He gives us each a go with his little plastic bottle of holy water, we throw some soil into the grave, and then everybody leaves me to whatever solitary thoughts I might have, which are not many, before we are driven back to Camden Town – life reasserted when the undertaker drops us handily outside Sainsbury's.

In the interval between Miss Shepherd's death and her funeral ten days later I found out more about her life than I had in twenty years. She had indeed driven ambulances during the war, and was either blown up or narrowly escaped death when a bomb exploded nearby. I'm not sure that her eccentricity can be put down to this any more than to the legend, mentioned by one of the nuns, that it was the death of her fiancé in this incident that 'tipped her over'. It would be comforting to think that it is love, or the death of it, that unbalances the mind, but I think her early attempts to become a nun and her repeated failures ('too argumentative,' one of the sisters said) point to a personality that must already have been quite awkward when she was a girl. After the war she spent some time in mental hospitals, but regularly absconded, finally remaining at large long enough to establish her competence to live unsupervised.

The turning-point in her life came when, through no fault of hers, a motorcyclist crashed into the side of her van. If her other vans were any guide, this one too would only have been insured in heaven, so it's not surprising she left the scene of the accident ('skedaddled', she would have said) without giving her name or address. The motorcyclist subsequently died, so that, while blameless in the accident, by leaving the scene of it she had committed a criminal offence. The police mounted a search for her. Having already changed her first name when she became a novice, now under very different circumstances she changed her second and, calling herself Shepherd, made her way back to Camden Town and the vicinity of the convent where she had taken her vows. And though in the years to come she had little to do with the nuns, or they with her, she was never to stray far from the convent for the rest of her life.

All this I learned in those last few days. It was as if she had been a character in Dickens whose history has to be revealed and her secrets told in the general setting-to-rights before the happy-ever-after, though all that this amounted to was that at long last I could bring my car into the garden to stand now where the van stood all those years.

Postscript (1994)

This account of Miss Shepherd condenses some of the many entries to do with her that are scattered through my diaries.

Unemphasized in the text (though deducible from the dates of the entries) is the formality of her last days. The Sunday before she died she attended mass, which she had not done for many months; on the Wednesday morning she allowed herself to be taken to be bathed and given clean clothes and then put to bed in the van on clean sheets; and that same night she died. The progression seemed so neat that I felt, when I first wrote it up, that to emphasize it would cast doubt on the truth of my account, or at least make it seem sentimental or melodramatic. However, the doctor who pronounced Miss Shepherd dead said that she had known other deaths in similar circumstances; that it was not (as I had facetiously wondered) the bath that had killed her but that to allow herself to be washed and put into clean clothes was both a preparation and an acknowledgement that death was in the offing.

Nor is it plain from the original account how in the period after her death I got to know the facts of her life that she had so long concealed. A few months before, a bout of flu must have made her think about putting her affairs in order and she had shown me an envelope that I might need 'in case anything happens to me, possibly'. I would find the envelope in the place under the banquette where she kept her savings books and other papers. What the envelope contained she did not say, and, when in due course she got over the flu and struggled on, nothing more was said about it.

It was about this time, though, that I had the first and only hint that her name might not be her own. She had, I knew, some money in the Abbey National, and periodically their bright brochures would come through my door – young and happy home-owners pictured gaily striding across their first threshold and entering upon a life of mortgaged bliss.

'Some post, Miss Shepherd,' I would knock on the window and wait for the scrawny hand to come out (nails long and grey;

fingers ochre-stained as if she had been handling clay). The brochure would be drawn back into the dim and fetid interior, where it would be a while before it was opened, the packet turned over and over in her dubious hands, the Society's latest exciting offer waiting until she was sure it was not from the IRA. 'Another bomb, possibly. They've heard my views.'

In 1988 the Abbey National were preparing to turn themselves from a building society into a bank, a proposal to which Miss Shepherd for some reason (novelty, possibly) was very much opposed. Before filling in her ballot form, she asked me (and she was careful to couch the question impersonally) if a vote would be valid had the purchaser of the shares changed their name. I said, fairly obviously, that if the shares had been bought in one name then it would be in order to vote in that name. 'Why?' I asked. But I should have known better, and, as so often, having given a teasing hint of some revelation, she refused to follow it up, just shook her head mutely, and snapped shut the window. Except (and this was standard procedure too) as I was passing the van next day her hand came out.

'Mr Bennett. What I said about change of name, don't mention it to anybody. It was just in theory, possibly.'

For some days after Miss Shepherd's death I left the van as it was, not from piety or anything to do with decorum but because I couldn't face getting into it, and though I put on a new padlock I made no attempt to extract her bank books or locate the necessary envelope. But the news had got round, and when one afternoon I came home to find a scrap dealer nosing about I realized I had to grit my teeth (or hold my nose) and go through Miss Shepherd's possessions.

To do the job properly would have required a team of archaeologists. Every surface was covered in layers of old clothes, frocks, blankets and accumulated papers, some of them undisturbed for years and all lying under a crust of ancient talcum powder. Sprinkled impartially over wet slippers, used incontinence pads and half-eaten tins of baked beans, it was of a virulence that supplemented rather than obliterated the distinctive odour of the van. The narrow aisle between the two banks of seats where Miss Shepherd had knelt, prayed and slept was trodden six inches deep in sodden debris, on which lay a top dressing of old food, Mr Kipling cakes, wrinkled apples, rotten oranges and everywhere batteries – batteries loose, batteries in packets, batteries that had split and oozed black gum on to the prehistoric sponge cakes and ubiquitous sherbet lemons that they lay among. A handkerchief round my face, I lifted one of the banquettes where in the hollow beneath she had told me her bank books were hidden. The underside of the seat was alive with moths and maggots, but the books were there, together with other documents she considered valuable: an MoT certificate for her Reliant, long expired; a receipt for some repairs to it done three years before; an offer of a fortnight of sun and sea in the Seychelles that came with some car wax. What there was not was the envelope. So there was nothing for it but to excavate the van, to go through the festering debris in the hope of finding the note she had promised to leave, and with it perhaps her history.

Searching the van, I was not just looking for the envelope; sifting the accumulated refuse of fifteen years, I was hoping for some clue as to what it was that had happened to make Miss Shepherd want to live like this. Except that I kept coming across items that suggested that living 'like this' wasn't all that different from the way people ordinarily lived. There was a set of matching kitchen utensils, for instance – a ladle, a spatula, a masher for potatoes – all of them unused. They were the kind of thing my mother bought and hung up in the kitchen, just for show, while she went on using the battered old-faithfuls kept in the knife drawer. There were boxes of cheap soap and, of course, talcum powder, the cellophane wrapping unbreached; they too had counterparts in the dressing-table drawer at home. Another item my mother hoarded was toilet rolls, and here were a dozen. There was a condiment set, still in its box. When, amid such chaos, can she have hoped to use that particular appurtenance of gentility? But when did we ever use ours, stuck permanently in the sideboard cupboard in readiness for the social life my parents never had or ever really wanted? The more I laboured, the less peculiar the van seemed – its proprieties and aspirations no different from those with which I had been brought up.

There was cash here too. In a bag Miss Shepherd carried round her neck there had been nearly £500, and peeling off the soggy layers from the van floor I collected about £100 more. Taking into account the money in various building societies and her National Savings certificates, Miss Shepherd had managed to save some £6,000. Since she was not entitled to a pension, most of this must have been gleaned from the meagre allowance she got from the DHSS. I am not sure whether under the present regime she would have been praised for her thrift or singled out as a sponger. Arch-Tory though she was, she seems a prime candidate for Mr Lilley's little list, a paid-up member of the Something for Nothing society. I would just like to have seen him tell her so.

Modest though Miss Shepherd's estate was, it was more than I'd been expecting and made the finding of the envelope more urgent. So I went through the old clothes again, this time feeling gingerly in the pockets and shaking out the greasy blankets in a blizzard of moth and 'French Fern'. But there was nothing, only her bus-pass, the grim photograph looking as if it were taken during the siege of Stalingrad and hardly auguring well for the comedy series she had once suggested I write on the subject. I was about to give up, having decided that she must have kept the envelope on her and that it had been taken away with the body, when I came upon it, stiff with old soup and tucked into the glove compartment along with another cache of batteries and sherbet lemons, and marked 'Mr Bennett, if necessary'.

Still looking for some explanation ('I am like this, possibly, because . . .'), I opened the envelope. True to form, even in this her final communication Miss Shepherd wasn't prepared to give away any more than she had to. There was just a man's name, which was not her own, and a phone number in Sussex.

I finished cleaning out the van, scraped down the aisle, and opened all the windows and doors so that for the first time since she had moved in it was almost sweet-smelling – only not, because sweet in an awful way was how she had made it smell. My neighbour, the artist David Gentleman, who ten years before had done a lightning sketch of Miss Shepherd watching the removal of an earlier van, now came and did a romantic drawing of this her last vehicle, the grass growing high around it and the tattered curtains blowing in the spring breeze.

2 May 1989. This afternoon comes a rather dapper salvage man who, fifteen years ago, refused to execute a council order for the removal of one of Miss Shepherd's earlier vans on the grounds that someone was living in it. So he says anyway, though it's perhaps just to establish his claim. He stands there on the doorstep, maybe waiting to see if I am going to mention a price; I wait too, wondering if he is going to mention a charge. Silence on both sides seems to indicate that the transaction is over with no payment on either side, and within the hour he is back with his lifting-gear. Tom M. takes photographs as the van is hauled like an elephant's carcass through the gate and up the ramp, the miraculous tyres still happily inflated; the salvage man scrawls 'On Tow' in the thick dirt on the windscreen; stood by the bonnet I pose for a final photograph (which doesn't come out);

1 A. B. (left) and elder brother Gordon (right) with Mam, Filey, 1937

2 Mam, A. B., Gordon and Dad with Mr Weatherhead, Byril Farm, Wilsill, 1940

3 Nidderdale, 1942

4 Aunty Kathleen, Grandma Peel, Mam and A. B., Morecambe, 1948

5 Upper Armley National School, Leeds

6 Armley Branch Library, Leeds

7 Redmire, 1952

8 With Michael Frayn, Bodmin, 19

9 Oxford, 1955

10 Otley Road, Leeds, the Bennetts' house and shop (far right)

11 Walking on the beach at Brighton, April 1961

12 and 13 Dudley Moore, Jonathan Miller, Peter Cook and A. B. in
Beyond the Fringe, May 1961

14 Dudley Moore, Jonathan Miller, Peter Cook and A. B. in
Beyond the Fringe, May 1961

and the van goes off for the last time up the Crescent, leaving the drive feeling as wide and empty as the Piazza San Marco.

5 May 1989. 'Mr Bennett?' The voice is a touch military and quite sharp, though with no accent to speak of and nothing to indicate this a man who must be over eighty. 'You've sent me a letter about a Miss Shepherd, who seems to have died in your drive. I have to tell you I have no knowledge of such a person.' A bit nonplussed, I describe Miss Shepherd and her circumstances and give her date of birth. There is a slight pause.

'Yes. Well it's obviously my sister.'

He tells me her history and how, returning from Africa just after the war, he found her persecuting their mother, telling her how wicked she was and what she should and shouldn't eat, the upshot being that he finally had his sister committed to a mental hospital in Hayward's Heath. He gives her subsequent history, or as much of it as he knows, saying that the last time he had seen her was three years ago. He's direct and straightforward and doesn't disguise the fact that he feels guilty about having her committed yet cannot see how he could have done otherwise, how they never got on, and how he cannot see how I have managed to put up with her all these years. I tell him about the money, slightly expecting him to change his tune and stress how close they had really been. But not a bit of it. Since they hadn't got on he wants none of it, saying I should have it. When I disclaim it too, he tells me to give it to charity.

Anna Haycraft (Alice Thomas Ellis) had mentioned Miss S.'s death in her *Spectator* column, and I tell him about this, really to show that his sister did have a place in people's affections and wasn't simply a cantankerous old woman. 'Cantankerous is not the word,' he says, and laughs. I sense a wife there, and after I put the phone down I imagine them mulling over the call.

I mull it over too, wondering at the bold life she has had and how it contrasts with my own timid way of going on – living, as Camus said, slightly the opposite of expressing. And I see how the location of Miss Shepherd and the van in front but to the side of where I write is the location of most of the stuff I write about; that too is to the side and never what faces me.

Over a year later, finding myself near the village in Sussex where Mr F. lived, I telephoned and asked if I could call. In the meantime I'd written about Miss Shepherd in the *London Review of Books* and broadcast a series of talks about her on Radio 4.

17 June 1990. Mr and Mrs F. live in a little bungalow in a modern estate just off the main road. I suppose it was because of the unhesitating fashion in which he'd turned down her legacy that I was expecting something grander; in fact Mrs F. is disabled and their circumstances are obviously quite modest, which makes his refusal more creditable than I'd thought. From his phone manner I'd been expecting someone brisk and businesslike, but he's a plumpish, jolly man, and both he and his wife are full of laughs. They give me some lovely cake, which he's baked (Mrs F. being crippled with arthritis) and then patiently answer my questions.

The most interesting revelation is that as a girl Miss S. was a talented pianist and had studied in Paris under Cortot, who had told her she should have a concert career. Her decision to become a nun put an end to the piano, 'and that can't have helped her state of mind' says Mr F.

He recalls her occasional visits, when she would never come in by the front door but lope across the field at the back of the house and climb over the fence. She never took any notice of

THE LADY IN THE VAN

Mrs F., suspecting, rightly, that women were likely to be less tolerant of her than men.

He says all the fiancé stuff, which came via the nuns, is nonsense; she had no interest in men, and never had. When she was in the ambulance service she used to be ribbed by the other drivers, who asked her once why she had never married. She drew herself up and said, 'Because I've never found the man who could satisfy me.' Mystified by their laughter she went home and told her mother, who laughed too.

Mr F. has made no secret of the situation to his friends, particularly since the broadcasts, and keeps telling people he's spent his life trying to make his mark and here she is, having lived like a tramp, more famous than he'll ever be. But he talks about his career in Africa, how he still works as a part-time vet, and I come away thinking what an admirable pair they are, funny and kind and as good in practice as she was in theory – the brother Martha to his sister's Mary.

Sometimes now hearing a van door I think, 'There's Miss Shepherd,' instinctively looking up to see what outfit she's wearing this morning. But the oil patch that marked the site of the van has long since gone, and the flecks of yellow paint on the pavement have all but faded. She has left a more permanent legacy, though, and not only to me. Like diphtheria and Brylcreem, I associate moths with the forties, and until Miss Shepherd took up residence in the drive I thought them firmly confined to the past. But just as it was clothes in which the plague was reputedly spread to the Derbyshire village of Eyam so it was a bundle of Miss Shepherd's clothes, for all they were firmly done up in a black plastic bag, that brought the plague to my house, spreading from the bag to the wardrobe and from the wardrobe to the carpets, the appearance of a moth the signal for frantic clapping and savage stamping. On her death my vigorous cleaning of the van broadcast the plague more widely, so that now many of my neighbours have come to share in this unwanted legacy.

Her grave in the St Pancras Cemetery is scarcely less commodious than the narrow space she slept in the previous twenty years. It is unmarked, but I think as someone so reluctant to admit her name or divulge any information about herself, she would not have been displeased by that.

Diaries 1980–1995

I have kept a sporadic diary since the early seventies. I don't write it up every day and often not for weeks at a time; I am most conscientious about it when I'm busy writing something else, so that as a rule when work is going well (or at any rate going) the diary goes well too. If there are problems with rehearsals, say, or filming, the diary gets the complaints, but this querulous litany makes for dull and (on my part) somewhat shamefaced reading. So that side of things doesn't figure much in these extracts, or in the rehearsal or location diaries which are reprinted here.

My diaries are written on loose-leaf sheets – sometimes typed, sometimes in longhand – and a year's entries make a pretty untidy bundle. The writing is often untidy too; immediacy in my case doesn't make for vivid reporting, which is why I've not had any scruples about improving and editing, though I've never altered the tone or the sentiments of what I've written at the time.

Most of these diaries were originally published in the *London Review of Books*, where for reasons of space they had to be compressed, the extracts run together and the gaps between eliminated. What had been a series of jottings became a continuous, if disjointed, narrative. In this version I've restored my original spacing, as one of the pleasures of reading diaries, it seems to me, is that they are in bits (titbits with luck) – are like conversations, in fact, even if the conversation is with oneself.

133

Wanting to hold such a conversation is one reason for keeping a diary; another is that it slows down time.

In the account I have given of Miss Shepherd, who for many years lived in a van in my garden, I describe (in an extract from my diary) how going along in her wheelchair she would seldom lift her feet off the ground and so any Good Samaritan who pushed her found themselves behind a wheelchair continually braked by Miss Shepherd's slurring, carpet-slippered feet. Particularly as one gets older and time begins to speed up, a diary has the same slurring effects.

Where no place is given the entry was written in Camden Town in London; 'Yorkshire' is a village in Craven to which my parents retired and where I still have a house; 'New York' is generally an apartment on Thompson Street in SoHo.

―――――

1980

Sunday, 13 January. A cold, sunny morning, my room smelling nicely of wood and books. A nun passes. Nuns now dress like nurses; gone the voluminous black, the starched coif, the twinkling rosy face; these days it's a nanny's uniform in a nasty shade of grey – papal policewomen.

Struggle through the streaming flux of the Sunday papers before beginning the day: cultural events that are about to happen, talents that will shortly startle and never thereafter disappear, and of course money. Novelists who with their first novel stumble into a swamp of dollars; actors sitting down at their scrubbed-pine tables to find their income amounts to £70,000 a year; playwrights who cannot even calculate theirs.

And the last interview with Goronwy Rees, in which Goronwy talks to Andrew Boyle. Talks to him and wastes some of his presumably precious breath on calling Andrew frequently by name. 'Yes, Andrew, Burgess did go to bed with Blunt, and in the process, Andrew, Blunt absorbed more of Burgess's Marxist principles.' In what process, one wonders? In the process of Burgess putting his cock up Blunt's arse? To each according to ability ('Does that feel nice?'), from each according to his means. 'Now if you did it to me would that help you to grasp the principle better?'

21 January. To the Serpentine Gallery for an exhibition of photographs by André Kertész. The park is empty, the sun warm, and the Albert Memorial is glinting through the trees. If this were New York I would be revelling in such a morning, but it's only London. Few people in the exhibition, just one or two students and an old couple discussing the human interest of the pictures. 'Your pictures talk too much' a New York picture editor told Kertész. So what can I remember, having left the exhibition half an hour ago? A recruit in the Austrian army writing a letter in a barrack room in 1915. A corner of Mondrian's house in Paris in the twenties. Washington Square under snow, and a boy holding a puppy's head towards the camera.

And, while on photographers, Cecil Beaton died on Friday. The obituaries mention his capacity for hard work but not his toughness. The toughness of the dandy.

31 January. To John Huston's *Wise Blood* with Ronald Eyre and Jocelyn Herbert. A beautiful film: Huston seventy-five, and yet it seems the work of a young man. His touch is so firm, the spell cast in the first moments when the young soldier is dropped off by the van he has hitched, reaches for his kitbag and seems about to leave the driver unthanked but suddenly leans in and says, boldly, 'I'm obliged.' The town, Macon in Georgia, a battered American small town, shot in bitter, blue sunshine; the hero mad as the figures in Dadd or Fuseli are mad – wide-eyed, bony, possessed.

We have a meal at Bertorelli's in Queensway, and Ron talks of how there may be a way of doing *Enjoy* in which the furniture is gradually removed during the last part of the second act, and the stage left wholly bare for the final speeches. Then to Jocelyn's house, where Ron plays some of the tunes her father A. P. Herbert wrote the lyrics for – 'Bless the Bride', 'Other People's Babies'. The house white and plain with no particular stamp on it, as designers' houses often are; the walls of the study crowded with photographs of George Devine and the great days at the Royal Court, and two vast models ready for the set of *Galileo*, which Jocelyn is designing for the National. Jocelyn is I suppose sixty-odd, with children and grandchildren, yet she seems a contemporary, with a wonderful regal face, drawling voice and effortless style.

1 February. To the Roundhouse for the Georgian State Theatre's *Richard III*. A handful of pickets on the steps hand out pamphlets, saying 'These will tell you what life in Russia is *really* like'; actually I'd have thought *Richard III* was a pretty fair picture (and certainly of life under Stalin). Seat 71 appears to be missing and I wander about the rows and stumble over Gaia Servadio.

'You strange man,' she calls out. 'Why do we never see you? I so liked your last.'

'You won't like my next,' I say ungraciously, and hurry by.

'Why are you so *sure*?' she wails after me.

The audience thick with actors – Ralph Richardson, Richard Pascoe, Ba Leigh Hunt, T. Nunn and co.

The nobles wear long-skirted overcoats, part boyar, part Regency buck, and the whole thing is done at tremendous pace and with great panache. Richmond is big and young and looks straight out of the Liverpool team; the rest are like taxi-drivers. It's difficult sometimes to assess what's happening, but it's easier to take Shakespeare done over like this when it's in a foreign language. Office chairs are wound in rags and bandages, a café orchestra plays silly lilting melodies, and in the exciting bits there's a rock accompaniment, the cast striding off the stage at high speed. The actor playing Richard III is hypnotic – all eyes and boots – and gets an enormous ovation at the end, when, as Ron Eyre had told me, one stands without constraint to shout and applaud, though doing so I note that it's some Russians in the audience who stand first, possibly on cue, and the ecstatic audience is filmed applauding, which makes one think uneasily of the pickets outside.

24 February, New York. Rose, the eighty-two-year-old lady in the apartment next door to K., is ill, maybe dying. Not much more than four feet tall, she has varicose ulcers on her legs, which are thick and stocky and generally bound in loose, telescopic bandages. Now she has taken off the bandages to let the ulcers heal, which they never will, two huge holes in her legs almost to the bone. 'I'm sick,' she shouts through the wall, 'I'm a sick girl.'

In this stronghold of private medicine there is a nurse who comes every day, probably paid for by the church. The doctor from St Vincent's brings his students, and most days she has a gentleman caller who announces his presence by crooning outside the door 'Hey there, you with the stars in your eyes'.

'Aw, quit fooling around,' shouts Rose through the door. 'I'm a sick girl. I can't talk to you. I'm too sick to talk to myself.'

Because she can never remember anybody's name, K. gives

his friends nicknames and I am Blackie. 'Bye, Blackie,' she says and kisses me on the lips, rubbing her head on my chest, which is as high as she comes. Rose de Nisco, who has never been more than three or four blocks from her building, an urban peasant.

'Pray for me,' someone has written up in the subway. 'Sure,' someone else has added.

6 March, London. I come through Heathrow and in the queue parallel to mine an Indian family is held up at Immigration, the father, thin, dark, with burning eyes, being questioned by a woman so stone-faced she could be at the East German border rather than at Heathrow. There are several sons, looking languid and beautiful, and the mother with a small child in her arms.

'Who are all these people?' says the official, jabbing at the passport. 'I want to *see* all these people.' Whereupon the father swiftly rounds up his family and marshals them in front of her. She does not even look up.

15 March. Finish a draft of my piece for the Larkin Festschrift, *Larkin at Sixty.** Parts of it I like and are what I want to say, but I detect a note of Uriah Heep-like self-abasement, which could be taken to denote (and maybe does denote) arrogance. I seem always to be saying 'What am *I* doing here? I'm not a literary person at all.'

Apropos of this I have just ordered a book I saw reviewed, a translation of Ernest Kris and Otto Kurz's *Legend, Myth and Magic in the Image of the Artist*, the main point of which is that there is a tradition, in which the artists themselves conspire, of making a painter's beginnings humbler and less sophisticated than in fact they were. The public liked to believe an artist had no training, that he astonished his elders, who picked out his

* See pages 498–503.

skill when he was in lowly or unlikely circumstances. This has always been the case, and K. and K. demonstrate it from many periods.

I suspect this is also true of literature. My contribution to the Larkin book discusses his poem 'I Remember, I Remember', in which he recalls what elsewhere he called the 'forgotten boredom' of his childhood and Coventry 'where my childhood was unspent'. He is trying to appear an artist without a past. And so am I in my piece, claiming I had little reading and no literary appreciation until I was in my thirties. This conveniently forgets the armfuls of books I used to take out of Headingley Public Library – Shaw, Anouilh, Toynbee, Christopher Fry. Many of the books, it's true, I took for the look of them, and lots I didn't even read, and those I did I've forgotten. Still I did read, though without knowing what I liked or was looking for, and certainly umpteen plays, but without ever thinking of becoming a playwright. This was the period from thirteen to sixteen, just before puberty, and I always wipe it from my mind.

23 March, Bristol. This evening Mam is convinced there are people outside the house and that they are waiting to take me away. I get her off to bed but she keeps coming down, anxious to be taken away in my place. At one point she gets outside in the bitter cold, and eventually I go to bed in order to stop her coming downstairs. I drift off to sleep three or four times, but each time she wakes me wanting to know if I am all right. I then put the camp-bed up in her room and sleep at the foot of the bed so as to stop her getting up and wandering about. But my presence in her bedroom now transforms me into Dad, and she keeps saying 'Walt, why don't you come to bed?' The next day she vaguely remembers I spent the night in her room and thinks that something 'went on', so that becomes another reason why there are people outside the house. And so we go on.

1 May, Yorkshire. W. and I walk from Buckhaw Brow over the fells to Smearsett to look at the Celtic wall. I had only read about it in Wainwright, but W. had come across it years ago without being sure where it was. We struck too far north at first, then saw it against the skyline to our right, running for about thirty yards; a thick wall, put together in a different way from the other drystone walls, almost *woven*, and much broader across the top, as if it were some sort of fortification. The thought that it is two thousand years old and more is duly impressive, and I put my hand on it and think conventional thoughts like 'This wall was new when the census was being taken in Judaea, already ancient when the Normans came,' and so on. But then so were the unshaped rocks, the earth we are standing on.

We walk to the top of Smearsett, and on to Feizor, where far away to the north-west there is a faint fuming haze that is the sea, which I first saw from here, or from the top of Ingleborough anyway, in 1953, when I was on leave from the Russian course. And for some reason it makes me smile, this glimpse of the sea, just as coming out at night and unexpectedly seeing the moon will make one smile.

17 June. All morning auditioning at the Queen's on the set of *The Dresser*, Ronald Harwood's new play and a much more popular evening than *Enjoy* is likely to be. I hate auditions and all the chat one has to go through; Ron explaining the play, tells the actors (wrongly to my mind) that the action could be thought to take place in their head – a direction that helps nobody. Then there is the putting of them at their ease, the enthusiasm one manages to squeeze out after they have read, all so that these young men can leave, as they are entitled to, with their self-respect intact. We see nine actors, and by the end of the morning I'm shattered.

I bike to the Royal Academy to look at the Wyeth exhibition, which is unexpectedly crowded, partly with the overflow from the Summer Exhibition but also, I suspect, with people hungry for naturalism. Some of the pictures are wonderfully delicate, particularly an open window with a curtain blowing through done in 1947 and a sexy nude boy. But the crowds in the gallery repel, and as always I wonder what they are there for and what I am there for. The blown-curtain picture is reminiscent of Edward Hopper's *Evening Wind*, and I come away thinking I like his paintings more, raw and unfinished though they seem by comparison with Wyeth's. Two myths of America here, though: Wyeth's rural America, weatherboarded barns, grey New England shores, models who turn their faces from the painter and search across empty fields for unseen visitors; Hopper's the world of B pictures, singles bars, lonely people in diners, middle-aged women waiting for love with a drink and a cigarette, bored usherettes, and lonely gas stations.

10 July, New York. Why American is a foreign language: we lunch in a café near Gramercy Park, sitting out on a heavy, overcast day. I order a screwdriver and drink it quickly and ask for another.

'I guess it's kind of hot,' the waiter says.

'Yes,' says Lynn, 'and the glasses are kind of small.'

'Yes,' says the waiter. 'That's true also.'

No Englishman would say 'That's true also' (although it's a perfectly grammatical sentence), because it's written not spoken English. Only Ivy Compton-Burnett would write it as dialogue.

21 July. Mary-Kay rings from Geneva to tell the children their grandfather has died. Sam answers the phone, is told the news, and then immediately announces to the room in his gruff eight-year-old voice, 'He's dead.'

William (six) now comes to the phone. 'Can I pretend that I don't know and you tell me all over again?'

19 August, Yorkshire. Wake at 5.30 a.m. and hear a cock crow. A cock, unaware that it has turned into a cliché, unselfconsciously goes on maintaining a rustic tradition, fulfilling its role in the environment. The corn mill is restored, the drystone-waller demonstrates his craft, the thatchers bind their reeds and the cocks crow. Country craft.

And somewhere between sleeping and waking G. knocks at the door. I had the chain on and look at him standing there in the dawn. But I am not surprised, and he comes in and sits in one of the green chairs in the living-room and talks. And he tells me, or I know, that he has murdered all his family. And, gentle and friendly as ever, he has come, I know, to murder me.

8 September, Leeds. 'Las Vegas,' says my cousin Arnold. 'Then in November it's Mombasa.' We are waiting outside the crematorium at Cottingley, where his father, Dad's brother Bill, is to be cremated. He's telling me about his retirement, the package holidays he and his wife go on. 'I've lost count of the number of times we've been to Majorca.'

All crematoriums are built on the loggia principle; long open corridors, cloisters even, the walls lined with slips of stone printed with the names of the burned. 'Reunited', 'Loved', and in one case 'He was kind', which is the sort of thing women who don't like sex say of a forbearing husband. Among the names I spot Mr and Mrs Holdsworth, who lived opposite us in the Hallidays during the war and from whose nasturtium border we used to collect caterpillars.

Now the vicar arrives in beige frock and rimless glasses and bounds out of his car to shake our hands.

Two women wait in the sunshine. They are from Mount Pisgah, the chapel Uncle Bill used to go to. 'Well, we still call it Mount Pisgah, only Mount Pisgah's actually a Sikh chapel now.' One is very tall, the other tiny, with kali legs. 'He was a grand feller, your uncle,' one of them says. 'And he had beautiful handwriting.'

The hearse and the attendant cars are grey and low-slung, so that it looks more like the funeral of a Mafia boss than of an ex-tram-driver. As we come out of the chapel cousin Geoff, who always takes the piss, shouts at my Uncle Jim, the last surviving brother, and who's deaf, 'Head of the clan now, Uncle'.

'Aye,' Uncle Jim shouts back. 'There's nobbut me now.'

'Nay, Jim,' somebody says.

Geoff nudges me. 'Give us your autograph.'

The funeral tea is held in the functions room of Waites, at the top of Gledhow Street. Cousin Arnold, who's a retired police photographer, tells me about a visit by the stripper Mary Millington to Blackpool, where he now lives, and how she committed suicide soon afterwards. 'I can't understand why she committed suicide. She had a lovely body.'

I call at Uncle Bill's house, 72 Gledhow Street, partly to refresh my memory as it's what I imagine the set of *Enjoy* should look like. But it's not as I remember it, all chrome and leatherette and the knight in armour holding the fire tongs on the hearth; now just a dull, cream-painted room that could be anywhere.

I take the train back. Through county after county the fields are alight. It's like taking a train through the Thirty Years War.

14 September. Supper with the Waltons and Russell Harty. William Walton has asked me to write a companion piece for his one-act opera *The Bear*, and I bring the synopsis along. Lady W.

thrusts it unread into her bag and only extracts it when Russell asks to read it. It's quite funny, but it transpires that Walton didn't want a funny piece so back it goes into her bag.

Walton is good for gossip, saying how badly Sargent conducted the first performance of *Troilus and Cressida*, how he had not read the score and conducted the second act at sight. Heifetz had been at supper with the Waltons and when the ladies had retired revealed he had been to rehearsal at Walton's invitation and had seen that Sargent was trying to wing the whole thing. Sargent was about to do his first American tour, and Heifetz warned him that he would personally see it was a disaster unless Sargent made more of an effort to present this new work properly. Whereupon Sargent wept. But it was still an indifferent production and, though well received, took an hour longer than it should have done. I actually saw it given by a Covent Garden touring company at the Leeds Grand in 1951 and remember being taken through some of the themes in a lecture by Ernest Bradbury. I heard my first operas that week, and a very odd trio they were: Vaughan Williams's *Pilgrim's Progress*, Walton's *Troilus* and Strauss's *Der Rosenkavalier*. Walton also says that Sargent had the original score of *Belshazzar's Feast*, which he kept after the first performance at the Leeds Festival in 1931 and which has never been seen since.

Draft libretto for William Walton, 14 September 1980

A grand seaside hotel in the twenties.

A young woman in black sits in the window, in sharp contrast to other guests in blazers and shorts on their way to the beach.

The hotel manager come in and tells the woman that unless her bill is paid that day she must leave the hotel. There is an argument.

Meanwhile waiters come in with very expensive luggage,

belonging to a millionaire whose yacht has just anchored in the harbour. The millionaire comes in and takes a seat while his room is got ready.

The young woman summons a waiter and tells him to move her seat further away from the millionaire. The millionaire is intrigued. He summons the same waiter, who is noticeably more polite to him than to the woman, and tells him to move his seat closer to her. The process is repeated. The increasingly disgruntled waiter has to move the chairs again.

The millionaire asks why she is moving. She says it is because she can smell money. She is allergic to the sight and smell of money.

The millionaire cannot smell money. He smells his hand but cannot detect it. He offers the young woman his hand to smell, and she very gingerly does so, and promptly collapses. The millionaire summons the waiter for some champagne. A glass revives her, but the sight of the millionaire tipping the waiter promptly makes her swoon again.

The millionaire asks her how she came to be like this. She says that she married a poor man, and they were very happy, but he worked very hard and gradually became rich. Making money took over his life. He used to come home smelling of money. They lived in a house that smelled of money. He dressed her in clothes, gave her jewels – all smelling of money. She began to suffer from asthma, rashes, fainting fits – all brought on by the sight and smell of money. Even signing a cheque fetched her out in spots.

Eventually her husband died, leaving her very rich. But, valuing her health, she could not touch the money, and besides it nauseated her.

The millionaire is overjoyed. He has spent all his life looking for someone who would love him for himself, regardless of his fortune. He approaches her, but she begins to feel faint.

Suddenly the manager appears with her bill. The millionaire orders the manager to strip, so he can put on his clothes. The manager, obsequious to a fault, does so and the millionaire, now dressed in the manager's clothes, which do not smell of money, is at last able to kiss the young woman's hand.

She says she cannot stand the hotel and wants to leave. Despite being in his underpants, the manager still insists that her bill be paid, but at the very mention of it the young woman collapses again.

The millionaire is furious with the manager, saying that he will settle her bill. She begins to revive, and as she does so the millionaire begs her to come away with him on his yacht.

'Will it,' she asks fearfully, 'will it smell of money?'

'No,' says the millionaire. 'It is a very petite yacht, and all it will smell of is the sea and freedom.'

The couple leave hand in hand, and as the yacht sails out of the bay the waiter clears away the champagne, complaining that neither of them has left him a tip.

18 September, Kenneth Tynan's memorial service. I wasn't intending to go. I never knew him well, and when we did meet, during *Beyond the Fringe* for instance, I was generally in the shadow of J. I sent him *Forty Years On* in 1967, when he was dramaturge at the National, but he sent it back saying he thought it was for the commercial theatre (this was before the National went commercial). After *Habeas Corpus* he asked me to adapt Willie Donaldson's autobiography and we had a meeting, but I was never easy with him or one of his fans. So I would have given the occasion a miss, only Kathy T.'s secretary phoned, ostensibly to inquire if I knew the time of the service had changed, which I took to be a three-line whip. So for the third time in three weeks I put on my grey suit, get on my bike, and go down to St Paul's, Covent Garden.

Hoping I'm not early, I find the church packed and a scrum in the doorway. Peter Hall and Peter Shaffer go in ahead of me and march boldly down the centre aisle, but spotting a seat in the back row I slip in as Michael White moves up and down the aisles like an usher at a wedding. Note Kingsley Amis across the way, Larry Adler sitting in front, and then see Larry Adler also walking down the aisle and realize one of them must be Bert Shevelove. Tom Stoppard stands up at the front and surveys the house, and just before we kick off a little figure in black is escorted down the far aisle – Princess Margaret, seemingly attended by Christopher Logue.

The priest is young and on the plump side and, were he playing the part, way over the top. He apologizes, as parsons tend to do these days, that we are in a church at all and says that though there will have to be a prayer at the end of the proceedings, it will not so much be a prayer as 'an opportunity for our private commemoration'.

Albert Finney reads a preface in his rich, plump actor's voice, then George Axelrod, who's inaudible. Alan Brien talks, but, as is the way of these occasions, more about himself than about the deceased. Then Penelope Gilliatt comes to the chancel steps, smiling, smiling and smiling. 'Your Royal Highness,' she begins – and that is the last we hear. It is as if a mouse is at the microphone. Still, she is plainly speaking, and the audience lean forward to catch the faint squeakings. People cough. A note is passed down the aisle, written as it turns out by Irving Wardle: 'Tell her to speak up.' It gets as far as Shevelove, who turns round and says in tones much louder than hers, 'I certainly will not!' and so Penelope whispers on before Tom Stoppard concludes.

Then out into the rain, with a vast crush in the doorway. Huw Wheldon grips my arm: 'An impressive service, I think.

A fitting tribute. Unfortunate about that woman. One couldn't hear.' Codron is ahead of me in a white suit, and I note the newly gilded panel to Richard Beckinsale. On the steps Peter Nichols had already lit up, and there are people asking for (and getting) autographs. As I go for my bike I see Peter Brook surrounded by reporters, and it is his picture that is in all the papers next day, standing under an umbrella with Mrs Tynan.

Back at rehearsal Joan Plowright makes no comment on my being in a suit. Olivier had apparently been asked to speak but had declined, saying that he was unable to come and if he had been he was not sure what he would have said. They do a run-through of the play which is excellent, much better than I could have expected, and I begin to wonder whether it might amount to something.

20 September. John Fortune was once in a TV show with Irene Handl. It involved colour separation, a technique then in its infancy, and the enthusiastic young director thought he should explain the process to Miss Handl at the outset.

Swathed in a fur tippet and carrying at least two Pekingese, the dumpy old lady listened patiently while he embarked on a lecture about electronics. Eventually she interrupts: 'Excuse me, dear, but I think you're confusing me with one of those actresses who gives a fuck.'

1 October. Telephoned by the *Evening News* to see if I have any comment to offer on the occasion of Harold Pinter's fiftieth birthday. I don't; it's only later I realize I could have suggested two minutes' silence.

10 October. Enjoy now in its second week at Richmond. See it tonight, after four days' absence, and find it has turned into *A*

Girl in My Soup, with the actors hopping from laugh to laugh with no thought for what's in between. Several people, including Tom Sutcliffe in the *Guardian*, describe the play as 'courageous'. Since the central character is in drag throughout, this presupposes that I spend my evenings idly running my fingers along a rack of strapless evening-gowns and adjusting my slingbacks. Now it can be told.

Next week a bad week for the play to open, as there are new plays opening practically every night, including one at the National by Howard Brenton, *The Romans in Britain*.

19 October. About the only person feeling more sorry for themselves than I am this Sunday morning must be Lady Barnett. She was convicted of shoplifting last Wednesday and I was convicted the same day, though of what? I don't quite know, since I haven't read the papers. But sentence was pronounced again today, this time unanimously; it will be carried out, and *Enjoy* close, in about three weeks' time. 'You have cut the umbilical cord,' says Lindsay A.

A ring at the door yesterday. A telegram from *In Britain*, a magazine for tourists. 'Feel you are the ideal person to interview Jonathan Miller. Reply prepaid.'

Reply, 'Sorry, already interviewing him for *Racing Pigeon Gazette*.'

17 November, New York. Shepherd R., K.'s lawyer, calls and asks me if I would care for a theatrical experience around seven. Lynn prophesies it will be something to do with AA, and so it proves. A church hall off Hudson Street, used by various community groups. Notices to do with the aged. The times of the crèche. A poster, 'Blossom where you are planted.' Three speakers at a table, miked: a drama teacher at Rutgers and part-time theatre critic of the *Village Voice*; Alice, the chairperson; and Tom, a priest (although you would not guess it – actually, maybe God would not guess it either). The room fills up, sexes about equally divided, more whites than blacks, one of the blacks a policeman in uniform. The most noticeable factor is that everybody smokes (and smokes and smokes), each chair with its individual tin-can ashtray.

A cadaverous white-haired woman stands up. 'My name is Barbara and I am an alcoholic.'

'Hi, Barbara,' everyone says.

Then Barbara recounts her experiences (while smoking): the blackouts, the pneumonia, the sickness.

The priest tells his story: how he got so pie-eyed at the Eucharist the congregation were lucky they got the wafer in their mouth, because generally they got it in the ear or even the eye.

One by one the people from the floor stand up and identify themselves.

'My name is Marvin and I am an alcoholic.'

'Hi, Marvin.'

'My name is Todd and I am an alcoholic.'

'Hi, Todd.'

Shepherd speaks too, and now there are so few people who haven't testified that I begin to feel distinctly out of it and note some kind, encouraging smiles willing me to take the plunge. ('My name is Alan and I'm English and I don't do this sort of thing.')

I'm saved by Alice, who, whenever there is a pause, gets hold of the mike and lets us in on her life. Alice's big problem is not that she's an alcoholic but that she's a bore. Maybe that's what drove her to drink, because as sure as hell it drives other people, a big guy in the front row falling fast asleep as she recounts her non-experiences when pissed. A lesson here, though, because whereas avowals of general degradation, such as Alice goes in for, are tedious, bad behaviour that is specific (e.g. the wafer in the ear) is interesting and funny.

Still, as so often with Americans, one comes away thinking that they do this kind of thing so much better than we do, and that, wanting irony, they show each other more concern.

11 December, New York. I am having supper at The Odeon when word goes round the tables that John Lennon has been shot. 'This country of ours,' sighs my waiter. 'May I tell you the specials for this evening?'

The Chinese cooks come and stand at the door of the kitchen as a radio is brought to one of the booths. At another table some diners call instantly for their check, hardly bothering to conceal their appetite for the tragedy (they are, after all, New Yorkers), and take a cab uptown to join what WNEW is already calling 'a vigil'. 'Would you describe the crowd outside the Dakota Apartments as a vigil?' asks Dan, our host. 'I would describe it', says the woman reporter, whose name is Robin, 'definitely as a vigil.'

In England this will mark New York down yet again as a violent and dangerous place, but I walk back up West Broadway, the street deserted except for a few drunks in doorways ('The slayer thought to be male, white') and feel perfectly safe. Already, though, there are candles burning in windows, and a girl weeps as she waits on this warm, windy night to cross Canal Street – 'Sixty-four degrees here on WNEW, the wind from the south-west', the wind and the warmth making it possible for the male, white slayer to wait however long he had to wait this unseasonable December night for the return of his victim.

Back in my building all is normal, which is to say that Rose is shouting up the stairs at the top of her eighty-two-year-old voice. 'My brain hurts,' she is bellowing. 'I'm a sick girl. Come on down here, you no-good four-eyed bastard. I'll kill you dead. Bouncing your goddamn ball – that ain't nice.' This ball, which she has been complaining about for twenty years, does not exist except as a sound in her own head, and, so far from sending *her* mad, her shouting about it has put the woman upstairs in Bellevue, so there is nobody in the apartment to bounce a ball anyway.

In England, where eccentricity is more narrowly circumscribed, Rose would have been long ago in hospital herself; but here in New York, where everyone is mad, she is tolerated, looked after as maybe the male, white slayer has been tolerated and looked after. She stands at the door of her apartment:

'She's no good, my dear fellow. She stinks. Bring my clothes to the Bendix tomorrow. It's a bad world, my dear.'

Meanwhile on WNEW, 'We're kind of staying together, keeping each other company through the night and just charting impressions here.' 'I guess', says Dan, 'that it's kind of futile to speculate on the motives of the screwball who committed this murder, or maybe I should say the alleged screwball who committed this alleged murder.' The body is now no longer believed to be at the Roosevelt Hospital and Yoko is thought to be back at the Dakota in 'what is believed to be a deeply distraught condition.' 'Which is', says Dan, 'kind of surreal.'

'Yeah,' says another reporter (also charting impressions). 'This night has much irony – irony that's added to if we remember that showing on TV this evening was *The Glenn Miller Story*.'

'I'd like to say', says a caller, 'that he had a zest for life. That's what I'd like to say as of this moment.'

'I don't want to take away from the gravity of this situation,' says another caller. 'If anything I'd like to add to it, and what I would say is that it's going to be hard to walk the streets of this town knowing he is not here with us. I once saw him on Madison Avenue.'

'Hold on, people,' says Dan. 'We're here. Hold on.'

1981

1 February. 'What is it', said Ariel C. today, 'that I've no need to do now that I'm an old lady? Oh, I remember: tell the truth.'

She has just seen the National's production of *The Caretaker*, which she hasn't liked because she didn't care for Warren Hastings. She means Warren Mitchell, and when the mistake is pointed out says airily (and Arielly), 'Well, he's the only Warren I've come across.'

24 February. Supper at Pat Heald's with Thora Hird, who tells stories of her childhood in Morecambe, where her father was the manager of the Winter Gardens. Morecambe had one prostitute, Nellie Hodge, who used to take her clients down the ginnel at the back of the Hirds' house, thus providing Thora with a fund of anecdote.

CLIENT: Nay, put a bit of feeling into it, Nellie.

NELLIE: I can't while I'm eating my fish and two.

And on another occasion:

CLIENT: Nay, Nellie, don't keep nodding your head.

NELLIE: I can't help it, you've gone and got my scarf fast inside.

Thora has just had both hips replaced by Mr Brian Roper, a handsome, taciturn surgeon whom she teased. When he was looking at her scars, she said, 'I suppose you've seen a lot of actresses' bottoms, Mr Roper.'

'I have, yes, Miss Hird.'

'Tell me, do character actresses' bottoms look any different from leading ladies'?'

He thought for a moment.

'No, Miss Hird. I don't think they do.'

14 May. 'Utter trust,' says Miss Shepherd this morning. 'I have utter trust. Look at you. I had utter trust when you were ill and you have recovered. More or less. Utter trust.' And she bangs her fist on her knee.

Not getting the gist, I change the subject. 'Have you heard about the Pope?'

'I'm *talking* about the Pope. Your trouble was in the stomach, and that's where he's been shot. Utter trust.'

23 May. Each time I come to New York I'm surprised that Rose is still around. Having arrived last night, I wake this morning to hear her singing, and in due course there is a thud on the door. 'Open!' she shouts.

Rose never rings the bell, just hurls herself at the door expecting it to be open, as her door always is. Look through the spyhole and there is nobody there, Rose coming well below security level.

Though I've not been here for six months, there are no preliminaries. 'I'm telling her, come on down, the dirty, nasty bitch. Bouncing a ball. It ain't nice. I'm a sick girl, I tell you. Come *on*!'

She stands shouting up the staircase, looking like Old Mother Riley girding herself for battle. 'I'll kill you dead, I tell you.'

At which point one of the other tenants comes slowly down the stairs. He smiles wearily at me (Rose a burden all the tenants share).

'Good morning, Rose.'

'Yeah, yeah. Go ahead, go ahead,' and he passes through. 'Come on down here, you bum. I'll fix you.'

Then, the other tenant now out of earshot, 'He's no good, my dear fellow. He stinks. He's had no luck with his sons. They're all crazy.'

Dependent on everyone's goodwill, Rose badmouths everybody and hasn't a scrap of loyalty.

'How are you, Blackie? Where's Peetie?'

'He's not here.'

'Ain't that a shame? That ain't nice. He's a bum.'

'He's OK.'

'Well, maybe he is. I don't know. You're nice to him; he's nice to you. One hand washes the other in this world.'

She gives the empty staircase a final shout before going inside. 'You come on down, you four-eyed bastard. I'll kill you dead.

'I can't see so good now, Blackie. Bring my clothes to the Bendix, will you?'

12 June. Drive down to Shipbourne for George F.'s father's funeral. It's a warm, misty day, almost foggy, and Kent, which I seldom see except *en route* for Dover, is rich and lush. I know many of the place-names – East Hoathly, Ightham, Wrotham – from Denton Welch's *Journals*, which I read when I was seventeen, the countryside still set in my mind as it was in those days, with barbed wire, Nissen huts and soldiers bathing.

George's father was sixty-eight and had a stroke last month while I was in UCH, and it converted him into the same helpless, chained creature that lay in the bed opposite me. I'm thankful George hadn't visited me and seen to what his dad might have come – a helpless hulk, rolling his eyes, grunting and roaring and trying to make himself understood. A second stroke finished him as (and today everyone keeps saying this) he would have wished.

Dick's life had been full of odd coincidences. Wounded at

Dunkirk, he was lying on the beach with the last boats gone, and as the Germans began to round up the remnants of the BEF he passed out. When he came to, he found himself looking up into the face of a German officer he knew: it was the man who had taught him German at school.

Having tried several times to escape, Dick ended up in Colditz, where he was Escape Officer after Pat Reid. Reid came to see him when he was dying, and took a turn at the bedside, sitting rigidly to attention while George went off and had a lie-down. George fell asleep, to be woken five hours later by a clap of thunder. Rushing back to the ward he found Reid sitting in exactly the same position, not having moved a muscle in five hours.

Dick died in Tunbridge Wells General Hospital, and all afternoon a drunken trumpeter was playing in the street outside – not, one would have thought, a common occurrence in Tunbridge Wells. As the afternoon drew to a close he signed off with the Last Post, shortly after which Dick died.

The village church is packed out. 'Armoured Division or friend of the family?' murmurs a ramrod figure on the door, and indeed half of the church is crammed with the men who won the war. Young officers then, now in their sixties, good, solid, old-fashioned faces, never wavering, never doubting, and singing their hearts out – 'For All the Saints', 'Immortal, Invisible'. It's like *Forty Years On* – all that one loves and hates.

The service over, the old soldiers turn and clap hands on familiar shoulders and there is a hum of talk as they troop out of the church, stilled suddenly as we see the family stood in a corner of the churchyard, gathered round the grave, people under the cedar trees watching.

2 July. McEnroe behaves badly at Wimbledon and in one particularly ludicrous moment shouts at a linesman, 'You're a disgrace to the human race.' Some group captain on the high chair then docks him a point and an argument ensues as to whether McEnroe was, as he insists, talking to himself and, if he was, whether it was in order to talk to oneself on court (or even breathe).

Of course, now that Wimbledon is all about money, behaving badly is exactly what is required, certainly of McEnroe, and all the claptrap about decency and fair play is just the English at their usual game of trying to have it both ways. Wimbledon is now a spectacle, just as a wrestling match, say, is a spectacle, and a spectacle needs a Hero and a Villain. It's a contest between Right and Wrong, not because McEnroe is particularly badly behaved but because the Wimbledon authorities have sold out to television and this kind of drama is just what viewers enjoy. So McEnroe doesn't really have a choice, only a role.

Many of McEnroe's critics point out how Connors has 'reformed': how three or four years ago he was the rogue, disputing calls, not attending the line-up, and how much better behaved he is now. This misses the point. Connors has to be better behaved, not because his character has changed or his tennis manners have improved but because he has no part in the spectacle. Or if he had (if he had beaten Borg in the semi-final for instance) he would have had to be cast in the Hero's role.

All this is written at five in the morning. I seem to get these impulses to argue first thing – another bout a few days ago being on English philosophy, a subject of which I know and care as little as I do about tennis. But it isn't just in the early morning. They go on all the time, these disputes with myself, and particularly when I'm cycling around. I catch passers-by looking at me, and it's not out of recognition; seeing my frowning face and my jaw working away, they are thinking, 'This is a lunatic.'

7 July. When I say goodbye to Mam after taking her back to the home at Weston, she gets out of the car saying, 'Thank you for all you've done for me, love.' And she means this; it isn't a remark intended to induce guilt. But in a film the next shot would be me looking down at the shaft of a spear protruding from my belly with the head stuck out a foot behind me.

3 August, Yorkshire. I know so little that writing is like crossing a patch of swampy ground, jumping from one tussock to another trying not to get my feet wet (or egg on my face). Of course at a distance no one can see the ground is swampy, and at a distance too one's movements are smoothed out, the hesitations diminished. Fifty years on, the anguished leaps may seem like confident strides. Except who will be looking?

Today is the anniversary of Dad's death, and I go down to the cemetery about half past twelve, which was around the time he died, and put flowers on the grave.

I would like to forward on to him beyond the grave a card David Vaisey sent me last Christmas. It's of a toy butcher's shop, *c.* 1885, and it would remind him of the butcher's shop he made for Gordon and me when we were evacuated to Wilsill in 1939. It had little wooden joints that hung on bent-pin meat hooks, a counter and a block, and he had made it sitting at his Hobbies fretwork machine by the fire at Halliday Place in those first weeks of the war.

The other item I'd send him would be Emanuel Hurwitz's valuation of the violin he bought at Barnoldswick in 1970 for £16. Hill's, the snooty violin shop in Bond Street, made him feel a fool for thinking it was of any interest and grandly offered him £20 for it. Hurwitz says it's worth £2,000, and with restoration much more.

What I wouldn't like to send him is Mam's address, or the

Orton script which I've been struggling with all this year [*Prick Up Your Ears*].

Standing by the grave, I fetch back a memory of him in his waistcoat with his sleeves rolled up, grinning all over his still young face. But no voice that says, 'It'll be all right eventually' or 'You'll get through this patch,' which is what he'd have said if he were alive.

22 *August, La Garde Freinet.* This villa is a farmhouse that has been converted so ruthlessly that only two buttresses of the original remain. It belongs to Reiner Moritz, the German TV mogul. My room is the so-called library and games room, one end of which holds the bookshelves. The books are a varied selection, but they have one thing in common: they have all been read with a view to turning them into TV programmes.

Apropos of books, I have just finished Robert Byron's *Road to Oxiana* in a new paperback edition with an introduction by Bruce Chatwin. It's a funny and enjoyable book, though I have reservations about both Byron and Chatwin – Byron contemptuous of other 'worthier' travellers, a (possibly invented) schoolmaster, Thrush, Chatwin of the hippies who have made much of the journey to Afghanistan commonplace. Both, though writing forty years apart, are acceptable figures socially. Embassies abroad are invariably outposts of snobbery of one kind or another, where one is welcomed if one is 'amusing' or a 'celebrity' but not otherwise. Boredom is the enemy, and diplomats, like aristocrats, wish to be diverted.

Chatwin irritates on another level. 'I can guess, too, what happened to Wali Jahn,' he writes. 'He took me to safety when I got blood-poisoning. He carried me on his back through the river, and bathed my head, and made me rest under the ilexes. But when we came back five years later he was coughing, deep retching coughs, and had the look of someone going down to the cold.' This is sheer Buchan, the permitted degree of male camaraderie – men caring and crying for each other, both nobly – plus the bit of Sapper–Buchan lore in 'the look of a man going down to the cold'. What is this look? Does he mean the man has TB or bronchitis?

I am a mean-spirited reader, though. 'One afternoon . . .' Chatwin writes, 'I took *The Road to Oxiana* into the mosque [of Sheik Lutf'ullah, in Isfahan] and sat, cross-legged, marvelling both at the tilework and Byron's description of it.' It's the 'cross-legged' I dislike, partly because five minutes of it and I'd be crippled. But why tell us?

28 August, La Garde Freinet. Ten years ago it was thought (or I thought it) quite daring for a girl to loosen her bikini top to brown her whole back. Nowadays girls bare their breasts and bake them openly just as a matter of course. Or girls with nice breasts do. Charlotte H., for instance, who sits across the swimming-pool from me now, has huge unexpected breasts with large, snub nipples; they look like the noses of koala bears.

I wear a pair of flip-flop sandals, the sort with a sole and one strap across – the biblical type, I suppose. When I was a boy and read of Jesus washing the feet of the disciples, I thought of their feet as like my own in 1943, sweating in grey Utility socks and encased in heavy black shoes with stuck-on rubber soles. Consequently I regarded Jesus's gesture as far more self-sacrificing, even heroic, than it actually was. After twelve pairs of such feet, I thought, the Crucifixion would have been a pushover.

11 November. An article on playwrights in the *Daily Mail*, listed according to Hard Left, Soft Left, Hard Right, Soft Right and

Centre. I am not listed. I should probably come under Soft Centre.

14 November, Bristol. Mam is now having difficulty putting names to objects, as much, I think, from disuse of her faculties as from actual decay. She was stood in front of the mantelpiece trying to think of the name for the clock. 'It's one of those things', she said, 'with things going round, and then when they get there they've had it for a bit.'

20 November, Yorkshire. The phone rings. 'Have I got the pox, darling?'

'I beg your pardon?'

'Have I got the pox? It's Coral Browne, dear. I've just got into London and found everybody else has left. Alec's not here. You're not here. The only person who is here, thank God, is John Schlesinger, and I'm going there to supper tonight.'

I ask her what it is she's doing. 'An American TV special. Are you sitting down, dear, because I'm about to tell you the title: "The Most Wonderful Woman in the World". I need hardly add, darling, that I am not playing the title role. About Eleanor Roosevelt. Being played by Jean Stapleton. No, not Maureen Stapleton – that would make sense. I'm playing Lady Reading. Ever heard of her? No, I hadn't. There's apparently only one photograph of her extant, and they've given it to make-up so I fear the worst. They've kitted me out in some Oxfam clothes, furs with alopecia, and they haven't even let me *see* the hat, saying its got to be "refreshed", plus I have to wear these invalid shoes. In the scene we do tomorrow I'm supposed to walk from Claridge's round the corner into Parliament Square. I've pointed out that Parliament Square is not round the corner from Claridge's, but they say it's all the footage will allow. Vincent is in Paris, getting some award for his services to horror, then we go to Rome for something similar only in Italian.'

We talk about the Burgess piece [*An Englishman Abroad*] and discuss who should play him, and we go through various names while it becomes increasingly obvious that we haven't talked about who is to play her. Eventually I hear myself saying, 'Would you like to do it?'

'But aren't I too *old*?'

'Well,' I say, 'what do you think?'

'I'm not sure, dear. You see, in a way, age didn't come into it' (which is true). 'And I was playing Gertrude at the time – mother to Michael Redgrave, who's several years older than me. I mean, I've played mother to them all, Redgrave, Gielgud, Alec. The only one whose mother I haven't played, thank God, is Ralph Richardson.'

I promise to keep her posted and send her the next draft, when there is a next draft, and that's where we leave it. It slightly alters the play, makes it less fictional, but I think I like that.

1982

17 January, New York. At The Odeon on our last evening A. and I sit on the banquette next to a couple in their late twenties, good-looking, though the woman over-attended-to – hair carefully coiffed, eyelashes curled, altogether too done-up. They are waited on by Helen, who is pretty and natural-looking (and also imperturbable). Their main dish is lobster, and the girl sends it back twice, the first time because it is cold, the second because 'it's like rubber.' The real reason, it seems, is that the boyfriend had noticed Helen and been pleasant to her while she was taking their order. Stephen C., who is *maître d'*, says this often happens, and, 'without being sexist *at all*, gays do not do that.' If a gay couple are served by a good-looking waiter and one of them fancies him, it's all part of the fun.

24 January. To the Lutyens exhibition at the Hayward, thinking (wrongly) that towards the end of a Sunday afternoon it will not be crowded. In fact the rooms are so full the only solution is to go round the wrong way, though no matter, since my impressions of exhibitions and galleries are always haphazard. As usual, I am struck more by who is doing the looking rather than by what they are looking at: worthy architects, with grey hair and bright ties, seeming younger than their age; pencil-slim architectural students dressed with casual care, functional in their persons; a lot of people who have probably had a decent salad for their lunch and come in their five- and six-year-old cars, reflecting that this is what architecture should be about – warm, idiosyncratic, cosy. Though in fact much of Lutyens's architecture is as contemptuous of the individual as the bleakest tower block. But more fun – particularly the follies of it: a wooden bridge over a gate, a pergola, a billiard table on a plinth of solid chalk, gingerbread housing, and some of it like the architecture of dreams. His furniture is beautifully curved and chamfered in bleached oak and lime, and in the crowded lecture hall, which I cannot get into, a glimpse of two chandeliers in painted wood, fat coloured hens and ladies fishing – nursery chandeliers from the Viceroy's House in New Delhi. I have a sense of uncompeting ease here, knowing what I like and what I don't like without being mystified or bewildered as I always am by first-rate pictures, and the feeling recurs that had I been a designer (though I would not have wanted to be an architect) I would have been a happier man.

I go upstairs to the second exhibition, the later paintings of Sickert. Some are thin and unfinished and (which always disqualifies a picture for me) with the grain of the canvas showing through the paint. A good one of George V at Aintree, with his dead Cambridge-blue eyes, and a superb boldly done picture of 'Lazarus Breaking His Fast'. Odd pictures I recognize from boyhood and Leeds ('Oh hello. Fancy seeing you here!') and are more friendly than any face in the gallery. But it's a foul little building, and its inadequacy emphasized by the photographs of Lutyens' delicious details – delicate finials, tiled floors, curved banisters. All the Hayward can boast in the way of decoration is the impress of boards on concrete. The staircase up to Waterloo Bridge is wet and stinks of urine, and rightly – it is properly pissed on.

10 February. I am walking in the Lower East Side in New York, strolling east through the Village. I am surprised by how much of it has been smartened up. Then I come out into an intersection between warehouses and railway buildings, where, across a large central triangle, I see a herd of mackintoshed derelicts, who are also convicts, each with a white oblong on his boots carrying his prison number. I turn and run, much as one might run to get out of the way of a herd of cows, for I know they are not individually dangerous.

Now I am walking back towards safety – east is danger, I know, and west is home – back along a narrow track beside fields of standing corn. A colourful character waves me on, and then I am confronted by a young man in a smart cavalry-twill coat, the coat slightly too big for him; he has a small head, with gummy, edgy hair. He wants money, and I reach into my right-hand back pocket, where I have several bills, and, taking them out, pull out one for ten dollars. I notice that all the colour has drained from the note. Knowing that I have only taken out one bill from many, he suddenly has a knife in his hand which he is holding before his face, a small knife, the blade of which I can hardly see. I know as we confront each other in the standing corn that this young man of twenty-six or so is going to kill me and that I had been misled by the cavalry-twill coat into thinking him a better class of person. Suddenly I see why the coat is too big – because that too is stolen. I look into the face of this cold-eyed runt and see as I wake and die that I will perish because I have been a snob.

23 March. When, like today, I feel I have got a little, little way with a plot and knock off for the day, it is like a climber going up a sheer face who pitches camp on a narrow ledge. Tomorrow he may get no further; he may even roll off during the night.

'That's a place I haven't been for some time.'

'Where?'

'On top of the world.'

1 April. To the Lyric Studio, Hammersmith, to record Roy Hattersley's *It's My Pleasure*, an evening of Larkin's poetry, with Judi Dench. 'Are you still writing your lovely plays?' she asks. Still, yes.

As always the simpler the programme the more one is called upon to rehearse, in this case all day from ten till five. Hattersley is decent and straightforward and with a sense of humour, but wastes much of his commentary by talking about how deeply the poems have moved him rather than riveting it to fact. He is more nervous of doing this programme ('not his job') than he is of addressing the House of Commons, and he takes up all sorts of points with the producer, thinking there is some sort of expertise involved, whereas really the knack is just to come through as oneself. On recording he is very nervous, and we have to do several retakes, the final one being when he ends up, 'And my thanks to Miss Judi Dench and Mr Alan Brien.'

'Alan would be very flattered,' he says.

'Why?'

'To think that his name is so much at the forefront of my mind.'

His choice of poems is dull, and I read indifferently; Judi as always with great sweetness and lots of light and air in her voice. She wears the same dress she wore when we did my *Evening With* thirteen years ago, and I am in the same suit. Happier then, I reflect (and much in the spirit of the poems); happier almost any time than now.

5 April, Yorkshire. I walk round the village at half past ten, the shadows from the barns sharp and clear under Larkin's 'strong, unhindered moon'. 'This must wait', is my foolish thought, 'until I have written something that permits me to enjoy it.'

27 April. Gavin Millar rehearses Julie Walters and me in our two main scenes from my television film *Intensive Care*. I play a shy schoolteacher, she a night nurse in the intensive-care unit where my father hovers between life and death. In the first scene, after a bit of palaver, I ask her to go to bed; in the second scene we do so, and in this brief absence from duty and the paternal bedside my father, of course, dies. The scene was suggested by an incident in the life of Gandhi, whose father died while he was actually screwing. I had had some thoughts while writing the play that I might act the schoolmaster, but coming to the bedroom scene I sighed with relief, knowing this was something I wouldn't be prepared to tackle – an experience that occurs too frequently when I am writing for it to be just accidental; i.e. I deliberately write myself out of my own work. In this case, though, Gavin hasn't been able to find anyone else to play the part, so here I am. It is a hard job because I have written myself very few lines, something I regularly do with the central character. Supporting parts I don't find difficult, either to invent or to supply with dialogue; the central character is a blank, a puzzle, and one which I hope the actor will solve for me. But now the actor is me and I don't know what to do.

16 May, Yorkshire. A racing pigeon comes down in the garden. It has been plucking its breast as pelicans were once thought to do and now just stands there, amber eyes unwinking, its beak full of fluff. It cannot fly, not even to help itself over the threshold of the hut, and, though we feed it on Ryvita and milk, A. finds it lying on its back this morning, fluttering and unable to right itself. I get the axe and, shutting my eyes, hit it on the head. Bright blood suddenly flows over the dust, though I seem to have made no wound, and its sharp-ringed eye is still. Gingerly I turn it over and it flutters again, so I give it another blow and as I lift it up there is a sound like a sigh as life leaves it. I put it in the bin. I cannot have killed more than three creatures in my life.

25 May, Airedale Hospital, Keighley. Neil, the dresser, has been arguing with Simon, the AFM, and Miri, the make-up assistant, about the colour problem. Simon and Miri are both Jewish (Miri an Israeli) and Neil is ill-equipped to argue with them.

'I just think,' he says, telling me of the argument afterwards, 'I just think there are too many coloured people in London now. And I don't like it. But it's only a preference. After all, some people don't like Bette Davis.'

4 June. We (we!) drop leaflets on the Argentine troops besieged in Port Stanley, urging them to lay down their arms. Were such leaflets dropped on our troops we would consider them contemptible and ludicrous; our leaflets are represented as a great humanitarian gesture.

15 June. Mrs Thatcher announces the surrender of Port Stanley in well-modulated tones. Film follows of the funeral of the commandos killed at Goose Green, the simple service and the youth of the wounded unbearable. A pilot of one of the Harriers talks about the effectiveness of the Sidewinder missiles. 'A bit of an eye-opener,' is how he puts it. A bit of an eye-closer too. Not English I feel now. This is just where I happen to have been put down. No country. No party. No Church. No voice.

And now they are singing 'Britannia Rules the Waves' outside Downing Street. It's the Last Night of the Proms erected into a policy.

Alan (Son of *Civilisation*) Clark MP wants the Argentinian prisoners paraded in front of the cameras with unlaced boots. I'm surprised he doesn't want them displayed in front of the cameras with no braces, like the July plotters.

16 June. A cease-fire with 250 of our forces dead, one for every twenty civilians of the Falkland Islands – the price, Madam says, of freedom. The ways the freedom of the Islanders seem to have been infringed before the outbreak of hostilities appear to be (i) they had to drive on the right, which, since their roads are mainly one-track, can scarcely have been a hardship; (ii) they were occasionally stood up against a wall, hands above their head, and searched, a humiliation suffered nightly by many citizens of this country – chiefly black – any protest about which is treated by the Conservative Party as humbug. The only actual atrocity seems to have been the death of a dairy cow. The man who would have had a field day with this war is Sydney Smith.

19 June. Supper at AG's with Evie Karloff, Boris Karloff's widow. 'Tell me,' I long to lean over and ask, 'what was Bela Lugosi *really* like?' She's admirably plucky and lives in an isolated cottage near Liphook, where she's in the telephone book. On two occasions bricks have been thrown through her windows at night. 'Well,' she says, 'I suppose they think, "He frightened me, so now I'm jolly well going to frighten her."'

20 June. The papers continue fatuous. Peregrine Worsthorne suggests that, having won this war, our troops emerging with so much credit, Mrs Thatcher might consider using them at home to solve such problems as the forthcoming rail strike or indeed to break the power of the unions altogether, overlooking the fact that this is precisely what we are supposed to object to about the regime in Argentina.

Since the war (the last war should we now call it?) there has been a noticeable increase in the use of the military metaphor in public debate. Tebbitt, the Employment Secretary, yesterday talked of campaigns, charges and wars of attrition. And the flag figures. The danger of such talk, of course, is that it presupposes an enemy.

8 July. A drunk comes round tonight shouting at Miss Shepherd and trying to get her out of the van. I go to the door and scare him off, saying, 'What sort of a man is it who torments old ladies of seventy-five?' This morning I am passing the van when her hand comes out. 'Mr Bennett. I'm not seventy-five. I'm seventy-one.'

10 July. Olivier is much given to excessive and almost laughably insincere flattery; he described *Enjoy*, I remember, as the best play he had ever seen – this from the balcony of Her Majesty's to the assembled company at the dress rehearsal, when some of the younger members of the company actually believed him. I saw M. today, who told me of a better instance. Spotting Tom Courtenay at some awards dinner, Olivier congratulates him on his role in *The Dresser*. Tom's current girlfriend is the ASM, whose duties include prompting. Tom introduces her. 'Oh, my dear,' said the Brighton peer, 'what wouldn't I give to be in your shoes! To be able to follow the text of this play *every night*!'

3 August. R. tells me that there has been a photo-call for Sefton, one of the horses injured by the IRA bomb in Hyde Park. However, Sefton has so far recovered that his wounds no longer register on camera. So make-up is applied.

6 September, Weston-super-Mare. To Weston to see Mam. We have lunch in the Cosy Café. Mam's teeth are loose, which blurs her speech, and she also talks quite loudly, as if she is deaf (and exactly the opposite of the hushed tones she and Dad would always use in cafés), so other diners are startled to hear 'I do love you, chick' shouted across the small room. I notice her watching what I do with my knife and fork at the end of the meal, then imitating me.

I drive her back. 'Have you got one of these of your own?' she asks as we are going along.

'What?'

'One of these things where you're in it by yourself.'

'A car?'

'That's it.'

7 September. Douglas Bader dies. I used to imitate him in *Beyond the Fringe* as part of the Aftermyth of War sketch, coming downstairs with a pipe in my mouth and exaggeratedly straight legs (though I never quite dared make them as stiff as they should have been). One night I was hissed and was very pleased with myself. He died after a dinner for Sir Arthur Harris, the destroyer of Dresden. 'Probably legless,' says R. Many other jokes possible, like the loss of his legs going to his head.

Certainly had he not lost them he would not have been heard so much of, which he was – and always on the right. Somehow his death is yet another feather in the cap of Mrs Thatcher, of whom he doubtless approved and who certainly approved of him. Describing his death, another veteran says, 'It was completely clean.'

24 September, Yorkshire. I blackberry up the lane that leads to Wharfe. A big heron in the beck takes wing and flies slowly away up to Crummock. My nightmare when blackberrying (or when I stop the car for a pee) is that I shall find the body of a child, that I will report it and be suspected of the crime. So I find myself running through in my mind the evidences of my legitimate occupation – where I started picking, who saw me park, and so on.

These days I even imagine Mozart as being arrayed against me – so safe, so consistent and now so universally esteemed, the centre of a great huddle (and a huddle of the great) at the Posterity Cocktail Party.

27 September. Russell invents a good parlour game: whose underpants would you least like to be gagged by? I say there would be many people jostling for first position. 'No,' says R. 'not jostling. Jockeying.'

8 October. On the platform at the Conservative Party conference this week sits Mrs H. Jones, the widow of the commando colonel killed at Goose Green. No one remarks on the inappropriateness of this. Even were she, as I imagine she is, a fervent supporter of the Conservative Party, to parade her sacrifice in this fashion makes it partial, not national, and in every sense diminishes it.

13 October. I am rehearsing *Merry Wives of Windsor* for TV, in which I play Justice Shallow. Today I go for a costume fitting to find I am dressed from head to foot in red brocade. I look like an animated tandoori restaurant.

22 November, New York. Struck by the completeness of New York, much of it still as it was in 1930. Today is Thanksgiving Day and the streets are emptied of humanity, Prince Street swept clean of people, every detail of the fretted fronts of warehouses clear and sharp, buildings cut up like cheese, segmented against the sky. It was like this the Thanksgiving Day after J.F.K.'s assassination, when I walked down a totally empty Seventh Avenue with not a soul to be seen.

4 December, New York. One change that has come over public manners was evident at the Falklands homecomings. Combatants (the only airman captured by the Argentinians, for instance), asked what is the first thing they are going to do when they get home, grin cheekily. One says, 'Well, what do you think?' and doubtless others actually do say, 'I'm going to fuck someone silly.' Once upon a time they would have *said*, at any rate, 'Have a nice cup of tea.'

6 December, New York. Ever since 1977, when I first stayed in SoHo, there has been a boutique on the corner of Watts and West Broadway. It's still there this year, and to the casual passer-by the stock looks much the same. But it isn't. Despite the flimsy-looking furs and dresses on display, this is now a shop that specializes in 'protective clothing'. The fur is bullet-proof.

Opposite, and a fixture there for many years longer, is a shop that sells live chickens (the hot smell of it always bringing back the hen coop at Wilsill where we were evacuated in 1939). The presence of the live-chicken shop and the boutique selling protective clothing would enable J. to make one of his 'waiting for the right circumstances' jokes – i.e. not bullet-proof but pullet-proof.

1983

8 February, Dundee. A day off from filming *An Englishman Abroad* and I go to Edinburgh with Alan Bates. We climb the tower near the castle to see the camera obscura. The texture of the revolving bowl and the softness of the reflection convert the view into an eighteenth-century aquatint in which motor cars seem as delicate and exotic as sedan chairs. The traffic is also rendered more sedate and unreal for being silent.

An element of voyeurism in it. The guide, a genteel Morningside lady, trains the mirror on some adjacent scaffolding where workmen are restoring a church. 'I often wonder,' she muses in the darkened room, 'if one were to catch them . . . well, unawares. I mean,' she adds hastily, 'taking a little *rest*.'

3 March, Yorkshire. I take a version of a script down to Settle to be photocopied. The man in charge of the machine watches the sheets come through. 'Glancing at this,' he says, 'I see you dabble in playwriting.' While this about sums it up, I find myself resenting him for noticing what goes through his machine at all. Photocopying is a job in which one is required to see and not see, the delicacy demanded not different from that in medicine. It's as if a nurse were to say, 'I see, watching you undress, that your legs are nothing to write home about.'

20 March, Weston-super-Mare. To see Mam at Weston. I sit in the dining-room of the home while they locate her coat. Two old ladies are waiting for their lunch, which won't happen for at least another hour. 'It went through my mind it was pineapple,' says one, 'but I wouldn't swear to it.' 'You have to watch her,' says the other, pointing to an empty place. 'She'll have all the bread.' Mam's memory has almost gone, leaving her suffused with a general benevolence. 'I've always liked you,' she says to one of the other residents and plants a kiss on her slightly startled cheek.

It is a beautiful day and we walk on the sands. 'Has Gordon been to see you?' I ask. 'Oh yes,' she says, happily. 'Though I'm saying he has, I don't know who he is.' 'Do you know who I am?' She peers at me. 'Oh yes, you're . . . you're my son, aren't you?' 'And what's my name?' 'Ah, now then.' And she laughs, as if this is not information any reasonable person could expect her to have. But it doesn't distress her, so it doesn't distress me.

We have our sandwiches on a hill outside Weston with a vast view over Somerset. She wants to say, 'What a grand view,' but her words are going too. 'Oh,' she exclaims. 'What a big lot of About.' There are sheep in the field. 'I know what they are,' she says, 'but I don't know what they are called.' Thus Wittgenstein is routed by my mother.

28 March. A 'vigorous but not bellicose' war memorial is to be erected by the Falkland Islanders. It has been on view in High Wycombe. On the news, pictures of three ex-servicemen being taught to ski in Nevada. All have lost feet in the Falklands conflict. The instructor is American. He leads them off down the slopes with the words 'All together now. Follow *moi*.'

17 April. George Fenton, who got an Oscar nomination for his *Gandhi* music, has been to Hollywood for the ceremony. By far the most striking people attending were young couples, faultlessly dressed and very glamorous, who stood in the aisles throughout the evening. When anyone in the audience left to go to the loo (the ceremony was interminable) their seat was immediately taken by one of these groomed and gorgeous creatures, who then gave it up without demur when the rightful seat-holder returned. Thinking they were hangers-on, George found himself slightly resenting them, as also their grooming and their glamour. Leaving for a break himself, George found a young man promptly sliding into his place and on his lapel a badge: 'Seat-Filler'. They were all extras employed by the organizers to make sure nothing so shocking as an empty seat should ever appear on the television screen.

6 May. A second session doing a voice-over for a commercial for Quartz washing-machines. I spend half an hour trying to invest the words 'This frog' with some singularity of tone that will distinguish this particular frog from the previous frog, with which it is otherwise identical. It defeats me, and the session is abandoned. Coming away, I feel just as badly as if I'd given a shoddy performance in a definitive recording of the Sonnets.

20 May. In the evening I often bike round Regent's Park. Tonight I am mooning along the Inner Circle past Bedford College when a distraught woman dashes out into the road and nearly fetches me off. She and her friend have found themselves locked in and have had to climb over the gate. Her friend, Marie, hasn't made it. And there, laid along the top of one of the five-barred gates, is a plump sixty-year-old lady, one leg either side of the gate, bawling to her friend to hurry up. I climb over and try to assess the situation. 'Good,' says Marie, her cheek pressed against the gate. 'I can see you're of a scientific turn of mind.' Her faith in science rapidly evaporates when I try moving her leg, and she yells with pain. It's at this point that we become aware of an audience. Three Chinese in the regulation rig-out of embassy officials are watching the pantomime, smiling politely and clearly not sure if this is a pastime or a predicament. Eventually they are persuaded to line up on the other side of the gate. I hoist Marie over and she rolls comfortably down into their outstretched arms. Much smiling and bowing.

Marie's friend says, 'All's well that ends well.' Marie says she's laddered both her stockings and I cycle on my way.

30 May, Yorkshire. A boy is paddling in the beck. He has rolled up his trousers but not taken his socks off, thus refuting the soldier's argument against contraceptives.

I talk to Graham Mort, a young poet who has come to live in the village. He has a wife and three small children and to make ends meet teaches at a prison, the mental hospital in Lancaster and a local school. He says that, compared with the school-children, the murderers and psychotics are models of good behaviour.

9 June, Yorkshire. On the day that Mrs Thatcher is elected for a second term I spit blood. Last night I was reading *Metamorphosis* and wondered that Gregor Samsa, having woken and found himself a beetle, could yet drop off to sleep again, or at any rate daydream and pretend it wasn't true. Yet somehow I manage to doze until around seven, when I come to and lie awake arranging my future, or lack of it.

At nine I go down to the Health Centre in Settle to see Dr. W., whom I first met twelve years or so ago when he was a student at Airedale Hospital. He examines me, finds some evidence of bronchitis, and sends me down to Skipton for an X-ray. By ten-thirty I am back at home, the whole process having taken less than two hours. The result ('nothing sinister') comes through later in the day. It's a model of how the NHS should work, and does in small communities like this, where the patients know the receptionists, the GPs know the hospital, and bureaucracy and waiting are reduced to a minimum. There can be very few private patients, I imagine, in our area because the NHS provides a better service.

12 June, Yorkshire. The verges full of gypsies these last two weeks, on the road to and from the horse fair at Appleby. Someone must have gone into business reproducing their traditional hooped carts, as there are far more this year than previously. I pass some of them on the back road to Settle, two horse-and-carts coming down the steep hill above Swabeck. To brake the carts they trail an old car tyre behind with a child perched on it.

23 June. As A. and I are walking in Regent's Park this evening we stop to watch a baseball game. A police car comes smoothly along the path, keeping parallel with a young black guy who is walking over the grass. The police keep calling to him from the car, but he ignores them and eventually stops right in the middle of the game. A policeman gets out and begins questioning him, but warily and from a distance. The baseball players, unfortunately for the suspect, are all white and they mostly pretend it isn't happening. Some laugh and look at their feet. Others break away and talk among themselves. Only a few unabashedly listen. Someone shouts, 'What's he done?' 'I want you to bear witness,' the man shouts. 'You all bear witness.' For his part the policeman ignores the players, sensing that he is at a disadvantage and that the middle of a game is some kind of sanctuary and too public for the law's liking. It's the sort of refuge Cary Grant might choose in a Hitchcock movie. Meanwhile reinforcements are on the way, and, as a police van speeds over the grass, another policeman gets out of the car and the two of them tackle the suspect. Still one watched, nobody saying anything, those nearest the struggle moving away, their embarrassment now acute. Eventually the police bundle the man into a van and he is driven off. The game is restarted, a little shamefacedly at first, then gathering momentum as we walk on. But the players must have lost heart, because five minutes later the pitcher passes us with his baseball mitt and a young man in a funny hat.

4 July. Recording *The House at Pooh Corner* for Radio 4. One story ends, ' "Tigger is all right, *really*," said Piglet lazily. "Of course he is," said Christopher Robin. "Everybody is *really*," said Pooh.' The true voice of England in the thirties.

8 July. Two strips of pale-blue shirt fabric arrive in the post with a letter asking me to wear them as an armlet on 25 August, which is Leonard Bernstein's sixty-fifth birthday. This will testify to my regard for Lenny and my desire for peace. Actually I don't know Lenny and fear that wearing a sky-blue armband is an opaque if not an ambiguous gesture, so I send my Van Heusen sample to Patricia Routledge, who does know Lenny and is as much concerned about dying from radiation as I am, but less concerned about dying of embarrassment.

1 October. I mend a puncture on my bike. I get pleasure out of being able to do simple, practical jobs – replacing a fuse, changing a wheel, jump-starting the car – because these are not accomplishments generally associated with a temperament like mine. I tend to put sexual intercourse in this category too. The contents of a puncture outfit are like a time capsule, unchanged from what they were when I was a boy, and probably long before that. Here are the rubber solution, the dusting-chalk, the grater on the side of the box, and the little yellow crayon I didn't use then and I don't use now. I ask the cycle shop if anyone has thought of making self-adhesive puncture patches. No one has.

15 October, Yorkshire. If Mr Parkinson and Miss Keays would only get together they could call their baby Frances Parkinson Keays.

20 December, New York. A sign on Seventh Avenue at Sheridan Square: 'Ears pierced, with or without pain.'

I am reading a book on Kafka. It is a library book, and someone has marked a passage in the margin with a long, wavering line. I pay the passage special attention without finding it particularly rewarding. As I turn the page the line moves. It is a long, dark hair.

1984

29 January. Russell has been given some beta-blockers which help to suppress the symptoms of nerves and stage fright. He had put one of them in a tissue, meaning to take it just before his programme, but when he came to do so he found it had dissolved, leaving a patch on the tissue. In the hope that some effective trace of the drug remained, he sucked this patch and within a few minutes felt calmer and came through with flying colours. A second attack of nerves he dealt with in the same way. It was only on the way home after the programme that he felt in another pocket and found the original tissue with the pill intact. What he had been sucking was some snot.

16 February, London. Forty Years On is to be produced at Chichester in May, sixteen years after it was first done. I am nervous about this. When I've written something, I'd quite like to have it adopted, put in someone else's name, and thus have none of the responsibilities of parentage or run the risk that at sixteen one's offspring doesn't turn out as well as one had hoped.

Apropos of which, a few years ago I adopted a Kenyan boy through Action Aid. Every three months or so I get an aerogramme covered with his drawings and a comment on his work from his teacher. The drawings have scarcely improved at all over the years: today's are 'house', 'pesil', 'bus' and 'boy', with the teacher's comment 'He is doing nice in all fields.' John Ryle, who has lived in Africa, says that these boys invariably end up in government service as petty officials.

23 February. Local elections are in progress and I have two posters in the window on behalf of the Alliance candidate. Today is polling day and around eight I am woken by the doorbell. Thinking it's the postman, I go down in my dressing-gown, open the door, and just catch Miss Shepherd scuttling back into the van. She has left a note on the mat:

Mr. Bennett. Urgent.
It has dawned on me I have not been given the Alliance Leaflet. If it should be the second one you have put in your window as my property I demand that it is *removed immediately*. Please put it through my window so that I can dispose of it as I think best.

Later I see she has stuck a Conservative poster in the back window of the van.

14 March. Two nuns in Marks & Spencer's studying *meringues*.

21 March. Malcolm Mowbray, Michael Palin, Mark Shivas and I go to Broxbourne, where we have three pigs being groomed for their role in the film *A Private Function*, due to be shot in May. The couple doing the grooming operate under the name 'Intellectual Animals', but our pigs are anything but intellectual, squealing to be let out and then trotting round on delicate little feet like buxom landladies tripping naked to the bathroom in their high-heeled shoes. Their bums are much more striking than their faces, constantly on the move and shivering with delicate erotic tremors. They are supposed to have been house-trained and taught to come when called, but they aren't and don't. None of us mentions this.

31 March, Oxford. In the morning to the Ashmolean, where I look at and dislike Leonardo's *John the Baptist*, the body so smooth and rubbery it makes one doubt the attribution. The face, with its ambiguous smile, and the hand raised in what is almost an insulting gesture make it look more like a whore than a saint, the mysteriousness of the smile not a natural mystery – the enigma of beauty, say – but one of deliberate provocation. If he weren't John the Baptist he'd be carrying a fan or peeping from under a parasol.

In the afternoon to Libby Vaisey's confirmation in the cathedral. Though it's not a large building, the bishop dons a mike in order to speak, but then, moving to the pulpit, forgets that he has done so and there is a terrible amplified slurring as he fouls the cable. However, the young, bearded priest who attends him (who is probably as much his sound man as his chaplain) disentangles his lordship so that he can get into the pulpit. Once there he unceremonially dons another mike, though presumably if this becomes a feature of the ordinary service it will end up being given ceremonial trappings and perhaps even a place in the liturgy.

The actual laying-on of hands has been personalized since that evening thirty-five years ago when H. H. Vully de Candole, the Bishop of Knaresborough, confirmed me in St Michael's, Headingley. Nowadays each candidate carries a card with his or her name on it in block letters, some, I imagine, with an aid to pronunciation in brackets. And there are Kims and Beckys and Mandys and Trevs, all blessed and admitted to communion by this miked-up bishop and with a casualness about it that nobody seems to find surprising and which I think myself a snob for even noticing. Few of the boys wear suits, and one of the older candidates goes up in almost doctrinaire Fabian undress in an anorak.

In the new form of service God is throughout referred to as You; only one Thou left in the world, and the fools have abolished it. Of course they can't do away with the vocative, which is every bit as archaic, so we still say 'O God'. It's a good job God doesn't have a name, or we'd probably be calling him Dave.

4 April. Commentators on Kafka tend to *enlist* him. Heller enlists him, holds him up to the rest of the literature class as a good example. How he would have squirmed! Canetti does the same, annexes Kafka for his own stringency.

Once upon a time K. remarked that he didn't understand why I complained about growing old. Look at the compensations. I was, after all, old enough to have known steam trains in daily use. I made fun of this at the time but today I come across the same point in Auden:

> Let your last thinks be all thanks:
>
> . . . . . .
>
> In boyhood
> you were permitted to meet
> beautiful contraptions,
> soon to be banished from the earth,
> saddle-tank loks, beam engines
> and over-shot waterwheels.
> Yes, love, you have been lucky.

13 April. Susan B. was in a traffic jam in Liverpool caused by a large car blocking the road. It only needed to reverse a little to clear the way, so a taxi-driver leaned out and shouted, 'if you'd just reverse the length of your *dick* we could all get through.'

16 April, Yorkshire. Between Stamford and Grantham *en route* home I pass a convoy of seven police vans and two coachloads from the Suffolk Constabulary on their way to the coalfields.

A bank clerk counts me out some notes and scarcely pausing in his counting, puts aside the more dog-eared ones as he does so. With about as much thought, and for exactly the same reason (the practical use of this object is almost over), the SS officer on the platform at Auschwitz separated out the sick for immediate extermination.

17 April. Bettany, the Ministry of Defence employee, is given twenty-three years for treason, and likely to serve the whole of it – and in isolation, because he has a photographic memory and so cannot be released until the information he has in his head is obsolete. Just as radioactive waste has to be sealed in drums and sunk in the depths of the ocean, so he has to be confined to his cell.

No one suggests this is barbarous. We are getting back (or Mrs Thatcher would like to get back) to a view of treason that is Elizabethan in its rigour. The Lord Chief Justice delivers a moralistic lecture about Bettany's inadequate character, saying nothing of course of those who, well aware of his inadequate character and its usefulness, recruited him into government service.

9 May, Ilkley. James Fenton has been recruited by *The Times* and today reviews Peter Nichols's autobiography, *Feeling*

You're Behind. Feeling you're behind is a feeling I share, though Fenton professes to be mystified by it. Nichols has written many excellent plays, Fenton protests; he is well thought of, prosperous, but at fifty-seven confesses to feeling that nothing he has done is much good, is not even 'writing'. In Nichols Fenton finds this ridiculous, though not presumably in Kafka, whose thoughts in much the same vein have made him revered. But Nichols is not Kafka. Precisely. That is what he is on about.

16 May, Ilkley. My function on this film [*A Private Function*], as on many of my productions, is to sit around and keep people happy. Much of today I spend in Maggie Smith's dressing-room while the pig is put through its paces downstairs. She talks about Noël Coward and how when she was in *Private Lives* her performance had got very mannered and self-indulgent. Coward was in one night and came round and told her off, but in the best possible way, wagging his finger and saying, 'You've got very common. Very common indeed. You're almost as common as Gertie.' To be compared with Gertrude Lawrence, if only for overdoing it, was such a compliment Maggie instantly mended her ways.

Maggie always refers to Malcolm (Mowbray) the director as 'our fearless leader'.

2 June, Bradford. Denys Hawthorne, who plays an undeservedly small part in the film as a hotel manager, comes from Belfast, where he knew Maurice Miles, whom I as a boy in Leeds used to see conducting the Yorkshire Symphony Orchestra. Miles was a balletic conductor who very much fancied himself on the rostrum, fond of shooting his cuffs and fetching the brass in with a flourish. Denys was chatting with him one night after a concert when Miles broke off to have a word with the leading horn-player, a dour Yorkshireman.

'What went wrong tonight, George? Something, I wasn't quite sure.'

'Well, let's put it like this, Mr Miles, it's very hard to come in on the fourth rattle of the cufflinks.'

The hierarchy on the film unit can be discerned much easier when the sun shines. The riggers and electricians regardless of whether they are fat or thin straightaway take their shirts off; the camera crew and the upper levels of production never.

Jim Carter, who plays the police inspector in the film, is a tall, dark, rather saturnine character, less effusive than most actors, and while the others tell stories he quietly does sleight-of-hand tricks and close-up magic. I am slightly nervous of him, feeling that he sees through me. And he does. I was leaving early today when he remarked, 'You can't go. You're Continuity Giggles'.

30 June. Prince Charles at Betjeman's memorial service. Never read the Bible as if it means something. Or at any rate don't *try* and mean it. Nor prayers. The liturgy is best treated and read as if it's someone announcing the departure of trains.

Giles Cooper, who died nearly twenty years ago, is described in today's *Times* as 'award-winning playwright Giles Cooper'. I'd have thought that one of the few things to be said in favour of death was that it extinguished all that.

9 July. After four days feeling under sentence of death, having found a small lump on my foot, I go to the doctor. 'Not a nasty,' says young Dr Macgregor cheerfully – 'just a thrombosed vein.'

Reprieved, I bike back home thinking of the people who are not reprieved and do not bike back home, resolving to do better, work harder, behave. But it's such a precarious business, life's peaceful landscape suddenly transformed, what look like green fields suddenly a swamp of anxiety.

I had said this to the doctor.

'No. It's quite natural. Most people are the same, particularly when they get to . . .' and he looks down at my notes.

'My age?' I supply.

'Yes. No way of saying that in a complimentary way, is there?'

2 September. M. Neve calls to say that a colleague of his has told him that while Goffman was writing *Asylums* his wife was an inmate of the institution where he did most of his research and that she died in that same institution.

Projects I have been sent in the last week: a life of Lola Montes; 'Survive' (an ordinary family wrecked in the South Pacific); Pierre Loti ('exotic, erotic and neurotic'); 'The Life and Times of Emanuel Swedenborg'. And then people ask, 'Anything in the pipeline?'

9 September, Yorkshire. The little boy opposite, who has the beginnings of muscular dystrophy, is leaning over the bridge watching his sister fishing. A tall, bald-headed man comes over the bridge, having been walking on the fells. He stops, looks over the wall beside the little boy, then tentatively pats his bottom. The boy takes no notice and continues to watch the fishing while the man looks sideways at him and touches the boy's blue anorak. There is a gap between the anorak and the top of his jeans, and he looks at that. Someone is coming. He pats the boy's bum again and, as the boy shyly looks after him, waves goodbye. The boy gets up and leans over the other side of the bridge, and a minute or two later his sister comes up from the beck with a tiny trout she has caught – the first time I have ever seen anyone actually catch a fish in all the eighteen years I have lived here. Together they come up the path to show the fish to their mother, the girl going slowly so that her brother can hold on to her and balance himself, moving in his odd dislocated way like a long-distance walker. He is very happy.

14 September. The working miners, particularly those working in villages which are largely on strike, would make an interesting sociological study. This conflict has distanced them from their neighbours, but I would guess that process had begun long before the strike. Some are social oddities – bespectacled young men living with their mothers – others are over-emphatic, even obsessive; and one is filmed against his bookshelf, an oddity in itself. He and his fellows were plainly on a different track before the strike even started.

18 September. In the inane publicity hand-out for *A Private Function* I find myself described as 'This Northern lad' – maybe even (I can't bear to read it closely) 'This flaxen-haired Northern lad'. Is Pinter ever described as 'This East End boy'? Has he ever been? I put this down not to my supposedly youthful appearance but to the attitude comic writing engenders. Any third-rate journalist putting together copy feels entitled to be matey simply because one makes jokes.

25 September. Gore Vidal is being interviewed on *Start the Week* along with Richard (*Watership Down*) Adams. Adams is asked what he thought of Vidal's new novel about Lincoln. 'I thought it was meretricious.' 'Really?' says Gore. 'Well, meretricious and a happy new year.' That's the way to do it.

13 October. Mrs Thatcher is achieving mythic status. Scarcely does her step falter than the gods intervene with some terrible event like this bomb at Brighton from which she emerges with her reputation enhanced. There is the sad sight of the injured Tebbitt trying to prevent the British public getting a glimpse of his balls; firemen arranging his dusty pyjama trousers to foil the ever-present cameras, as ministers in varying states of undress wait on the front. If the IRA had really wanted to succeed they should have left a sniper behind and he would have had an easy task. Much comment on Mrs T.'s courage the next morning, when she arrives at the Conservative conference on the dot, but it's not difficult to appear calm and unruffled in such circumstances, as any actor could tell you. The majority of people perform well in a crisis and when the spotlight is on them; it's on the Sunday afternoons of this life, when nobody is looking, that the spirit falters.

28 October. Truffaut dies – an oddly personal loss. I sometimes haven't liked his films but could always understand their language, share his concerns, sense his humanity. Like Woody Allen's films, though in a different way, they were *within range*. I watch a *South Bank Show* repeat in tribute.

   'My films,' he says, 'are about timidity. My characters want to take part. They want to belong, and be like everybody else.'

I have supper with Russell. A few weeks ago on his programme, which is filmed at the Greenwood Theatre, he interviewed Billy Graham and had at one point to escort him to the lavatory. At the Greenwood these are all cubicles. The following week he went into the same cubicle Dr Graham had used, where he saw at eye-level and in very clear handwriting, just where the Doctor's eyes must have rested, the message 'The only pussy worth licking is young pussy.'

6 December. Agents are like doctors: they prefer dealing with one another. Clients, like patients, are secondary – there to be soothed and comforted and lied to while the real business is done in straight talking between professional men. This is after all what a professional man is: someone who can talk to other professional men without feeling, or feeling only a precise measure of concern that will pass for feeling. This is why voters distrust politicians, a prisoner his lawyer, and, at this particular moment, why I am unhappy with my agent. I am a graceful appendage to his list, I make enough money but nothing spectacular, and I make no trouble. Result: when I do have a success I end up being underpaid (as with *An Englishman Abroad* – £3,000) or the play comes off (*Forty Years On*). Meanwhile my contemporaries who have learned how to be hard-nosed and fifty, even to make telephone calls and speak their minds, get themselves disliked but make money. Whereas I prefer to be liked and thought a nice man. But I'm not. I'm just as bad as the rest of them, only I don't like to show it.

7 December. To a party at the Department of the History of Medicine at University College. I talk to Alan Tyson, who's like a figure out of the eighteenth century: a genial, snuff-taking, snuff-coloured, easy-going aristocrat – Fox, perhaps, or one of the Bourbons. He is a fellow of All Souls, and when Mrs Thatcher came to the college for a scientific symposium Tyson was deputed to take her round the Common Room. This is hung with portraits and photographs of dead fellows, including one of the economist G. D. H. Cole. Tyson planned to take Mrs Thatcher up to it saying, 'And this, Prime Minister, is a former fellow, G. D. H. Dole.' Whereupon, with luck, Mrs Thatcher would have had to say, 'Cole not Dole.' In the event he did take her round but lost his nerve.

15 December. Filming this week for *Man and Music* at Penshurst Place, the home of Lord de L'Isle and Dudley. Everything one imagines an English country house should be – a hotchpotch of different periods, medieval hall, eighteenth-century courtyards, Gothic front, solid green walls of yew and parterres of box. We film in a room adjoining the drawing-room, part of the private wing, with photographs of Lord D. at Cambridge, in India as a young man and ADC to Wavell, and now stood beside Macmillan as he unveils a plaque to Lord Gort. On a coffee-table are back numbers of *The Economist*, *Country Life* and the *TLS*, with drinks at the side.

'Ah,' one thinks – 'a glimpse here of the private life.' But is it? Is this really a private room or just a private room for public consumption? These drinks (and the bottle of vitamin pills beside them), have they been artfully arranged to suggest a private life? Is there somewhere else, another flat, which is more private? And so on. And so on. This impression is confirmed by the hall table, on which are all the Viscount's hats: his green Guards trilbies, his bowler, his lumberjack's hat that was plainly presented to him on some sort of ceremonial visit. Surely all this is meant to be *seen*.

31 December, New York. I leave The Odeon around eleven, the place already a frenzy of streamers and horn-blowing. Back at the apartment all is quiet, but as firecrackers go off in the street and the noises in her head are blotted out by the whistles and bangs, Rose sings in the new year with a love song:

> I love you
> And I find it to be true
> And the whole world smiles at you.

Except that five minutes into 1985 the fireworks stop, the noises come back, and once more she thinks there is a boy bouncing his ball on her ceiling. No matter that she has thought this for twenty-five years and if there were a boy he would now be a middle-aged man, for Rose he is still bouncing his ball.

'Stop it. Stop it,' she shouts. 'I can't have this. Stop it, you goddamn filthy bum.'

1985

6 January. The revival of *Forty Years On* closes after a five-month run. Houses are good and it has made a decent profit, but it now makes way for Charlton Heston in *The Caine Mutiny*. The classified ad reads, ' "The Queen's Theatre will not have seen the last of this play for many a long day." Final week.'

25 January. The chaplain of Chelmsford Prison has recently died of Aids, since when maiden ladies of irreproachable morals have been inquiring of their doctors whether they stand to have caught the virus from the communion chalice. I remember having the same problem when I was seventeen and a fervent Anglican, though then my fear was only of catching dear old VD. The regular Sunday Eucharist was no great worry, as those with whom one shared the cup were of blameless life. The problem arose at the great festivals of Christmas and Easter, when the church was thronged with the promiscuous multitude. All too easy to catch something you couldn't get rid of from such once-or-twice-a-year Christians, particularly at the watch-night service, when many of them were half-drunk. I was contemptuous of these opportunistic worshippers who didn't know the service backwards like I did, never knew when to stand and when to kneel, and, when they did kneel, didn't kneel on their knees but just leaned forward with their head in their hands as if they were on the lav. I didn't feel the clergy despised them, though – knowing without ever acknowledging it to myself that, like doctors with hypochondriacs, their faint contempt was reserved for regular attenders like me. Mindful of the parable of the lost sheep, they were happy to see the church packed out with the once-a-year crowd, and me and the pious hard core swamped.

12 February. I am buying daffodils in a shop in Camden High Street. An oldish woman asks for some violets, but they aren't quite fresh. 'Never mind,' she explains. 'I only want to throw them down a grave.'

My TV play *The Insurance Man* has come back typed and duplicated by the BBC. It's about Kafka. In various places I had included a note, 'Cut or shift elsewhere'. This is transcribed, 'Cut or shit elsewhere.'

13 March, Los Angeles. The Pig Film [*A Private Function*] is due to open the British Film Week at the LA Film Festival. A limousine which will fetch the director Malcolm Mowbray and myself from our hotel to the cinema doesn't arrive. Eventually we are rushed down Hollywood Boulevard in the hotel van, which smells strongly of fish. The opening is at Grauman's Chinese Theater. There are searchlights and what appear to be a troop of Horse Guards on duty. Close inspection reveals that none of the troops is under sixty. A few passers-by watch the arrival of the celebrities, of which there seem only to be two, Michael York and Michael Caine (who later slags off the film). The audience is not star-studded either and heavily sprinkled with those freaks, autograph-hunters and emotional cripples who haunt the stage doors of American theatres. A troop of 'Highlanders' file on to the stage but with trumpets, not bagpipes. They stand about awkwardly for a few minutes, blow a discordant fanfare, then another endless pause before they shuffle off again. The British Ambassador now stands up to introduce the evening, but his microphone doesn't work and the audience start barracking. The producer Mark Shivas, Malcolm Mowbray and myself are sitting in different parts of the cinema, and we are to be introduced to the audience. Mark is introduced first, the spotlight locates him, and there is scattered applause; then Malcolm similarly. When my turn comes I stand up, but since I am sitting further back than the others the spotlight doesn't locate me. 'What's this guy playing at?' says someone behind. 'Sit down, you jerk.' So I do. The film begins.

16 March, New York. K. wants to make a seafood salad, so we go into a fishmonger's on Bleecker. A young, fat guy sits by the door, an old, grey one at the back, and, doing all the work, a Puerto Rican.

K.: I want a dozen mussels.

FAT GUY: We don't sell them by the dozen.

K.: How do you sell them?

FAT GUY: Sell them by the pound.

K.: OK. A pound. (*Pause.*) How many are there in a pound?

FAT GUY (*triumphantly*): 'Bout a dozen.

12 May. Opposite the Libyan Embassy in St James's Square a woman is photographing the newly unveiled memorial to WPC Fletcher. Will she show it as one of the slides of her London visit, one wonders. The Beefeaters, the Horse Guards – 'Oh, and here's the memorial to that policewoman who was shot.'

During the miners' strike we heard nothing of the Lebanon. Now the strike is over the first item on the news is once again the Middle East. Did the Shiite Muslims liaise with Mr Scargill? Was the Christian militia apprised of the efforts of Mr Michael Eaton in that suit with the persistent check? Do murders cease in Beirut because the pickets are out in Bolsover? I suppose to

The World at One and the rest of the hyena crew of newsmen this is what's called 'a sense of priority'.

20 May. Money begins to pour in for the victims of the Bradford football ground fire. Cash the poultice: not for the injuries of the victims or the feelings of the bereaved but for the memory of the public. Give now in order to forget. Though there is no denying it helps. The squabbles about the amount of money to be distributed are already beginning; once greed has been reawakened we know that all is well.

Apropos the safety measures now required of soccer clubs, it is pointed out to Mrs Thatcher that many of them are too poor to afford such outlays. She then expresses surprise that clubs of this kind have survived at all. The same argument could of course be applied to churches. It's a good job Mrs T. isn't Archbishop of Canterbury, or we would just be left with the cathedrals and a few other 'viable places of worship'.

30 May. Writing a review of *Auden in Love* [see pages 504–16], I come across Stephen Spender's story of how Auden made Spender pay for the cigarettes he had bummed off him on Ischia. Spender points out that at other times Auden could be conspicuously generous, on one occasion giving Spender £50 towards a pony for his daughter. This isn't uncommon. Michael Codron will spend vast sums on entertaining the cast, but resents replacing an actress's cardigan. If someone stays overnight I count the cost of laundering the sheets but never think about the price of dinner. This kind of inconsistency is enshrined in the language: it's 'a mean streak'.

3 June. A bizarre accident in Camden Town. Shooting the lights at the foot of Chalk Farm Road, a fire-engine swerves to avoid a car and plunges straight through the front of a shop. It happens first thing in the morning and no one is hurt – the call turned out to be a hoax. All day the fire-engine has been stuck inside the shop, and so neatly, long ladder and all, with only the rear wheels visible, it's as if it has been deliberately garaged. Scaffolders toil till dark to shore up the building lest, when the engine is withdrawn, it will fetch the building down with it. Were the shop a newsagent's or a greengrocer's it would be bad enough, but the premises in question are those of an extremely select antique shop, which fastidiously confines itself to art deco. There are mirrors tinted a faint pink, lamps in frail fluted skirts. Suddenly in the pearly light of dawn in bursts this red, bullying monster.

I read biographies backwards, beginning with the death. If that takes my fancy I go through the rest. Childhood seldom interests me at all.

7 June, Yorkshire. Driving to Giggleswick on the back road, I see a barn-owl. It is perched, eponymously, on a barn and at the very tip of the gable, so that at first I take it, stone-coloured and still, to be a finial. I stop the car and gaze up at it, whereupon it doesn't take flight but edges delicately back out of view. I stop again at the top of High Rigg, the sun low behind Morecambe and the sky full of flying clouds. It's nine o'clock, but they are still haymaking above Eldroth, the newly mown fields fresh and green. Then down into Giggleswick to a silly supper and a game of Trivial Pursuit. To play Trivial Pursuit with a life like mine could be said to be a form of homeopathy.

30 June. To supper at the Camden Brasserie. It's a hot night and the shutters have been folded back so that the room opens directly on to Camden High Street. In France or New York this would excite no comment. In London, or in Camden Town at any rate, it draws the jeers of every passing drunk. Kids on their way to the Emerald Ballroom stop and stare. To dine like this in England is somehow to advertise one's status. Though the restaurant is neither expensive nor exclusive, fold back the shutters and suddenly we are in a 'Let them eat cake' situation.

17 July, Southport. A sign on the road to this still rather genteel seaside resort reads, 'You are now entering Southport.' Someone has added, 'Eat shit.' I've come here because I am weary of Liverpool, where we are filming. Every Liverpudlian seems a comedian, fitted out with smart answers, ready with the chat and anxious to do his little verbal dance. They are more like Cockneys than Lancashire people, and it gets me down.

25 July, Yorkshire. T. R. ('Tosco') Fyvel, friend of Orwell, has died. The *Telegraph* obituary is headed 'T. R. (Tesco) Fyvel'.

Supper at Warwick and Susan's. We have fish and chips, which W. and I fetch from the shop in Settle market-place. Some local boys come in and there is a bit of chat between them and the fish-fryer about whether the kestrel under the counter is for sale. W. takes no notice of this, to me, slightly surprising conversation, and when the youths have gone I edge round to see if I can get a glimpse of this bird, wondering what a cage is doing under the counter and if such conditions amount to cruelty. I see nothing, and only when I mention it to W. does he explain Kestrel is now a lager. I imagine the future is going to contain an increasing number of incidents like this, culminating with a man in a white coat saying to one kindly, 'And now can you tell me the name of the Prime Minister?'

30 November. My dustbin has been on its last legs for some time, and after the binmen have called this morning I find no trace of it. Never having heard of tautology, the binmen have put the dustbin in the dustbin.

1986

6 January. Isherwood dies. *The Times* obituary, with a discretion amounting to insult, makes no mention of his homosexuality. The *Telegraph* has no scruples on this score though the obituary, written by a critic (David Holloway) mentions *I Am A Camera* as notable only for occasioning a critic's joke. Which it misquotes (Holloway: Me no lika; Tynan: No Leica). In both obituaries the note is the familiar one of 'Could have done better'.

I met Isherwood in 1962. He had seen *Beyond the Fringe* and I went out to supper with him and Don Bachardy at Chez Solange in Cranbourne Street. He wanted to tell me about the sermons and ceremonies he and Auden used to perform in a disused quarry near their school at Hindhead. I was incurious and so shy I scarcely remember speaking. It was the first time I had come across a couple who made no bones about their homosexuality. The difference in their ages stunned me.

30 January. A meeting at the Royal Court about *Kafka's Dick*, now put off until September. Their next play is an adaptation by Howard Barker of *Women Beware Women*, and the production after that *The Normal Heart*, an American play about Aids. This is referred to at the theatre as 'Men Beware Men'.

14 February, New York. Lunch with S. at the Harvard Club. Grander (or certainly loftier) than any London club at lunchtime, it is as busy as a railroad station. Afterwards we sit in the library. Smack opposite the vast window of this superb room, in which sleep several distinguished senators, is a cheap clothing store and a neon sign winking 'Crazy Eddy's'.

I go into a pharmacy and ask for some Interdens. The girl behind the counter does not understand but the handyman who is stocking the shelves guesses I mean Stim–U–Dent and says they have a new brand just in. 'I didn't put them on the shelves yet. Guess I didn't want to *inundate* the public.'

4 March. Read *Winnie the Pooh* to an audience of children at the Tricycle Theatre, Kilburn. Many have never been in a theatre before. I battle against the crying of babies and the shouts of toddlers and end up screaming and shouting myself hoarse. It is *Winnie the Pooh* as read by Dr Goebbels.

28 March. (*Easter Sunday*), *Yorkshire*. To church at eleven for the Eucharist, where I hit Rite B. This is a new one on me. It mysteriously adheres to some of the old forms then suddenly we're onto a bit of dual carriageway that by-passes lots of the old prose and fetches us up at the altar rail by a new route entirely. I think back to Easter at St Michael's in Leeds, the great lilies on the altar, the copes and the candles and the holy ladies plummeting to their knees at any mention of the Virgin's name. Today nice Mr Dalby, the bearded plain-spoken vicar of Austwick, guides us through the ruins of the Book of Common Prayer ('turn to page 189 and then to foot of page 192') no more the great rhythmic prayers, the majestic rise and fall of the service to the hushed 'Then in the same night he was betrayed.'

'Many there?' Dad would always ask after church. About thirty today, well wrapped-up farmers' wives, cheap fur coats and bobble hats and all the little niceties of devotion I had forgotten, like the couple at the front, more fastidious worshippers than the rest, who wait until the queue has subsided before going up 'to receive'.

Tell Mary-Kay about the service, who says that she knows of a church in France where the rite is sung as in the patristic church and people flock. It's like Real Ale. And if the C of E were differently organized that would be one way to revivify it, advertise the type of worship and the quality of the service provided. Real God.

29 March, Yorkshire. It is Bank Holiday, and the cave rescue gets called out to find some students who have gone pot-holing and not come up. A young caver from our village, David Anderson, is one of the rescue team. The water is rising, and as he is going down he slips into a narrow gulley. Though he is roped up, the force of the torrent is too much for his companions: as they struggle to pull him out, his light still shining through the water, he drowns. The students are later found unharmed. What the feelings of the rescuers must be when, having lost one of their colleagues, they come upon the students is hard to imagine. Some harsh words spoken, or no words spoken at all more likely, pot-holers being a pretty laconic breed. The boy himself was very shy, blushing if his leg was pulled and cautious to a fault. Putting a TV aerial up on Graham Mort's cottage roof, he got into a complete safety harness. He is the first cave rescuer ever to have died. Four hundred cavers turn up for his funeral and follow the coffin down the village to the graveyard. It is like a scene from Northern Ireland. The students who were rescued have gone down again today.

8 April. A helicopter crashes near Banbury. The pilot, four children and a woman are killed. An eager reporter on *P.M.* interviews an eyewitness, who describes what happened. 'But what did it look like?' persists the reporter. What he means is, 'What did it look like seeing six people burn to death?'

19 April, Bruges. After seeing Uncle Clarence's grave at Ypres* we drive to Bruges for the weekend. Drenching rain. Sea Scouts are putting up two wooden stakes near the Fish Market as once upon a time, in this city of cruelties, other more sinister stakes were often erected. Later we pass by; it is still raining and two figures in oilskins have been lashed to the stakes and a Sea Scout waits with a bucket of sponges for anyone wanting to pay for a shot.

The Groeninge is a good small museum with the rooms set on a circular plan so that the final room is next door to the first. They cover the whole span of Flemish painting. In the first room hang the Van Eycks and Van der Weydens. In the last room the chief exhibit is a large canvas which has been partially cut away to incorporate a bird-cage. The bird-cage contains a live bird, and the whole is reflected in a mirror opposite.

1 May. When Denholm Elliott is sent a script he opens it in the middle and reads a few pages. If he likes it, finds the characters interesting, he goes back to the beginning and reads it through. 'You soon enough decide whether these are the kind of people you want to spend any time with. Reading a play, going into a pub – same thing, old boy.'

11 May, Yorkshire. A day or two after the accident at Chernobyl Barry Brewster, our local doctor, rang the Department of Health and various other authorities wanting information about the likelihood of contamination. Getting none, and indeed no help whatsoever, he called all the local farmers and told them to keep

* See page 29.

their cows indoors and alerted all the schools to stop them drinking the milk. On such people will survival depend.

14 May. When stuck in hospital (I am thinking of Sam) it is irritating to find that, though on the one hand you are an object of pity and concern, on the other one is a social catalyst. Friends meet around the bed, discuss where they can 'go on' after the hospital, supper possibly, then a movie, all pleasures which one's illness has made possible but from which the illness excludes you. The last glimpse of the world as one goes through the gates will be of friends making plans what to do afterwards.

25 May, Gloucestershire. Walking in the bleak, deodorized fields round Blockley, we pass a large modern barn. Barns used commonly to be compared with cathedrals, and this, too, is not unlike a cathedral – but one of the terrible present-day ones at Bristol or Liverpool. The metaphor has kept pace. Of course, to say a barn is like a cathedral is different from saying a cathedral is like a barn.

26 May, Weston-super-Mare. To Weston. Mam and I sit in the sun lounge and she holds my hand, hers now so thin and fine it is like an anatomical illustration, every vein visible. She has had her hair done, her face is plump and happy, and she talks gibberish.

Other residents pass through. 'I hate it here,' says one. 'I hate it here, only my mother died.' She is about sixty.

'Can you remember your mother?' I ask Mam. 'No. I don't think she had done then.' Pause. 'I am glad to see you. You are a love.' She kisses my hand. 'You're beautiful.'

'You're beautiful too. Do you know how old you are?'

'Was it?'

While we sit there a younger woman helps lay the tables. She has straight white hair, a red rustic face, long socks pulled up almost to her knees, and trainers. 'It's 26 May,' she says, not unhappily, 'so I've been here one year, one month, and six days'.

'I haven't seen you,' says a much older woman, 'but then I'm upstairs most of the time. Just thought I'd come down for a trot round. I'm from Cirencester. Most people I know are from Westbury-on-Severn. Too far for them to come. I've only been here five weeks. My son's off to Portugal tomorrow.'

She is quite sensible, and when Mam responds in one of her garbled sentences I am apologetic, but the woman takes no notice. Occasionally Mam takes hold of her hand and kisses it.

It is time for lunch, so Mam is taken upstairs, though not on the chair lift. A few years ago, when she was still talking sensibly and getting about, I was with her as one of the other ladies sat on the chair and slowly ascended. Mam was not impressed. 'I've been on that thing,' she said. 'It's nowt.' It might have been the Big Dipper.

I go and sit with her in the bedroom and help her with her lunch. She shares the room with two other old ladies, one the small Lancashire woman who always used to hang about the hall and keep trying the door. Now she is very frail, and with her little square face and beaked nose she looks like a finch. The third woman has rather a distinguished face and seems to be asleep, then suddenly without opening her eyes she shouts, 'Help! Help! Help!' Neither of the other two takes any notice. The handyman puts his head round the door, sees there is a responsible person present, grins, and goes away. 'Who was that?' Mam says, and laughs.

When I go she blows me a kiss.

27 May. Roger Lloyd Pack is to play Kafka in *Kafka's Dick*. We also see Mark Rylance, an actor whom I don't know and who is also very good. Totally self-absorbed, to the point of eccentricity, he's the first actor we've read who makes sense of Kafka's desire to be somebody and nobody at the same time. Roger L.–P. will be funnier and is physically more striking (and looks like Kafka), but Rylance has a lovely, appealing face and marvellous directness. He has played Peter Pan and many roles at the RSC (all, of course, unseen by me) and has had his own company presenting potted Shakespeare. Born in Kent, he was brought up in Milwaukee but talks like a northerner who has lost his accent.

1 June. Mary-Kay has been dining at All Souls and comes back with a nice Alan Tyson story. One of the Fellows is a vegetarian and was telling Tyson how he had to arrange himself special food at a dinner. He was to start off with Jerusalem artichoke soup which would be followed by a salad of Jerusalem artichokes. 'Surely,' said Tyson, 'Once in Royal David's City is enough.'

3 June. The harrying of the hippies continues. Turfed off a farm, they now camp on a disused airfield belonging to the Forestry Commission. The FC protest, saying the convoy will be injurious to wildlife, as if – with all those millions of acres of factory firs they've planted – they have ever given a toss about wildlife. The Chief Constable of Hampshire issues a statement: 'If only they would return to a conventional way of living there would be no problem.' It is the cry of the police the world over. I'm surprised there's no such thing as an international police conference (perhaps there is). I can see the Hampshire Police and the KGB getting on like a house on fire. Later, on *The World at One*, the same Chief Constable, a drab accountant-like figure, describes the hippies as 'rebels'. Nobody queries his use of the word. Meanwhile Mrs T. sets up a special committee of the Cabinet to deal with the problem and the threat to property. No Cabinet committee to deal with the problem on the other flank, the daily attacks on Asians and the threat to property there. No monitoring of that by the police.

The Guards beat the retreat to the signature tune from *East Enders*.

When Larkin says his childhood was a forgotten boredom, what he means is that he has nothing to write home about.

14 July. First day of shooting a film based on the life of Joe Orton. We begin with the childhood scenes, Thornton Heath standing in for Leicester. The film is announced in *Variety*. The title, *Prick Up Your Ears*, presents a problem, as *Variety*'s cryptic style demands the film be known as *Prick*. But no: the headline reads, '*Ears* lenses Monday'.

Those best at saying what they mean aren't always best at meaning what they say.

I am reading Ryszard Kapuscinski's *The Emperor*, the story of the last days of Haile Selassie. The accounts by the lowliest of the palace officials are the most interesting. Something of Oliver Sacks in the other 'verbatim' accounts. It's not always easy to believe these articulate and over-literary witnesses, or to trust that words are not being put into their mouths. The most curious feature of the account are the names: Tenene Work, Asfa Wossen, Teferra Gebrewold. Are they Germanic or Scandinavian? Makonen, Zera Yakob: who would guess these were Africans?

A boy and a girl in Marks & Spencer's, she punk, he gay. They take the lid off a prawn cocktail, shove their noses in it, sniff, then put it back on the shelf. Marks & Spencer's now sell freshly-squeezed ruby orange juice. Delicious, it is of course blood-orange juice, only the word 'blood' is thought to be unmarketable. It will doubtless not be long before the Church of England takes note of this and amends the already much-amended communion service, so that the priest, proffering the chalice, will say, not 'This is my blood which is shed for thee,' but, more palatably, 'This is my ruby liquid.' And while we're at it, why not 'This is the fibre-enriched bread of the New Testament'?

20 July. What is written all over Gary Oldman's muddy, slightly spotty face of Joe Orton at fifteen is a forgotten disease. It is that look of guilt and cunning you used to see thirty years ago on the faces of thirteen- and fourteen-year-old schoolboys, wankers doom. Look at old school photographs and it's there in the faces of half my form because most of us were using every spare moment to wank ourselves silly and thinking nobody else knew. Nowadays everybody knows. Wanking is authorized, joked about on television. Not every boy is a wanker but everybody wanks and there is no doom.

27 July, Yorkshire. The annual street market in the village and I take out piles of stuff for the junk stall. At home this clearing-out process was always known as 'wuthering' and Dad used to love it. 'What's happened to such and such?' I would, ask Mam. 'Ask your Dad. He's probably wuthered it.'

And it does become a fever as I search each room for any object worthy of being wuthered. It's like cutting a play, the zeal and pleasure of finding a cut far exceeding the joy of writing the stuff in the first place.

Among the junk I put out are piles of Mam's old *Ideal Home* magazines and as I am about to hand them over a photograph falls out. It's a portrait of the four of us in *Beyond the Fringe*, taken and signed by Cecil Beaton.

31 July. To St Mary's College, Strawberry Hill, to speak to a summer school. My vanity is nicely exposed at the outset when I am introduced by the principal. A few nights ago, he tells the audience, he was playing a parlour game with some friends in which one pretended to be a famous person. He was a playwright beginning with B and he was asked whether he was one of the most profound, influential (and here a modest-seeming smile begins to play shyly across my face) ascetic and un-self-regarding writers of our time. By now my smile is sickening in its humility.

'And I said, "No",' says the principal, ' "I am not Samuel Beckett." '

5 August. Neville Smith plays the police inspector in the Orton film. He was an undergraduate at Hull and is un-impressed by the current canonization of Larkin. He came across him twice. Once, waiting at a bus-stop in torrential rain, Neville edged closer and closer to Larkin, who had an umbrella. Finally the poet spoke: 'Don't think you're going to share my umbrella, because you're not.' Another time Larkin in his role as librarian collared Neville as he was slipping in with an overdue book: 'Don't you know there's a queue for this book?' Neville swears the last time it had been taken out was in 1951.

1 September. A group of drunks in the back doorway of the *Odeon* on Inverness Street. Another drunk, somewhat younger, sways across the street to join them. One of the drunks staggers to his feet. 'Go away. We don't want you jumping on our bandwagon.'

Play snooker with Sam. It is just before his bedtime and when I am not looking he keeps moving the white to a worse position so that the game can go on longer. One of the lines I have cut from *Kafka's Dick* is about the games of cards he used to play with his parents. Eventually his father refuses to play with him because his son used to cheat. 'But only', says Kafka, 'in order to lose.'

24 September, Yorkshire. Kafka's Dick opens at the Royal Court, and Richard Eyre rings at noon with the gist of the notices. They are mixed, with only the *Standard* and the *Financial Times* wholehearted in its favour. Wardle in *The Times* strikes his usual 'Bennett has bitten off more than he can chew' note, just as he did years ago with *Forty Years On*. What he means is that I have bitten off more than he can chew. Billington trots out his school essay on Kafka, and few of them bother to say that it is a funny evening. I walk in the fields above Austwick looking for mushrooms. Find none. Well, one must take it like a man. Which means that one must take it like a woman – i.e. without complaint.

26 September, Ljubljana. Here playing a small part in a BBC drama series, *Fortunes of War*, an adaptation of Olivia Manning's *Balkan Trilogy*, Yugoslavia standing in for Romania, Ljubljana for Belgrade. The people here are Slovenians, tall, fine-looking and Roman in their grace and self-assurance. A few (Croats?) are small and fierce and heavily-moustached, and look as if they are taking a day off from herding the goats. 'Ah, partisans!' I find myself thinking. There is a good deal of smoking, and they kiss as if it had just come off the ration. At the next table in our restaurant tonight, two couples in their late twenties. One couple cock their cigarettes, go into a clinch, and kiss long and lingeringly. The meal is on the table, but their companions wait, watching without impatience or embarrassment as the kiss goes on, the cigarettes burn down, and the food gets cold.

Through a gateway I see student actors in a garden rehearsing a play. I can't hear the dialogue and would be no wiser if I could, but it only takes a minute to see that it is *Hamlet*. A tall young man stands centre-stage watched by an older couple. Two actors come on, have a word with the older couple, then saunter innocently over to the lone figure and chat before scurrying back to report. Hamlet is in jeans and bomber jacket. He looks tiresome, but I can't tell whether this is because he is a tiresome actor, or because he is playing Hamlet tiresome, or whether, divested of the poetry, tiresome is what Hamlet is.

1 October, Grado. Two days off from filming and I drive into Italy. Still depressed about *Kafka's Dick*, I come by chance on the village of Aquileia. Knowing nothing about the place, I go into the church (a cathedral, as it turns out) and find a huge mosaic floor laid down in the fourth century. To read Kafka is to become aware of coincidence. This is to put it at its mildest. His work prefigures the future, often in ways that are both specific and dreadful. Sometimes, though, these premonitions are less haunted. In my play Kafka is metamorphosed from a tortoise and is also sensitive about the size of his cock. So to find here, by the west door, a mosaic of a cock fighting a tortoise feels not quite an accident. In Aquileia, the guidebook says, they represent a battle between the forces of light and darkness. I buy a postcard of the mosaic, and the postcard-seller tells me there is a better example in the crypt. This takes some finding: the tortoise isn't in the crypt so much as in a crypt beyond the crypt, and even there hidden behind the furthest pillar, just where Kafka would have chosen to be. It seems if not quite a nod then at least a wink, and I drive on in better spirits.

13 November. The notice has gone up for *Kafka's Dick*, so Richard Eyre and I take the cast out to supper. Alison S. and Vivian P. particularly ask not to be put next to Charles L. (who is eighty-six next week), because he tries to touch them up. Coming offstage at one point in the show he always likes to get in a salacious remark to A. which sends her on stage flurried and blushing. He's very good, though, on anti-memoirs. 'You worked with Edith Evans, Charles. What was she like?' 'She was a miserable cow.' More theatrical memories are of this nature than is ever let on.

20 December. Run into stately, plump Don Warrington moving slowly up the Crescent. Says he has to go to Newcastle for Christmas. I say I like Newcastle. 'Why? It's all vomit and love-bites.'

24 December, Yorkshire. I find a little artificial Christmas tree in a box in the junk room and put it up. It's not the tree we had as children, but some of the ornaments are the same, including the fairy that went on top, back to back with Santa Claus. Santa has long gone, and the fairy is pretty battered, a slit in her celluloid head for a tiny cardboard tiara, her wings bits of kitchen foil Mam put on ten years ago, along with a skirt made of lampshade fringe. Her painted hair-do is a twenties shingle, and I suppose she must be about as old as I am. Perhaps through being suspended by the neck from the top of the tree every Christmas for fifty years, the look in her painted eyes is of sheer terror.

1987

2 January. Reg, who kept the junk stall in the market, has died, and today is his funeral. Where his stall stood outside The Good

Mixer there is a trestle-table covered with a blue sheet, and a notice on a wreath of chrysanthemums announces that Reg Stone passed peacefully away on Boxing Day and that his cortège will be passing through the market at three o'clock. Until I read the card I'd never known his last name.

Reg's stall was a feature of the market long before I moved here in 1961. Then he had two prices, sixpence and a shilling. In time this went up to a shilling and five shillings, and latterly it had reached 50p and £1. To some extent he shaped his price to the customer, though not in a Robin Hood sort of way, the poorer customers often getting charged more, and any attempt to bargain having the same effect. I have two American clocks, both in working order, that were five shillings apiece, and an early Mason's Ironstone soup dish that cost sixpence and hangs on the wall of the kitchen. Local houses used to be full of treasures from Reg: model steam engines, maple mirrors, Asian Pheasant plates, rummers – all picked up for a song. Once I saw a can of film (empty) with 'Moholy-Nagy' round the rim, and only this last year Harriet G. got some Ravilious plates for 50p. Money didn't seem to interest Reg. Scarcely glancing at what one had found, he'd take the fag out of his mouth, say 'A pound,' then take a sip from his glass of mild on the pub window-sill and turn away, not bothered if one bought it or not.

I go down at three. The table is now piled high with flowers, mostly the dog-eared variety on offer at the cheap stall in the market, petals already scattering on the wind. One or two of the long-established residents stand about, old NW1 very much in evidence. Thinking the cortège will arrive from the Catholic church, we are looking along Arlington Road when it comes stealing through the market itself. It is led by a priest in a cape and an undertaker bearing a heavy rolled umbrella that he holds in front of him like a staff of office or a ceremonial cross. The procession is so silent and unexpected that it scarcely disturbs people doing their normal shopping, the queue at Terry Mercer's fruit stall gently nudged aside by the creeping limousines. The priest stops at the top of the street, turns, and stands looking down the market as if the street were a nave and this his altar. The flowers are now distributed among the various cars, more petals falling. In one of the limousines a glamorous blonde is weeping, and in other cars there are children. Just as I never thought of Reg as having a name, so a family (and a family as respectable as this) comes as a surprise. And for a man I never saw smile or scowl, laugh or lose his temper, grief, too, seems out of place.

8 January, Egypt. To Cairo to film another scene in *Fortunes of War*. The Ramses Hilton is on the site of the demolished Anglican cathedral, the view from the sixteenth floor taking in the Nile, the back of the Cairo Museum, three flyovers and, dim shapes beyond the tower blocks, the Pyramids. On stand-by for filming, we take a trip down the Nile by three-decker river boat, on which we have lunch. The boat never reaches even the outskirts of Cairo, and, since many of the buildings on both banks are in the process of demolition or construction, it's like a boat trip down the Harrow Road. The streets are filthy, the pavements torn up, no architecture of any distinction, and all of it in the same dusty, dun-coloured stone. And yet it is a delightful place, wholly redeemed by the people, who are open and friendly, the men tall and handsome, the women of a ripe biblical beauty, heavy-eyebrowed, voluptuous and bold, none of them veiled and on seeming equality with the men. As for beggars, there are now more in London than in Cairo.

The most striking feature of the boat trip is an entirely rural island of lush green fields and primitive cultivation with a mud-brick farmhouse at the edge of the water where boatmen are mending nets, women washing clothes, and the farmer trots round the fields on a mule, all this virtually in the middle of the city. It looks almost as if it has been laid on for passing tourists, and in the West that's just what it would be: a folk park or an urban farm.

9 January, Cairo. When they are not called for filming, the cast spend much of the day lounging round the hotel swimming-pool. P. is wearing a bikini, and whispers to her neighbour that before putting it on she has had to shave a little. She reckons without the blind and therefore sharp-eared Esmond Knight (eighty-two), who is on the other side of the pool, and he calls across, 'Could I inquire, my dear, what you did with the clippings?'

I spend the day with Magdy, a student who turns out to be a Muslim fundamentalist. He has left his temporary job at the Cairo Museum because the scantily clad foreign ladies put wicked thoughts into his head: 'They come in with their closes very high up on their legs and no closes on their shoulders, and I find something in me that desire them.' He also thinks that chopping people's hands off for theft is not entirely a bad thing. We take the river bus to Old Cairo. Magdy has never been on the river and insists on sitting next to a lifebelt in case we capsize. We see some of the Coptic churches, and I try to explain to Magdy about Jesus. 'We believe he was the Son of God.' 'God have a son? That is stupid. Does he have an aunt, an uncle? Who is his mother?' I point to a picture of the Virgin. 'Who her husband?' 'She was a virgin.' 'Of course. All women virgin till married. I marry virgin' (though presumably not one with closes that come high up on her legs).

Down the Nile float gobs of vegetation which I take to be clumps of rushes or some kind of water lily, but so rich and fertile-looking that one knows as soon as they hit land they will take root and grow. Swallows swoop low over the water and at dusk cluster in the dusty eucalyptus trees. Some may have summered in Craven.

10 January, Cairo. One of the company, Diana H., spent her honeymoon in Cairo. The marriage did not last long, and when she learned she was to be filming in Cairo she wondered where the unit would be staying. It was the Ramses Hilton, where she had spent her honeymoon. When the desk handed her her key it was the same room.

Every day in the late afternoon the hotel fills with tourists, and after breakfast empties again as they depart for Luxor and the boat up the Nile. Many are English. 'Palm trees are nothing to us,' one said today – 'we're from Torquay.'

12 January, Cairo. To Gizeh, where, in hot sunshine, we ride camels and horses around the Pyramids. Not expecting much, I am not put off by the litter and trash, and even the dead dog my camel steps round does not seem out of place. The Sphinx, like a personality seen on TV then met in the flesh, is smaller than one had imagined, and it's quite hard to tell how tall the Pyramids themselves are. In the distance stand the towers and skyscrapers of Cairo, in the misty morning sunshine a sight every bit as remarkable as the Pyramids. Odd that one marvels at stone piled up in one shape but not in another, both of much the same height. Were our world largely wiped out, would tourists flock to Croydon as they do to Cairo?

Beyond the Sphinx, on the edge of the desert, is a Coptic cemetery, and, as we ride past, a funeral arrives. Painted green and looking like an ammunition locker, the coffin is handed out from an old Commer van to be passed over the heads of the crowd into the graveyard, the shrieks with which the women urge it on towards the grave not much different from the shouts the men use to encourage the camels. Mine farts continuously, and on one occasion manages to spit down my neck.

A discussion of sex life uncovers the fact that in this unit of fifty and more people, most of them quite young, no one is known to be having an affair.

14 January, Luxor. Here by overnight train, waking as the sun comes up and farmers on donkeys scurry along paths beside barriers of tall sugar cane and, somewhere over the flat fields, the Nile. By cab from the ferry to the Valley of the Kings. What I had been expecting, I realize afterwards, was a landscape out of *King Solomon's Mines*, but it proves to be not much more than a large quarry, whatever shape and grandeur it may have had now obscured by the huge heaps of excavated spoil, among which are the shafts going down into the tombs. I traipse dutifully round three or four, but am soon weary. Struck by the freshness of the colours, the dark-blue ceilings thick with stars and the hair of the Pharaohs chiselled in tiny regular diamonds as sharp and fresh today as when they were done three thousand years ago. Still, a long way to come for that. Handicapped too by ignorance. Luxor is Thebes, but is it Oedipus's Thebes or Tiresias's 'Thebes below the wall'? I don't know, the guidebook doesn't say, and if it did I don't suppose it would insert the place into my memory. It's not nine o'clock and yet the place is already crowded with parties picking their way over the hard flints under a cloudless sky. What are these jaded tourists looking for? Some flicker of wonder, some sensation or reminder of a sensation they once had, perhaps as children when they first gazed on the world? Is tourism like pornography – blue films and the holiday slides both a search for lost sensation? I can see some (serious) point in guided tours with a very particular interest – the sex life of the ancient Egyptians, say, or hairdressing under the Pharaohs. One would pick up more because incidentally. It's Forster's 'Only what is seen sideways sinks deep.'

Our cab takes us on, and we stop at the edge of a field to look at the Colossi of Memnon, but so sated am I with antiquities (after two hours only) I do not even get out to look. In any case these statues have been so quarried and defaced their heads are just jumbles of masonry, a reality disguised by the artful photography of the guidebooks, the world never as pretty as it is photographed.

15 January, Luxor. Tea on the terrace of the Winter Palace Hotel, a brown stucco building no different from the Winter Gardens of many an English seaside town because built around the same time and nowadays as run-down and deserted as they are. We watch the sun set over the Nile, a scene captured by dozens of tourists with film cameras, who wait as if for the passage of royalty.

19 January, Cairo. Early at Cairo Airport, we wander round the departure lounge, where Christopher S. discovers a museum. It's just one room, looking out on to the tarmac, and has a score or so showcases of various periods – Ancient Egypt, the Copts, the Mamelukes – with only a few exhibits in each: a wooden tablet of a saint in glory, vases for viscera with smiling dogs' heads, a fragment of Greek alabaster labelled 'Man carrying something on his shoulder'. There's more satisfaction in these few (I'm sure) inferior artefacts than in a morning spent traipsing round the tombs. It's partly because we have time to kill and here is just one room and nothing else – no other objects queuing up for attention, no visions of rooms unvisited, treasures overlooked. (Madame de Sévigné on sightseeing: 'What I see tires me and what I don't see worries me.') It's also that the museum itself is something discovered, a found object, an oddity.

It saves its best surprise until last: a painted limestone statue, *c*. 3000 BC, of two monumental figures: Iuh and his wife Mary. They sit enthroned in their ceremonial wigs, the woman's real hair peeping out from underneath, their expressions, insofar as they have expressions, solemn and unsmiling. Except that Iuh has his left arm round his wife's shoulder, which is, according to the label, 'a mark of affection'. It is another version of what inspired Larkin's poem 'An Arundel Tomb', where the effigies lie hand in hand. That turned out to be a bit of sentimental nineteenth-century restoration, whereas this husband from the Old Kingdom has had his arm round his wife for four thousand years. I think. I hope. As maybe Larkin hoped.

Our flight is announced, and when I come out of the museum the domestic departure lounge has emptied, travellers and airport workers gathered at the far end of the room kneeling in prayer.

18 February. Children are less coy than the Department of Health. In the playground at Primrose Hill, Aids is referred to as 'the bum disease'.

1 March. The tabloids full of some 'Russell Harty is gay' shock horror. The first inkling of it came last week in Giggleswick when Mrs Walton, Susan Brookes's mother, went upstairs to get ready for her stint at the Oxfam shop in Settle. Her house overlooks the recreation ground, where she saw four men seemingly playing football, though rather on the old side to be doing it. The recreation ground borders on Russell's garden, and the men were kicking the ball once or twice then deliberately booting it over the wall. They would then take it in turns to climb over and retrieve it, meanwhile spying on the house. Mrs Walton watched this curious game for a while and couldn't make it out until she saw the spread in the papers this morning.

The youth in question describes Russell's flat as 'scruffy . . . it had plates on the shelves and the paint was a dirty orange'. So much for R's Staffordshire figures, carefully chosen decor and expensively distressed paintwork.

14 March, Oxford. To Oxford to cast my vote for Roy Jenkins as Chancellor. Only 9.30, but the line of voters is already round the Sheldonian and the atmosphere that of a cocktail party. The average voter is about my age, tall and armed with a beaming wife, both determined to make a day of it. Never was there such a feast of complacency, so many silly men showing off to their womenfolk in their robes. Some have got themselves up not simply in gowns but in hoods as well, remaining gowned long after they have voted and probably only to be persuaded out of them when they get into their pyjamas. And oh what a convivial queue, merry with the prospect of drinks in Oriel and lunch in Wadham, jokes shouted to friends, contemporaries spotted – isn't this *fun*! It's like the theatre at Chichester, the same tall families, the same assurance of happiness and their place in the world. That is Theatre, this is University, both their birthright. Inside the Divinity Schools there is a scramble to fill in the voting-form, with a pig-faced university official bullying any dawdlers. We line up finally before the Vice-Chancellor, Patrick Neill, who looks about as lively as the mercury in a thermometer. He tips his hat, and twenty minutes later I'm heading back down the M40.

9 April. Seeing the flag blowing over the Polish Embassy in Portland Place reminds me how as a child I found flags of other nations a disappointment. The Stars and Stripes was OK, but, that apart, in the Union Jack we did seem to have bagged all the best colours. The flags of other nations were the genteel shades of ice-cream, and as often as not with a fiddling little motif to distinguish them from other flags to which they were all too similar. Ours was best.

16 April. A letter from the director of the Thorndike Theatre at Leatherhead, where they are producing *Forty Years On*. The title of the play within the play is 'Speak for England, Arthur' and the schoolboy cast hold up letter-boards to spell it out for the audience. Part of the stage directions is that, before getting it right, one or two of the boys should get their letters jumbled. One of the eighteen local schoolboys doing it at the Thorndike has discovered that if jumbled still further they can come up with 'O Grandfather, Real Spunk'. This is not incorporated into the production.

13 May. Colin Haycraft and I are chatting on the pavement when a man comes past wheeling a basket of shopping. 'Out of the way, you so-called intellectuals,' he snarls, 'blocking the fucking way.' It's curious that it's the intellectual that annoys, though it must never be admitted to be the genuine article but always 'pseudo' or 'so-called'. It is, of course, only in England that 'intellectual' is an insult anyway.

28 May. Mary Hope's sister-in-law has cancer and is in intensive care at the Royal Free. Because of staff shortages her ward has to close down at weekends, and on Friday she was wheeled across the hospital to a ward where, with men on one side, women on the other, there was scarcely room to move between the beds and several patients were dying. Here she stayed all weekend. If the Labour Party could fight the election on the state of the Health Service alone, it would win hands down.

29 May. A letter from David [Ned] Vaisey at Oxford saying that

John Carey thinks my 'Kafka at Las Vegas' too 'ruminative and ambling' to qualify for a university-sponsored lecture. Ned, though finding it 'a good read', tends to agree, and suggests an undergraduate society might leap at the prospect. Or I could take my stand alongside the seller of *Socialist Worker* in Camden High Street on a Saturday morning and deliver it there.

7 June. With Mrs Thatcher safely ahead in the polls, that voice and the little scuttling walk threatening to lead us into the next century, Conservative commentators like P. Worsthorne feel it now safe to admit that perhaps there is just a little truth in the general distaste for Thatcherism, the decay of manufacture, the throttling of the Health Service etc., and in the last few days of the campaign it might be as well to look at these details. The well-being of half the country, and all it is now is an election garnish: 'Conservative Party: Serving Suggestion'.

17 June. Lord Hailsham, the Arthur Negus of the English law, is at seventy-nine put out of office. Not before time, some might think, but on *News at Ten* he is feeling a bit sorry for himself. He was just the same the only time I met him, after one of Ned Sherrin's shows in the sixties, but then his complaint was not neglect or ingratitude but poverty. Very much one of the 'You must grin and bear it' school (inequities dismissed with a chuckle), he doesn't like it when he gets the mucky end of the stick. Not that most people would consider the House of Lords and the Lord Chancellor's pension exactly mucky.

20 June. A list of queries comes from the German translator of *Kafka's Dick*:
Q. Who is Nurse Cavell, a figure from a movie or a play? I
   think I know her, but I cannot remember from where.
A. You shot her.

Other questions:

'For a long time I used to go to bed early.' This Proust
quote, where?
Ivy Compton-Burnett: who or what is that?
Gas oven: do you mean the gas chamber of the Nazis or the
kitchen stove, which is used for suicide?
Altar: do you mean marriage or sacrifice?

2 July. All the life has gone out of politics. I switch on the
televised debates from the House of Lords and it is like a clip
from a Hollywood epic of Ancient Rome. While Nero or
Caligula rules, the footling Senate goes through the motions.
Like the trams at Beamish or the mills of Ironbridge, demo-
cracy, once part of the English heritage, will soon be part of
English Heritage – a property of the Department of the
Environment.

3 July. My TV film *The Insurance Man* has won the Beautiful
Human Life Award in Japan, and Robert Hines, the young actor
who starred in the film, has been out to Tokyo to collect the
citation. He calls round with a souvenir for me. It is a headband
as worn by Kamikaze pilots.

In the market today: 'Listen, there's nothing you can teach me
about road-sweeping.'

16 July. Watch the first of two programmes by Tony Harrison
about death. It begins at Blackpool, where Harrison was
conceived in August 1935. Harrison comes from Leeds, as I
do, and August Bank Holiday at the seaside was when I was
conceived. So, too, was my brother: three years older than me,
he has the same May birthday. With us it was Morecambe not
Blackpool, which my mother always thought a bit common. If

we ever went to Blackpool she made sure we stayed at Cleveleys or Bispham – 'the refined end'. The era of package holidays came too late for my parents and they never went abroad, but had they done so the same standards would have applied. Mam would soon have sussed out the refined part of Torremolinos or a select end to Sitges.

2 September. Evidence of madness: a woman entering Marks & Spencer's and saying brightly 'Good morning!'

A young mother passes the house wheeling a pram. She is wearing headphones. The baby is crying desperately.

14 September. A.'s dog is run over and she takes it to the vet. The dog's name is Lucky, and in this particular practice people are called in not by the name of the owner but by the name of the pet. So the receptionist comes into the waiting-room and says, 'Lucky Davies?'

1 November, Switzerland. On the train from Gstaad to Montreux. It is the *train panoramique*, and since this is Sunday it's crowded out, with people standing in the aisles. In front of me sits a man, about forty, French or possibly American, reading a magazine of pornographic stories in English. 'Her body arched to receive his quivering member' is one paragraph heading. Beside him sits a businessman, who glances curiously at the magazine and once or twice at its reader but makes no comment. He eventually gets off at the same moment as the porn-reader decides to go to the buffet car for some coffee. The porn-reader leaves his magazine on the seat to keep his place. Not having seen him go, a middle-aged couple take the seats, and the husband picks up the magazine and starts leafing through it. He shows it to his wife, and they are still looking at it when some time later the French/American returns with his coffee. 'I see you're having a good time with that,' he says in French, completely unabashed. Equally unembarrassed, they agree that they are, and some discussion of the magazine follows. In the middle of this the magazine-owner points out without rancour that the husband is actually sitting in his place. The husband promptly gets up, the porn-reader sits down, and he and the wife (ankle socks, anorak, a schoolteacher possibly) carry on their amicable conversation about the magazine, with the husband occasionally joining in. It's a curious scene for a Sunday afternoon, and one hard to imagine taking place in England. In its directness it is like the beginning of a film by Bertrand Blier, except that there sexual connections would be being made. There is none of that here, just human beings confronting each other without judgement or preconception. Not so much humanity as specimens of humanity. And not what the Swiss are supposed to be like at all.

15 November, Yorkshire. This Week's Cause of Cancer in the *Sunday Times* is bracken, the spores of which are said to affect the lungs. The Department of Health is reported to be concerned about 'how to get this message across' without causing a mass exodus from the countryside. One reason for mass exodus being as good as another, it's also been disclosed that, after Chernobyl, an area of fifty miles centring on Skipton, and therefore including our village, was (and possibly still is) a radiation blackspot. The weekend after Chernobyl the local CND had organized a barbecue, and I remember Graham M. telling me how it had rained so hard he and his family (three children under six) had given up trying to shelter and got happily soaked. It was this rain that carried the radioactivity which is now said to be still present in the bilberries on the moors. Along with the bracken spores, of course.

1 December. Read a poem by Tony Harrison about his childhood in Leeds in which he recalls that the slang for the rhubarb which filled the fields in and around the city was 'tusky'. I recall it too, reading his poem, but cannot remember when I was a boy in Leeds ever calling it that myself. Other boys did, I remember. Other boys nicked rhubarb from the field's edge. Though I did it too, it was more fearfully than the others. They were part of the gang as I never was, quite, and not being part of the gang (the last to be picked, the first to be turned out) I never felt easy using their language. So with me it wasn't 'tusky'; I stuck to 'rhubarb'. In later years, and for the same reason, I never said 'bird' or 'screw', and today hearing myself say 'guy' I winced and felt it an imposture.

Being picked, though, reminds me of Russell's account of his childhood. As usual he was the last to be chosen, and as the two captains dithered as to who should have him the master in charge lost his temper and cut it short: 'Right. That's it. You have him.'

'Oh, sir, sir. No, sir. We had him last week, sir.'

21 December, Yorkshire. In a bookshop in Ilkley – ASSISTANT: Is that *Geoffrey* Chaucer?

1988

10 January. The newly privatized tow-away trucks are now operating in Camden and make regular visits to our street. The crews display a fearsome zeal, scrambling to get the slings and chains around the offending car before the owner (just doing five minutes' shopping in the market) returns. They are like a gang of executioners hurrying the victim to his doom before a reprieve arrives.

The pound is only at the top of the street, and the crews find it handier (and, if they are on piecework, more profitable) to tow our cars away rather than go questing for them in the outlying areas of the borough.

That the operation is on the dubious boundary between commerce and law-enforcement could be deduced from the jaunty demeanour of the policeman in charge, who wears his flat cap tilted to the back of his head. 'Distancing', the late Erving Goffmann would have called it, the cap enough to call the whole activity into question.

17 February. To Cambridge with A. to see an exhibition at the Fitzwilliam on the conservation of pictures. I skimp the actual exhibition, my aim just to get the catalogue and study it at leisure – i.e. sitting down. The Backs are full of snowdrops and crocuses, school parties, Japanese and dozens of retired couples – undergraduates almost an event.

Then to Ely, where I have not been since I cycled there thirty-five years ago when I was at Cambridge on the Russian course, the then empty fen now cluttered with gas stations and chicken farms, an industrial park and all the litter of modern agriculture. In 1953 the cathedral was damp and empty, looming like a liner out of the fog. Now there is a desk inside the door and it costs £1.60 to go in, which I don't mind much – less, anyway, than the information display that spills, as it does in all such places, halfway down the north aisle, like 'Who's Who in the Diocese of Ely', a montage of photos from bishop to verger, all flashing fluorescent smiles. 'That's nice,' says a visitor, and I suppose it's just me that minds, even A. not understanding my grumpiness. Still there (though doomed, I'm sure) are the great black Gurney stoves, lit and warm and as much monuments as the reclining alabaster figures of nineteenth-century deans and professors of divinity.

The painted roof is half covered over, in process of restoration, the colours pastel as if done in chalk. And there are the features that always move and disturb: the regimental chapel and the war memorials, the threadbare nets of colours long ago laid up. Note the absence of the old black-garbed, proprietary vergers – just more ladies sitting at the information desk and helpful retired gentlemen doing their duty as Friends of the Cathedral. How once in this huge hangar I would have knelt and prayed and hoped to hear the Voice of God, or some twitching of my teenage sensibility that would convince me I might one day turn out to be – what? Not a grumpy middle-aged playwright anyway.

6 March. A wet Sunday afternoon, and A. and I walk round the edge of Inverforth House on Golders Hill. Noting a number of condoms in the bushes I assume it's a Lovers' Lane, but gradually we become aware of a number of single men wandering slowly round and realize we have hit a cruising-ground. We walk up into the gardens, empty on this cold, grey afternoon, and up the steps to the huge pergola that stretches round the house and which is now threatened with demolition. From here we have a grandstand view of the wood below.

A young man in white with a rucksack, whom we saw outside, is still hanging about. He is passed by three or four men, none of whom go far but wait and look back so that eventually he is ringed by admirers, all of them at a radius of twenty yards or so. But nobody actually approaches him, and he seems unaware that he is being watched and eventually drifts away. Occasional decorous family groups pass through the middle of this cruising-ground, civilians crossing a battlefield under the white flag of respectability, but no one who watches for more than two minutes could fail to be aware of what is going on. Though nothing *is* actually going on – just men watching and waiting. Driving home, we speculate why no one approached the young man in white and decide it was because he was (or was thought to be) a policeman.

7 March. Three IRA terrorists shot in Gibraltar, dreadful mayhem averted. It's fairly plain that the terrorists were shot in cold blood by the SAS, though this, of course, is not stated in the Commons and no one dares query Geoffrey Howe's bland version of events except, to his credit, Eric Heffer.

Some high-ranking general pointed out only last week that a live terrorist is much more use than a dead one, but nobody thinks to bring this up either. Instead we take one more step down the road to barbarism, the real damage the IRA does in making us their mirror image. But of course the mirror is thickly veiled in English hypocrisy – 'making movements which might seem to threaten life and limb' is how it's justified.

Celebrations in the mess at Shrewsbury tonight, no doubt.

12 March. Watch the *South Bank Show* on Kafka, which falls into the customary mistakes, Tim Roth playing Joseph K. in the usual style – blank-faced, anonymous, *cosmic*. There are long, featureless corridors and lofty rooms, distorted camera angles and all that, and, though the actual trial is set in an attic, as it should be, it's an attic so vast it could be a tithe barn.

The mistake in dramatizing Kafka is always the same (and we didn't manage wholly to sidestep it in *The Insurance Man*): actors and directors don't play the text, they play the implications of the text. So Joseph K., instead of being just a bank clerk, wrongly accused, becomes emblematic of everyone who has been wrongly accused. What Kafka writes is a naturalistic account of ordinary behaviour, and that is what actors should play and let the implications take care of themselves. Directors similarly. Or, as Arthur Miller says somewhere, 'Just play the text, not what it reminds you of.'

19 March. A wet weekend in the country, where I gather armfuls of branches of balsam poplar. To look at the balsam poplar isn't much of a tree, with none of the shimmer (the 'dazzle' Gerard Manley Hopkins called it) or the grace of the Lombard variety, but for a few weeks in spring it comes into its own.

For years I didn't know of its existence, only that around this time of year one occasionally caught a whiff of something so intoxicating that it seemed to promise opportunity, fresh beginnings, the turning-over of new leaves; it seemed the very breath of spring. Once I thought it was daffodils (the daffodils were under the tree); in Rome I thought it was a waiter's aftershave (we were dining outside); once I even thought it was sweat and that the person concerned (we were walking in the Parks at Oxford) must be like a saint and have the odour of sanctity. It was only a few years ago that I came upon a line of these poplars in the grounds of Alec Guinness's house and was told by Alec that it was a tree on the site that had decided them to live there.

The buds of the balsam poplar secrete a gum which, as the buds burst, releases its scent. It lasts only a couple of weeks, but once the leaves have begun to open they can be dried to retain their scent throughout the year and long afterwards. There's no elaborate procedure, like making pot pourri: I just put them on a newspaper on top of the central-heating boiler. I once took a branch from the tree into Penhaligon's, hoping they manufactured something similar. They didn't, but a dreamy look came into the assistant's eye as she sniffed, and she called in her colleagues, who were similarly entranced.

There's a scene at the end of Patrick Suskind's novel *Perfume* when a mob clamouring for a murderer's execution falls instead into a frenzy of lust and adoration because he has drenched himself in some specially concocted essence. I imagine that was balsam poplar.

21 March. I listen to the debate in the Commons on the lynching of two British soldiers by an IRA mob. 'The House of Commons at its best' is how the papers will put it, but no one dares get up and say that had we captured the terrorists in Gibraltar and not shot them out of hand there would have been no funerals and no lynchings.

Meanwhile the inquest on the Gibraltar dead is set for *June.* The *Sun*'s headline this morning: 'String 'Em Up.'

15 April. An exchange at the Cashpoint. I put my card in the dispenser only to have it returned with the display reading 'Card wrongly inserted'. I try again and the same thing happens, so I join the other queue. One of two men in their thirties – estate agents in their lunch hour maybe – now tries the same machine, with the same result. 'Let me,' says the other. 'It'll know a good insertion from a bad one.' There is a general snigger, but his card comes back too. 'It doesn't know when it's lucky,' he says, joining our queue.

17 April. Drive back from Yorkshire, calling at Giggleswick to see Russell, who has jaundice. He is lying in bed, surrounded by the Sunday papers which are full of bad reviews of his *Grand Tour* programme. In profile he looks thinner and somehow *papal.* I only stay five minutes or so, while he drifts in and out of sleep, before I go, saying 'Is there anything you want?'

'Yes. Pie and chips.'

18 April. The news about Russell has reached the papers. The

Sun claims (I'm sure reluctantly) that he hasn't got Aids but the hepatitis-B virus, 'which is passed in the same way. Harty is a bachelor.' His secretary, Pat H., hasn't made things easier by saying he has 'catarrh of the liver', a wonderful nineteenth-century diagnosis. He is now in Airedale Hospital, where the nurses have told the papers they have been asked not to talk about it. And so on.

27 April, Harrogate. In a break from filming *Dinner at Noon** at the Crown Hotel, I walk across to St Wilfred's, which I cycled over from Leeds to see forty years ago with John Totterdill. Having remembered it as Ninian Comper, I find it's by Temple Moore, Early English cathedral architecture miniaturized – tiny clerestory passages, sweeping steps up to the organ, and lots of Arts and Crafts rood-loftery stuff which I just about liked then but which looks much nicer now. Modern I thought this church was once. Now it's antique, the pewter-coloured door bound in iron and as rutted and heavy as its medieval model.

Half expecting it to be locked, as churches generally are nowadays, I find evensong is being said (and in the BCP version too), with three men sitting in the Lady Chapel – one I imagine the priest in charge, and a third (bearded) who is possibly the curate. I sit and listen for a while but don't wander round as I'd have liked to do, not wanting to be roped in or (when they've finished) welcomed. The same conflict in church (particularly when a service is being said) that I feel in art galleries, a need to stay and go at the same time. (Watching a sunset the same.) It's a sense that there is something to be had here and I ought to have the patience to wait on it, while the other (and generally stronger) urge is get out and think about it later. Which, having signed the book, I do.

* See page 39.

Walk back through the suburbs of Harrogate: wide empty streets, huge houses, girls' schools, private hotels, homes.

28 April, Harrogate. Mike Fox, our cameraman, once filmed on Concorde sitting on the flight deck. He spotted an out-of-the-way dial and asked its function. It was the radiation meter, which the plane needed because it goes near or beyond the limits of the earth's protective layer.

'Does it ever go off the dial?' Mike asked.

'No,' said the pilot. 'Or not for that reason anyway. The one time it does is coming in over the Bristol Channel. It's the Berkeley nuclear power station.'

This is just the kind of odd information cameramen often have – their experience of the world more various than almost any profession I can think of, and also more oblique. It's what would make a cameraman a good character in a play, and a useful one (all worlds known, all walks of life visited) in a thriller.

1 May. Miss Shepherd asks me to stick a notice on the back of her wheelchair. It reads, 'Please help push me. Sometimes.'

6 May, Leeds. Some signs yesterday that Russell was coming out of his coma, and today he is sitting up and taking notice, even trying to write notes. Intensive Care, though actually the busiest and most fraught section of the hospital, is also the most carefree. Though everyone has so much to do, dodging round each other in their green pyjamas like Olympic gymnasts, they all have time to stop and explain what it is they are doing. There are no obvious signs of rank. We were told we could wave at R. through the glass by a young man in green who might have been a nurse, a doctor or just someone there cleaning the floor. The consultant himself is in shirt sleeves and pullover and looks as if he might have come in to adjust the radiators. He says R. is not yet out of the wood.

7 May, Leeds. It's now thought that R. has turned the corner, and St James's is planning a press conference to announce this, in the hope it will get rid of the reporters camped in the car park and also the group in the flat opposite with a telescope trained on the window of the ward. A nurse inadvertently mentions the press conference to Russell, who since then can think of nothing else and keeps scribbling indecipherable notes on the lines of 'Tell the world I am grateful to the doctors of St James's Hospital and all staff and cleaners on Ward 17.'

These signs of life, far from producing sighs of relief from his assembled friends, just make them think that Russell has done it on them again. Schooled in the tactics of the Harty family, they have been fooled so often before and vowed never to be fooled again but once more they have been CONNED.

Meanwhile the press continue at their games, and Mrs Thatcher attacks media ethics. But of course she doesn't mean Mr Murdoch (whom she regularly invites to Christmas Dinner); what she means is the investigative reporting of the Gibraltar shootings.

10–20 May. I spend ten days in Russia on a visit arranged by the Great Britain–USSR Society. My colleagues are the novelists Paul Bailey, Christopher Hope and Timothy Mo (who also writes for *Boxing News*), the poet Craig Raine (who doesn't) and the playwright Sue Townsend, of *Adrian Mole* fame. I have many misgivings about the trip, particularly in regard to creature comforts. I wonder, for instance, if the Russians have got round to mineral water. John Sturrock reassures me. 'Haven't you heard of Perrierstroika?'

The Writers' Union is a pleasant one-storeyed nineteenth-century building set round a leafy courtyard and currently being refurbished against Mr Reagan's visit. He is to have lunch here. We are never going to have lunch, it seems, as this introductory session of talks began at ten and it is now 1.30 with no sign of it ending. We sit down one side of a long green-baize-covered table with the Soviet writers on the other, the most eye-catching of them the playwright Mikhail Shatrov, a stocky middle-aged man with a pallor so striking Sue Townsend insists it owes something to Max Factor. Shatrov is seemingly contemptuous of these proceedings; he arrives late, ostentatiously reads a newspaper during the speeches, and from time to time points out items of interest to his colleagues. Sceptical of the purpose of formal discussions like these, I find Shatrov's attitude not unsympathetic, particularly when the talk turns to the writer's role in society. I feel like a not very expert motor mechanic taking part in a discussion on national transport policy. Presiding over the meeting is Professor Zassoursky, who holds the chair of journalism at Moscow University. He is an urbane and elegant figure (in what looks like a Brooks Brothers suit), and witty with it. The talk among the Soviet writers is all of the coming Party Congress, which they hope will enforce the retirement of the heads of the Musicians' and Writers' Unions, both notorious hard-liners. 'But if they resign,' says Zassoursky, 'it could even be worse. After all, they might start writing again.'

The Hotel Ukraina, where we are staying, looks like the Gotham or the Dakota, those monstrous nineteenth-century mansions on New York's Central Park West, though this and dozens of buildings like it were built fifty or sixty years later by Stalin. Like the Writers' Union, the Ukraina is being refurbished against The Visit, the refurbishment taking the form of new three-ply cabinets to encase the (old) TV sets. My room has a fridge which lights up nicely but otherwise just makes the contents (one bottle of mineral water) sweat. An engineer comes and looks at it but is baffled. It is hard to understand, with simple technology such a mystery, why they haven't blown us all up years ago. 'Be fair,' says Sue Townsend: 'I believe they do a very good smelter.'

I am disturbed to find Melvyn Bragg working in the hotel as a doorman. He pretends not to recognize me.

To Massenet's *Werther* at the Bolshoi. It is an indifferent production, the scenery and sets almost music-hall, but the house is packed, and Nina and Galina, our guides, say that this is the first time for years they have managed to get a ticket – which makes us all feel worse for not enjoying it. Someone who is enjoying it is Melvyn Bragg, this time in the back row of the chorus.

Though food is pretty basic, I find meals the high points of each day, just as they are when filming. One talks about food, thinks about it, and tonight, returning from the opera, we are mortified to find we are too late for supper. Anne Vaughan, our organizer, braves the kitchen, and eventually a waitress takes pity on us and gives us some bread and ham and a bit of dog-eared salad, which we take upstairs in plastic bags. 'You must be very hungry,' says a man in the lift. 'What country are you coming from?'

Another session at the Writers' Union. Most of the writers we talk to are likeable, decent people and it is this that makes it difficult to raise potentially embarrassing issues like dissidence. If these were fanatical hard-liners it would be easy to ask the hard questions, but they are not. One tells us how she has just translated *Animal Farm* ('Not a good book,' one of us says prissily), and they are so obviously thrilled with what is happening that to inquire, say, about psychiatric punishment seems tactless. What one does not get from them is any sense of what they think of each other. They hear out each other's speeches without comment or dissent, and only when Boguslavskaya (Mrs Voznesensky) makes a long self-regarding speech and shortly afterwards sweeps out does one get some hint that they think she is tiresome too.

Breakfast (food again) is self-service and is generally a relatively tranquil meal, but this morning I come down to find we have been invaded by the American Friendship Society ('Lois Ravenna Jr,' says the name tag of the lady opposite). They are a middle-aged to elderly group, ladies whom I would call 'game' (and Barry Humphries 'spunky'). They know they cannot expect the creature comforts on offer at the Wichita Hilton, but they are determined not to complain or be defeated. This sometimes leads them into absurdity. One old lady, not noticing the nearby pile of plates, assumes the plate is just another refinement the Soviet Union has not got round to. No matter. She grits her teeth and piles meat balls on one corner of her tray and porridge on to another, a practice she can only be familiar with from Hollywood prison movies.

Another visit to the Bolshoi, this time for an evening of ballet excerpts. Note the universal presence, even here at the ballet, of small, square old men, their jackets buckling under the weight of medals and ribbons, and looking like the Eastern Front in person. By now I am unsurprised to find Melvyn is in the ballet as well as the opera, and he even takes a curtain call, accompanied, as ballet calls are the world over, by a deadly hail of tulips.

I have seen only one bit of graffiti in Moscow, a faint felt-tip scrawl on the huge revolving doors of the Ukraina: 'Be Attention. Aids!'

To the Novodevichnaya Cemetery to see the grave of Chekhov.

However, today is Saturday, relatives' day, and, since we are only tourists and no one, not even Timothy Mo, is related to Chekhov, we are not admitted. Galina, the sterner of our guides, goes into the gateman's office to argue it out. 'I have a delegation of British writers outside.' The man shrugs. 'But these are *writers*.' 'So? I am a reader.' One had not thought deconstruction had reached so far.

After lunch at the Georgian State restaurant near Pushkin Square we stroll back through the Arbat, a pedestrian precinct crowded with shoppers and sightseers this Saturday afternoon. With its seats and bulbous lamp-standards, street pedlars and guitar-players, it could be a precinct anywhere in Western Europe. ('The Russians are like us; they have precincts.') The difference, of course, is that there is virtually nothing in the shops. There are queues for ice-cream and queues for coffee, but, that apart, no one is selling anything resembling food.

I go into a stationer's to buy an exercise book (the word *tetradka* surfacing unbidden from my Russian learned and forgotten thirty-five years ago). Even in the stationer's there is a queue, and a bored shop-girl serving a little boy has him trembling on the edge of tears, so I come out.

Going into the shop has made me lose the others, and hurrying to catch up I pass a middle-aged woman stood at a podium improvised from a cardboard box. It has something written on the front in pencil, and on a bench nearby sit a man and a boy whom I take to be her husband and son. She is making an impassioned speech to which no one is listening, the husband looking shamefaced and the boy turning away in embarrassment. Not wanting to contribute to their discomfort, I do not listen to her either, or try to read what is written on the box. It is only after I have walked on that I wonder if this is a political protest and think maybe that is what dissidence is like –

embarrassing to the general public, shaming for the immediate family, getting a dose of freedom like getting a dose of Jesus.

By overnight train to Orel. It is a bad night, and we have to be up at six. Me: 'There are two men playing chess in the next compartment.' Craig Raine: 'One of them isn't Death by any chance?'

None of us has ever heard of Orel, and when we come out of the station we realize why: it is Loughborough. We are met by our Intourist guide, Marina, a youngish woman, sturdy, solid and with a wide-eyed humourless look I find familiar but hard to place. Of course: what is missing is the wimple. She is a nun. 'Now', she says briskly, 'we have arrived at our place of destination.' We get into our bus and she seizes the intercom. 'Allow me to compliment you on your choice of season for coming to our city. It is spring and, as you see, everything is not yet bare still. After your breakfast we will pick up, so to speak, some other writers from the centre of our city and visit the war memorials.'

Even on the short journey to the motel one detects the difference in atmosphere between here and Moscow. There we had scarcely seen a slogan, and Sue thought that even the pictures of Lenin were not as common as a few years back. Here he is very much in evidence, and every factory and public building is still surmounted by calls to action. 'All Power to Soviet Youth.' 'Long Live the Working Class.' Marina drives the point home. 'Let me say something of Orel centre. The city was a witness to many historical events. It has a prolonged form along the river, and was one of the fifteen most ruined cities by the Fascists. On the right is a monument not to any concrete personality, so to speak, but to the distinction of Orel Steel Rolling Mill, which outports to sixty countries in the world.' It is seven o'clock on Sunday morning.

The morning having been devoted to war, the afternoon is set aside for art. 'Here is our museum of Orel writers,' announces Marina as our bus draws up. 'Now we are getting out and coming in.' The Orel writers turn out to be Fet, Bunin, Andreev, Novikov and (somewhere out in the country) Turgenev. What they all have in common, having been born in Orel, is that they got out of it at the earliest opportunity. The museum is full of dark Edwardian furniture. It is like a succession of dentists' waiting-rooms. Soon I am moaning aloud with boredom and I begin to realize what the Queen must feel like.

A tea party to meet the present-day writers of Orel – the ones who haven't managed to get away, that is. My neighbour is a burly playwright who looks more like a butcher. 'Do you like Orel?' I begin vapidly. He shrugs. 'He says it is nice,' Marina explains – 'less rushing than in Moscow.' 'Were you born here?' I ask. 'No. He was born in Siberia.' Maybe it is the mention of Siberia that galvanizes Marina, but she decides we have spent long enough on the social chit-chat and ought to get down to business. 'What is love?' she asks firmly. 'That is good question to discuss. Love is, so to speak, many things. Let us discuss that as writers.' Instead we discuss literature, and in particular Jerome K. Jerome's *Three Men in the Same Boat*.

We drive sixty kilometres to the east to visit Turgenev's birthplace. Wide-verged roads, thin woods, rolling countryside: the tanks must have had a field day. Marina has the mike again. 'Permit me to say a couple of words about the vegetation of Orel region. There are oak trees, pine trees, birch trees. There are in all many grown-up trees.' Two of the local writers accompanying us take a fancy to Sue Townsend, taking turns to sit next to her, and these manoeuvres generate a sense of hysteria in our party.

Lunch is taken at a ranch-style roadhouse in a room hung with chandeliers used for banquets and weddings. We have scarcely started on the food when the toasts begin, the writers popping up one after the other to give long rambling speeches about peace and friendship and the Russian soul. I remember the Russian soul. It was much in evidence thirty-five years ago when I was on the Joint-Services Russian course at Cambridge; it was always a useful theme to pad out one's weekly essay. None of the writers in Moscow had mentioned it, but here it was in Orel, still alive and kicking. When the lengthy meal is finished, we climb wearily back into the bus, whereupon Oleg, the leader of the Orel writers (and one of the suitors for Ms Townsend), proceeds to harangue us further on the Russian soul. We become more and more hysterical. 'I had been told the English were reserved people,' says Marina, 'but you laugh all the time.' And of course knowing we are behaving disgracefully doesn't help.

When we reach Turgenev's villa, Sue Townsend, Craig Raine and I avoid the guided tour and wander by the lake. We then do a perfunctory tour of the house (more dentists' waiting-rooms) and sit by the village pond just outside the gates. The back gardens of some wooden cottages run down to the pond, and a peasant woman stands on a little jetty washing some buckets. Children play by a lower pond, and geese usher their goslings down to the water. It could be a theme park, of course, but it doesn't look to have changed much since the nineteenth century. It's the sort of scene that youth or love would print on the heart, but with nothing to make one remember, no agent to develop the snapshot, one notes the pond and the peace this warm spring day and that's all.

The coach returns and, as we draw near to Orel, Sue's admirers become increasingly desperate and try to get her to go for a walk in the woods. One of them (the playwright) coyly opens his briefcase to reveal two bottles of wine. He has his son with him, a shy boy who is about to go into the army and who speaks a little English. He has to translate his father's ogling remarks. Were the seduction to go according to plan, he would presumably have to stick around until actions began to speak louder than words. In its potential for filial embarrassment it reminds me of a Chekhov short story in which a father and son, sailors on a freighter, draw the winning lots to the cabin spyhole through which they watch a honeymoon couple.

At an embassy cocktail party back in Moscow I talk to the BBC correspondent Jeremy Harris, who has been at Philby's funeral. He says the first evidence that it was happening was a phone call to a Reuter's colleague to say that Philby's funeral was taking place at the Kurskaya cemetery. 'When?' 'Now,' said the voice, and rang off. They piled into a taxi, got to the cemetery, and found it deserted, the only evidence of the coming ceremony an open grave lined with red and black silk. Eventually a procession threaded its way among the graves, with the coffin borne aloft. As it was lowered, they saw that it was open, and there was Philby, smiling slightly, and, waiting at the graveside, fresh from the airport, Philby's son.

Novy Mir had printed bootleg extracts from Sue Townsend's *Diary of Adrian Mole*. Now it is to be officially translated, and the translator is to take her out to supper. We go off to a restaurant, where eventually she joins us. The translator has stood her up. Next day he calls to say he had the day confused and thought Tuesday was Thursday. Paul Bailey remarks that this augurs ill for the translation, which will probably read, 'Friday. Got up early and went to Sunday school.'

To Lvov by Aeroflot. It is a two-hour flight, and the only refreshment served is a cup of faintly scented mineral water. The stewardess waits while one drinks (not enough cups), this making it seem even more like medicine. Spirits rise as we see another stewardess coming through with a trolley and the passengers falling on the contents. They turn out to be dolls. A second pass through the plane brings little brown bears and plastic carrier bags, and a third the Russian equivalent of Knight's Castile. I imagine if the flight went on long enough we'd be down to Brillo pads and plastic sink tidies.

The woman in front is nervous of flying. She is sweating a lot, and eventually removes her coat. Sitting by the emergency door and not finding anywhere to put her doubtless precious coat, she tries to hang it on the emergency door handle. In an unaccustomed moment of decision I clasp both arms round her and shout, 'Stop!' She doesn't even look round, just meekly puts the coat across her lap and goes on sweating.

On the flight Paul Bailey reads Gibbon, I read Updike, Sue Townsend reads Paul Bailey, and Timothy Mo chats to Volodya, our senior representative. He is translating John le Carré and asks Tim for help with some idiomatic phrases. 'What is "Down the hatch"? This is an invitation to drop the liquid, no?' Some of Tim's explanations are as inaccurate as Volodya's guesses. 'At Oxford, what is Port Meadow?' Tim describes a rich green pasture where cows stand up to their bellies in the lush grass – a far cry from the patch of scrub bordered by factories and allotments that it really is.

Lvov turns out to be an enchanting place, a seventeenth- and eighteenth-century city that is largely intact, with architecture so cosmopolitan one could be anywhere in northern Europe or even Austria. The city was Polish until 1939, when it came to Russia in the carve-up after the Nazi–Soviet Pact, and is now a centre of Ukrainian nationalism. We are taken to meet the mayor, a large ironic man who gives us coffee in his parlour and tells us of the contacts the city maintains with expatriate Ukrainians, particularly in Canada, where he has just been visiting Winnipeg. I mention that most of the Russians in *An Englishman Abroad* were played by members of the Ukrainian colony near Dundee. 'What a pity,' he says. 'Next time maybe they'll play Ukrainians.'

Lvov is full of churches – Catholic, Orthodox and Uniate – and all of them are packed this Thursday morning because it is Ascension Day. Sue and I go into the cathedral. Although the service is over, women are kneeling not only in the pews and before the altars but in the aisles, against pillars, anywhere where there is a spare patch of flagstone (which some of them kiss). We are younger than most of the congregation, and a kindly old granny, assuming that it is all mumbo-jumbo to us, starts to explain about the Ascension and Pentecost. She is stopped by a mean-looking old woman who tells me I should not be sitting with my legs crossed in a church. Sue is upset by this attack and starts crying, whereupon the nice granny shoos the old witch away and takes us off behind a pillar in order to continue the lesson.

Such fervour is disturbing. Lvov is still Polish in spirit, which explains part of it, but one realizes there is no easy equation between political liberty and religious freedom, and that faith as blind as this is no more democratic than the regime that would suppress it. It is incidentally very anti-Semitic. We ask our guide whether there is a synagogue in the city. There may have been, he says, but he thinks it has been destroyed. Further questions are met with a shrug. Later we discover that during the war Lvov had a large concentration camp on its outskirts.

An afternoon spent in discussions at the local Writers' Union. The most striking person here is a French-speaking Ukrainian woman. She is in her sixties, but chic and smartly dressed, almost a caricature of a Frenchwoman making the most of herself. Her job was to translate approved novels from the French. The approval had its limitations, however, and she was sentenced to ten years in a camp at Magadan. When the official interpreter translates this, she doesn't actually say 'a camp', but 'somewhere far away'. I am not sure if this is because of censorship, voluntary or otherwise, or because it wasn't a camp, just a kind of exile. Or maybe it's just that she's naturally embarrassed in an atmosphere of cordial discussion to admit that there are such places.

There are plenty of cafés in Lvov, more food in the shops than in Moscow, and in the evening the place takes on an Italian atmosphere with the whole town out walking the streets round the main square. On park seats old men play chess, dominoes and a kind of stand-up whist in which the players hurl their cards down on to a low table.

Later we go to the opera to see an epic of Ukrainian nationalism, Gulak-Artemosky's *The Ukrainian Cossack beyond the Danube*. It is a simple tale, given once a month by the company and greatly appreciated by the audience, who applaud it way beyond its merits. The orchestra are plainly bored stiff with it, openly reading newspapers and chattering loudly during spoken passages. A pigeon now gets into the roof and gets trapped against the glass. The chorus discuss this while singing, and step out of line to look up at the source of the disturbance, as in their unoccupied moments do the leading singers. At the end, bouquets are brought on to the stage and there is the usual hail of tulips and ten minutes of rhythmic applause. Nice to see, though, that Melvyn has caught up with us again, this time giving a somewhat overstated performance as a eunuch in the retinue of the Sultan.

Beer was unobtainable in Moscow except at the hard-currency shop, and before coming to Lvov I bought a dozen or more cans to see me through the trip. However, beer is plentiful in Lvov (though about as alcoholic as dandelion and burdock), so when I board the plane for Moscow I am still carrying a dozen cans of Heineken. It is, I suppose, the closest I shall ever come to being a football hooligan.

26 May, Leeds. There is a sense in which the dying *shake off* the concerns of the living, play them like a salmon plays the rod – seeming to get a little better so that relief replaces concern, then worsening again so that anxiety returns. It needs only a short dose of this before the living are quite glad to see them go. Lady Bracknell's 'It is high time that Mr Bunbury made up his mind whether he was going to live or to die' is not altogether a joke.

11 June, Yorkshire. The evening of Russell's funeral A. and I go down to supper in Giggleswick, thinking we will also take a look at the flowers on the grave. But as long as the light lasts and well past eleven o'clock there are visitors threading their way by the church and through the opening in the wall to the huge mound of wreaths, and so we give it a miss.

At one point after supper I go up to the bathroom at W.'s, which overlooks the graveyard, just to see if it's quietened down. There are myths in friendship, and one of ours was that I envied Russell his life and he envied me mine. He certainly had his much better sorted out – had a housekeeper, someone to cook and to clean, took lots of trips abroad, and always with a car to take him wherever he wanted to go. Whereas what he envied about me was that I could point to the work I'd done and that I caught much less critical flak than he did (who caught more than most). The truth is, of course, that I wouldn't have wanted his life or he mine.

My grave will, I imagine, be in the next village, a few miles north of Giggleswick. It's a fairly anonymous spot, as our churchyard is full and burials are in the overflow cemetery on the road to the station. It's where my father is buried, pleasant enough and surrounded by trees and fields, but without much character. Russell's grave is in the churchyard itself, Giggleswick church an ancient one, the setting picturesque, the graveyard grazed by sheep beneath the fell. He lies on the edge of the playing-fields, a stone's throw from the village street and within sight and sound of the school where he was so happy. The church clock strikes ten as I look out of the bathroom window in the dusk. Not a bad place to be, I think. Then it comes to me that what I am doing is envying him his grave.

12 June. Simon Callow calls suggesting *Single Spies* as a title for the double bill of Burgess and Blunt plays. While I'd hoped to get rid of spies altogether, it's a much better title than any I've thought of and so *Single Spies* it is.

19 June. Various quotes from today's *Sunday Telegraph*:

that evil decade the 1960s . . .

Four-letter words replaced the classics as the language of the 1960's Royal Court Theatre. Nobody well-washed had a chance of advancement . . .

. . . lots of families are now trying to buy back their stately homes from the National Trust. This is an excellent sign. The life of the country house was very much part of a civilizing process.

all Peregrine Worsthorne

[When Mrs Thatcher's satellite revolution comes] it will be rare for an entire saloon bar or dinner party to have all watched the same television programme the night before. There will then be a healthy decline in the importance of the programme chiefs.

Frank Johnson

That there will also be an unhealthy decline in the standard of the programmes televised does not of course concern him.

27 June, Paris. To the Brasserie Bofinger near the Bastille. As we are finishing our supper a party rises from a distant table. It is Francis Bacon and his little entourage. A sharp narrow-trousered suit like the ones Peter Cook used to wear from Sportique in 1960, hair in a slick modified DA, and no sense at all that he is in his mid-seventies.

As Bacon and his party wait on the pavement outside, the waiters gather and look out of the window, paying their unashamed respects to a great man in a way I can't imagine waiters doing in England. It recalls the dining-car attendant Harold Nicolson encountered who joined him and Vita Sackville-West in a toast to Sainte-Beuve as their train passed through Boulogne.

Kafka could never have written as he did had he lived in a house. His writing is that of someone whose whole life was spent in apartments, with lifts, stairwells, muffled voices behind closed doors, and sounds through walls. Put him in a nice detached villa and he'd never have written a word.

Someone writes asking advice about where to send a TV script. 'We sent it to Kenneth Williams and he was extremely enthusiastic about our script but he committed suicide soon after.'

20 August. Watching Barry Humphries on TV the other night I noticed the band was laughing. It reminded me how when I used to do comedy I never used to make the band laugh. Dudley [Moore] did and Peter [Cook], but not me. And somehow it was another version of not being good at games.

The Foreign Secretary says that with regard to the use of chemical weapons against the Kurds Britain is in 'the forefront of anxiety'.

September. Watch Tony Palmer's film on Richard Burton, a morality tale about the perils of art. Less effective with me because I never went for the Welsh-wizardry and didn't like the way he cultivated or acquired the Olivier mannerisms – the sudden fortissimos, the instant access to the emotions, and all the characteristics of the shouting school of acting. In 1968 the Burtons came to *Forty Years On*, coming round afterwards to see Gielgud together with a posse of black-suited hairdressers, make-up artists and, I suppose, bouncers. Then at a party at the Savoy a few months later Liz Taylor perched momentarily on my knee (and pretty uncomfortable it was too). In an earlier connection I knew Burton's first wife, Sibyl, when we were in New York with *Beyond the Fringe*, and the night the divorce from Sibyl and the marriage to Liz was announced Sibyl asked me to accompany her to the film première of *The Criminal* with Stanley Baker (more Welsh-wizardry). Even at the time I realized I had been chosen because I was someone with whom no one could seriously imagine she had a romantic link. But what really impressed me about the evening was that, while I had Sibyl Burton on my right, on my left was Myrna Loy.

21 September. I have started working on a play about George III, but I fear it may just have been brought on by being about to do another play [*Single Spies*] in which royalty figures and that it will accordingly come to nothing. This often happens. When I was waiting for *Forty Years On* to be produced I was trying to write a farce which was also about a school. *Enjoy* was preceded by months of fruitless work on another play about old people, *Gerry Ward*; and, though it's hard to say which came first, I suppose *The Insurance Man* and *Kafka's Dick* are similarly related.

25 October. Russell's memorial service* belatedly attacked in the *Daily Telegraph* by Peter Simple. Its inaccuracy ('A friend tells me . . .') and the toadying omission from censure of Ned Sherrin suggests that the author is C. Booker. The *Telegraph*'s obituary of R. was equally vile.

The kind of memorial service the *Telegraph* likes is on the same page: the Prime Minister, flanked by her favourite bishop, Dr Leonard, looking caring at the service for T. E. Utley, for whom no one in the Tory world has a wrong word, though the presence at the service of the Chief Constable of the RUC plus the South African Ambassador suggests that a different view is possible.

11 November. To Weston to see Mam. Two of the other old ladies in the home are having their hair done. One of them shouts above the noise of the dryer, 'They keep telling me I ought to have been a Trappist nun. I didn't want to be a Trappist nun. My father had Friar's Balsam in the medicine chest, but that's as far as it went.'

The train back is crowded, and at Bath a bunch of schoolboys get on, either from a prep school or from the lower forms of a public school, Monkton Combe probably. They are talking of the football team. 'Tim's in the A team,' says one, 'but he's only

* See page 63.

hanging on by a needle and thread.' There is a pause. 'Actually,' says the other. 'I think it's just "thread". You don't have to say "needle".' This is said with perfect solemnity and kindness.

21 *November.* A girl of twenty-five is kept in solitary confinement for two hundred days in conditions which induce a breakdown, before being brought to trial for conspiracy, when she is sentenced to twenty-five years' imprisonment.

A vote in which those voting in favour of an official proposal lose the vote to those voting against it but are declared the winners because those abstaining are deemed to have voted in favour.

Both incidents happen here: one to Martina Shanahan, convicted in the highly dubious conspiracy trial at Winchester, the other in a dispute over council-house sales in Torbay.

And Mrs Thatcher refuses to allow the Queen to visit Moscow until Mr Gorbachev has shown more genuine concern for human rights.

I am allotted my dressing-room at the National – not unlike a cell at Risley Remand Home. I share it with Michael Gambon. There is no evidence of his occupancy at all; not even a razor blade.

Four preview performances of *Single Spies* do not diminish my stage fright, the worst moment being when one pushes through the double doors from the dressing-room corridor into the staircase well and hears for the first time the amplified roar of the audience. They are only chatting together before the curtain, but it sounds like the crowd waiting for the Christians in the Colosseum. Still, both plays produce lots of laughs, the biggest always for HMQ's remark 'Governments come and go. Or don't go', which one night is even cheered.

1 December. I am reading Alan Hollinghurst's novel *The Swimming Pool Library*, which is about a rampant homosexual Wykehamist. The Wykehamists I knew at Oxford were all rather cold fish – famously so in fact – but it may be that Hollinghurst's novel explains something that happened when I went to the Age of Chivalry exhibition at the Royal Academy.

'You've only an hour,' says the ticket lady. More than enough for me, who finds shovelling coal slightly less exhausting than traipsing round an art gallery. I generally put down my fatigue to my ignorance of the contents but in this instance that doesn't apply as, being a former medieval historian, I know all about Richard II's character and Edward III and what Bastard Feudalism is. In fifteen minutes I'm shattered, so conclude it must just be art that exhausts.

I marvel at the statue of St Michael brought from Norway (or is it Sweden?), at the painted screen from some Suffolk church, and at the jewellery and swords and armour that have survived – the survival as much a miracle as the handiwork.

Of course these days my eyes are going, or altering anyway, and I catch myself joining in the bifocal minuet in front of the showcases: glasses on to see the item, one pace back and glasses off to read the card, glasses on and in to look at the item again. At one point I am bending down and peering at the information card alongside an old county lady (plenty of those about). 'This exhibit', the card reads, 'was lent by the Master and Scholars of Winchester College', to which someone (presumably a Wykehamist) has added in a beautiful italic hand, 'all of whom have big dicks'. I leave the old lady to it and bury myself in a pipe roll.

1989

January. The Government 'profoundly rejects' the report of the inquiry into the Thames TV programme *Death on the Rock.* 'Firmly' one could understand, and 'passionately' even, but *profoundly?* Of course what they actually mean is 'contemptuously'. Or, in Mrs Thatcher's case, 'furiously'.

A man rooting in the dustbin opposite stops suddenly and looks at his watch.

24 February. *Single Spies* has transferred from the National to the Queen's and is now previewing, though not without incident. Stage-hands in West End theatres are used to long runs and find it hard to turn productions round as deftly as they do in repertory. Tonight, as the lights go down at the end of the first scene of 'A Question of Attribution', I wait on the sliding truck for the projection screen to rise before the truck carries me upstage in the blackout. However, the screen does not rise and the truck moves inexorably upstage, which means that the screen demolishes everything in its path. I flatten myself on my desk and hear it swish over my head before catching me a heavy blow on the shoulder. Then, in a sequence reminiscent of *A Night at the Opera*, thirty or so slides flick rapidly through on the wildly swaying screen, a bookshelf collapses, and the Buckingham Palace set descends amid the chaos. When eventually I manage to get off, expecting to find myself the hero of the hour for having sat there as the world collapsed about me, I find that nobody realizes I've been hurt at all.

Later I run into Judi Dench, who says that when she was in *The Good Companions* she caught her foot in the revolve. It was agonizing, but she carried on, with the result that nobody was much interested in her injury. Finally she took to limping, in order to enlist some sympathy, but gave that up when the director, noticing it for the first time, thought it was part of a developing insight into her character and said, 'Love the limp, darling.'

10 March. A fat woman stops me in Parkway and puts out her hand. 'The council's put me in a hotel, me and my three kids. They said they'd send me my books, but they haven't.' I give her the coins in my pocket and come away thinking, 'Well, at least she reads. I'd miss my books too, if I were stuck in some hotel.' It takes me a time to realize that she is not talking about her treasured copies of Anthony Burgess but her social-security books.

11 March. Wake up from a dream saying, 'I have no faith in him as a sort of cricketing Velázquez, if *that's* what you mean.'

Lent is now 'the run-up to Easter'.

12 March. Names of the Albanian Football Team:
The Interpreter: Ilir Agolli.
The Manager: Shyqri Rrelli.
The Goalkeeper: Blendi Nallbani.

2 April. Hotel Terminus, Marcel Ophuls's documentary on Klaus Barbie, includes an account of how Barbie was spirited away to South America, having been recruited by the FBI, and in their comfortable suburban homes various old FBI agents recount the arrangements they made for Barbie some forty years ago. Similar revelations here would be illegal under Douglas Hurd's new Secrets Bill. But then, of course, we are a decent nation; we don't do things like that.

16 April. The ninety-eight Liverpool fans crushed to death at
Sheffield bring back memories of a similar disaster at Bolton in
1946. We never took a Sunday paper at home but sometimes saw
the *News of the World* when we went down to Grandma's on a
Sunday night, and I think I knew at eleven years old that there
was something wrong about the gusto with which the tragic
story was written up, and something prurient about the way I
gobbled up every word. Today I read very little, and because of
being at the theatre see nothing of the live coverage on
television. But already the process begins whereby terrible
events are broken down and made palatable. They are first
covered in a kind of gum: the personal reactions of bystanders,
eyewitnesses giving their inadequate testimonials – 'It was
terrible'; 'I'll never forget it'; 'Tragic. Bloody tragic' – and the
wreaths inscribed 'You'll never walk alone'. Then the event
begins to be swallowed, broken up into digestible pieces, minced
morsels: the reaction of the football authorities is gone into, then
the comments of the police, the verdict of the Sports Minister
and so on, day after day, until by the end of the week it will begin
to get boring and the snake will have swallowed the pig. Then
there are all the customary components of the scene – the
establishment of a memorial fund (always a dubious response)
and the bedside visits by the Prime Minister. I find myself
thinking, It *would* be Liverpool, that sentimental, self-dramatiz-
ing place, and am brought up short by seeing footage of a child
brought out dead, women waiting blank-faced at Lime Street
and a father meeting his two sons off the train, his relief turned
to anger at the sight of their smiling faces, cuffing and hustling
them away from the cameras.

30 April, Yorkshire. W. tells me that the Misses Blunt – Violet
and Dorothy – lived near Settle and were cousins to Sir
Anthony, a relationship of which they made much (at any rate

before his downfall). Miss Dorothy had a moustache and an eye-patch, and Miss Violet worked for a time at Giggleswick School.

They decided to leave their house and move to a bungalow at Austwick. On the morning of the removal the men arrived and began taking the furniture out. Then one of them came downstairs white-faced and took Miss Violet to one side. 'I'm afraid', he said, 'there's a woman dead in the bedroom upstairs.'

'Yes, I know,' said Miss Violet. 'It's Dorothy. She died in the night. I'm expecting the undertaker shortly.'

14 May. Resist various appeals to go down to the South Bank, where Dames Peggy and Judi are holding a vigil to protest against the bulldozing, starting tomorrow, of the site of the Rose Theatre, on the stage of which Shakespeare played. Like most archaeological sites it's closer to dentistry than it is to architecture – just a pit with some gap-toothed masonry – though doubtless the developers will capitalize on its associations and feel they are paying their debt to history by naming the building Rose House and installing a Shakespeare Carvery. Had Jerusalem been builded here and the site of the Crucifixion discovered, it would promptly be built over and christened the Golgotha Centre.

29 May. Oliver Sacks is about to set off for Japan to look at some patients suffering from Tourette's syndrome, a condition that results in an involuntary stream of abuse and obscenity. 'Japanese, you see, has no expletives. I'm most curious to know how the complaint expresses itself.'

1 June. From time to time middle-aged couples walk past the house arm-in-arm and looking around them with more than ordinary interest, as if this were a foreign town and they were visiting it. There is a house for sale up the street, and, having looked round it, they are walking down the street and trying to imagine living here. Today, though, there is a girl weeping by my wall and trying to get into a car. Now her boyfriend comes up, a tall young man in shorts, with a muscular face. They get in the car and he puts his arm round her, but she starts to argue, banging her hand on her knee and gesturing with the fingers of the hand open in a way that looks Italian. All he offers her in the way of consolation is his bag of peanuts, which in terms of consolation *is* peanuts. Still, she takes them, so that's a good sign. All it needs to end the quarrel is for her to put her hand on his knee, which she does just as my telephone rings. It is K. in New York, and I describe the scene to him, how they are now getting out of the car, the quarrel ended and the boy with something of an erection, which he adjusts in his shorts before putting his arm round his girlfriend and walking her back to Camden Lock.

2 June. A helicopter swoops low over Camden Town as President Bush departs from the American Ambassador's house, the President having left Mrs Thatcher 'holding the reins of history'.

9 June. Apropos George III I am reading Namier's *England in the Age of the American Revolution* and come across this: 'Similarly in Brueghel's *Fall of Icarus* the true humour of the tragedy is not so much the pair of naked legs sticking out of the water, as the complete unconcern of all potential onlookers: not even the fisherman who sits on the shore notices what has happened.' It pre-dates Auden's '*Musée des Beaux Arts*' by eight years or so.

11 June. In the evening to the Savile with Mary-Kay for the Hawthornden Prizegiving. I sit between Anthony Quinton and

15 *Evening Standard* Drama Awards, 1961

16 Camden Town, 1968

17 A. B. with Sir John Gielgud and some of the cast of *Forty Years On*,
Apollo Theatre, October 1968

18 *A Day Out*, Fountains Abbey, May 1972

19 and 20 Miss Shepherd's first van, Camden Town, 1973

21 *Habeas Corpus*, Lyric Theatre, May 1973

22 Gemma Fripp, George Fenton and A. B., Morecambe, September 1976

23 *Our Winnie*, Rochdale, 1982

24 *Our Winnie* with Innes Lloyd

25 With Kirk Wild, *Intensive Care*, Bradford, 1982

Iris Murdoch and am grateful for the worldliness of one and the unworldliness of the other, Quinton chatting easily and with seeming gusto and also being very funny despite having flown back from Boston that day, while Dame Iris keeps up a constant flow of questions ('Where do you live?' 'Do you drive a car?' 'What colour is it?' 'Where have you parked?'), a nice purling stream as she tucks into the Savile's duck, followed by apple sorbet. Others within earshot are Grey Gowrie, Dirk Bogarde and Thora Hird. It's less daunting than I imagined, and I manage some sort of speech and think the worst is over. But no. Dru Heinz has detailed a dozen of the men to stand up and say a few words about me, or tell a theatrical anecdote. So I sit there while these poor sods – Piers Paul Read, John Bayley, P. J. Kavanagh – all fetch out some theatrical memoir while obligatorily praising my perception, wit, humanity etc., all of them obviously hating it, but no one hating it quite as much as me.

Nicholas Henderson manages to avoid this indignity by denying he's been asked to speak, so poor Colin Haycraft is put up in his place. Gowrie talks a little about Blunt, saying that his brother Wilfrid knew nothing of the rumours until stories started appearing in *Private Eye*. After one particularly pointed story Wilfrid rang his brother and said that, simply for the sake of the family, they should do something to scotch these tales. There was a pause. 'I think', said Anthony, 'I should come and see you.' Two days later he was exposed.

3 July. After the show [*Single Spies*] I take A. to pick up Trevor, who's gone fishing with his friend Martin up Hampstead Ponds. One or two boys are pitched by the dark water, sitting under the obligatory umbrellas (though it's a warm and cloudless night), and drifting in the water their luminous blue floats. We find Trevor and Martin just as they're packing up, not having caught anything, and we walk behind them across the embankment, Trevor a gangling, old-fashioned boy in oilskins and all the gear and the woolly cap he insists on wearing, Martin smaller and younger and more of a Cockney. They chat quietly, like two old men coming back from the allotment.

'Have you caught anything?' A. asks some other boys who are still pitched by the pond. 'Yes,' says one: 'a cold.' It's a joke he probably got from his father.

5 July. A middle-aged couple walking along the cliffs in Wales are 'brutally murdered'. The dead man's brother, unable to believe it could have happened to them, says, 'They were perfect parents, churchgoers, *non-smokers'*.

12 July. Coral [Browne] rings, having had another operation to remove a tumour from her leg. 'I tell you, darling, I feel like a fucking sieve. I've got a hole under my arm from the last operation and now another hole in my leg. And that's in addition to the holes that nature gave me.' I say how brave she is. 'No, dear – you just have to get on with it. Mind you, I've had seven operations for it now, and it just gets boring.' Then she says how Vincent [Price] has lost a lot of weight but is still insisting on going on some long trip to open an exhibition: 'But you know Vinny. He'd travel halfway across the United States to open a manhole.'

Says that despite all her radiation therapy and last week's operation she is looking wonderful. 'It's heartbreaking, dear. When I was young and needed to look wonderful I was like something the cat brought in. Now I'm seventy-six and it doesn't matter I look better than I've ever looked in my life.'

Continuing appreciations of Olivier, all of them avoiding the unspoken English question: 'But was he *nice*?'

23 July. 'On comedy Ken Dodd has read Schopenhauer, Wittgenstein, Kant, Malcolm Muggeridge, Stephen Leacock and Freud, though he is always careful not to appear a Clever Clogs' (today's *Observer*). Taking a leaf out of Isaiah Berlin's book, I suppose.

20 August. Steven Berkoff, who is currently everywhere, is quoted as saying that critics are like worn-out old tarts. If only they were, the theatre would be in a better state. In fact critics are much more like dizzy girls out for the evening, just longing to be fucked and happy to be taken in by any plausible rogue who'll flatter their silly heads while knowing roughly the whereabouts of their private parts. A cheap thrill is all they want. Worn-out old tarts have at least got past that stage.

22 August. Many drowned in the Thames when, in the early hours of Sunday morning, a dredger runs down a pleasure boat. The circumstances are bad enough – the party in full swing, the huge black dredger tipping the boat on its side before running it down, but this doesn't stop the reportage from making it worse. 'Revellers', says ITN, 'were tipped into the freezing waters.' 'Left struggling in the icy waters of the Thames' is another report. It was actually one of the hottest nights of the year, and one of the rescued says that the water was warm, only very dirty. One sane girl, whose Italian boyfriend is missing, refuses to give her name to reporters because 'she doesn't want to become a news item.' Undeterred by becoming a news item, Mrs Thatcher, in her capacity as Mother of Her People, circles the spot in a police launch and is filmed bending caringly over a computer screen in the incident room.

27 September. K. has been auditioning extras for his film, including a woman who had put down among her special accomplishments 'Flirting with Japanese men'. Had this been a joke it would almost certainly have got her the job, but it turns out to be true. She is irresistibly drawn to the Japanese and has learned the language in order to flirt more effectively. Passing Japanese in the street, she will sometimes murmur (in Japanese), 'I would like to cut your toenails in the warmth of my own home' – apparently a standard come-on in the Land of the Rising Sun. 'And does it work?' asks K. 'Oh yes. Quite often.'

28 September. Watch a TV programme in which it is said that ambulance drivers undergo a high degree of stress and that *en route* to a call their pulse habitually rises from a normal 60 to 90. Not *en route* to a call but slumped in my chair, I check my own pulse. It is 82. Note that after a successful round even show-jumpers now punch the air. Croquet next.

16 October. Trying to write with a bit more precision this morning and to come up with the right word, I remember a machine that used to be in every seaside amusement arcade. A big mirrored drum in a glass case slowly revolved and on it some (not very) desirable objects – cigarettes, lipstick, tins of talcum powder. One slid in a penny that activated a grab which one had to manoeuvre over one's chosen prize before at the critical moment releasing the grab to grip the object. Except that it never did. Either the grab moved or failed to grip or the drum revolved what one wanted out of reach. That was what happened this morning. The talcum powder, the cigarettes and the lipstick and the world and everything that is the case went on turning, the grab came up with nothing, and I wasted my penny.

4 November. More humbug from Lord Hailsham (apropos the Guildford Four): 'I cannot see how you can blame the piano if someone strikes the wrong note.' Then that complacent chuckle. If by piano he means the system of justice, then the metaphor is inaccurate. The 'wrong note' (all fifteen years of it) was struck by the police and Crown Prosecution Service – i.e. part of the workings of the piano. The thing that's wrong with the judicial system is that at the moment it isn't a piano. It's a pianola.

13 December. An article in yesterday's *Independent* says that, fanciful though it may seem, it is now pretty well accepted that a deep crease in the ear lobe indicates a propensity to heart disease. I forget about the article until I am brushing my teeth, then glance out of idle curiosity at my ear lobes, wondering how they could be creased anyway. But mine *are*, with a definite crease in one and the beginnings of a crease in the other. Of course, as the article says, such creases are quite common and often mean nothing at all, but I go gingerly to bed and today find myself looking at the world in an entirely different light, all the time waiting for the thunderbolt. It could be a punishment for having written a book about Kafka. His ear lobes were one of the few parts of his body that he was happy with; and indeed I have never had any quibbles about mine – or much interest in them. But now all that has changed. I look at ear lobes on the tube; I look at ear lobes on TV. The Archbishop of Canterbury was on tonight, and all I was interested in was his ear lobes. Which I could see. Now I can't wait for Mrs Thatcher.

Modern Life. I ring A. and Ben answers. I ask A. why he is not at school. 'Ben. Why are you not at school?' 'Asbestos in the art room.'

28 December. A respectably dressed middle-aged woman outside the post office clutches a collecting-box. About to drop a coin in

it, I see in the nick of time that it is not a collecting-box but a can
of Holsten Pils.

1990

2 January. I seem to be the only Western playwright not
personally acquainted with the new President of Czechoslovakia. I envy him though. What a relief to find oneself head of state
and not have to write plays but just make history. And no
Czechoslovak equivalent of Charles Osborne snapping at your
ankles complaining that the history you're making falls between
every possible stool, or some Prague Steven Berkoff snarling
that it's not the kind of history that's worth making anyway. I
wonder whether Havel has lots of uncompleted dissident plays.
To put them on now would be somehow inappropriate. Still, he
could write a play about it.

Though I like the sound of Havel, I'm put off by the chic of the
kind of people who are now flocking to Prague. I suppose
revolutions always attract the wrong people. When I was at
Oxford in 1956 some smart Balliol undergraduates felt that the
Hungarian uprising would benefit from their presence. They
sent round an appeal for funds, pointing out that a contingent
was going from Cambridge, so it was important that Oxford
should not be unrepresented, history for them simply the Boat
Race carried on by other means.

28 February. At the National Theatre to discuss a possible
adaptation of *The Wind in the Willows*, I run into Tony Harrison.
He talks about *Trackers*, the play he has written and is directing
about two papyrologists who piece together the fragments of a
satyr play and then take on the central roles, cocks and all. It is to

open first in a warehouse at Saltaire, near Bradford, and Tony had to meet the local press to tell them something about the play, the issues it discusses, and how it relates to subsequent cultural history. The papers came out the next day all more or less saying the same thing: 'Mucky Play for Bradford'.

17 May. Sitting outside a café in Regent's Park Road, A. and I see a transvestite striding up the street with a mane of hennaed hair, short skirt and long, skinny legs. It's the legs that give him/her away – scrawny, unfleshed and too nobbly for a girl's. He/she has also attracted the attention of someone in the snooker hall above the pub, and there's a lot of shouting. Later, as we are getting into the car, Gary, a young man crippled with arthritis, calls out to A. from the snooker hall. She knows him and asks if it was him that was doing the shouting. 'Yes,' he says proudly. 'You shouldn't.' 'Why?' he asks. 'Because', I put in weakly, 'it's a free country.' 'No, it isn't.' 'Well you shouldn't.' A. says again: 'I should think about it' – meaning, I suppose, that if it's all right to shout at transvestites, next on the list will be cripples with arthritis. This is lost on Gary, who starts to shout at us too. It's a comic encounter, and the liberal dilemma it poses impenetrable. We mustn't abuse sexual deviants, but must we also be tolerant of the handicapped who do?

28 May. As I am coming out of the house around six o'clock a young man runs past, half-naked and brandishing a hammer. He is in leather trousers and boots, and his head is shaved except for a little tuft at the back. He pauses outside number 20, at which point, the man in full view, a police car roars up the street. 'Oh, so it's not him they're looking for' is my reaction, confirmed when a second car hurtles round the corner, past the man and up the street. The young man has run across the road and hidden in the garden of number 64 as a third police car speeds past. An old man who has been observing the proceedings points a shaking hand at the garden where the young man is hiding, but the police car takes no notice of him either. More police cars arrive until there are seven in all, all full of policemen, not one of whom has yet got out to take a look. There is now a lot of high-speed manoeuvring, flashy reversing, zooming and stopping as the rear cars begins to turn round. In the course of this James R. goes over to one of the cars and asks them if they are looking for the man with a hammer, whereupon a policeman leaps from the car and, ignoring the open gate, vaults theatrically over the garden wall of number 64 shouting, 'Here, we want you!', and the young man is taken away without a struggle.

The presence of seven cars, and at least twenty policemen, not one of them with the sense just to walk up the street, makes me feel the young man deserved to get away with it. And, hammer or no hammer, I think he wasn't really a skinhead. Then I realize, absurdly, that what made me think of him as somehow more sensitive, a creature of conviction even, was that little knot of hair at the back.

5 June. R. has won his first ever prize at school. It is for the boy who kept his head in the hole longest while the others threw wet sponges at him.

27 June. To a recording session at the BBC to lay down music tracks for a short film I have written about Proust, *102 Boulevard Haussmann*. The Delmé Quartet play extracts from the César Franck String Quartet and the Fauré Piano Quartet, both possible models for the Vinteuil sonata that recurs in *À la Recherche*. Striking about the musicians is their total absence of self-importance. They play a passage, listen to it back, then give each other notes, and run over sections again. George Fenton, who is coordinating the music, also chips in, but he's a musician. David H., the director, chips in too, but he isn't a musician, just knows what atmosphere he wants at various points in the film. In the finish even I chip in, just because I know what I like. And the musicians nod and listen, try out a few bars here and there, then settle down and have another go. Now one could never do this with actors. No actor would tolerate a fellow performer who ventured to comment on what he or she was doing – comment of that sort coming solely from the director, and even then it has to be carefully packaged and seasoned with plenty of love and appreciation. Whereas these players, all of them first-class, seem happy to listen to the views of anyone if it results in them doing a better job.

We are videoing the performance for the benefit of the actors who will play the string quartet in the film, and it transpires that the Delmé Quartet have been videoed once before, by the BMA. The readiness of players in a string quartet to absorb criticism from their colleagues had been noted by doctors, and the BMA video was made to be shown to businessmen as a model for them to emulate. Perhaps it should be shown to Mrs Thatcher.

17 July. Supper with Don Sniegowski and his wife, Barbara, and with David and Maureen Vaisey. They have all recently visited Poland, where they were taken to see the church of the murdered priest Father Popieluszko, which is in the process of being turned into a shrine. Here in the church is the car in which the young priest was driven to his death; here are the clothes he was wearing when he was murdered; and around the walls, as it were the stations of his particular cross, are scenes leading up to the murder. At Christmas the crib is placed in the boot of the car, the Christ-child curled up in the same position as Father Popieluszko was curled up as he was driven to the reservoir to be murdered. Day by day the devout bring in further relics. David, who began life as a medieval historian, is excited by all this, as it shows exactly how medieval cults must have started: the accumulation of relics, the elevation of the martyr's life to the status of myth, until finally comes the sanctification, as in due course it will come for Father Popieluszko.

Don, who is American and the son of second-generation Polish immigrants, takes a less detached view, believing that it's still in the interest of the Church in Poland to foster ignorance and idolatry, and that bigotry will now flourish.

10 August. An invitation from the Vice-Chancellor at Oxford to a fund-raising dinner at Merton. 'It will be an opportunity', he writes, 'to tell you something about the university's current achievements.' Since one of the university's current achievements is the establishment of the Rupert Murdoch Chair in Communications, I feel disinclined to attend, and write back that if the university thinks it's appropriate to take Rupert Murdoch's money perhaps they ought to approach Saddam Hussein to found a chair in Peace Studies. [A pained letter eventually came back saying the university had been most careful to ensure the money came from *The Times* and not from the less reputable sections of the Murdoch empire. A visit to the university Department of Economics would seem to be in order.]

15 August. To Weston-super-Mare. A young couple get on at Reading, returning from a holiday (and possibly their honeymoon) on the Isle of Wight.

SHE: We been on a bus, a boat and two trains. The only form of transport we not been on today is a plane.

HE: Yeah.

SHE: Did I tell you that when I went to the toilet this morning
there was a pigeon on the window-sill and it was still there
when I came out?
(*Pause.*)
HE: No. You didn't tell me that.

23 August. Saddam Hussein poses with the children of the
hostages on TV, thereby producing outrage in the Foreign
Office and Downing Street. 'Nauseating,' says Douglas Hurd,
and Mrs Thatcher is said to have thrown up her hands in horror.
There's some hypocrisy here. The programme was foolish, the
propaganda crude, and Saddam H. an obvious villain, but
politicians have always made a beeline for babies. This
'nauseating obscene exhibition' (Gerald Kaufman) is only an
extension of the 'caring' image they all like to project, and with
about as much truth in it.

5 October. An article in the *Independent* entitled 'The Gate-
crasher's Guide to Berlin': 'Now is the time to visit Berlin while
the shock of the Wall is still evident, consumerism' – of which
the *Independent* is wholly innocent – 'has yet to take over and
freedom means more than a new microwave oven. Berlin in 1990
is extraordinary; go there before it becomes plain ordinary' – i.e.
before the readers of the *Mail* get round to it.

8 October. Rehearsals for *The Wind in the Willows* begin this
week. The cast are having movement classes to teach them how
to move like the animals they are representing – rabbits, weasels
and so on – and as a first step have been watching videos and
nature films. Michael Bryant, who plays Badger, is sceptical
about this, as older actors tend to be. However, Jane Gibson,
who is teaching them movement, thinks she has made a
breakthrough when Michael asks if he can take away the videos

and study them at home. He comes back next day and takes her on one side. 'I've been watching these films of badgers and the way they move . . . and the thing is they all move exactly like Michael Bryant.'

7 November. I film at a TV studio in Harlesden where Gary Lineker had been filming the previous day. The girls in the crew have still not recovered from the beauty of his thighs. 'They were so big. And so *smooth*. You could land a helicopter on them.'

11 November. A young man sets himself on fire during the Two Minutes' Silence and, as he lies on the ground burning, shouts, 'Think about the people today.' Closer in feeling and in genuine agony to what is being commemorated than anyone else on the parade, he is bundled away to be treated for 60 per cent burns at Roehampton, and nothing more will be heard of him. If Jan Palach had put a match to himself in Whitehall and not Wenceslas Square, the same would have happened. It's not called 'martyrdom' in England, just 'going too far'. Still, 'it is thought that the Royal Party were unaware of the incident,' and that's the important thing.

22 November. Phoned by the *Guardian* in a round-up of what people think of the departure of Mrs T., I say that I'm hopeless at this kind of thing and am simply relieved I shan't have to think about politics quite so much. They print this fairly uninspired comment but preface it with 'Oo 'eck' and systematically drop all my aitches. I suppose I should be grateful they didn't report me as saying: 'Ee ba gum, I'm reet glad t'Prime Minister's tekken her 'ook.' Actually, now that she has gone, what it does feel like is the week after Christmas.

24 November. In all the welter of comment on the Tory leadership crisis, no one seems to have noted how eighteenth-century it all is. Namier would have found Michael Heseltine a familiar figure: the leader of a group of 'outs' numerous enough to have to be taken into the government but who cannot be taken in without the administration being reconstructed. Hence the departure of Mrs T.

Of course the difference between politics then and politics now is that in the eighteenth century there were few issues that really divided the House, leaving members time and energy to squabble over patronage and place. Not yet quite the same, but 'the structure of politics in the age of Charles III' may be getting on that way.

28 November. Two young men come down the Bristol train, unshaven and in track suits. Looking up from my book, I wonder vaguely if they're football hooligans. They knock on the conductor's door and have a word with him, and when they go back up the train I notice one of them is carrying a policeman's helmet. All is explained when the conductor announces over the Tannoy that there are two policemen on the train, doing a twenty-four-hour rail marathon in aid of the Bristol Children's Hospital, and would we all give generously. There is a general reaching into pockets, but as the carriage awaits their return, certain questions occur. What if the collectors had not been policemen but students collecting for Amnesty, say, or Action Aid, or the Terrence Higgins Trust? Would the conductor have acquiesced so readily in a collection for them? Besides which there's the other nagging thought that hospitals ought not to have to depend on charity, and that by forking out for a hospital fund one is just playing the government's game and getting it out of the hole it has dug for itself. But now the policemen have returned and the helmet is under my nose. A pound seems the average gift, so I put one in meekly and say nothing.

8 December. Richard Briers tells me how he was going up the steps from the National on to Waterloo Bridge when he was accosted, as one invariably is, by someone sitting on the landing, begging. 'No, I thought,' said Richard – 'not *again*, and walked on. Only then I heard this lugubrious voice say, "Oh. My favourite actor." So I turned back and gave him a pound.'

That particular pitch is known to be very profitable, partly because of actors and playgoers being more soft-hearted than the general run. The beggars have got themselves so well-organized as to ration the pitch to half an hour apiece on pain of being beaten up. I find it easiest to think of Waterloo Bridge as a toll bridge, and resign myself to paying at least 50p to get across, thus sidestepping any tiresome questions about need or being taken advantage of.

11 December. I am taking A.'s three children to *The Wind in the Willows*.

TREVOR: How long does it go on?

ME: It finishes at ten.

ROBIN: Are there any of those things when they let you out for a bit?

BEN: He means intervals.

ME: Just one.

ROBIN: Oh. Those are the bits I like best.

1993

4 January. On BBC's *Catchword* this afternoon, one of the
questions is on anagrams of playwrights. Mine is Annabel Tent.
Nobody guesses it.

A joke about the Queen Mother, who in an old people's home
finds herself not treated with the proper respect. She
approaches a nurse:

QM: Don't you know who I am?
NURSE: No, dear, but if you go over and ask the lady at the desk
    she'll probably be able to tell you.

14 January. Most of the headlines this morning quote Bush's
remark that they have given Saddam Hussein 'a spanking' – a
homely term which nicely obscures the fact, nowhere mentioned, that people were killed, spanked, in fact, to death. A
couple of days ago one of our peace-keeping troops was shot in
Bosnia, and he is pictured everywhere. Maybe the Serbs or the
Croats, or whoever it was shot him, think this was just a bit of a
spanking too.

16 January. Now the papers are full of the latest scandal, the
bugged phone call between the Prince of Wales and Mrs Parker-
Bowles. I read none of it, as I didn't read the earlier Diana tapes,
not out of disapproval or moral superiority, just genuine lack of
interest. I wish it would all go away.

I am sickened by the self-righteousness of the newspapers,
which, though it takes a different form, is as nauseating in the
Independent as it is in the *Sun*. Depressed too by the continuing
corruption of public life, ex-members of the Government
moving straight on to the boards of the ex-public utilities they
have helped to privatize and reckoning to see nothing wrong in
it. Meanwhile the Government keeps at it, relentlessly paring

and picking away at the proper functions of the State; 'lean' is how they like to describe it, but it's gone beyond lean – now it's more like the four-day-old carcass of the Christmas turkey. Then an item today about babies born without eyes in Lincolnshire makes me want never to read a paper again and go and live in the middle of a field.

20 January. Collected by *The New Yorker* and taken to be photographed by Richard Avedon, now a grey-haired faun of seventy-two who says he's bored with taking snapshots in the studio (this morning Isaiah Berlin and Stephen Spender) and wants to photograph me outside. 'Outside' means that eventually I find myself perched up a tree in Hyde Park. Avedon's assistants bustle round with lights, Avedon himself scarcely bothering to look through the lens, just enquiring from time to time where the edge of the frame is. He explains he wants me to seem to sit on the branch but actually to lean forward into the camera at the same time. I try.

'You're game,' says Julie Kavanagh of *The New Yorker*. Actually I'm not game at all, just timid, and – short of taking my clothes off – ready to do anything, even climb trees, rather than be thought 'difficult'.

A propos of which is Whitman's description of himself to Edward Carpenter: 'An old hen . . . with something in my nature *furtive.*'

2 February. Late for a final rehearsal for the tour of *Talking Heads*, I rush out of the house on this bright spring-like morning to be confronted by a large pile of excrement on the path. Thinking it's a dog, I swear and am about to go in and get a bucket to swill the path when I see that shit has been smeared on the car, and the paper whoever it is has used to wipe his or her bum has been carefully stuffed into the door-handle. I swill the flags, wash the car, and, returning home this evening, wash it again with Dettol, reflecting that if my mother were in a state to know of this she would never get into the car again, would want it sold or at the very least a new door fitted. Wonder if the person who did the shitting is the same person who stove in the car window on Saturday night, but decide this is paranoia.

8 February, Newcastle. Coming back to the hotel from the dress rehearsal, I call in at the cathedral – the parish church as it must have been until about 1900. A grand medley of Church and State, the army and the professions, it's an old-fashioned place too in that you're not blitzed with information, exhibitions and outreach as soon as you set foot in the door. Here are Collingwood, Nelson's admiral, and an eighteenth-century general in the Deccan Rifles, dead on the voyage out; surgeons and solicitors of the town; neat, kneeling Tudors; plump Augustan divines; and an atmosphere of piety, property and Pledge never quite caught by anyone – even Larkin, whose life I must get on and review. I wanted *Forty Years On* to be like this cathedral, studded with relics and effigies, reminders and memorials, half-forgotten verses and half-remembered hymns. Everything fits: the crypt chapel nicely restored in the thirties, the memorial to Danish seamen dead in the war, the brasses rubbed to extinction before a lavish twenties altar rail – time and what it has deposited.

11 February, Yorkshire. Am periodically sent statements of profits (*sic*) by Hand Made Films, which produced *A Private Function*. Each year the loss escalates, and it now runs at some £2 million for a film that cost two-thirds of that. Write back suggesting they submit the statement as an entry for this year's Booker Prize for fiction and saying that if it won they'd probably be able to convert the prize money into a loss too.

Remember at supper in Giggleswick that, when I was a boy in Armley, the clothes-horse was called the 'winter edge' – actually the 'winter hedge'. W. suggests, poetically, that it was because, laden with clothes, it would look like a hedge covered with snow. More plausibly, it was because in summer clothes could be spread on the hedge (though not in sooty Armley) and in winter on the horse. The other name for it, remembered by W.'s eighty-five-year-old mother, is 'clothes maiden'.

16 February. A child lured away by two boys in Bootle and found battered to death and run over by a train. A boy is taken in for questioning, and crowds gather outside his house, jeering and hurling stones, so that the family have to be taken away to a place of safety; the boy is later released. The ludicrous Mr Kenneth Baker blames the Church, and in particular the Bishop of Liverpool, David Sheppard – probably because he's the only socialist in sight.

22 February. A large crowd gathers outside Bootle Magistrates Court to jeer as the vans carrying the two ten-year-olds accused of the toddler's murder are driven away. One man eludes the police cordon and manages to bang on the side of the van, and six others are arrested. Yesterday Mr Major appealed for 'less understanding', as indeed the *Sun* does every day of the week.

> The single and peculiar life is bound
> With all the strength and armour of the mind
> To keep itself from noyance.

Come across this, said (I think) by Resencrantz. As so often with Shakespeare, you wonder what sort of life he led, how he came to know this. It takes in most of Larkin's life.

A regular from Arlington House walks down the crescent, stiff as a ramrod, upright, respectable. By his side and pressed as firmly into the seam of his trousers as the thumb of a Guards sergeant-major is a can of McEwen's lager.

10 March. The *Independent* pursues its campaign against John Birt over his tax arrangements. On another page it boasts its acquisition of Jim Slater as its Stock Exchange commentator.

13 March. To Weston to see Mam, who is dull-eyed, expressionless, absent. The sun is hot through the blinds, and the radio full on. 'My,' says a nurse (who's not really a nurse), bending over the wreck of some ex-Somerset housewife, 'it's 12.30. Doesn't time fly when you're having fun!' Downstairs comes an uninterrupted lamentation from some caged creature. 'Well,' says the nurse, spooning another dollop of rice pudding into a gaping mouth, 'what I say is, If you've got lungs, why not use them?'

20 March, Yorkshire. Late on Saturday afternoon I drive over to the Georgian Theatre at Richmond and do my piece. Half the audience are in dinner-jackets, part of a group paying extra to dine afterwards with the Marquis of Zetland, thus raising more money for the Dales Museum. Nobody comes round, and since I've cried off the dinner I come away feeling unthanked but also obscurely pleased, as it shows I'm just the entertainment, below stairs the proper place for the actor, and which I'm in favour of if only because the opposite can be so dire. So, while half the audience are dining at Aske with the Zetlands, I am sitting in the Little Chef at Leeming Bar having baked beans on toast. Which is what I prefer, so it isn't a grumble. But I catch myself here doing a Larkin (or being a man) – i.e. claiming I don't want something, then chuntering about not getting it.

9 April, Good Friday. 'It's *Good* Friday!' shouts the ginger-haired young man who presents *The Big Breakfast*, as if the goodness of the day were to do with having a good time.

What nobody seems to say (and what I didn't say) about Larkin's idea of the artist – lonely, unpossessed and unpossessioned – is that it's both romantic and conventional. Pearson Park was a garret.

15 April. Lady Thatcher back on the scene, lecturing the world about Bosnia, with 'Bomb the Serbs' her solution. She doesn't begin by saying, as any fair-minded person would, 'I admit I supported the Serbs to start with,' just hoping no one will remember that (and having some glib answer if they do).* Most people would also say that the fewer arms there are on the market the easier these conflicts would be to settle, and that anyone whose family is involved in arms-dealing would do better to pipe down about the moral issues. Nobody points this out – least of all to her.

18 April. A seventieth-birthday party for Lindsay Anderson in St Mary's Church Hall, Paddington. Lindsay in one of his presents, a silk dressing gown ('I'm wearing it to show that I am quite happy to direct Noël Coward if asked'). A wheelchair has been provided for a ninety-year-old guest who hasn't turned up, so Lindsay commandeers it and is wheeled around the room getting older by the minute. The room is full of all sorts of people, with show business probably in a minority, and offhand I can't think of any other director who'd be given a birthday party like this, and with such lovely parish-hall food. 'A very English occasion' is how it would be described. The church hall was

---

* I was told at the time I was wrong about this and that she hadn't supported the Serbs. I felt (and feel) pretty unrepentant about this, accuracy never having been Lady Thatcher's strong point either.

built after the parish had discovered that it owned the land on which the A40 flyover had been built and so was compensated with several millions – a real-life Ealing Studios plot.

11 May. To Weston. Besides the women, Mam's room now has two men: Cyril and Les. Cyril is small and plump with a little secret smile, as if he's sitting on an egg; Les has a bad chest and does what Mam would once have called 'ruttles', i.e. gargles with phlegm. He can't speak except as part of a routine he does with the cleaner. She says, 'Les, Les,' and, having got his attention, 'Boom tee bum bum.' And Les (sometimes) says, 'Bum Bum.' This is as much laughed at and applauded as if he were an elephant that had got on its hind legs.

15 May, Yorkshire. Sitting in the car at Richmond, waiting while R. has a look round, I see out of the corner of my eye a middle-aged woman crossing over towards the car with a broad smile on her face. I assume I have been recognized and am about to be accosted, and compose my features in a look of kindly accommodation. Even so I am a little taken aback when the woman, without even knocking on the window, actually opens the car door. Still, I don't show any surprise – this is a fan, after all. But not merely does she open the door, she gets in, sits down beside me, and closes the door. Still I make no protest. She settles herself, then finally turns to me, still smiling. 'Only in Yorkshire . . . Bloody Hell! I'm in the wrong car!' and bolts, running back along the pavement to her by now wildly gesticulating husband. The person who is really shown up by the story is, of course, me.

Tony Cash tells me that he saw *A Lady of Letters* done on French TV. When Miss Ruddock is watching the young couple who live opposite her, she remarks, 'The couple opposite just having their tea. No cloth on. Milk bottle stuck there, waiting.' This has been translated as 'The couple opposite just having their tea. No clothes on. Milk bottle stuck there waiting.' It's the milk bottle that intrigues.

8 June. Man overheard in Oxford Street: 'Can that cow shop! Jesus!'

18 June. Alan Clark's *Diaries* mention being smiled on in the lobby by the Prime Minister. Idly opening Chips Channon's *Diaries* I find a similar note, re Chamberlain. Courts do not change whether the court is at Westminster, Versailles or even British Airways – Lord King's rare smiles presumably a high favour. But that grown men should garner a little hoard of smiles from Mrs Thatcher and find something to comfort them there makes me thankful this dull morning to be sitting at my desk, watching the rag-and-bone man push his cart past the window, his Jack Russell stood eagerly in the prow as if waiting to strike land.

On *Any Questions* on Radio 4 tonight are Roy Hattersley and Edward Heath, Janet Cohen and Jonathon Porritt. Neither Heath nor Hattersley is a particular favourite of mine but, because no one on the panel is extreme in their views, discussion is sensible and without point-scoring and one has the feeling by the end of the programme that the topics have been properly aired and some understanding achieved. Contrast this with *Question Time* on BBC1 last night with Norman Tebbit, Shirley Williams and some unidentified industrialist. Tebbit played his usual role of a sneer on legs, snarling and heaping contempt on any vaguely liberal view, and the discussion – which was no discussion at all – was rancorous and rowdy and left all concerned as far from enlightenment and understanding as they had been at the start. It is *Any Questions* of course that is the exception, *Question Time* with its shouting and ill-temper very much the norm. And for this we have to thank the ex-Mrs Thatcher and her cronies: they have un-civilized debate and denatured the nation.

25 June. Walking in the park, we pass some young black boys playing football. One gets a shot at goal which the goalie, in the way of goalies, does not think the so-called defenders should have allowed him. However, he manages to save the ball and throws it back into play, shaking his head and saying, as a reproof to his own team, ' 'Ave a word, 'ave a *word*.' I take this to mean 'Pull your socks up' or, as they would say in Yorkshire, 'Frame yourselves.'

Having espoused the attitudes of the thirties, the *Spectator* now seems to be aping their style: 'Her mind was as sharp as any I have known.' Thus Charles Moore on Shirley Letwin. Buchan is alive and editing the *Sunday Telegraph*.

11 July. An ex-prisoner turns up at the Drop-In Centre in Parkway. He is violent, and the Centre telephones for help to Social Services, who tell it to send him round. The Centre does so, phoning to say that he's on his way and that he's armed, though not saying with what. It's actually a syringe filled with blood, which he claims is Aids-infected, and he makes his way through Camden Town brandishing this at horrified passers-by. At Social Services he says it's not his own blood but that he bought it at Camden tube station for £1, and when a social worker bravely tries to persuade him to give it up he takes the cap off as if he's cocking a gun. Eventually he is coaxed into a taxi, the social worker goes with him and *en route* for the Royal Free persuades him to give up the syringe, which is then flung out of the window.

Had Harriet G. not told me the story I would put it down as an urban myth. But it isn't, the most chilling part of the saga the syringe changing hands for £1 as a profitable investment. The social worker who took him to hospital deserves the George Medal, but he's more likely to be dismissed by Mrs Bottomley as just another ancillary worker bleeding (*sic*) the Health Service dry.

18 July. Lord (ex-Chief Rabbi) Jakobovits is in favour of genetic engineering to rid the world of homosexuality. I wonder whether he's always been in favour of medical experiments.

11 August. Neville Smith sends me a menu from Virginia Woolf's, a restaurant and bar in the Russell Hotel, which tells prospective diners that Virginia Woolf was 'a modernist writer', a member of the Bloomsbury Group 'which used to meet at 46 Gordon Square where topics for discussion were Philosophy, Religion and the Arts'. Dishes include Jacob's Burger (a burger in a creamy mushroom sauce), Mrs Dalloway's (sauce poivre, pink and green peppercorns, cream and brandy) and Orlando's (hot chilli sauce). As a dessert you can have 'Virginia's favourite: deep-fried banana with vanilla ice-cream, real maple syrup and cream. Irresistible.' Carol Smith says, 'Well, if that was her favourite I'm not surprised she sank like a stone.'

25 August. Asked to write the entry on Russell Harty for *The Dictionary of National Biography*, I duly send it off. A card from Ned Sherrin says he has been landed with Hermione Baddeley on the same principle – i.e. if he didn't do it nobody else would. His contribution had been returned to him because it lacked the full name of her second husband – something she didn't know herself, as she always referred to him by his initials.

Shot of a dead whale being slowly winched up a ramp. Men with satchels of knives move in and slit it open. Titles come up: 'The Art of Biography'.

6 September. Work in the morning, get my lunch – cold chicken and beetroot – then bike down to Bond Street. I look in Agnew's, buy some soap in Fortnum's, and end up in the Fine Arts Society, where there is an exhibition of American prints. I chat to two of the partners about F. Matania, an illustrator I have remembered from my childhood and whom I'd like to know more about. Then I get on my bike, having spent a civilized afternoon – the kind that leisured playwrights are supposed to spend. Except that when I get home T. says, 'What are those red stains on your chin?' And all the time I have been dallying in Fortnum's and idling in Agnew's and chatting in the Fine Arts Society my chin was covered in beetroot juice so that I must have looked as if I'd been sucking an iced lolly.

15 September. There are three reporters. The woman is smartly dressed, hair drawn back, hard-faced and ringing the bell at this moment (and now rattling the letter-box). They have been outside the house for two hours, since eight o'clock this morning, and, though there has been no sign of life or anything to indicate I am at home, madam periodically strides briskly up to the door and rings the bell as if it were the first time she has done it. She is at it again now, and clip clip go her little heels as she trips back down the path. Across the road her companion waits – a solid middle-aged man with bright white hair and glasses: a sports outfitter perhaps, the secretary of a golf club, even chairman of the parish council, though there is something slightly seedy or lavatorial about him, but nothing to suggest he is a reporter or a photographer on the *Daily Mirror*. I'm mildly surprised that both of them *read* the *Mirror*: they sit in their car drinking coffee and looking at their own paper, pigs wallowing in their own shit. The third, slightly forlorn, figure is a balding young man in a Barbour who rang the doorbell last night to say he was from the *Daily Mail* – the first time I was aware I had done anything to attract any attention. I closed the door in his face then and now he is back, but with no car to sit in he stands disconsolately on the pavement, picking his nails. Meanwhile the phone rings constantly.

All this is because in a profile in *The New Yorker* a week or so ago I made a few unguarded remarks about my personal life. These are apparently reprinted and amplified in this morning's *Mail*, as if I had approached the paper anxious to come clean.

'Hello?' The balding young man is calling through the letter-box. 'Hello, Mr Bennett. Can I have a chat? I just want to clear up one or two misconceptions.'

Periodically the chairman of the parish council pokes his little lens through the car window and takes yet another photograph of the mute house.

Around four the shifts change and Ms Hardface and the chairman of the PCC go off, leaving a bearded young man to do duty for them both.

'I don't want to make your life a misery,' says one of the notes put through the door.

I think of George Steiner, who asked Lukács how he got through so much work. 'House arrest, Steiner. House arrest.'

16 September. A. N. Wilson thoughtfully weighs in, this time in the *Evening Standard*, comparing me with Liberace and Cliff Richard and saying I have been boasting about my sex life. 'You silly prat' is what I feel, wondering how anyone who writes for such a rag as the *Standard* feels in a position to say anything about anybody. The littleness of England is another thought. All you need to do if you want the nation's press camped on your doorstep is say you once had a wank in 1947.

26 September. Six days in France, much of it in drenching rain, driving round Provence. Most towns and villages now meticulously restored – Lacoste, Les Baux, Arles, Uzés, the cobbles relaid, the stone cleaned and patched, everywhere scrubbed and made ready – for what? Well, for art mainly. For little shops selling cheap jewellery or baskets, for galleries with Provençal pottery and fabrics, bowls and beads and 'throws'. Better, having done the clean-up, to put a machine-shop in one of these caves, a butcher's where a butcher's was, a dry-cleaner's even. But no, it's always art, dolls, kitchenware, tea-towels. And people *throng* (myself included), Les Baux like Blackpool.

Arles is better because a working place still, and with a good museum of monumental masonry – early Christian altarpieces, Roman gravestones – and beneath it a labyrinth of arcaded passages that ran under the old Roman forum. The Musée Arlaten, on the other hand, is rather creepy, the walls crowded with primitive paintings of grim females – Arlésiennes presumably – and roomfuls of nineteenth-century folkish artefacts, collected under the aegis of the trilby-hatted poet Frédéric Mistral, whose heavily moustached image is everywhere. Many of the rooms contain costumed dummies which are only fractionally less lively than the identically costumed attendants, some of them startlingly like Anthony Perkins's mother in *Psycho*.

Then to an antique fair in the middle of some *zone industrielle*, every stall stocked with the appurtenances of French bourgeois life: great bullying wardrobes, huge ponderous mirrors and cabinets of flowery china. For the first time in my life I find myself longing for a breath of stripped pine.

12 October, Baltimore. Edward Kemp, the National Theatre's staff director, goes into a diner. 'How do you like coffee?' asks the waitress, who is black.

'White, please,' said Edward.

'Excuse me?'

'White . . . with milk.' The explanation notwithstanding the waitress marches away into the kitchen, refusing to serve him.

Another waitress comes out, also black.

'All I want,' says the hapless Edward, who has not twigged, 'is a white coffee.'

'No,' says the waitress. 'You want a brain.'

26 October. The queue outside the post office this morning trails right up past the (now closed) Parkway Cinema, where half a dozen people are sleeping in the doorway. Sunley, who demolished the St James's Theatre back in the early sixties, are still at it thirty years and a clutch of knighthoods later. I suppose Mr Major would cite the redevelopment of the cinema as evidence of 'the recovery'.

8 November. The Government is preparing to sell off the forests and nature reserves. I wonder whether it ever occurs to the fourteen-year-olds who staff the Adam Smith Institute that such seemingly unrelated policies have something to do with the rise in crime and civil disorder generally. Paid to think the unthinkable, do they not see that unless the State is perceived as benevolent – a provider of amenities, parks, art, transport even – how should it demand respect in its prescriptive and law-giving aspect? Particularly when the law is represented by Group 4.

24 November. Some junior minister blames the Bulger murder on the Church of England's failure to teach the difference between right and wrong. Poor Church. It's supposed to hold the Government's coat (and its peace) while the Government kicks the shit out of society, and then it has to take the blame for the damage that's been done.

28 November, Leeds. Fewer beggars in Leeds than in London, though I notice today a young man approach a woman asking for some change. 'Oh, *don't*!' she wails in a tone so heartfelt it's as if his necessities are the day's last straw.

Forty years ago beggars in Leeds had specific locations. Bond Street was patrolled by the smarter prostitutes but also by Cigarette Liz, an old gypsyish woman in half a dozen coats and with a stained tab end always dangling from her lips. Outside Trinity Church on Boar Lane was a man with a flat cap and deformed legs, his hands resting on what as a child I took to be blocks of Sunlight soap which I thought he was selling, but which were the grips on which he hauled himself along. No one seemed to give him anything, perhaps because, like me, they just thought of him as a feature of the street.

Someone I took for a long time to be a tramp wasn't at all. Dirty, often drunk, in a greasy overcoat and very Jewish, he would hang around the art gallery or slump over a book of paintings in the reference library, where he would be periodically woken up by the staff and told, 'No sleeping.' This was the painter Jacob Kramer, an early Vorticist and contemporary of Nevinson, William Roberts and Wyndham Lewis. I had often looked at his portrait of Delius in the art gallery without knowing that, like Proust's Elstir, this down and out was the painter.

Roberts, who was Kramer's brother-in-law, was often to be seen in Camden Town in the seventies. An apple-cheeked man, he looked like a small rotund farmer but wasn't at all amiable and if one got in his way on the pavement he would unleash a torrent of abuse. Knowing his wife slightly, I was once asked back to tea but made to promise that should Roberts appear I was to show no interest in painting. When he didn't I was both relieved and disappointed.

29 November. In one strategem for not working today I find myself carefully cleaning off the accumulation of dried ointment from the nozzle of the Vaseline Derma Care hand-lotion dispenser.

1994

13 January. Having supper in the National Theatre restaurant are Lindsay Anderson and Gavin Lambert. 'I suppose you like this place,' says Lindsay. I do, actually, as the food is now very good. I say so, and Lindsay, who judges all restaurants by the standard of the Cosmo in Finchley Road, smiles wearily, pleased to be reassured about one's moral decline.

Gavin L. is *en route* for Tangier to see Paul Bowles. I say that Bowles must be quite old now.

'Yes,' says Gavin. 'Eighty-two.'

'That's not so old,' says Lindsay.

'Well it's a funny age, eighty-two,' says Gavin. 'I've known several people of eighty-two who haven't made it to eighty-three.'

I don't think this is meant as a joke.

15 January. I go into the chemist in Camden High Street and find a down-at-heel young man not quite holding the place to ransom but effectively terrorizing the shop. He keeps pulling items off the shelves, and waving them in the face of the blonde assistant saying, 'This is mine. And this is mine. The whole shop's mine. It's bought with my money. So don't you order me out of the shop, you fucking cow. I *allow* you to work here.' The mild, rather donnish Asian pharmacist is a bit nonplussed, and as he serves me I offer to go next door to Marks & Spencer's for their security man. But the blonde assistant is pluckily standing her ground. The young man has a really mean face, and the pharmacist thinks the best thing is to wait until he goes. Which he is about to do when he spots a small woman in her sixties at the other end of the counter, looking at cosmetics. 'And that goes for you too,' he says, shoving his face into hers and taking a handful of eyeliners.

Suddenly the little lady erupts.

'Right,' she says, 'I'm a policewoman,' and she brandishes her identification in his face as they do in police series. 'You're nicked.'

She isn't exactly an intimidating figure and he's practically out of the shop now anyway, but it seems to decide him – he darts off into the bustle of the High Street.

'I wasn't having any truck with that,' says the unlikely policewoman, putting away what quite plainly was her bus pass, and gets on with buying some face cream.

The moral I suppose, is that you can get good behaviour off the television as well as bad.

20 January. At Paddington a throng of bewildered travellers gaze up at the Departures board, where there's a bland announcement saying that, due to building work at Heathrow, many services have been rescheduled *earlier* than in the timetable – i.e. everybody misses their train. I sit down meaning to have some coffee from my flask, only to find it's broken (an old-fashioned accident, breaking flasks something I associate with the forties). I wander round the station with the dripping flask looking for a litter bin, but because of the risk of bombs there are none. I can't just put the flask discreetly down lest it be mistaken for a bomb itself and the whole station grind to a halt, so it's ten minutes before I find a railwayman who will take it off me, by which time my train is in.

25 January. Having spoken at Norwich, I trek across England to Birmingham to speak there, never more conscious of Larkin's strictures about going round the country pretending to be oneself. It's a beautiful morning, the flat fields made dramatic and Dutch by floods and huge skies, but the whole journey is ruined by two schoolboys going off for university interviews. They try to impress one another with their knowledge of current affairs and hone their interview techniques. 'I like that Michael Howard,' says one. 'And Kenneth Clarke's a good bloke too.' Neither boy, I suppose, has ever known anything but a Tory government nor by the sound of it ever wants to.

At Birmingham I have a session with David Edgar's playwrights' class, then do another 'Our Alan' performance for a more general audience.

26 January. Run into Tristram Powell. Andrew Devonshire (*sic*) has done a diary for the *Spectator* mentioning the memoir of Julian Jebb (edited by Tristram) as one of the books he was putting in the guest bedroom at Chatsworth. 'I wish he'd leave a copy in *all* the bedrooms,' drawls Tristram. 'Then it would be a best-seller.'

Take the second draft of the filmscript of *The Madness of George III* to be printed. Nick Hytner has the good idea of fetching the King back from Kew to Westminster to prove to the MPs that he has recovered from his madness. Of course, it never happened, but the nearer one gets to production the bolder one gets. I hope it's boldness anyway.

23 February. Derek Jarman has died. I liked his writing more than I did his films, though I wish he had made the film which he once asked me to write about his father, a Battle of Britain pilot who turned kleptomaniac in his old age. Jarman dies on the eve of the fudged Commons vote which reduces the age of male consent to eighteen not sixteen. Anyone in any doubt should have compared the speech by the civilized and courageous Chris Smith with that of the bigot Tony Marlow. 'Predatory' is a word much in evidence, the frail faltering flame of heterosexuality always in danger of being snuffed out by the hot homosexual wind.

1 March. It seems pretty well accepted now that much of one's life, including the length of it and the weaknesses to which one will be prone, is decided in the womb. This would please Kafka, or at any rate confirm his worst fears: to be sentenced to death before one is even born would be for him a kind of apotheosis.

25 March, Yorkshire. Drive over into Wensleydale for the view of a sale at Tennant's. Leyburn turns out to be a High Recognition Area, and as I walk past the church two middle-aged WI-type ladies come out and their faces light up. 'Oh, do come and have a Lenten Lunch. Very simple. Delicious soup. All home-made!' Actually I wouldn't have minded the soup but I can't face the chat, though in the event I can't settle on anywhere else to eat either. Tennant's, which was a small country auctioneer's twenty years ago, with sales in church halls etc., is now a huge concern with a vast custom-built South-Forks-like pavilion complete with restaurant (where again I don't eat), changing-room for babies, computer terminals and all the paraphernalia of big business. There are some nice bits of furniture, but the atmosphere (well-heeled retired couples, women in sharp little Robin Hood hats, men in Barbours) puts me off, and, having driven fifty miles to get there, I spend ten minutes looking round then beat a quick retreat.

I drive back over Upper Wharfedale to Kettlewell on a road that used to be deserted and scarcely signposted, though this was probably twenty years ago too. Now it's obviously a scenic tour for Sunday afternoons and another outing for retired leisure. I stop and look in Hubberholme church, and sitting in a pew see a plaque on a pillar recording that the remains of J. B. Priestley are buried near this spot. I look at the war memorial to the dead of the 1914–18 war (ranks not given) and think of boys going on carts down the dale once the harvest was in. Dennis Potter's impending death is announced this morning, and I wonder where his ashes will lie. Potter's health, or lack of it, has always been a factor in his fame, so that, like Kafka, he visibly conformed to what the public thinks artists ought to be – poor or promiscuous, suffering or starved. And perhaps that's why Priestley was treated so condescendingly: because he was none of these things.

21 April. A lunch party at the Connaught for John Gielgud's ninetieth birthday given by Alec Guinness. John G. in an olive-green corduroy suit, elbows pressed firmly into his sides, hands clasped over his tummy, smiling and giggling and bubbling over with things to say and (except for a small fading of the voice) no different from when I first met him twenty-five years ago. Dame Judi is here and Michael Williams, Dame Wendy, Lindsay A., Ron Pickup and Anna Massey, Keith Baxter, Percy Harris – who's ninety herself – and Ralph Richardson's widow, Mu. I am seated between Jocelyn Herbert and Merula Guinness, with both of whom one can be happily silly.

'You see,' says Jocelyn, 'I look down this table at all these distinguished people and think, What am I doing here?' Same here, but as soon as one loses the sense of being in grand places on false pretences it ceases to be fun. Lindsay, who is on Jocelyn's other side, is amiable but made more combative by the circumstances. 'Is this very grand? I suppose it is. Jocelyn insisted I put on a tie, didn't you, Jocelyn? I thought that was very bourgeois. And she told me not to wear my leather jacket.' Since he's now a bit deaf one has to shout, and I see J. G. giving our end of the table uneasy glances as we seem to be making a lot of noise.

'*Othello*'s a silly play, I always think,' says Lindsay. 'You designed Olivier's *Othello*, didn't you, Jocelyn? *Winter's Tale* is much better. What do you think, John? Is *Winter's Tale* better than *Othello*?' 'I see no reason to make the comparison,' says John G. crisply, then snuffles, as he does when he's made a joke. Lindsay then provokes some talk about how, before doing David Storey's *Home*, John thought Lindsay disliked him. 'You *did* dislike me,' John wails. 'Take no notice, John,' calls Mu Richardson. 'This is your birthday. Shut up, Lindsay.'

Lindsay playing the bad boy only serves to emphasize how jolly the rest of it is, with John G. still able to produce stories one has never heard – how during rehearsals for *The Good Companions* the leading lady had been reluctant to come down the stairs and step on a trapdoor at the bottom for fear she'd fall through. Whereupon Jack Priestley climbed up the stairs, lumbered down the steps . . . and promptly went through. They stood round aghast gazing at the open trapdoor, when there came a voice from under the stage: 'I 'eard you laughing.'

Percy Harris talks about the stable behind St Martin's Lane where the theatrical designers Motley used to function in the thirties: it was in Garrick Yard and had been Chippendale's workshop, and when Douglas Byng first used the stable for a nightclub in the twenties Chippendale's lathe was still hanging from a beam. All Motley's costumes were stored there, and when it was blitzed early in the war John G. came down the morning after and found nothing left, just the firemen sweeping up in the *Hamlet* hats.

Alec G's hospitality is, as always, princely, Jocelyn saying she'd never tasted such wine, and when I come away there is a line of cars he's hired waiting to take all the old ladies home.

1 May. 'He/she died in my arms' is an odd phrase. M. used it of Tulip, the last of her goats, who snuffed it a few weeks back. 'She was so clever,' M. said, 'waiting until we got back from Rome, then dying in my arms at 10.30 the next morning.' It may be quite a comfortable way for a goat to go, but it must, I imagine, be most uncomfortable for a person – particularly if you're not feeling quite up to it, as presumably you aren't if you're on the way out. Or is it a general statement of things that might mean holding the dying one's hand or just being there at the bedside at the time? Because, without actually getting into the bed behind the person in question, how can he or she die in one's arms? It's as difficult to envisage as that other deathbed posture – 'He/she turned his face to the wall.' What if the bed isn't by a wall? Actually it's only men who turn their faces to the wall: women face up to things, peeping over the blanket to the last.

26 July. Upset and angered by the extradition of the two British women who've been accused of conspiracy to murder ten years (and another life) ago and now sent to face trial in Oregon. Police wait for them outside the court, but they are allowed bail in order to make their own way to Heathrow. I would make my own way to Sweden or Denmark, one of the decent countries. The original decision to extradite them was taken by nice, tubby, hail-fellow-well-met Kenneth Clarke.

I stroll round the block later thinking about this. The heat is almost tropical. Certainly it's like the South of France, because somewhere along Regent's Park Terrace there is a cricket singing – something I don't remember ever hearing in England before.

10 August. Do two interviews for *Writing Home*. In each case I find myself telling stories to the interviewers and, seeing them slightly glaze over, realize I am simply repeating stories that I have included in the book. Note that this is something to be careful of for the future. It's the same state of affairs I noticed once when having supper with Stephen Spender, namely that he was telling me lots of stories I knew already. But of course I only knew them because he had already published them in book form. There's very little in the back of the shop is the message: now that it's all out on the shelves the best plan is to pipe down.

25 August. Second day shooting a documentary on Westminster Abbey. Henry VII's Chapel, which the Abbey prefers (and the pious Henry VII would, I'm sure, have preferred) to call the Lady Chapel, is to be closed at the end of the week for cleaning and repairs, so we have two days to film all our set-ups there, which we can only do once the last visitors have gone. The set-ups include a piece on Dean Stanley's quest for the body of James I which began at the grave of his queen, the six foot five Anne of Denmark, where he ought to have been buried, and finished in the vault below the tomb of Henry VII, where James finally ended up, the founder of the Stuart dynasty snuggling up as of right to the founder of the Tudors. With the excuse of looking at the shot, I go up on the camera crane high above the bronze outer wall of Henry VII's tomb to look down on Torrigiano's effigies of Henry and his queen, Elizabeth of York. And wonderful it is, except that there is also something of the top of the wardrobe about it, the ramparts of the tomb quite dusty, with a few old planks lying about and odd bits of flex. One half-expects to see a suitcase or two.

Alfie, the grip on the crew, worked on *A Day Out*. We sit around at dinner-time swapping stories of what the BBC used to be like, deploring in particular the security men who now man the gates and know nobody, remembering the BBC commissionaires of old and one in particular, of famous surliness, who had one arm. He guarded the car park as if it were sacred ground. Once, when told it was full, Sid Lotterby, the director of *Porridge*, became so infuriated he wound down his window and shouted, 'Let me in, you old bugger, or I'll tear your other arm off.'

Alfie has a better story. The same commissionaire was a big fan of Morecambe and Wise, to whom even he deferred. As they drove in one day he stopped their car and asked if there was any chance of a ticket to one of their shows.

'No,' said Eric. 'We don't want you.' 'Why?' said the one-armed commissionaire. 'I'm your biggest fan.' 'But you can't clap.'

26 August. A fire on a cross-Channel ferry. On the *World at One* this is announced as 'a fire on a cross-flannel cherry'. The newsreader pauses, then decides the error is irretrievable and passes on, a slight tremor in his voice. Fortunately he is just finishing the news and gives way to the presenter, who talks about some slight fall in the trade figures with a degree of intensity and concentration utterly unwarranted by the importance of the subject. It's exactly what would happen on the stage.

1 September. Lindsay Anderson dies. Unusually, the obituaries are quite fair and catch the essence of him, all of them regretting that he had made so few films but praising him as a critic and a conscience. Had he been born ten or fifteen years earlier, and worked under a studio system that demanded he direct three or four films a year as a matter of routine, he might have made more rubbish but there would have been more first-rate films as well. As it was, he was too fastidious – enabled to be so, it was said, by a small private income from an aunt with a stake in Bell's Scotch whisky. The pity was that so much of his time was taken up not with working in the theatre but in futile development deals that never came to anything.

None of the obituaries mentions how consistently and constructively kind he was, shouldering other people's burdens (albeit with a sigh), housing the homeless, his flat in Swiss Cottage always sheltering someone down on their luck.

He wasn't a person it was wise to go to the theatre with, as he tended to groan aloud. 'Oh, *honestly*,' he would mutter, and turn to look in wonderment at his neighbours who were so lacking in discriminations as to be actually enjoying themselves. If in the interval you said you were quite liking it too, his eyes would close in a fastidious despair reminiscent of Annie Walker in *Coronation Street*. 'Well of course, Alan, you would. These are your people.' Then (the clincher in most arguments) a sad shake of the head and: 'England!'

He had never, so far as I know, been a schoolmaster, but there was a lot of the schoolmaster in him – sceptical, sarcastic, given to provocative exaggeration, and able to generate in his associates, as good teachers do, a longing to please. He was schoolmasterly, too, in his loves, his loyalty to a few chosen actors setting him apart as a perpetual romantic in what is a pretty hardbitten profession.

Anyone who was his friend will miss those instantly recognizable postcards with their capitals, underlinings and exclamation marks, like the one he sent me from Moscow in 1987: 'I have been standing for PEACE and MR GORBACHEV with Gregory Peck and Yoko Ono and Gore Vidal and Fay Weldon. Where were you?!'

26 September. And as I am correcting the proofs of this piece comes the death of my next-door neighbour, the publisher Colin Haycraft. He was like Lindsay A. in many ways, standing at the same ironic angle to the universe, though his anarchism was of the right rather than the left. Worn down in his last years by his efforts to retain control of Duckworth's, he never ceased to be perky and good for a laugh, my best memory of him being at the funeral of Miss Shepherd, who had lived in a van in my drive. As the hearse doors closed on the coffin, Colin loudly remarked, 'Well, it's a cut above her previous vehicle.'

1995

13 January. One of Peter Cook's jokes, several times quoted in his obituaries, is of two men chatting. 'I'm writing a novel,' says one, whereupon the other says, 'Yes, neither am I.' And of course it's funny and it has a point, but Peter, I suspect, felt that this disposed of the matter entirely. That people did write novels or poetry and were heartfelt about it didn't make much difference: literature, music – it was just the stuff of cocktail-party chatter; nobody really did it, still less genuinely enjoyed it when it was done. Forget plays, pictures, concerts: newspapers were the only reality – not that one could believe them either.

16 January. Listening to Michael Heseltine justifying the £475,000 of Mr Brown, the chairman of British Gas, I remember Joe Fitton. During the war Dad was a warden in the ARP, his companion on patrol a neighbour, Joe Fitton. Somebody aroused Joe's ire (a persistent failure to draw their blackout curtains perhaps), and one night, having had to ring the bell and remonstrate yet again, Joe burst out, 'I'd like to give them a right kick up the arse.' This wasn't like Joe at all and turned into a family joke – and a useful one too, as Dad never swore, so to give somebody a kick up the arse became known euphemistically as 'Joe Fitton's Remedy'. With Dad it even became a verb: 'I'd like to Joe Fitton him,' he'd say. And that's what I felt like this lunchtime, Joe Fittoning Michael Heseltine, and Mr Brown too.

20 January. I note how much pleasure I get from anemones. I love their Victorian colours, their green ruffs and how, furry as chestnuts, the blooms gradually open and in so doing turn and arrange themselves in the vase, still retaining their beauty even when almost dead, at every stage of their life delightful.

I used to like freesias for their scent, and when I was at Oxford and bought them in the market two or three flowers would scent a room. But florists (and certainly Marks & Spencer) have now bred a strain which has no scent at all except faintly that of pepper. Considering this is a flower which is not much to look at, the whole point of which is its scent, this must be considered a triumph of marketing.

24 January. Somebody writes from the *New Statesman* asking me to contribute to a feature on Englishness, the other contributors, the letter says, 'ranging from Frank Bruno to Calvin [*sic*] MacKenzie'. I wish, as they say.

26 January. The papers are full of the beastliness of Eric Cantona, who kicked some loud-mouthed, pop-eyed Crystal Palace supporter and got himself suspended for it – for ever, some soccer-lovers hope. Currently Walker's Crisps are running a TV advert in which Gary Lineker, returning home from Japan, sits on a park bench beside a little boy and then, saying 'No more Mr Nice Guy,' steals the child's crisps. If Walker's were smart they would make a sequel in which Lineker, making off with the bag of crisps, is stopped in his tracks by Cantona, who kicks him and makes him give the crisps back. Then the British public would be thoroughly confused.

13 February. To Westminster for the last two days of shooting The Abbey documentary. Happily they coincide with one of the rare showings of the thirteenth-century Cosmati pavement in the Sanctuary. Knowing it only from photographs, when the carpets have been rolled back I'm slightly disappointed to see the original. Portions of it – particularly the bits of *opus sectile* in black and white – I'd like to grub up and frame, but some of it seems crude and the colours vulgar, and I've no means of knowing whether the parts I like are the original stones and the vulgar bits Victorian renovation or the other way round. Certainly the much later tiles round the altar are more faded and pleasing than the harsh reds and blues of ancient glass in the original work (which probably come from medieval Islam); and the purple and green porphyry, which must of its nature be original, isn't to my taste at all.

During the day the pavement is roped off, but once the Abbey is closed I am allowed to walk across it in my stockinged feet.

14 February. A courier, a good-looking dark-haired boy, comes this Valentine's Day with a single rose for someone next door. Having rung the bell, he waits with his rose and clipboard: today's Rosenkavalier needs a signature.

Huge crowds at the Abbey for the unveiling of the Oscar Wilde window: both transepts full, with people standing (some on chairs) to catch a glimpse of the speakers. The most notable is of course the ninety-year-old Gielgud – black overcoat, velvet collar, a half-smile always on his lips as of someone prepared to indulge the world in its fondnesses but with his thoughts already elsewhere. Michael Denison and Judi Dench do the handbag scene from *The Importance*, J. G. reads from *De Profundis*, and Seamus Heaney gives the address. The congregation look sober and worthy, Gay Pride not much in evidence, with the wreath laid by Thelma Holland, Wilde's daughter-in-law, a link which vaults the century.

After the congregation clears we do cutaway shots of the window, 'the little patch of blue', and that's the end of our filming in the Abbey, which has been going on, on and off, since last September.

As the crew packs up, I go and have another look at the tomb of Henry III's children in the south ambulatory, which I've just read incorporates one of the medieval relics of the Abbey – the stone supposedly with the imprint of Christ's foot when he took off for the Ascension. I'm not sure if this is the square stone on the front of the tomb or the roundel on the top, but I lay my hand on both – as maybe pilgrims did once – though why I'd find it hard to say. It's a beautiful tomb, the arch still with traces of vermilion paint and black and green foliage, the top studded with bits of mosaic. Not expecting any elegiac feelings (I will, after all, be coming back to record the commentary), I am surprised to find how sad I am that the shoot is over and that I shan't be coming here regularly as I have the last five months.

17 February. To Leeds, where the decent cupolaed building on Woodhouse Moor that housed both the public library and the police station has been converted into a pub, The Feast and Firkin. The Woodman, the pub opposite St Chad's, has been renamed Woodies Ale Bar, in homage, I suppose, to *Cheers*. The more real community has dwindled in the last twenty years, the more cheap marketing versions of it have multiplied.

20 February. In the evening to the National Gallery for a private view of the Spanish Still Life exhibition, which I don't expect to like but do, very much – particularly the Cotáns, vivid vegetables of horticultural-show proportions (tight cabbages, huge cardoons) strung up in dark boxes as if for the strappado. There are some ravishing Zurbarán still lives, the most appealing – a beaker on a dish with a rose – belonging to the Saltwood Bequest and so to Alan Clark, who is somewhere about, though I don't see (or hear) him. Then there are lots of terrible flower paintings before some wonderful Goyas in the last room, including a heap of dead fish. The look in the eye of one of the dead bream seems familiar, then I realize it's also the look in the eye of the man throwing up his hands before being shot in *The Third of May*. Find no one to hand with whom I can quite share this (probably mistaken) perception, so come away.

22 February. Switch on *Newsnight* to find some bright spark from, guess where, the Adam Smith Institute proposing the privatization of public libraries. His name is Eamonn Butler, and it's to be hoped he's no relation of the 1944 Education Act Butler. Smirking and pleased with himself, as they generally are from that stable, he's pitted against a well-meaning but flustered woman who's an authority on children's books. Paxman looks on undissenting as this nylon-underpanted figure dismisses any defence of the tradition of free public libraries as 'the usual bleating of the middle classes'. I go to bed depressed, only to wake and find Madsen Pirie, also from the Adam Smith Institute for the Criminally Insane, banging the same drum in the *Independent*. Not long ago John Bird and John Fortune did a sketch about the privatization of air. These days it scarcely seems unthinkable.

28 February. There have been football riots in Bruges, where Chelsea have been playing. Responsible for their suppression was the commissioner of police for Bruges, one Roger de Bris. This gives quiet pleasure, as it's also the name of the transvestite stage director in Mel Brooks's *The Producers*, who makes his appearance bare-shouldered and in a heavy ball gown.

7 March. Our pillar box is now emptied at 9 a.m. not by the Royal Mail van but by a minibus marked Portobello Car and Van Hire.

10 March. To Bradford for the provincial première of *The Madness of King George*. The Lord Mayor is present, and R. sees him afterwards in the gents, mayoral chain round his neck, trying to have a pee. His badge of office dangles just over his flies, so that he has to take great care not to piss on it. Eventually he slings it back over his shoulder rather like a games mistress and her whistle.

29 March. Nell Campbell calls from New York to say that Don Palladino, *maître d'* at the Odeon and Café Luxembourg, died last night. He was very gay in his concerns, even the historical ones. 'Yes,' Nell says, 'we like to think he's with Marie Antoinette now.'

17 April. Easter Monday. On Saturday with T. and R. to Oxford, where we find most places (the University Museum, the Ashmolean) closed. Also all the colleges – and not just not open to visitors, but the gates actually locked. I ring the bell at Exeter, but there is no answer so we hang about until an undergraduate goes in (entry now by swipecard). An expressionless figure in the lodge, looking like a middle-ranking police inspector, says the college is closed. I say I'm a Fellow, which produces no change of expression but at least procures us admission, and we go into the garden and look at the

WRITING HOME

grandstand view of Radcliffe Square, – now, without cars, much improved.

The day is redeemed when, going back via Dorchester, we call in at the Abbey to look at the thirteenth-century crusader tomb of a knight struggling to draw his sword in death. The naturalism of the pose and the fall of the draperies make it extraordinarily impressive and modern-seeming. I've no notion whether the sculptor was English or French, though, as R. says, if it were in a German church he would certainly be known as the Master of the Crusader Tomb. What contributes to its freshness is that, whereas a nearby fifteenth-century tomb is covered in centuries of graffiti, the knight, perhaps because he was originally under a grille, is virtually untouched.

24 April. The Tories are now in a great hurry to mop up any corners of the state that have not been privatized, presumably against probable failure at the next election. Next on the list is the nuclear industry – not a popular project, as the decommissioning of the older nuclear power stations has no commercial attractions and safety considerations are likely to be skimped. But of course it will provide the Government with some election pin-money, which is what it wants. The real driving force, against all common sense and reason, is ideology. When the Germans were withdrawing from Italy in 1944 and were short of trains, troops and every other resource, priority was given when crossing the Po not to military formations but to the transports involved in the last-minute deportation of the Italian Jews. The analogy will be thought offensive, but it is exact. Ideology, as I think Galbraith wrote, is the great solvent of reason.

1 May. A drunk clinging on to the railings in Inverness Street gathers himself up to speak.

300

'Excuse me, squire, but how far has yesterday gone?'

'Sorry?'

'How far has yesterday gone?'

I say helpfully that it's six o'clock.

'Six o'clock? Six o'clock? What sort of fucking answer is that?'

Of course I could have said, What sort of fucking question was it in the first place?

3 May. Invited to speech day at Giggleswick, where the guest of honour is to be Lord Archer. I write back and say I can't come but I look forward to being invited next year, when doubtless the guest will be Bernard Manning. Giggleswick doesn't have many distinguished old boys, though one which it never seems to acknowledge was the critic James Agate. This reticence may be on account of Agate's well-known propensity to drink his own piss.

13 June. Three police acquitted in the case of Joy Gardner, who died after being gagged with thirteen inches of tape, a restraining belt and leg irons. It's not unexpected. I can't offhand recall any serious case in the last ten years in which the police have been found guilty and punished. Or even sacked.

20 June. Three jokes from George Fenton.

1. A man has bad pains in his bum. A friend says it's piles, so he applies various creams which do no good. Another friend says; 'No, creams are useless. What you want to do is have a cup of tea then take the tea leaves and put them up your arse. It's like a poultice. Do the trick in no time.' So whenever the man has a cup of tea he puts the tea leaves up his bum. No joy. When at the end of the week he's no better he goes to the doctor. The doctor tells him to take his trousers down, looks up his bum, and says,

'Yes. Well, there are two things to say. One is that you're quite right, you do have piles. And the other is you're going to go on a long journey.'

2. A devout Jewish man is desperately anxious to win the lottery. He goes to the synagogue and prays that he may win. Saturday comes round, but he doesn't win. Goes to the synagogue again and remonstrates with God, pointing out how often he comes to the synagogue, how devout he has been, etc., etc. Saturday comes round again and again he doesn't win. Back he goes to the synagogue and prays again to God, this time in despair. Suddenly the clouds part and there is a figure with a grey beard leaning down between the clouds: 'OK. So you want to win the lottery. But please, meet me halfway: *buy a ticket.*'

3. A man buys a green bottle at a car-boot sale. He rubs it. Out pops a genie and offers him one wish. The man asks to be the luckiest man in the world. The wish is granted and the genie disappears. Next week the man wins millions on the football pools and takes his mates out to celebrate. He explains about his luck but they don't believe him, saying, 'Right, if you're so lucky, try pulling that beautiful Indian bird.' So the man goes over and chats her up and sure enough she's all over him, they go back to her place and have a fantastic time. In the morning he wakes up and looks down at her beautiful naked body and thinks how lucky he is. She is still fast asleep, and as he gazes at her sleeping face he sees the little red spot she has on her forehead. Gently he scratches it – and wins a Renault 5.

All these come from musicians, George being the only one of my friends who still hears jokes or moves in circles that tell them, or make them up.

27 June. Most adverse comments on John Redwood's appearance remark on his resemblance to Mr Spock or someone from outer space. Actually he looks like Kenneth Williams in one of those roles (Chauvelin, for instance) when the eyes suddenly go back and he goes wildly over the top. The smirking crew around Redwood are deeply depressing, Tony Marlow and Edward Leigh both fat and complacent and looking like two cheeks of the same arse. It's all so sixth-form – the prefects in revolt.

14 July. A letter this morning saying the Tokyo production of *Wind in the Willows* is to be revived for two weeks in August, the revival to be supervised by a Nigel Nicholson. Mole and Ratty as Harold and Vita now (and Violet Trefusis as Mr Toad).

29 July, Ménerbes. Stripping some redcurrants this evening reminds me how when I was writing both *Getting On* and *The Old Country* I could never think of something for the wife to do while the husband was talking. In *Getting On* I think I made Polly top and tail gooseberries, and in *The Old Country* I even gave Bron some flowers to press (I go hot with shame at the thought). Of course, if I'd had any sense I would have seen that if it was so hard to think what it was the woman should be doing then there was something wrong with the plays or that this was what the plays should have been about, as in a way it was. Neither of the wives had seemingly ever had a job – an omission I had to some extent rectified by the time I got to *Kafka's Dick*, when the wife had at least been in employment at some period (she was an ex-nurse). But again the men did the jobs and most of the talking. In *Enjoy*, which is set in Leeds, the women do most of the talking, which is how it always used to be when I was a child. It was only when I got to London that the men started talking and the women fell silent.

8 August. A new strategy for not working: empty the fluff not only from the sieve on the dryer door, which is routine, but from the grilles on the machine itself. This involves prising off the plastic covers and poking about with a skewer to dislodge the fluff that has fallen through. A quarter of an hour can be made to pass in this way.

9 August. Surprised to find from today's *New Yorker* that Madame Chiang Kai-shek is still alive at ninety-seven. My surprise is less surprising when I realize I have her inextricably confused with the Duchess of Windsor, who I know is dead – both, in Geoffrey Madan's words, 'part governess, part earwig'.

11 August. In the yard at the back of Camden Social Services, in Bayham Street, a mound of tangled Zimmer frames.

14 August. Toothache, and I make an appointment for the dentist. The trouble is almost inevitably deep under one of my many caps and bridges. It will be like having to go through the dome of St Paul's in order to repair the floor of the crypt.

16 August. Life in Camden Town. As I come in this afternoon two young men are sitting by the garden wall drinking cans of beer. One looks like a Hong Kong Chinese; the other is Australian, fair, brown and not unlike the actor Jack Thompson, who used to figure in sheep-shearing films. I sit and work at my table, where I can hear the murmur of their talk. Then the Australian, slightly reluctantly but egged on by the Chinese, goes over and has a piss in the gateway of number 61. Before they go, the Chinese does the same. Had they not seen me come in, mine would doubtless have been the gateway they would have used. I groan inwardly at the loutishness of it all (the beer cans just left on the pavement), but a couple of hours later I am coming up Inverness Street when a large Mercedes draws up outside the Good Mixer and the two pavement drinkers get out. I suppose they're from the fashionable music fraternity which now heavily patronizes the pub, the crowd at weekends spilling right across the road, which means the street is seldom effectively cleaned and always littered with cans and broken glass first thing in the morning when I go down for my paper. The pleasures of drinking here must be diminished (or, who knows, heightened) by the squalor of the setting: the recycling bins opposite, every doorway a urinal, the pavements caked in the market's grease and muck. Such squalor is these days about average for Camden Town, the end of Inverness Street now a haunt for drug dealers.

17 August. 'Grounded', meaning a withdrawal of privileges, is a word I dislike. It's off the television (*Roseanne* notably), but now in common use. (I just heard it on *Emmerdale Farm*, where they probably think it's dialect.) I would almost prefer 'gated', deriving from forties public-school stories in *Hotspur* and *Wizard*.

Other current dislikes: 'Brits', 'for starters', 'sorted' and (when used intransitively) 'hurting'.

9 September. Drive into Oxfordshire, stopping first at Ewelme to look at the church. The village is too manicured for my liking, though the mown lawns and neat gardens don't quite eliminate an air of rural brutishness I often sense in Oxfordshire. I note features in the church I'd forgotten – the gilded angel with outstretched wings which acts as part of the counterweight for the font cover, and the angels that spread their wings to support the aisle roof. Then on through terrible Didcot to Faringdon and Buscot Park, which belongs to the National Trust. The house is well set, with beautiful long vistas down alleys of trees to water gardens and a lake, and from the terrace at the back vast views over Oxfordshire. Inside, though, it's disappointing, with a Rembrandt that I'm sure isn't, a nice

Ravilious of the house, but none of the rooms informed by vision or individual taste and like a rather dull country-house hotel.

As we're going out, a scholarly man, whom I'd seen carefully studying the catalogue, pauses by the desk. 'Could you tell me,' he asks of the lady on duty, 'how the first Lord Faringdon made his money?' She gives him a vinegary look as if the question were in very bad taste: 'I've no idea.'

11 September. Nick Leeson, the errant young man from the Singapore Stock Exchange, is interviewed in his Frankfurt prison by David Frost, the interview, made by Frost's production company, broadcast by the BBC at ten this evening. The papers, which have had a preview, are full of Leeson's self-justifications, but nobody seems to question the propriety of broadcasting such an interview in the first place. Like so many of the interviews Frost is involved with, it's a pretty seedy affair. Not that Frost isn't highly respectable, but his rise as a political commentator is in direct proportion to the decline of respect for politicians. Major, Blair and Ashdown meekly trot along to be lightly grilled by the heavily made-up Frost, and indeed use the occasion for statements of policy and matters of national importance. It's as if Jesus were to undertake the feeding of the five thousand as a contribution to *Challenge Anneka*.

[Much is explained when in October the filming of the Leeson story is announced, starring Hugh Grant and produced by D. Frost.]

14 September. The house next door is empty, and I have got its mice. Having watched a mouse last night gambolling away among the poison pellets behind the gas oven, I find this morning that it (or a colleague) is in one of the humane traps. I have been told mice have a good homing instinct, so I take the

306

trap up to the railway bridge, give the box a shaking to disorientate the occupant (and teach it a lesson), then empty it on to the railway line. I find I am a little cheered by this.

19 September. A young man walks up the street dressed with casual care in blue T-shirt and narrow jeans and with the loose, bouncing walk I associate with an (albeit humble) assumption of moral superiority. Say this to K. 'Yes. He walks like a vegetarian flautist.'

28 September. Pass a gown shop off Manchester Square called Ghost and Foale. Mention this to Mary-Kay as seeming an unusual name. Not at all, apparently, as both names are famous and fashionable in the world of frocks. More amusing to her was my calling it a gown shop.

19 October. To Accord near Poughkeepsie in New York State, where Don Palladino had a house which Lynn has been clearing out before the new owner takes over next week. It's a little clapboard cottage, idyllically situated on the bank of a broad shallow river backed by woods and looking across meadows to the distant Catskills. A huge catalpa shades the house, and beyond it is a derelict canal. We roll up matting and put it on top of the van along with two bikes, then pack the inside with bedding and books and lampshades. When it's done I sit on the brick terrace in the warm sunshine looking across the river and watching the dozens of birds, most of them strange to me – even the pheasants looking more like turkeys, as they peck about among the sweetcorn.

Emptied, the little house still manages to be a temple to Marie Antoinette. Her bust is on the mantelpiece, books about her line the stairs, and there are French wallpapers incongruously on the walls and a few damp tapestried chairs marooned in the dining-room. Most of this is to be left for the new owner, though a garrulous handyman hangs about hoping to pick up what he can. 'Of course he loved it here, only I gather he got sick.' We walk along the dried-up canal for a bit, before driving to Rhinebeck for some tea, then back along the Taconic Parkway through the famed autumn tints to a huge red sun setting over New York.

21 October. Lynn has some firewood delivered – around thirty neat boxes, panniers almost which, stacked in the hall, look so tidy and pleasing they might be an installation or an art object. These thirty or so boxes apparently constitute a *cord* of wood (128 cubic feet), which is how wood is still ordered in this old-fashioned city. I doubt if it is in London, and certainly not in rural Yorkshire.

Language: Disabled Toilet in America becomes Handi-capped Bathroom.

22 October. We pick up a cab at Lincoln Center tonight and drive to Nineteenth Street. The cab-driver says into a small microphone, 'The fare is five dollars fifty. Would you please pay the cashier?', whereupon a white rabbit, presumably a glove-puppet, appears in the interconnecting hatch and makes a bow. Lynn pays the rabbit, the rabbit bows again, the cab-driver says, 'Have a good evening,' and off he goes.

31 October. At the bottom of the moving walkway in the local Marks & Spencer's there often lurks a security man. He will be squinting under the plastic partition at the upper floor, keeping an eye on putative shoplifters (or, at any rate, their ankles). This particular corner of the store is where they sell underwear, the theft of which is, I suppose, more common and more of a thrill than nicking the broccoli, say. The security men wear beige uniforms, short-sleeved shirts and peaked caps with that steep neb which I still associate with redcaps, the military policemen who, when I was in the army, were one of the hazards of mainline stations, always lying in wait for timid and slipshod soldiers like me. The other paramilitary force in Camden are the parking wardens, who are also kitted out in peaked caps, theirs having scarlet ribbons. Though inoffensive-looking, there's something not quite right about them either. They remind me of the forces of the wicked Regent in films like *The Prisoner of Zenda*: decent enough, but misled.

12 November. The judicial murder of Ken Saro-Wiwa and his colleagues in Nigeria properly outrages world opinion. Quite apart from the merits of his case, the death of this writer has more readily caught the public imagination for a very simple reason – the euphonious nature of his name. Ken is a good ordinary start, but with Saro-Wiwa the name takes flight and, unlike many African names, is both easy to say and brings with it an almost incantatory pleasure. So in the last few days many people have been enjoying saying his name. Not, of course, that this did him any good.

28 November. Cycling down to the West End, I'll often cut out the boring windswept stretch of Albany Street by going the back way along Stanhope Street, through the council estate that was built in the fifties over what was once Cumberland Market. The tower blocks are named after beauty spots: Derwentwater, Dentdale – all of them (I see the connection now) places in what was Cumberland. Between two of the blocks is a grass plot, and in the far corner of it a curved concrete screen about ten foot high with a doorway opening on either side, this screen, and the slightly raised platform on which it stands, converting the unkempt patch into a kind of auditorium. There's no sign that it's ever used as such, but I imagine that this is what it was intended for – part of some vision for this estate back in those still-hopeful days after the war. Did the architect, I wonder, in his presentation to the planners, sell this podium as a place where pageants could be held, bonny babies paraded, or even Shakespeare performed? Probably, as architects fleshing out their bleak vision are ever sanguine and never modest. Nowadays this little Epidaurus off the Hampstead Road looks a touch forlorn; the scrubby grass is strewn with litter and matted with dog-dirt, the shops opposite operate behind steel shutters, the estate is riven with racial conflict, and nobody takes the stage.

8 December. Trying to find someone a Meccano set for Christmas, I'm reminded of a couple, friends of Russell H., who had a son of twelve or so who they were worried might be growing up gay. However, they were greatly heartened when the boy said that what he wanted for Christmas was a Meccano set. Delighted by what they saw as an access of butchness, they bought him the biggest set they could find; it was a huge success, and he took it to his room and played with it for hours. The day came when the boy asked to show them what he had been making, and they were made to wait with their backs turned while he manoeuvred it carefully into the room. When they turned round, the boy stood there shyly peeping at them from behind a vast Meccano fan.

Prefaces to Plays

Forty Years On and Other Plays

In 1969 I had a letter from a producer in BBC Radio saying he'd fished out an old script of mine from the pool and thought it might have possibilities for a radio play. I liked the idea of a producer at Portland Place dredging up drama from a pool of old paperwork, but he was six months too late and I smugly wrote back to point out that the play in question, *Forty Years On*, was already running in the West End.

In fairness, the version of the play put on at the Apollo in 1968 was very different from the one I'd submitted to the BBC two years before. There was no mention of Albion House, the run-down public school which is the setting for the play, nor of the Headmaster, whose retirement is the occasion for the presentation of 'Speak for England, Arthur', the play within the play. The memoirs of T. E. Lawrence and Virginia Woolf occur in the original script, and the visit to the country house on the eve of the First War, but these are presented as the memoirs of Hugh and Moggie, an upper-class couple who sit out the Second World War in the basement of Claridge's. The transitions in time and the representation of memory, which are hard to bring off on the stage, are the stock-in-trade of radio, but I'm thankful now that the BBC put this first script on the discard pile, thus forcing me to rewrite it in the version eventually produced on the stage. What the letter did remind me of was the struggle there'd been to find the play a shape.

To begin with, most of the parodies in the play I'd written separately and stockpiled, hoping vaguely to put together a kind of literary revue. When I began to think in more narrative terms these parodies proved a stumbling-block, as I found I had to create characters who could conceivably have had memories of, say, the age of Oscar Wilde, Lawrence of Arabia and Bloomsbury. Hence the Claridge's couple, Hugh and Moggie. When I subsequently hit on the (fairly obvious) idea of a school play, with the school itself a loose metaphor for England, it resolved much that had made me uneasy. It had all been too snobbish for a start, but once in the context of the school play, which guyed them just as much as it celebrated them, Hugh and Moggie and Nursie, their nanny, became more acceptable. They're still *quite* snobbish, of course, and certainly not the common man. But to put a play within a play is to add another frame which enables one to introduce more jokes, and also more irony as references within the play find echoes outside it. Jokes like the Headmaster's 'Thirty years ago today, Tupper, the Germans marched into Poland and you're picking your nose'; ironies like Churchill announcing peace in Europe in 1945 just as the boys in the present day fling themselves into a fierce fight.

The play enshrines some terrible jokes. One way of looking at *Forty Years On* is as an elaborate life-support system for the preservation of bad jokes. 'Sandy will accompany you, disguised as a waiter. That should at least secure you the entrée.' One of the boys is called Lord. It's true that there was such a boy at Giggleswick School, from whose prospectus I pinched some of the names, but he's only so called in order to furnish the Headmaster, wandering about holding his empty coffee cup, with the blasphemous exchange 'Lord, take this cup from me.' The child does so. 'Thank you, Lord.' But I like bad jokes and always have, and when an audience groans at a pun it's often only because they wish they'd thought of it first, or at any rate seen it coming in time to duck.

Besides, these bad jokes were the survivors; even worse jokes had bit the dust along the way. When the play opened in Manchester it included a piece about the first London visit of the Diaghilev ballet in 1911.

A boy got up as Nijinsky, dressed as the faun in L'Après-Midi, *dances behind a gauze, while downstage the practice pianist reminisces:* Ah yes. Nijinsky. I suppose I am the only person now able to recall one of the most exciting of his ballets, the fruit of an unlikely collaboration between Nijinsky on the one hand and Sir Arthur Conan Doyle on the other. It was the only detective story in ballet and was called *The Inspectre de la Rose*. The choreography was by Fokine. It wasn't up to much. The usual Fokine rubbish.

Ordinarily, good taste in the person of the Lord Chamberlain would have put paid to that last joke. But this was 1968, and *Forty Years On* was one of the plays on his desk when the Lord Chamberlain's powers expired and stage censorship was abolished.

There were other jokes, equally bad but more 'satirical'. At one point Field Marshal Earl Haig strode on, in bright red gloves: 'As you all know, I have just this minute returned from the First World War. Indeed, so recently have I returned I haven't had time to wash my hands.' And much more in the same vein. The play was such a ragbag I even considered including a story about Earl Haig at Durham Cathedral. The Field Marshal was being shown round by the Dean when they paused at the tomb of the Venerable Bede. Haig regarded it thoughtfully for a moment, then said, 'Of course. Bede. Now he was a woman, wasn't he?' It's a good example of scrambled memory, but the laborious explanations that I had to go into with the cast decided me against inflicting it on an audience.

Hugh and Moggie were suggested by – but not modelled on – Harold Nicolson and Vita Sackville-West. In 1968 Nicolson's diaries had just been published, with his passionate account of the fight against Appeasement in the thirties and how, come the war, appeasers like Chips Channon conveniently forgot to eat their words about Germany and pretended they'd been right all along.

The play is stiff with quotations. The readings from the lectern enable actual quotations to be incorporated into the structure of the play, but there are umpteen more, some lying about on the surface in mangled form and others buried in shallow graves. 'Patience is mine: I will delay saith the Lord.' 'They are rolling up the maps all over Europe. We shall not see them lit again in our lifetime.' Some quotations I have lost track of. I thought I'd invented the phrase 'snobbery with violence' to describe the school of Sapper and Buchan (and Ian Fleming, for that matter), but then I was told it had been used before, but where and in what circumstances I have forgotten.*

The form of *Forty Years On* is more complicated than I would dream of attempting now. It is a play within a play in which the time-scale of the first play gradually catches up with the time-scale of the second, one cog the years 1900–39, the other 1939–45, and both within the third wheel of the present day. What doesn't seem to have worried me at the time is what kind of educational institution it is that would mount such a production. This didn't seem to worry the audience. After all, it is only a play. Or a play within a play. Or a play within that. Plenty of jokes anyway (too many, some people said), and it's hard to fail with twenty-odd schoolboys on the stage. I've a feeling they (and the set) came via a Polish play, *The Glorious Resurrection of Our Lord*, that I saw in the World Theatre

* It is the title of a book by the New Zealand eccentric, Count Potocki de Montalk, for whom see *The Diary of Virginia Woolf* (ed. Bell) vol iv, p. 76n.

season at the Aldwych in 1967, in which choirboys sang above a screen that ran across the stage. I saw *Zigger Zagger* that year, too, with the stage a crowded football terrace, which made me realize how theatrical a spectacle is an audience watching an audience.

Because *Forty Years On* employs a large cast, and also because it is as much a revue as a play, it seldom gets performed. Schools do it from time to time, and ironically, in view of the Headmaster's strictures, sometimes find it necessary to cut the confirmation class. This raises the dizzy possibility of the pretend headmaster rushing on to the stage to put a stop to 'this farrago of libel, blasphemy and perversion' only to find the real headmaster hard on his heels, bent on putting a stop to him putting a stop to it.

Forty Years On had been such a happy experience that when, in 1971, I wrote my second play it was natural that Stoll Theatres, who'd put the first one on, should want to keep the winning team together. Accordingly, we had the same director, Patrick Garland, and the same designer, Julia Trevelyan Oman, and the management even contrived that we should begin rehearsing on the same stage, Drury Lane, and on the same day, August Bank Holiday, as three years before. In some cultures they would have slit the throat of a chicken. In view of what was to happen it would have been just as effective.

Getting On is an account of a middle-aged Labour MP, George Oliver, so self-absorbed that he remains blind to the fact that his wife is having an affair with the handyman, his mother-in-law is dying, his son is getting ready to leave home, his best friend thinks him a fool and that to everyone who comes into contact with him he is a self-esteeming joke. Nowadays one would just say, 'Oh, you mean he's *a man*,' and have done with it. But in 1971 the beast was less plain, the part harder to define, and casting the main role proved a problem. The script was turned down by half a dozen leading actors, and I had begun to think there was something wrong with the play (there was: too long) when Kenneth More's name came up. Kenneth More was, to say the least, not an obvious choice. As an actor and a man he had a very conservative image, and to many of my generation he was identified with one of his most famous parts, that of Douglas Bader in the film *Reach for the Sky*. It was one of the films we were making fun of in the Aftermyth of War sketch in *Beyond the Fringe*.

I had a pretty quiet war really. I was one of the Few. We were stationed down at Biggin Hill. One Sunday we got word Jerry was coming in, over Broadstairs, I think it was. We got up there quickly as we could and, you know, everything was very calm and peaceful. England lay like a green carpet below me and the war seemed worlds away. I could see Tunbridge Wells and the sun glinting on the river, and I remembered that last weekend I'd spent there with Celia that summer of '39.

Suddenly Jerry was coming at me out of a bank of cloud. I let him have it, and I think I must have got him in the wing because he spiralled past me out of control. As he did so . . . I'll always remember this . . . I got a glimpse of his face, and you know . . . he smiled. Funny thing, war.

Some nights, greatly daring, I would stump stiff-legged around the stage in imitation of Douglas Bader, feeling priggishly rewarded by the occasional hiss. Douglas Bader, that is, as played by Kenneth More; and here we were casting him as a Labour MP. It seemed folly. But was it? A veteran of many casting sessions since, I have learned how the argument goes. When all the obvious choices have been exhausted, a kind of hysteria sets in as more and more unlikely names are suggested. The process is called Casting Against the Part, and it's almost a parlour game; a winning combination would be, say, Robert Morley as Andrew Aguecheek.

All of which is to do an injustice to Kenneth More, who was a fine naturalistic actor, and, although he had never stepped outside his genial public stereotype, Patrick Garland and I both thought that if he could be persuaded to do so it might remake him as an actor. The example of Olivier and Archie Rice was invoked, with high-sounding phrases like 'taking his proper place in the modern theatre'. In retrospect it seems silly, conceited and always futile. Kenneth More had no intention of remaking himself as an actor. Why should he? His public liked him the way he was. It would be much simpler to remake the play, and this is what he did. However, all this was in the future. We had lunch, he was enthusiastic about the play, seeing it as a great opportunity, and so the production went ahead, with Mona Washbourne, Gemma Jones and Brian Cox in the other parts.

I didn't attend many of the rehearsals. I still wasn't certain that one should. The question had not arisen in *Forty Years On*, since I was there anyway as a member of the cast. Practices differ. Some playwrights attend the first read-through (and sometimes *do* the first read-through), then aren't seen again until the dress rehearsal. Others are at the director's elbow every day. There is something to be said for both. When one only puts in an occasional appearance the actors tend to think of the author as the Guardian of the Text, an uncomfortable and potentially censorious presence before whom they go to pieces. On the other hand, a playwright who is at every rehearsal soon ceases to be intimidating but has to exercise a corresponding tact. The temptation to put one's oar in is strong. Actors come to a performance slowly; blind alleys have to be gone down, toes slid gingerly into water. To the playwright (the brute) the cast seem like small boys stood shivering and blowing into their hands on the side of a swimming-bath. Why don't they just dive in and strike out for the other end with strong and perfect strokes? After all, it's perfectly obvious to the playwright how to do the play. He could do it himself if only he could act.

It seemed easiest to keep away, which is what I did. When I'm asked these days why I invariably go to rehearsals and on location with films, I have some nice answer ready. But if I'm honest it's because that autumn with *Getting On* I made a wrong decision. I wrote in my diary:

The saddest thing about this production so far is that it is getting on quite well without me. I go down to the theatre from time to time, sneaking into the auditorium without being seen in case my presence should make the actors nervous. If they do see me they ply me with questions about the text. 'Would he say this?' asks Kenneth More, pointing to an inconsistency. 'No, *he* wouldn't,' is what I ought to say, 'but *I* would.' Instead I construct a lame theory to justify the inconsistency. 'What is she doing upstairs at this time?' asks Gemma Jones. 'Why did you send her off?' Why indeed? Because I'd run out of things for her to say, probably. 'Maybe she's putting the children to bed,' is what I answer. When a play's being cast it might be as well to pick someone to play the author too for all the help he can give them.

Even with the final dress rehearsals no alarm bells rang. The play was too long, admittedly, and ought to have been cut in rehearsal or, better still, beforehand, which is another lesson to be learned: if there are to be cuts, get them over with before rehearsals begin. But there was still a fortnight's tour in Brighton when all this could be done. No panic.

Now Brighton is a dangerous place. It is the home or the haunt of many theatricals, who take an entirely human pleasure in getting in first on plays bound for the West End. They come round, proffer advice, diagnose what is wrong, and suggest remedies. That is one section of the audience. The other consists (or did in 1971) of playgoers for whom the theatre has never been the same since John Osborne, and if they don't like a play they leave it in droves. Indeed, it sometimes seems that their chief pleasure in going to the theatre in Brighton is in leaving it, and leaving it as noisily as possible. In *Beyond the Fringe* the seats were going up like pistol shots throughout the performance so that, come the curtain, there were scarcely more in the audience than there were on the stage. On the other hand, *Forty Years On* had done well. Brighton was where Gielgud had got his second wind and the play came into focus. But that was familiar ground. Audiences at Brighton like what they know and know what they like, and one person they did like was Kenneth More.

Until he was actually faced with an audience Kenneth More was scrupulous about playing the part as written (and some-times overwritten). It's true he flatly refused to say 'fuck' since it would ruin the matinées, but this didn't seem to me to be important, so long as he continued to play George Oliver as the kind of man who did say 'fuck' (the play maybe just happening to catch him on a day when he didn't). Kenny himself, of course, said it quite frequently in life, but that was neither here nor there. The first night in Brighton didn't go well, and I was surprised (it is evidence of my own foolishness) how nervous the audience made him. Nothing in his debonair and easy-going exterior prepared one for the vulnerable actor he became that night. It was plain he had been expecting the audience to love him, and when they didn't he felt lost.

That first week the Brighton audience lapped up the jokes but yawned at the bits in between. We made some cuts, but found it hard because it was now plain that Kenneth More saw the piece as a comedy while I was trying to keep it a serious play. At the beginning of the second week in Brighton, and without there having been any warning or disagreement, he called a rehearsal to cut the play to his own taste, while instructing the management not to allow me into the theatre until this had been done. The following day I found myself barred from the theatre altogether, and in fact never saw the play in its entirety from that day until it closed in the West End eight months later. When it was playing at the Queen's I'd sometimes slip in to see how it was going, find he'd introduced more new lines to make his character more acceptable to the audience, and come away feeling the piece had nothing to do with me at all. The younger members of the cast were fine, but there seemed to be an alliance between Kenneth More and Mona Washbourne to make it all nice and palatable, and with no ambiguity. I've always felt the play is too plotty, but it wasn't plotty enough for them. George is meant to be so self-absorbed that he has a diminished sense of the existence of others. Finding it unbearable that he should be playing a character who doesn't care that his mother-in-law may be dying, Kenny had inserted his own line: 'I'll go and see her doctor tomorrow.' I wrote in my diary at the time: 'It's as if after Tuzenbach's death in *Three Sisters* Irena were to come on and say, "I have three tickets for the 11.30 train to Moscow tomorrow. I have rented us a beautiful apartment and I already have my eye on several possible husbands."' But not really, because, alas, it isn't *Three Sisters*. I took it all very seriously. Two more diary entries:

It has been my experience that when directors or management start talking about the importance of the text it is because they are about to cut it. In the same way the people who talk most about the sanctity of human life are the advocates of capital punishment.

Seeing this production of my play without having attended the rehearsals or had anything to do with it until I actually saw it on stage is like going to see a relative who has been confined in an institution. A parent in a home. A son at boarding-school. Their hair is cut differently, they are wearing strange clothes; they have a routine with which one is not familiar, other friends, other jokes. Yet the features are the same. This is still the person I know. But what have these people done? What right have they to dress him up like this, cut off his hair, put her in that shapeless garment. This is my child. My mother.

All I was complaining about was that it had been turned into 'a lovely evening in the theatre'.

There was a comic side to all this. *Getting On* is set in George Oliver's North London home and furnished in a style that was becoming generally fashionable in the early seventies. I knew the style well, having parodied it as part of a TV series in 1966, *Life in* NW1. This was a period when stripped pine was in its infancy, and the customary objects of such a household – the jelly moulds, the cane carpet-beaters, the Seth Thomas clocks and Asian Pheasant plates – were not so readily available as they have since become. Attics were still unexplored, tallboys unstripped, and the nightdress potential of Edwardian shrouds not yet fully exploited. My own house was of course stuffed with such objects. Rather than scour the junk shops of Brighton and Portobello Road, it seemed easier to transfer my own possessions on to the set. But I was barred from the theatre. So while a lookout was kept for the star rehearsing on the stage I smuggled in my precious *objets trouvés* at a side door.

The question will, of course, be asked: What was the director, Patrick Garland, doing during all this? It was a question that kept occurring to me at the time, when I felt betrayed by him and by the management. In retrospect I think that, by concentrating on Kenneth More and leaving my feelings to take care of themselves, Patrick probably did the right thing, though I found it hard to take when it was happening. A leading actor is like a thoroughbred horse, to be coaxed and gentled into the gate. One false move and his ears are back and he's up at the other end of the paddock. With a West End opening large amounts of money are involved, and where there is money there is always bad behaviour. In films, where more money is at stake, the behaviour is much worse, and the writer traditionally gets the mucky end of the stick. Nor should one ever underestimate the courage required of actors. To go out in front of a first-night audience bearing the main brunt of a new play is a small act of heroism. Actors must always have a sense that they are there to do the author's dirty work. He may have written it, but he doesn't have to go out there and *say* it. They are in the trenches, he is back at base.

In the event, the play won an *Evening Standard* award for the best comedy of 1971. It had never seemed to me to be a comedy, and at the ceremony I said it was like entering a marrow for the show and being given the cucumber prize.

Kenneth More is dead, dying courageously and very much in the mould of the parts he liked playing. I still think that he could have been, if not a better actor than he was given credit for, certainly a more interesting one. He wasn't the simple, straightforward good-natured guy he played: he was more complicated than that. But because he wanted so much to be liked he left a large tract of his character undeveloped. Acting is a painful business, and it's to do with exposure, not conceal-ment. As it is, the play still remains uncut. It's far too long, too wordy, and probably reads better than it performs: a good part but a bad play.

The third play in this collection, *Habeas Corpus*, was written in 1973. It was an attempt to write a farce without the paraphernalia of farce – hiding-places, multiple exits and umpteen doors. Trousers fall, it is true, but in an instantaneous way as if by divine intervention. I wrote it without any idea of how it could be staged, and rehearsals began with just four bentwood chairs. The big revolution occurred after two weeks' rehearsal, when the director, Ronald Eyre, decided we could manage with three. Remembering *Getting On* I had worked hard on the text beforehand, and together we cut it to the bone before rehearsals started. The bare stage specified in the stage directions is essential to the bare text. Reintroduce the stock-in-trade of farce (as the Broadway production tried to do) and the play doesn't work. There is just enough text to carry the performers on and off, provided they don't dawdle. If they have to negotiate doors or stairs or potted plants or get anywhere except into the wings, then they will be left stranded halfway across the stage, with no line left with which to haul themselves off.

Neither *Getting On* nor *Habeas Corpus* is what Geoffrey Grigson called 'weeded of impermanence' – a necessary condition, apparently, if a play or a poem is to outlast its time. Topical references are out. Of course plays don't become timeless simply by weeding them of timely references, any more than plays become serious by weeding them of jokes. But the jokes in *Habeas Corpus* about the permissive society do date it, and some of the other jokes make me wince. Still, *Habeas Corpus* is a favourite of mine if only because it's one of the few times I've managed not to write a naturalistic play. It's also the only one of my plays to be done regularly by amateurs. I can see why. It's cheap to put on, there are plenty of good parts, mostly out of stock – henpecked husband, frustrated wife, lecherous curate, ubiquitous char – and everyone is slightly larger than life, which helps with the acting. But it's not altogether farce. Death doesn't quite lay down his book, and poor Dennis ends up doomed. The original production ended on an even blacker note, explaining what to anyone who didn't see the original production must seem a mysterious stage direction: 'Wicksteed dances alone in the spotlight until he can dance no more.' The original version of the play had no dance and ended with the quip:

Whatever right or wrong is
He whose lust lasts, lasts longest.

Putting music to the play was the idea of Ronald Eyre. Carl Davis recorded some rumbustious incidental music on a fairground organ and, hearing it, Alec Guinness wanted to add a coda to the play. In top hat and tails he begins a debonair dance number, which slowly shudders to a halt as the spotlight dwindles, a real dance of death. It was the idea of this dance that helped him to reconcile the otherwise uncongenial character of Wicksteed to his own. It was a great bonus to the play, and the exact opposite of what had happened in *Getting On*, an actor adding something to the play, enlarging it to accommodate his talents. I can't imagine anyone else bringing off that dance, or how to describe it in a stage direction. I imagine most amateur productions turn it into a knees-up, which is very different but no bad way to end.

Sometime in 1989 I read in the *Guardian* that the Victorian school at Burley Woodhead in Yorkshire was to be taken down stone by stone and re-erected in Bradford Museum, where it is to be visited by, among others, patients suffering from Alzheimer's disease, in the hope, one presumes, of jogging their memories. This school transport came handily at the end of the decade to remind me of the last play in this collection, *Enjoy*, which I wrote as the decade opened and which had predicted just such an event.

The title is possibly a mistake: *Endure* would probably have been better, though hardly a crowd-puller, or even, despite the implicit threat of chorus girls, *Look on the Bright Side*. Still, *Enjoy* it was, and I can't change it now.

It's the story of an old couple who live in one of the last back-to-backs in Leeds. Mam's memory is failing, and Dad is disabled. While he lands up in hospital, the end of the play sees Mam still happily living in the back-to-back, now lovingly reconstructed in a museum. The fact that one of the social workers who effect this transformation is their long-lost son in drag may have had something to do with the less than ecstatic reception the play received, but, that apart, the whole notion of the play was dismissed at the time as far-fetched – expressionistic even. A back-to-back in a museum! I was told in future to stick to the particularities of dialogue and the niceties of actual behaviour that I was supposed to be good at, and leave social comment to others.

Of course, there are things wrong with the play – the title certainly; the drag maybe, particularly since it persuaded some critics that I cherished a shamefaced longing to climb into twin-set and pearls. James Fenton, I was told, even referred to the drag character as 'the writer'. Mr Fenton's subsequent abandonment of dramatic criticism to become the *Independent*'s correspondent in the Philippines was one of the more cheering developments in the theatre in the eighties, though when President Marcos claimed to be a much-misunderstood man I knew how he felt.

However, if only in a spirit of 'I told you so', I noted in the course of the eighties various news items, like the reconstruction of the school at Burley Woodhead, which bore out the central thesis of the play and proved it to have been, though I say so myself, prophetic. For instance, a room was created in 1984 at Park Prewett Hospital in Basingstoke furnished as it would have been forty years ago in order to assist elderly patients in 'reminiscence therapy'. There was the exhibit, also in 1984, at the Miami Zoo of urban man in his natural habitat: a man in a sitting-room in a cage. There was the proposal, later abandoned, to reconstruct part of the Death Railway in Thailand as a tourist attraction. Most pertinent of all (and, of course, this is the cutting I have lost, so you will have to take my word for it) was the devoted reproduction in a museum somewhere in England of the last of the prefabs, with the couple who had lived in it doing a regular stint as curators.

Whether or not I got it right, I still like the laying-out scene in Act 2, because it is one of the few occasions when a character of mine has done what characters in plays and novels are supposed to do – namely, take on a life of their own. Until the two women started to lay Dad out I had thought Mr Craven was dead, and his erection (on the typewriter) took me as much by surprise as it did them. It is such a farcical scene it perhaps belongs to a different play, though the setting and the atmosphere of it owe something to Peter Gill's season of D. H. Lawrence plays which I saw in the seventies at the Royal Court.

With the exception of *Habeas Corpus*, all these plays are too long – well over an hour each way, which is all I can ever take in the theatre – and in performance they should be cut. As Churchill said, 'The head cannot take in more than the seat can endure.'

An Englishman Abroad

A few years ago a stage play of mine, *The Old Country*, was running in the West End. The central character, Hilary, played then by Alec Guinness, is an embittered, ironic figure living in the depths of the country. Visitors arrive, and in a small *coup de théâtre* halfway through the first act the audience suddenly realize that the country is Russia. Hilary is a traitor, a former Foreign Office official now in exile. At the end of the play he is induced to return home and face the music.

The play had some success, with Hilary being understandably, though to my mind mistakenly, identified as Kim Philby. Indeed soon after the play opened the *Daily Telegraph* correspondent in Moscow found himself sitting next to Philby at the opera and mentioned the play. The spy said he'd been told about it, but that it didn't sound at all like him. This wasn't surprising, since if I'd had anybody in mind when writing the play it was not Philby but W. H. Auden, the play seeming to me to be about exile, a subject that does interest me, rather than espionage, which interests me not a bit. Still, Philby or Auden, the play ran, and who was I to complain? It should perhaps be said that this was a couple of years before the unmasking of Professor Blunt and the great spy boom.

During the run of *The Old Country*, as happens, friends and well-wishers would come round after the performance to greet Alec Guinness, often with personal reminiscences of Philby and of his predecessors, Burgess and Maclean. Hints would be dropped as to the identity of spies still ensconced in the upper reaches of the Foreign Office or the Diplomatic, and when I next dropped into the theatre I would be given a précis of these titbits, though necessarily at second hand. I remember feeling rather out of it; I may not be interested in espionage, but I am a glutton for gossip.

Happily, I did get to hear one story at first hand. Coral Browne came to the play, and afterwards Alec Guinness took us both out to supper at the Mirabelle. I mention the restaurant only because the mixture of Moscow drabness and London *luxe* was a part of the telling of the tale, as it is a part of the tale told. It was over a meal very like the one that concludes *An Englishman Abroad* that Coral told me of her visit to Russia with the Shakespeare Memorial Company in 1958, and the particular incidents that make up this play.

The picture of the elegant actress and the seedy exile sitting in a dingy Moscow flat through a long afternoon listening again and again to Jack Buchanan singing 'Who Stole My Heart Away?' seemed to me funny and sad, but it was a few years before I got round to writing it up. It was only when I sent the first draft to Coral Browne that I found she had kept not merely Burgess's letters, thanking her for running him errands, but also her original notes of his measurements, and even his cheque (uncashed and for £6) to treat her and one of her fellow-actors to lunch at the Caprice.

I have made use of Burgess's letters in the play, but another extract deserves quoting in full. His first letter, dated Easter Sunday 1959, begins: 'This is a very suitable day to be writing to you, since I also was born on it . . . sprung from the womb on April 16 1911 . . . to the later horror of the Establishment of the country concerned.' Coral had apparently urged him to visit Paul Robeson when the singer visited Moscow:

In spite of your suggestion and invitation to visit Paul Robeson, I found myself too shy to call on him. You may find this surprising, but I always am with great men and artists such as him. Not so much shy as frightened. The *agonies* I remember on *first* meeting with people I really admire, e.g. E. M. Forster (and Picasso and Winston Churchill, but not W. S. Maugham).

There is some irony in these remarks, particularly with regard to Paul Robeson, when one recalls a quip of Burgess's in happier days. When he was sent to Washington as Second Secretary at the British Embassy his former boss, Hector McNeil, warned Burgess to remember three things: not to be too openly left-wing, not to get involved in race relations and above all not to get mixed up in any homosexual incidents. 'I understand, Hector,' said Burgess. 'What you mean is that I mustn't make a pass at Paul Robeson.'

I have put some of my own sentiments into Burgess's mouth. 'I can say I love London. I can say I love England. I can't say I love my country, because I don't know what that means,' is a fair statement of my own, and I imagine many people's, position. The Falklands War helped me to understand how a fastidious stepping-aside from patriotism could be an element in the make-up of characters as different as Burgess and Blunt. Certainly in the spy fever that followed the unmasking of Professor Blunt I felt more sympathy with the hunted than with the hunters. In the play it is suggested that Burgess was a spy because he wanted a place where he was alone, and that having a secret supplies this. I believe this to be psychologically true, but there is a sense too that an ironic attitude towards one's country and a scepticism about one's heritage are a part of that heritage. And so, by extension, is the decision to betray it. It is irony activated.

In his essay 'The Well of Narcissus' Auden imagines Narcissus not as young and beautiful but as fat and middle-aged. Drunk, he gazes at himself in the glass, and says, 'I shouldn't look at me like that if I were you. I suppose you think you know who I am. Well, let me tell *you*, my dear, that one of these days you're going to get a very big surprise *indeed*!' That seems a fair description of Burgess's character, and one not unfamiliar to the people among whom he was to end up. 'He exemplified that favourite type in the classical Russian novel, the buffoon; the man always playing the fool, not only for his own amusement and love of exhibitionism, but also with the object of keeping everyone in the dark as to his own inner views and intentions.' Not Burgess, but the poet Yevtushenko as described by Anthony Powell.

In the play Burgess says, 'I lack what the English call character, by which they mean the power to refrain.' The remark was actually made by the Oxford aesthete Brian Howard. The contradictions in the Cambridge Burgess turned him to treachery, the Oxford Howard to art. Howard's drunken, outrageous behaviour flouted convention much as Burgess's did, but with a conventional excuse: he was a failed writer. Burgess had no ambitions in that department, and, diplomacy being a less crowded field than literature, his failure turned out more of a success. As a second-rate poet or novelist, not a Second Secretary at the Washington Embassy, Burgess would have seemed, if not commonplace, at any rate not unfamiliar. He would also have been much easier to forget.

So far as the general issues in the play are concerned, I find it hard to drum up any patriotic indignation over Burgess (or any of the so-called Cambridge spies for that matter). No one has ever shown that Burgess did much harm, except to make fools of people in high places. Because he made jokes, scenes and most of all passes (though not at Paul Robeson), the general consensus is that he was rather silly. It is Philby who is always thought to be the most congenial figure. Clubbable, able to hold his liquor, a good man in a tight corner, he commends himself to his fellow journalists, who have given him a good press. But of all the Cambridge spies he is the only one of whom it can be proved without doubt that he handed over agents to torture and death.

Auden's name keeps coming up. Burgess wasn't a close friend, but the night before he left the country in May 1951, and before it became plain that he would have to go the whole hog and accompany Maclean, Burgess thought of lying low with Auden on Ischia. There would have been a nice appropriateness in this, secret agents and sudden flight being potent elements in Auden's poetic myth ('Leave for Cape Wrath tonight'). However, the projected visit didn't come off. On the crucial evening Auden, then staying with Stephen Spender, failed (or forgot) to return Burgess's call. And this omission was also appropriate. Auden's poetry in the thirties often sounded like a blueprint for political action, but set against subsequent events some of his verse rang hollow. Or so Auden began to think while in America during the war. Burgess 'running naked through Europe' and turning up on Ischia would have been like a parody of early Auden, a reminder of a poetic past, some of which Auden was anxious to forget, or at any rate re-edit. Burgess on Ischia would have been an artistic as much as a social embarrassment. Though that too would make a nice play.

I have taken a few liberties with the facts as Coral Browne told them to me. The scene in the British Embassy, for instance, did not occur; but since the Shakespeare Company were warned by the British Ambassador to 'shy away from that traitor Burgess, who's always trying to get back to England' it seemed no great liberty.

When I wrote the script I had no idea where it would be filmed, and while I included some exterior shots I kept them to a minimum, thinking that, without going abroad, Moscow-like settings would be hard to find. In the event the film's designer, Stuart Walker, came up with some very convincing locations in Glasgow and Dundee, enabling John Schlesinger to open up the film and include many more exteriors. We see the outside of the theatre (Caird Hall, Dundee) and the front of the British Embassy (back of Glasgow Town Hall), and the final shot of the film, vaguely described by me as 'Moscow streets', has Burgess strolling in his new togs across the Suspension Bridge in Glasgow, luckily in a snowstorm.

Searching for locations educates the eye. The Suspension Bridge on Clydeside doesn't look particularly Russian in itself. What makes it seem authentic is a long Georgian building on the far bank of the river, which is in the very back of the shot. This building happens to have been painted in two shades of pink in a way that maybe looks more like Leningrad than Moscow but which certainly suggests Eastern Europe. The exterior of Burgess's flat was filmed at Moss Heights in Glasgow, an early post-war block of flats, and the interior was built in the small concert room at the Caird Hall. The magnificent marble staircase of the British Embassy is in Glasgow Town Hall, but when Coral Browne leaves the two young diplomats and goes down the staircase she travels five hundred miles between frames, as the room in the Embassy is actually at Polesden Lacey in Surrey.

A poignant exchange occurs as Coral and Burgess are coming away from Burgess's flat and he casually enquires whether she had known Jack Buchanan, whose record he has been playing her. 'Yes,' says Coral. 'We nearly got married.' Burgess gives her a second look, not sure that she isn't pulling his leg. She isn't. It had come out casually in conversation with Coral just before we started filming. Slipped in right at the end of the sequence it focuses what has gone before, both of them listening to a record that to Burgess means something general and to Coral someone very particular. It's the kind of coincidence which, had it been invented, would have seemed sentimental.

It was pointed out, appropriately in the *Daily Express*, that it was not in Coral's dressing-room that Burgess was sick, but in that of Michael Redgrave next door. This is true and was part of the story as Coral originally told it to me, Redgrave having called her in to help clean up an Englishman who was being sick in his room, but without introducing him. In an article about the Moscow visit in the *Observer* in 1959 Redgrave mentioned Burgess coming round, but did not mention him being ill. The kernel of our film is the meeting in the flat, and, wanting to centre the story on Coral and leave Hamlet out of it as far as possible, I transferred the incident entirely to her dressing-room. In Sir Michael's autobiography, *In My Mind's Eye*, which came out in 1983, after the film had been made, he recalled the incident as it actually happened, which might suggest that Coral had plagiarized the story. She hadn't. I had rearranged it for dramatic reasons.

There was only one point in the interpretation of the script where John Schlesinger and I differed, and that was at the conclusion of the scene in the pyjama shop. Snobbish though I'd made the salesman, I felt he did have a point and that the balance of the scene ought in the end to go his way. When he revealed that the shop was Hungarian I wanted the tone of the scene to change and for it suddenly to cease to be about snobbery and to reveal real issues. The film is set after all in 1958, only two years after the Hungarian uprising. John felt that an audience would not grasp this. We argued and left it open until the last moment, when I deferred and gave the scene a jokier ending. On reflection I still think I was right and that those Mayfair scenes should end on a sourer note. But it was an amicable disagreement, and our only one on what to make was a very enjoyable film.

Postscript

An Englishman Abroad was transmitted in 1983. In *A Question of Attribution* (1988) I wrote about Anthony Blunt and a suspect Titian, put the plays together as a double bill under the title (suggested by Simon Callow) *Single Spies*, and they were put on at the National Theatre and later at the Queen's. Although the preface I wrote for *Single Spies* in 1989 was substantially the same as the one printed here for *An Englishman Abroad*, I note that it ended more harshly. The five years that separated the two plays were also the prime of Mrs Thatcher, and my attitudes had hardened:

It suits governments to make treachery the crime of crimes, but the world is smaller than it was and to conceal information can be as culpable as to betray it. As I write, evidence is emerging of a nuclear accident at Windscale in 1957, the full extent of which was hidden from the public. Were the politicians and civil servants responsible for this less culpable than our Cambridge villains? Because for the spies it can at least be said that they were risking their own skins, whereas the politicians were risking someone else's.

Of course Blunt and Burgess and co. had the advantage of us in that they still had illusions. They had somewhere to turn. The trouble with treachery nowadays is that if one does want to betray one's country there is no one satisfactory to betray it to. If there were, more people would be doing it.

The real solution for Burgess would have been to live until he was eighty; then he would have been welcomed back with open arms. You only have to survive in England for all to be forgiven. This was more or less what happened to Oswald Mosley, whose offence seems to me much greater, and would have happened to Burgess, had he lived. He would have gone on chat shows, been a guest on *Desert Island Discs*, and dined out all over London. In England you only have to be able to eat a boiled egg at ninety and they think you deserve the Nobel Prize.

The Wind in the Willows

Some time in 1987 Richard Eyre, newly appointed Director of the National Theatre, asked me if I'd think about writing a play that would combine *The Wind in the Willows* with some account of the life of its author, Kenneth Grahame. I had one or two similar approaches around that time, including a proposal for a film in which Bob Hoskins was to play Rat and Michael Caine Toad. Kenneth Grahame died in 1932, so this flurry of interest could be put down to money and managements waking up to the fact that, fifty years on, here was a best-seller that was now out of copyright.

Cut to December 1990, a week before the opening of the play I eventually wrote. Passing the British Museum, I ran into Bodley's Librarian, David Vaisey, who was taking a gloomy breather from some unending committee on the impending transfer to the new British Library. As I told him about rehearsing *The Wind in the Willows*, he became gloomier still. What I had not known was that Kenneth Grahame's long love-affair with Oxford had led him to bequeath the copyright in the book to the university, and a good little earner it had proved to be. Now the National Theatre's gain was about to be the Bodleian Library's loss.

I don't recall reading *The Wind in the Willows* as a child, or indeed any of the classics of children's literature. This was partly the library's fault. In those days Armley Junior Library at the bottom of Wesley Road in Leeds bound all its volumes in heavy maroon or black, so that *The Adventures of Milly Molly Mandy* was every bit as forbidding as *The Anatomy of Melancholy*. Doubtless *The Wind in the Willows* was there somewhere, along with *Winnie the Pooh* and *Alice* and all the other books every well-brought-up *Children's Hour*-listening child was supposed to read. Actually, I think I do remember looking at *Alice* and being put off by the Tenniel illustrations. 'Too old fashioned,' I thought – 'looks like a classic,' and back it went on the shelf.

It was only in the sixties, when I was rather haphazardly reading round the Edwardians with some vague idea of writing a history play (which eventually turned into *Forty Years On*), that I read Kenneth Grahame's *The Golden Age* and *Dream Days*. I left *The Wind in the Willows* until last, because I thought I had read it already – this being virtually the definition of a classic: a book everyone is assumed to have read and which they often assume they have read themselves.

One consideration that had kept me away from the book for so long, that gave it a protective coating every bit as off-putting as those black and maroon bindings of my childhood, was that it had *fans*. Fans are a feature of a certain kind of book. It's often a children's book – *Winnie the Pooh*, *Alice* and *The Hobbit* are examples – or it is a grown-up children's book such as those of Wodehouse, E. F. Benson and Conan Doyle. But Jane Austen and Anthony Trollope are nothing if not adult and they have fans too – and fan clubs – so children are not the essence of it.

What is common to all these authors, though, is the capacity to create self-contained worlds; their books constitute systems of literary self-sufficiency in ways that other novels, often more profound, do not. It is a kind of cosiness. Dickens is not cosy; he is always taking his reader back into the real world in a way that Trollope, who is cosy, does not. So it is Trollope who has the fans. In our own day the same distinction could be drawn

338

between the novels of Evelyn Waugh and those of Anthony Powell – Powell with fans, Waugh not. And though exceptions occur to me even as I write – the Brontës? (fans of the lives more than the books) Hardy? (fans of the scenery) – I have always found fans a great deterrent: 'It's just your kind of thing.' 'Really? And how would you know?'

Back in 1988, I set to work trying to interweave Grahame's real and fictional worlds, but I soon ran into difficulties. Grahame's life had not been a happy one. Born in 1859, he never had (as he put it) 'a proper equipment of parents', and was effectively orphaned at the age of five when his mother died of scarlet fever and his drunkard father packed him off to Cookham in Berkshire to live with his grandparents; he never saw his father again. He was sent to St Edward's School in Oxford, where he did moderately well, and was looking forward to going up to university there when the family – or the 'grown-ups', as he thought of them all his life – decided he should go into the City as a clerk ('a pale-faced quilldriver') in the Bank of England.

Disappointed though he was (and it was a disappointment that did not fade), Grahame did well at the Bank, and eventually became Secretary at the early age of thirty-nine. Still, for all his conventional appearance (and despite the 'Kitchener Needs You' moustache), he was hardly a conscientious clerk, and even in those relaxed days he soon acquired a reputation for sloping off early. When he was at his desk he was often not doing the Bank's work but writing articles for the *National Observer* and *The Yellow Book*. Pretty conventional for the most part, his pieces deplored the creeping tide of suburbia and extolled the charms of the countryside, sentiments that have been familiar and fashionable ever since, although nowadays Grahame's style is somewhat hard to take.

Grahame himself comes over as a sympathetic character who,

even when he begins to acquire a literary reputation, still has about him the air of a humble clerk, tied to his desk and longing to escape – like those little men on the loose that crop up in Wells or, later, in Priestley and Orwell. Of course, it is easier if you are an animal: his draper's shop has to burn down and his death be assumed before Mr Polly can escape; with Mole, it is just a matter of flinging aside his duster and brush, saying, 'Hang spring-cleaning!', and then up he comes into the sunlight and finds himself in 'the warm grass of a great meadow' – and a new life.

A new life of a different sort began for Grahame in 1899, when he was forty. Hitherto very much the bachelor, he suddenly – and to the surprise and consternation of his friends – became engaged to Elspeth Thompson, whom in due course he rather resignedly married. A Scot like himself, she was fey as well as formidable – insisting, for instance, on wearing a daisy chain to their wedding – but though their courtship had been conducted largely in baby talk there does not seem to have been much talk about babies afterwards. Sex did not come up to the expectations of either of them, but before it was discontinued they had one quick child, Alastair, who was born premature and half-blind.

He was a precocious boy, though – Elspeth, in particular, insisting on his charm and ability – with the result that he was much spoiled and given to tantrums, during which he would beat his head on the ground in fits of grief and rage. When his father started to write letters to him telling the stories that, in 1908, became *The Wind in the Willows*, Mr Toad's tantrums were intended to ring a bell.

The book was far from being an immediate success ('As a contribution to natural history,' wrote the *Times* critic, 'the book is negligible'), but at least this saved Alastair Grahame from the fate of A. A. Milne's son Christopher Robin, dogged always by his fictional counterpart. Still, there was not much else that went right for Alastair. Since his father had longed to go to Oxford, Alastair was sent there, but as the child of eccentric parents and lacking any social skills he was as unhappy as he had been at Eton, and in 1920 he was found dead on the railway line that runs by Port Meadow.

The ironies are dreadful: the river-bank, setting of the father's idyll, scene of the son's death; the train, Mr Toad's deliverer, the instrument of the real-life Mr Toad's destruction. Though these tragic events were made the substance of an excellent radio play – *The Killing of Toad*, by David Gooderson – I found it impossible to imagine them incorporated in *The Wind in the Willows* without casting a dark shadow over that earthly paradise, and so the project lapsed.

In March 1990, at the suggestion of Nicholas Hytner, the National revived the idea of an adaptation of Grahame's book, only this time in the form of a Christmas show that would be virtually all sunlight and would display to advantage the technical capabilities of the Olivier stage.

My theatrical imagination is pretty limited; it is all I can do to get characters on to the stage and once they are there, I can never think of a compelling reason for them to leave – 'I think I'll go now' being the nearest I get to dramatic urgency. So I was too set in my ways to be instantly liberated by the technological challenges of the commission.

'But there's a caravan in it,' I remember complaining, 'what do we do about that?'

'I'm sure it's possible,' comforted Nicholas Hytner, who is accustomed to launching 747s from the stage. 'Just write it in.'

'But it's drawn by a *horse*,' I persisted. 'We can't have a real horse and we can't have a pantomime horse or else we'll have to have a pantomime Rat and Mole and Badger.'

'Who is this idiot?' would have been a permissible response, but Nicholas Hytner patiently explained that there were several actors who looked like carthorses and who would take the part very well. It was all so simple, just as long as one used the imagination.

I set this down more or less as it happened, in case there should be any budding playwrights more tentative than I am. It's unlikely. I've been at it now for twenty-five years, and if I still can't stretch my mind to envisage a man playing a horse what have I learned?

After that, though, it all came much easier. When the motor car appeared, I just wrote '*A motor car comes on*', and likewise with the barge. The only thing the designer Mark Thompson was dubious about – on grounds of expense – was the railway train, but by that time I had got the bit between my teeth and wrote the scene in which Toad is rescued by the train with the note 'I think you can suggest a train with clouds of steam, hooters, etc.' Etcetera.

These props, and particularly the car and the train, were splendidly done and handsomely finished. As Griff Rhys Jones (who played Toad) remarked, most stage props look worse the closer you get to them, whereas these stood up to the actors' closest scrutiny, being beautifully detailed in places (such as the dashboard of the car) that the audience can scarcely hope to see.

To understand the technical side of the production, one needs to know that the stage of the Olivier comprises an inner circle and an outer circle. The meadow on which much of the action takes place was built on the inner circle; round and slightly crumpled in appearance, it was generally referred to by the crew as 'The Poppadum'. Around this, the outer circle – a rim about six and a half feet wide – did duty as river or road. Both inner and outer circles can revolve in either direction, and the inner circle can rise or fall, either one half at a time or in one piece, when it resembles a huge hollow drum. Thus when the scene changed to Rat's house the inner circle revolved and the drum rose at the same time, to reveal the interior of the house beneath the meadow, the combination of the stage rising and revolving making the scene appear to spiral up into view. A similar transformation took place when Rat and Mole were taken into Badger's house, with the bonus that, while Badger, Rat and Mole were sitting cosily by the fire on a level with the audience, one could still see, up above, the Chief Weasel and Weasel Norman keeping their chilly watch in the Wild Wood.

Mark Thompson's costumes incorporated some of the animals' natural appearance – Rat's tail, for instance, and his outsize ears – but not so as to obliterate the actors' human features. Jane Gibson taught the cast the movements of the various creatures they were representing: the linear shufflings of the hedgehogs, the dozy lollopings of the rabbits, the sinuous dartings of the weasel and so on.

Younger actors take to this kind of thing more readily than their seniors. Michael Bryant, playing Badger, was initially sceptical and avoided the movement classes; then, in an apparent access of enthusiasm, he asked if he could take home the various videos depicting badger activity. When he came in the next day, he handed back the videos, saying, 'I've studied all these films of the way badgers move, and I've discovered an extraordinary thing: they move exactly like Michael Bryant.' But to most of the actors, some of whom were doubling as different creatures, the animal-movement classes were of great value. For example, one could see in David Bamber's Mole that his get-up as an old-fashioned northern schoolboy did not entirely displace the shy, scuttling creature with splayed hands and feet, who people were always after for a waistcoat.

I have tried to do a faithful adaptation of the book while, at the same time, not being sure what a faithful adaptation is. One that remains true to the spirit of the book, most people would say. Well, *The Wind in the Willows* is a lyrical book, and the first casualties, for the book to work on the stage, were those descriptive passages that give it its lyrical flavour. The splendid music Jeremy Sams wrote helped to compensate for this loss and his lyrics too – which he dashed off with such speed that I felt, had he had a couple of hours to spare, he could have adapted the whole thing.

Still, the play is nowhere near as gentle and atmospheric as the book. No matter, other people would say: its special charm lies in the characters. But to adapt the text on that principle is not straightforward either, as the tale is very episodic. Rat and Mole disappear for long stretches, as does Badger, and it is not until Toad's adventures get under way that there is anything like a continuous narrative. It was for this reason, I imagine, that A. A. Milne called his adaptation *Toad of Toad Hall*, whereas to many readers of the book it is Rat and Mole who hold the story together.

The most substantial cut I made had been made by Milne too – namely the chapter entitled 'Wayfarers All', in which Rat encounters a sea-going cousin. Milne also omitted the mystical chapter 'The Piper at the Gates of Dawn', but this I did include, though I'm not sure what children made of it in the play – or made of it in the book, for that matter. In the play, Pan was heard but not seen, which is just as well: Grahame's description – 'the rippling muscles, on the arm that lay across the broad chest . . . the splendid curves of the shaggy limbs disposed in majestic ease on the sward' – makes him sound too much like Mellors the gamekeeper. Both chapters, incorporated into *The Wind in the Willows* at a late stage, recall the kind of pieces Grahame began writing when he worked at the Bank, and which were collected in his first book, *Pagan Papers*.

I ended up making the play the story of a group of friends, with the emphasis on Mole. He is the newcomer who takes us into this world of water and woods and weasels, and whose education is the thread that runs through it all. *The Wind in the Willows* is Mole's *Bildungsroman*. Mole is the only one of the characters I have allowed to have doubts. He doubts if he is having a good time, doubts if he is happy with Rat. He likes Toad as he is, and when the old show-off reforms it all seems rather dull – have they done the right thing by taking him in hand? Rat and Badger have no doubts, but at the finish, Mole is still wondering.

Jokes apart, the only element in the production that I brought up to date was the Wild Wooders. In the book, they are an occasional presence, but for the play Nicholas Hytner felt that they should be a constant threat, lurking in the background even at the most idyllic moments, and at one point going so far as to carry off a baby rabbit for their supper – an incident that shocked adults in the audience more than it did children.

In Grahame's day the Wild Wooders were taken to represent the threat to property posed by the militant proletariat – a view, whatever one's political persuasion, that it would be hard to maintain today. Our Wild Wooders ended up as property speculators and estate agents, spivs and ex-bovver-boys, who put Toad Hall through a programme of 'calculated decrepitude' in the hope of depressing its market value. Their plan is to turn it into a nice mix of executive dwellings and office accommodation, shove in a marina and a café or two, and market it as the 'Toad Hall Park and Leisure Centre' – 'The horror! The horror!' groans Badger. But the reformed Toad's vision of his ancestral home as a venue for opera, chamber concerts and even actors' one-man shows does not commend itself to Badger either. 'Actors!' he moans, and we know that, before long, he will be loping back to the Wild Wood.

Albert the horse is a nod in the direction of A. A. Milne. Grahame has a horse in the book to pull Toad's caravan, but he does not give him a name or a voice. In *Toad of Toad Hall*, the horse is called Alfred and is a bit of a pedant. I have made him, in another nod to Milne, extremely lugubrious – Eeyore's Wolverhampton cousin. Toad can never remember his name and keeps calling him Alfred, which is not surprising as he is probably remembering him from the other play.

In the blurb written for his publishers, Grahame said that his book was 'clean of the clash of sex'. What this means is that women do not get a look in. There are only three of them to speak of – the washerwoman, the bargewoman and the gaoler's daughter – and only the last is seen in a kindly light. One reviewer of the play described these three as 'coarse human females, coarsely characterized; they seem to come from another production.' No, just from the text, much as Grahame wrote it, where the female sex is generally rubbished. One of the indictments against Toad is that, owing to his car crashes, he had to spend weeks in hospital 'being ordered about by female nurses'. In addition, he has been 'jeered at, and ignominiously flung in the water – by a woman, too!' Even Toad, who rather fancies the gaoler's daughter, joins in the game. 'You know what *girls* are, ma'am,' he says to the bargewoman. 'Nasty little hussies, that's what *I* call 'em.'

Toad is pretending, but not so Rat, Mole and Badger, all of them confirmed bachelors. Bachelordom is a status that had more respect (and fewer undertones) in Grahame's day than it has now, and certainly he seems to have regarded it as the ideal state from which he had disastrously fallen. Of course, some bachelors are more confirmed than others, and the bachelordoms of Mole, Rat and Badger differ – or I have made them differ. Mole is a bachelor by circumstances, taking his cue from his surroundings. Rat is a single creature and so Mole is happy

346

to be single, too, and set up home with his new friend – though as properly as Morecambe with Wise or Abbott with Costello. But had Mole popped up on that spring morning and found Rat in a cosy family set-up he could have fitted in there just as well. Judging by the way he makes himself readily at home at Rat's and then at Badger's, Mole is a natural *ami de maison*.

Rat is solitary by circumstance but also by temperament. He could be played like Field Marshal Montgomery, and, as with Monty, there may once have been a great love in his life that he has had to bury. He is certainly a romantic, but his rules and rigidities protect him – have perhaps been devised to protect him – from his own feelings. He's not quite a Crocker-Harris, but certainly a Mr Chips.

Badger has something of the old schoolmaster about him, too. He's less buttoned up than Ratty and, because not repressed at all, more innocent. All he gets up to is pinching Mole's cheek and rubbing his little toes – behaviour that was quite common-place in old gentlemen when I was a boy, when such things were not thought to matter much and were shrugged off by the recipient as just another of the ways that grown-ups were boring.

To fans of the book, even to discuss these well-loved characters in such terms might seem, if not sacrilege, at any rate silly. But an adapter has to ask questions and speculate about the characters in order to make the play work. If presented on stage in the same way as in the book, Rat, Mole and Badger would find it hard to retain an audience's attention, because they are so relentlessly nice. Badger is a bit gruff, and Rat can be a little tetchy, but that is as far as it goes; all the faults that make for an interesting character are reserved for Toad.

I felt that the atmosphere of the River Bank had to be less serene, and that, while retaining their innocence and lack of insight into themselves, Rat and Mole – and to a lesser extent

Badger – should be prey to more complicated feelings, particularly jealousy. Thus Mole's arrival on the River Bank to become Rat's new friend is not quite the untroubled idyll it is in the book. It is not long before Mole wants to meet Badger, and of course he turns out to be a big hit there too. So now Mole is Badger's friend as well as Rat's, and we go into a routine of 'He's more my friend than he is yours – and anyway, I met him first!' It is a routine children are accustomed to, and it is not unknown to grown-ups, particularly in some of life's backwaters – and the River Bank, despite Rat's protestations, can be a bit on the dull side. Newcomers there are eagerly gobbled up, as newcomers always have been in novels of provincial life, from Jane Austen to Barbara Pym.

Toad presents a different problem, and as much for the actor as for the dramatist. It is not that, like Mole and Rat, he is too nice, though Grahame is at pains to emphasize that he *is* nice and, for all his boasting, a good fellow underneath. It is just that we are told before he appears that he is conceited, a show-off and a creature of crazes; then, when he does arrive, he is all these things and goes on being all these things, with none of his disastrous adventures resulting in any disillusionment at all, still less self-knowledge. Finally, and suddenly, at the end of the book he is confronted by the trio of friends and overnight becomes a changed character.

Now this is no use to the dramatist at all, and no pushover for the actor either. Characters in a play need to go on a journey, even if it's only from A to B. Mole's journey is a graduated schooling at the hands of Rat in the ways of the River Bank; Rat's journey (in my adaptation) is an emotional schooling at the hands of Mole; Badger's journey is from solitude to society. But Toad does not go on a journey at all – he goes on his travels, but he does not go on a journey. Until his transformation, he is the same at the end of the book as he is at the beginning; life has taught him nothing. But, unchanging as he is and in defiance of all the rules of drama, children love him, and, since Toad has so much of the action, even adults don't mind, until by the end, nobody – adults or children – wants him to change. Nor does he in my version – he just learns to keep it under.

'Keeping it under' is partly what *The Wind in the Willows* is about. There is a Toad in all of us, or certainly in all men, our social acceptability dependent on how much of our Toad we can keep hidden. Mole, by nature shy and humble, has no trouble fitting in; Toad, with neither of these virtues, must learn to counterfeit them before he is accepted. It is one of the useful dishonesties he might have learned at public school (where it is known as 'having the corners knocked off'). Humphrey Carpenter says of Toad that one could imagine him having a brief spell at Eton or Harrow before being expelled – too soon to have learned the social lie that the play teaches him.

TOAD: I say, Ratty, why didn't you tell me before?
RAT: Tell you what?
TOAD: About not showing off, being humble and shy and nice.
RAT: I did tell you.
TOAD: Yes, but what you didn't say was that this way I get
       more attention than ever. Everybody loves me! It's
       wonderful!

When I first read the book it seemed to me that Grahame meant Toad to be Jewish. He had endowed him with all the faults that genteel Edwardian anti-Semitism attributed to *nouveaux-riches* Jews. He is loud and shows off; he has too much money for his own good and no sense of social responsibility to go with it, and this sense of social responsibility is another lesson he has to learn. The fact that whenever Grahame has the animals discuss Toad's character they end up saying what a decent fellow he is underneath it all only seemed to confirm this analysis, and I thought that Grahame must have been thinking of characters like Sir Ernest Cassel and the Sassoons, the friends and financiers of Edward VII, who moved at the highest levels of society but were still regarded as outsiders. So when I read *The Wind in the Willows* for the BBC I gave Toad something of a flavour which if not Jewish, was at least exotic – trying to make his r's sound like Tom Stoppard's, for instance. I expected some criticism for this (not from Tom Stoppard), but none came, and now, having adapted the book for the stage, I am less sure anyway. The text is so full of inconsistencies. Grahame himself may not have known – 'He is and he isn't' as so often the proper answer to such questions.

The nearest Oscar Wilde got to the River Bank was his remark about ducks. 'You will never be in the best society,' he had a mother say to her ducklings, 'unless you can learn to stand on your heads.' In Toad there are echoes of Wilde, and not only in his disgrace and imprisonment. Many of Wilde's epigrams would not be out of place at Toad Hall – 'If the lower orders don't set us a good example, what on earth is the use of them?' or 'I live wholly for pleasure; pleasure is the only thing one should live for.' I am not sure that Toad thinks of himself as an artist (though he has been told that he ought to have a salon), but if he did, it would only be as a motorist ('Is motoring an art?' 'The way I do it, yes.') Occasionally he manages an epigram of his own that is worthy of Wilde. 'I have an aunt who is a washerwoman,' says the gaoler's daughter. 'Think no more about it,' replies Toad consolingly. '*I* have several aunts who *ought* to be washerwomen.' But then Toad's gaol cannot have been far from Reading.

At the finish I have the gaoler's daughter kiss Toad, who does not turn into a prince but straightaway wants Rat to taste the joys of kissing, just as he had once wanted him to share the joys of caravanning. Rat, of course, is reluctant, but finds to his surprise there may be something in this kissing business after all, and, generous animal that he is, he wants Mole initiated too. So the play ends with a hint of new horizons. It is a large departure from the text, of course, where all four of our heroes are left in bachelor bliss, but this alteration is not entirely without justification, echoing as it does the course of Grahame's own life. Courtship and marriage were late joys for him, too – and not such joys either – but that's another story but, as I said at the start, not one that I managed to tell.

My additions and alterations to *The Wind in the Willows* are, I am sure, as revealing of me as the original text is of Grahame. Grahame knew this very well. 'You must please remember,' he wrote:

that a theme, a thesis, is in most cases little more than a sort of clothes line on which one pegs a string of ideas, quotations, allusions and so on, one's mental undergarments of all shapes and sizes, some possibly fairly new but most rather old and patched; and they dance and sway in the breeze and flap and flutter, or hang limp and lifeless; and some are ordinary enough, and some are of a private and intimate shape, and rather give the owner away, and show up his or her peculiarities. And owing to the invisible clothes line they seem to have some connexion and continuity.

Peculiarities or not, I imagine most writers are gratified that there is an invisible clothes line, if only because it suggests there are things going on in their heads that they are unaware of. Who knows, these unintended recurrences might amount if not to Significance then at least to Subtext. The only other piece of mine that has been performed at the National Theatre was my double bill *Single Spies* in 1988. However, it was not until I was adapting *The Wind in the Willows* that I remembered that Guy Burgess, the protagonist of *An Englishman Abroad*, had, in his final rumbustious days at the Washington Embassy, acquired a twelve-cylinder Lincoln convertible in which he had frequent mishaps. 'He drove it', said Lord Greenhill, a fellow diplomat, 'just like Mr Toad.' Poop-poop.

The King and I

I've always had a soft spot for George III, starting all of forty years ago when I was in the sixth form at Leeds Modern School and reading for a scholarship to Cambridge. The smart book around that time was Herbert Butterfield's *The Whig Interpretation of History*, which took the nineteenth century to task for writing history with one eye on the future, and in particular for taking as the only path through the past the development of democratic institutions. On the Whig interpretation, historical characters got a tick if they were on the side of liberty (Cromwell, Chatham), a cross (Charles I, James II) if they held up the march of progress. Because he went in for active royalty and made some attempt to govern on his own account rather than leaving it to the Whig aristocracy, George III had been written up as a villain and a clumsy tyrant. This view Butterfield had helped to discredit, so a question on George III was thought likely to turn up in the Cambridge examination, which it duly did. Sitting in the freezing Senate House in December 1951, I trotted out my Butterfield and, though I didn't get a scholarship, counted myself lucky to be offered a place at Sidney Sussex – that Christmas when the college letter came the best Christmas of my life.

Before university, though, there was national service to be got through, regarded at best as a bore, but for me, as a late developer, a long-dreaded ordeal; it was touch and go which I got to first – puberty or the call-up. I served briefly in the infantry, then, like many university entrants at that time, was sent on the Joint Services Language Course to learn Russian, first at Coulsdon, then at Cambridge. So what I had dreaded turned out a happy time and, although I didn't realize it till later, far more enjoyable than my time at university proper. However, I began to think that, since I was now spending a year at Cambridge studying Russian, the gilt was off the gingerbread so far as Cambridge was concerned and I might get the best of both worlds if I were to go to Oxford. This wasn't altogether the beady-eyed career move it might seem, in that I had a hopeless crush on one of my fellow officer cadets, who was bound for Oxford – that his college was Brasenose, then a mecca of rowing and rugger, somehow exemplifying the futility of it. Still, I suppose I ought to have been grateful: he might have been going to Hull – or even back to Leeds.

So now in the evenings, after we'd finished our Russian lessons, I started to read for a scholarship again, biking in along Trumpington Road to work in the Cambridge Reference Library, a dark Victorian building behind the Town Hall (gaslit in memory, though it surely can't have been), where George III was about to make his second entrance. Sometime that autumn I bought, at Deighton Bell in Trinity Street, a copy of *George III and the Politicians* by Richard Pares, a book I have still, my name written in it by a friend, as I disliked my handwriting then as I do now. It was a detailed, allusive book, demanding a more thorough knowledge of eighteenth-century politics than a schoolboy could be expected to have, but I mugged it up. Like the good examinee I always was I realized that to know one book well is a better bet than having a smattering of several. A year in the army had made me more flash too, so this time I did get a scholarship, to read history at Exeter College, where I went when I came out of the army six months later.

The Oxford history syllabus takes in the whole of English history, beginning at 'the Beginnings' and finishing (in those days) at 1939. This meant that one didn't get round to the eighteenth century until the middle of the final year. Seeing that Pares, of whom I knew nothing other than his book, was lecturing at Rhodes House, I went along to find only a sparse attendance, though, curiously for a general lecture, I saw that quite a few of the audience were dons.

When Pares was brought in it was immediately plain why. Propped up in a wheelchair, completely paralysed, nodding and helpless, he was clearly dying. Someone spread his notes out on a board laid across his knees and he began to lecture, his head sunk on his chest but his voice still strong and clear. It was noticeable even in the eight weeks that I attended his lectures that the paralysis was progressive and that he was getting weaker. I fancy that in the final weeks, as he was unable to turn his head, someone sat beside him to move his notes into his line of vision.

Now, the eighteenth century is not an inspiring period. Whether by the Whig interpretation or not, there are none of those great constitutional struggles and movements of ideas that animate the seventeenth and dramatize the nineteenth. The politics are materialistic, small-minded, the House of Commons an arena where a man might make a name for himself but where most members were just concerned to line their pockets. That Pares, with death at his elbow, should have gone on analysing and lecturing on what I saw as such a thankless time made a great impression on me – the lesson put crudely, I suppose, being that if a thing is not worth doing it's worth doing well. As it was, these must have been the last lectures Pares gave – he died the following year – and, when I found I was able to stay on after taking my degree to do research and teach a little and possibly become a don, the memory of those lectures cast for me a romantic light on what is a pretty unromantic profession.

Pares kept cropping up in subsequent years. As the memoirs and letters of the twenties began to be published, it turned out that as an undergraduate he had been one of the group round Evelyn Waugh and Harold Acton. But, whereas most of that charmed circle went down without taking a degree, Pares turned his back on all that, took a First in Greats and was elected a fellow of All Souls. Thirty years later, in December 1954, Evelyn Waugh wrote to Nancy Mitford:

I went up to Oxford and visited my first homosexual love, Richard Pares, a don at All Souls. At 50 he is quite paralysed except his mind and voice, awaiting deterioration and death. A wife and four daughters, no private fortune. He would have been Master of Balliol if he had not been struck down. No Christian faith to support him. A very harrowing visit.

My vision of myself pursuing an academic career did not last long, though as a postgraduate I was supervised by the medieval historian K. B. McFarlane, who had, incidentally, shared a flat with Pares when they were both drafted into the Civil Service during the war. McFarlane was a great teacher, and yet he scarcely seemed to teach at all. An hour with him and, though he barely touched on the topic of my research, I would come away thinking that to study medieval history was the only thing in the world worth doing. McFarlane himself had no such illusions, once referring to medieval studies as 'just a branch of the entertainment business', though when with the onset of *Beyond the Fringe* I eventually abandoned medieval studies for the entertainment business this did not make him any less displeased. Still, it meant that when a couple of years ago I began to read about George III it was the first systematic historical work I'd done in twenty years.

In the meantime I found that George III's rehabilitation had proceeded apace. No longer the ogre, he had grown altogether more kindly – wiser even – and in his attachment to his people and his vision of the nation over and above the vagaries of politics he had come to seem a forerunner of a monarch of the present day. But it was a joke that made me think of writing about him – just as when a few years ago I thought of writing about Kafka what started me off was a joke that Kafka had made on his deathbed. Less poignant, George III's joke also occurred during his illness. He had an equerry, Colonel Manners, who, bringing him his dinner one day, discovered the King had hidden under the sofa. A Jeeves before his time, Manners imperturbably laid a place for His Majesty on the carpet and put down the plate. He was retiring discreetly when the King said (still *sous bergère*), 'That was very good . . . Manners.' The pun was thought to signal a further stage in the King's recovery. The anecdote hasn't found its way into the play, but it did make me think that George III might be fun to write about.

My interest in the King's story had also been rekindled by reading some of the medical history that was being published in the eighties, particularly by Roy Porter. Michael Neve and Jonathan Miller separately suggested that the madness of George III would make a play, and Neve lent me *The Royal Malady* by Charles Chenevix Trench, which is still the best account of the King's illness and the so–called Regency Crisis. I also read *George III and the Mad Business* by the mother-and-son partnership Richard Hunter and Ida Macalpine, who first put forward the theory that the King's illness was physical not mental and that he was suffering from porphyria. I found it a difficult book to read, convincing about George III himself but less so about the other historical cases the authors identify, the slightest regal indisposition being seized on to fetch the sufferer under porphyria's umbrella.

From a dramatist's point of view, it is obviously useful if the

King's malady was a toxic condition, traceable to a metabolic disturbance rather than due to schizophrenia or manic depression. Thus afflicted, he becomes the victim of his doctors and a tragic hero. How sympathetic this would make him to the audience I had not realized until the previews of the play. I had been worried that the climax came two-thirds of the way into the second act, when the King begins to recover, and that there was no real dramatic development after that. What I had not anticipated was that the audience would be so wholeheartedly on the King's side or that when he does recover it would prove such a relief of tension that the rest of the play, in which little happens except that various loose ends are tied up, would go by on a wave of delighted laughter. 'The King is himself again' means that the audience can once more take pleasure in his eccentricities and enjoy the discomfiture of the doctors until in a nice sentimental conclusion Mr and Mrs King are united in regal domesticity.

Having been working on the play for a year or so, I had eventually got it into some sort of order by April 1991, when, knowing it was far from finished, and in some despair, I put it through Nicholas Hytner's door. Coming away from the house, I felt rather like one of those practical jokers who arrange for an unsuspecting victim to be landed with a load of slurry. That Hytner was then enthusiastic about the script and with him the Director of the National Theatre, Richard Eyre, cheered me up so much that I forced myself to reread it. No, I had been right: slurry at that moment it was. Later I discovered that Hytner had a gap in his schedule and Richard Eyre had a gap in his, so that the script had come as the answer to both their prayers.

Reading the play for the first time and knowing only a little of the period, Nicholas Hytner had been surprised when the King recovered. With this in mind, his first suggestion was that I should make the play more of a cliff-hanger, relying on the fact that most people would know there was a Regency without quite knowing when it began or that the Prince of Wales would have to wait another twenty years before he finally got his hands on the government. This was just the first of many invaluable suggestions he made, and in the course of the next three months the play was completely reshaped. The role of a director at this stage of a play is more like that of an editor, and directors who can fill this role are few and far between.

Though it began and ended much as it did in the finished version, the original manuscript meandered about quite a bit, so the two rewrites I did between April and August cut out a good deal in an effort to make the progress of the King's illness and his recovery more clear. In August 1991 a reading of the text was set up in the National Theatre Studio, actors working at the National taking the various parts almost on a first-come-first-served basis, the purpose being for us to hear the text and see how it played. The only actor already cast was Nigel Hawthorne, and it was plain from his reading how he would transform the part. That said, to sit and hear the play read, knowing it was unfinished, was both depressing and embarrassing, and I fear that some of the actors, who seldom see a play at this stage, must have wondered why we were bothering. But I then began a third rewrite, which solved many of the problems the reading had thrown up and gave the play more dramatic thrust: this was the script we began to rehearse at the end of September.

That we were able to rehearse for ten weeks was a great luxury, and one only possible in a subsidized company. However, in that time Nicholas Hytner had also to rehearse the new production of *The Wind in the Willows*, so it was Pitt and Fox in the morning, Rat and Mole (and Fox) in the afternoon. When at the end of the seventh week we were able to run the play, it was immediately clear that, while the course of the King's illness and recovery was plain and worked dramatically, the political crisis it brought with it lacked urgency. So the final bout of rewriting was only a couple of weeks before the play went on stage. I have never worked on a play where so much reconstruction has been required. That it was unresented by the actors, who by this stage in rehearsal are naturally anxious for a finished text, says a good deal both for their forbearance and for the atmosphere in which the rehearsals were conducted. Not since *Forty Years On*, which is, I suppose, my only other historical play, have I enjoyed rehearsals so much.

One casualty of the rewrites was strict historical truth. In the early versions of the play I had adhered pretty closely to the facts: the Prince of Wales, for instance, was originally a more genial character than presented here, and more reluctant to have it admitted in public or in the press that his father might be mad. However, the play works only if the antipathy between father and son, never far below the surface with all the Hanoverian kings, is sharpened and the Prince made less sympathetic. In the original Fox, too, was a more ambiguous character, much troubled by his own lack of scruple, and the votes in the Commons were not so narrow, the government majority never as low as ten. In other respects, though, events needed no sharpening, the King's recovery, for instance, being only slightly less dramatic than it is in the play; certainly it took the politicians by surprise. This was because the King's illness was such a political football that no one was quite sure what information was to be trusted. Even when the King was plainly on the mend the doctors could not guarantee that he would maintain the improvement (and there were some alarming lapses).

In this process of recovery the 'what-whatting' was crucial. This verbal habit of the King's was presumably the attempt of a nervous and self-conscious man to prevent the conversation from flagging – always a danger in chats with the monarch, since the subject is never certain whether he or she is expected to reply or when. The onset of the King's mania delivered him from self-consciousness and so the 'what-whatting' went; the King was in any case talking too fast and too continuously for there to be need or room for it. When he began to calm down and come to himself again he came to the 'what-whatting' too, the flag of social distress now a signal of recovery. As Greville wrote, 'though not a grace in language, yet the restoring habits of former days prescribed a forerunner of returning wisdom.'

I have no experience of royal persons, some of whom I think may still 'what-what' a little. Today, though, it's easier. What royalty wants nowadays is deference without awe, though what they get more often than not is a fatuous smile, any social awkwardness veiled in nervous laughter so that the Queen moves among her people buoyed up on waves of obliging hilarity. How happy we must all seem! Such tittering would have been unthinkable at the court of George III, reputedly the dullest in Europe, where no one laughed or coughed, and where it was unthinkable ever to sneeze.

Had the King insisted on such formality outside the court he would not have been as popular as he was. A stickler for etiquette at home, he and the Queen remained seated while his courtiers stood for hours at a time, drooping with boredom: but outside the court, often riding unattended, the King would stop and chat with farm labourers, road-menders and anybody he came across. When they went to Cheltenham he promised the Queen, with a lack of formality that not so long ago was thought to be a modern breakthrough, that they would 'walk about and meet his subjects'.

One difficulty when writing the play was how to furnish the audience with sufficient information about the political set-up at the end of the eighteenth century for them to understand why the illness of the King threatened the survival of the government. Nowadays, of course, it wouldn't, and the fact that there were seemingly two parties, Tories and Whigs, could mislead an audience into thinking that nowadays and those days are much the same.

What has to be understood is that in 1788 the monarch was still the engine of the nation. The King would choose as his chief minister a politician who could muster enough support in the House of Commons to give him a majority. Today it is the other way round: the majority in the Commons determines the choice of Prime Minister. Though this sometimes seemed to be the case even in the eighteenth century, a minister imposed on the King by Parliament could not last long: this was why George III so much resented Fox, who was briefly his Prime Minister following a disreputable coalition with North in 1783. All governments were to some degree coalitions, and a majority in the Commons did not reflect some overall victory by Whigs or Tories in a general election. Leading figures in Parliament had their groups of supporters; there were Pittites, Foxites, Rockingham Whigs and Grenvilles, who voted as their patron voted. A ministry was put together, a majority accumulated out of an alliance of various groups, and what maintained that alliance was the uninterrupted flow of political patronage, the network of offices and appointments available to those running the administration. In the play Sir Boothby Skrymshir and his nephew Ramsden are a ridiculous pair, but, as Sheridan says (though the phrase was actually used by Fox), they are the 'marketable flotsam' out of which a majority was constructed. At the head of the pyramid was the King. All appointments flowed from him. If he was incapacitated and his powers transferred to his son, support for the ministry would dwindle because the flow of patronage had stopped. If the King was mad, it would not be long before the Ins were Out.

As I struggled to mince these chunks of information into credible morsels of dialogue (the danger always being that characters are telling each other what they know in their bones), I often felt it would have been simpler to call the audience in a quarter of an hour early and give them a short curtain lecture on the nature of eighteenth-century politics before getting on with the play proper.

The characters are largely historical. Margaret Nicholson's attempt on the King's life was in 1786, not just before his illness as in the play; but it is certainly true, as the King remarks, that in France she would not have got off so lightly. As it was, she lived on in Bedlam long after the witnesses to her deed were dead, surviving until the eve of the accession of George III's granddaughter, Queen Victoria.

I thought I had invented Fitzroy but discover that in 1801 George III had an aide-de-camp of this name, who was later the heart-throb of the King's youngest daughter, Amelia. He was 'generally admitted to be good-looking in a rather wooden sort of way, he had neither dash nor charm and seems to have been on the frigid side into the bargain,' which describes our Fitzroy exactly. That he was playing a double game and was an intimate of the Prince of Wales is my invention.

Greville is a historical character, his diary one of the most important sources for the history of the royal malady. However, Greville was not in attendance throughout as he is in the play. A fair-minded though conventional man, and clear-sighted where the King's illness was concerned (and often appalled at its treatment), Greville along with the King's other attendants was excluded when Dr Willis, 'the mad doctor', took on the case. Willis brought with him some of his own staff, presumably from his asylum at Greatham in Lincolnshire, and took on other heavies in London. In the play they appear only once, when the restraining-chair is brought in at the end of the first act, but in fact they remained at Windsor and Kew in constant attendance on the King until Willis eventually went back north. This was not, as in the play, immediately before the thanksgiving service in June 1789, but some months later.

The number of physicians attending the King varied. They were known as the 'London doctors', to distinguish them from Dr Willis and his son. I have restricted them to three, but there may have been as many as ten. Nor have I included Willis's son, who was also a doctor and in charge of the King during his next attack in 1802.

The pages who in the play bear so much of the burden of the King's illness were probably older than I have made them, the youngest and kindest, Papandiek, being the King's barber, with his wife another of those who kept a diary of this much journalized episode. Some pages were sacked when the King recovered, because 'from the manner in which they had been obliged to attend on Him during the illness, they had obtained a sort of familiarity which now would not be pleasing to Him. However, these were not Papandiek and Braun. In the play depicted as a heartless creature, Braun was in fact one of the King's favourites, and still in his service ten years later. The other page, Fortnum, left to found the grocer's, and in the seventies, I remember, one used to be accosted in the store in far-from-eighteenth-century language by two bewigged figures, Mr Fortnum and Mr Mason – actually two unemployed actors.

I found the Opposition (an anachronistic phrase for which there is no convenient substitute) much harder to write than the government. 'What can they *do*?' Nicholas Hytner would ask, which is the same question of course that Opposition politicians are always having to ask themselves, even today. Pitt, Dundas and Thurlow carry on the government; Fox, Sheridan and Burke can only talk about the day when they might have the government to carry on. And drink, of course. But, as the King says, 'they all drink.' Pitt was frequently drunk before a big speech, and on one occasion was sick behind the Speaker's chair.

With Pitt I had first to rid myself of the picture I retained of him from childhood, when I saw Korda's wartime propaganda film *The Young Mr Pitt*. Robert Donat was Pitt, kitted out with a kindly housekeeper, adoring chums and maybe even a girlfriend. At one point in the play he talks of when he was a boy, though boy he never really was, brought up by his father to be Prime Minister, destined always for 'the first employments'. The son, the nephew and the first cousin of Prime Ministers, the only commoner in a Cabinet of peers, perhaps he was arrogant – but no wonder. Long, lank and awkward, he made a wonderful caricature, and if he was the first Prime Minister in the sense we understand it today it was because, as Pares says, the cartoonists made him so.

Pitt's career ran in tandem with that of Fox, though Fox was the older man. Meeting the boy Pitt, he seems to have had a premonition that here was his destiny. They are such inveterate and complementary opposites – Pitt cold, distant and calculating; Fox warm, convivial and impulsive – that they are almost archetypes: save or squander, hoard or spend, Gladstone and Disraeli, Robespierre and Danton, Eliot and Pound. Pitt had his disciples, but Fox, for all his inconsistencies and political folly, was genuinely loved, even by his opponents (though never by the King). His oratory was spellbinding, as Pitt ruefully acknowledged ('Ah,' he said to one of Fox's critics, 'but you have never been under the wand of the magician'). Burke, whom posterity remembers as a great orator, was in his day considered a bore, his speeches often ludicrously over the top, and known as 'the dinner bell' because when he rose to speak he regularly emptied the House.

Fox had charm, even at his lowest ebb. 'I have led a sad life,' he wrote to his mistress:

sitting up late, always either at the House of Commons or gaming, and losing my money every night that I have played. Getting up late, of course, and finding people in my room so that I have never had the morning time to myself, and have gone out as soon as I could, though generally very late, to get rid of them, so that I have scarce ever had a moment to write. You have heard how poor a figure we made in numbers on the slave trade, but I spoke I believe very well . . . and it is a cause in which one cannot help being pleased with oneself for having done right.

Baffled as to how to convey Fox's charm, I included much of this letter in the first draft of the play, the speech originally part of the much altered final scene. 'A danger this is becoming Fox's story,' noted Nicholas Hytner, so I took it out again.

I made Sheridan a man of business, a manager of the House, and he was certainly more canny than Fox, whom he regularly scolded and who, he always said, treated him as if he were a swindler. I began by peppering his speeches with self-quotation, which is never a wise move. I had done the same with Orton in an early draft of the screenplay of *Prick Up Your Ears*, and that hadn't worked either; one thinks, too, of all the movies about Wilde in which he talks in epigrams throughout. There was originally a parody of the screen scene in *School for Scandal*, in which the Prince of Wales and his doctor are discovered hiding from the King. It had some basis in fact, but it was an early casualty. I give him two shots at explaining it, but what I find hard to understand is why, having made a name for himself in the theatre, Sheridan should have wanted to go into politics at all. On the rare occasions I have talked to politicians I have found myself condescended to because I'm not 'in the know'. (Political journalists and civil servants do it too.) So perhaps that was part of it. Poor Sheridan never quite managed to be one of the boys, even in death. In Westminster Abbey, Pitt, Fox and

26 Camden Town, 1982

27 *An Englishman Abroad*, Dundee, 1983, Coral Browne and Alan Bates

28 *An Englishman Abroad* (left to right: Alan Bates, Innes Lloyd, Ken Pearce, A. B. and John Schlesinger)

29 *Kafka's Dick*, Royal Court Theatre, September 1986 (left to right: Andrew Sachs, Jim Broadbent, Roger Lloyd Pack, Geoffrey Palmer)

30 *Kafka's Dick*, Jim Broadbent and Roger Lloyd Pack

31 *A Private Function*, Barnoldswick, May 1984 (left to right: A. B., Denholm Elliott, Bernard Wrigley, John Normington, Richard Griffiths, Michael Palin)

32 *A Private Function*, Bradford Art School (left to right: A. B., Maggie Smith, Michael Palin)

33 *A Private Function*, Ilkley, with Betty

34 Keith McNally and Russell Harty, New York, 1979

35 With Craig Raine, Sue Townsend and the Orel writers, USSR, May 1988

36 and 37 Miss Shepherd, 1988

38 With Simon Callow rehearsing *A Question of Attribution*,
Royal National Theatre, November 1988

Burke are buried clubbily together, whereas Sheridan has landed up next to Garrick. His distaste for this location was another casualty of the final scene of the play. Of course what I really wanted to include, but didn't dare, was the playwright's bane: a conversation (with Thurlow, it would be), beginning, 'Anything in the pipeline, Sheridan?'

Dundas was much older than I have made him, but, dramatically, Pitt needs a friend or else he would never unburden himself at all. Thurlow, foul-tongued and 'lazy as a toad at the bottom of a well', was well known to be a twister. When he made the speech on the King's recovery, quoted in the play – 'And when I forget my sovereign, may God forget me' – Wilkes, who was seated on the steps of the throne, remarked, 'God forget you? He'll see you damned first!'

Queen Charlotte was every bit as homely and parsimonious as she's presented, stamping the leftover pats of butter with her signet so that they would not be eaten by the servants. Her name is preserved in Apple Charlotte, a recipe that uses up stale bread. I thought I had caught her rather well until Janet Dale, who was playing her, said that the game little wife was a part to which she was no stranger: not long ago it was the first Mrs Orwell, and more recently Mrs Walesa. ' "Have another cup of tea, Lech, and let Solidarity take care of itself . . ." Solidarity, *Animal Farm* or porphyria, I'm always the plucky little woman married to a hubby with problems.'

There are some fortuitous parallels with contemporary politics; and had the play been written before the downfall of Mrs Thatcher there would have been more. Pitt's 'kitchen principles' were not dissimilar to hers, and one can see that Dundas having Willis redraft the bulletin while Pitt keeps his hands clean is reminiscent of Mrs Thatcher's conduct in the Westland affair. Thinking that the Regency Bill must pass and that he faces imminent dismissal, Pitt says that he needs five more years.* The audience laughs. But what politician doesn't? Pitt of course got them, but what he actually meant was five more years of peace, and these he didn't get. Mrs Thatcher's fortunes were made by a war that came just in time, Pitt's ruined by a war which (as Fox thought) should not have come at all. The audience applauds again when Pitt, reviewing his seemingly bleak future, says that having been Prime Minister he does not now intend to sit on the back benches and carp. This isn't an easy gibe at Mr Heath, for whom I've got some sympathy. Pitt had always aspired to be Prime Minister, but on his own terms; in 1783 he had even refused the King's invitation to form a ministry because he was not yet ready; defeated, he would never have played second fiddle to anybody.

Any account of politics, whatever the period, must throw up contemporary parallels. I think if I had deliberately made more of these it would have satisfied or pandered to some critics who felt that that was what the play should have been more about. But it is about the madness of George III – the rest amusing, intriguing, but incidental. Mention of the critics, though, reminds me that one of the jokes when we were rehearsing the play was that it would take audiences ten minutes to reconcile themselves to the fact that it wasn't set in Halifax. Such jokes tempt fate, and I'm told that the critic of the *Independent* spent most of his notice regretting that it wasn't more Trouble at t'Mill.

Though I have known sufferers from severe depression, I have had little experience of mental illness or of the discourse of the mentally ill, since depression, though it can lead to delusions, doesn't disorder speech. Of course, as Greville cautions Willis in the play, the King's discourse is slightly disordered to begin with, not normal anyway, and his idiosyn-

* When the play was put on in America the line only worked when altered to '*four* more years'.

cratic utterance has to be established in the audience's mind before it gets more hurried and compulsive and he starts to go off the rails. Even then Willis has to tread warily, because behaviour which in an ordinary person would be considered unbalanced (talking of oneself in the third person, for instance) is perfectly proper in the monarch. Some of the contents of the King's mad speech I cribbed from contemporary sources, such as John Haslam's *Illustrations of Madness*, an account of James Tilly Matthews, a patient in Bethlem Hospital in 1810. Other features of the King's mad talk – his elaborate circumlocutions (a chair 'an article for sitting in'), for instance – are characteristic of schizophrenic speech.

What was plain quite early on was that where mad talk was concerned a little went a long way; that while it is interesting to see the King going mad, and a great relief to see him recover, when he is completely mad and not making any sense at all he is of no dramatic consequence. Since what he is saying is irrational it cannot affect the outcome of things, and so is likely to be ignored: thus an audience will attend to what is being done to the King but not to what he is saying. There was also a difficulty with the sheer quantity of the King's discourse (on one occasion he was reported as talking continuously for nine hours at a stretch). Two minutes' drivel, however felicitously phrased, is enough to make an audience restive, and, though what the King is saying is never quite drivel, the volume of it has to be taken down to allow other characters to speak across him – subject sense taking precedence over regal nonsense. Of course speech is not the half of it, and without Nigel Hawthorne's transcendent performance the King could have been just a gabbling bore and his fate a matter of indifference. As it is, the performance made him such a human and sympathetic figure the audience saw the whole play through his eyes.

The final scene of the play proved the most difficult to get right. I knew from the start that the play must end at St Paul's, when the nation gave thanks for the King's return to health. As originally written, the doctors emerged still quarrelling as to who deserved the credit for their patient's recovery. Then Dr Richard Hunter, joint author of *George III and the Mad Business*, materialized in modern dress to tell the eighteenth-century doctors that they were all wrong anyway and that the King was not mad but suffering from porphyria. The discussion that followed was long and detailed – too much so for this stage of the play – and was made longer when the politicians emerged and started quarrelling too. Finally the King himself came out, found the doctors disagreeing over the body of the patient and the politicians disagreeing over the body of the state, said to hell with it all, and, taking his cue from Hunter, described how he would eventually end up mad anyway.

Nigel Hawthorne felt, I think rightly, that he couldn't step out of his character so easily and that if he did the audience would feel cheated. It was Roy Porter who suggested that Richard Hunter's mother, Ida Macalpine, was as much responsible for *George III and the Mad Business* as her son and that in the interest of literary justice (and political correctness) she should be the voice of modern medicine. Accordingly I wrote the brief scene just before the finale where she explains to the sacked pages (who had been the only ones to take notice of the King's blue piss) what this symptom meant. Whereas in a film one could deal with this explanation in the final credits, I felt at the time the play opened that the facts had to be set out and the matter settled within the play. Now I'm less sure, though the scene has a structural function as it enables the King and Queen to nip out of bed and into their togs ready for the finale.

One ending I was fond of, though it was determinedly untheatrical, and perhaps just an elaborate way of saying that too many cooks spoil the broth; still, it's the nearest I can get to extracting a message from the play. The King and Queen are left alone on the stage after the Thanksgiving Service and they sit down on the steps of St Paul's and try to decide what lessons can be drawn from this unfortunate episode.

KING: The real lesson, if I may say so, is that what makes an illness perilous is celebrity. Or, as in my case, royalty. In the ordinary course of things doctors want their patients to recover; their reputations depend on it. But if the patient is rich or royal, powerful or famous, other considerations enter in. There are many parties interested apart from the interested party. So more doctors are called in, and none but the best will do. But the best aren't always very good, and they argue, they disagree. They have to, because they are after all the best and the world is watching. And who is in the middle? The patient. It happened to me. It happened to Napoleon. It happened to Anthony Eden. It happened to the Shah. The doctors even killed off George V to make the first edition of *The Times*. I tell you, dear people, if you're poorly it's safer to be poor and ordinary.

QUEEN: But not too poor, Mr King.

KING: Oh no. Not too poor. What? What?

The Madness of King George

The first draft of *The Madness of King George* (then called *The Madness of George III*) was prefaced with this note:

The Windsor Castle in which much of the action takes place is the castle before it was reconstructed in the 1820s. The eighteenth century wasn't all elegance, and there should be a marked contrast between the state rooms, in which the King's life was largely spent, and the back parts of the building, those tiny rooms and attics, cubicles almost, where, because the court was so crowded, most of the courtiers had to lodge. This was certainly the situation at Versailles and, I imagine, at most of the courts of Europe. Greville is lucky to have a little room to himself, and the pages sleep stacked in a cupboard like a scene from *Alice in Wonderland*.

It's not simply a contrast between public opulence and private squalor. I don't imagine the living-quarters of the court, cramped though they were, to have been particularly squalid; I think of them as being long boarded passages lined with doors, with narrow staircases and abrupt changes of level – accommodation not unlike that in the colleges at Oxford and Cambridge or on the top floors of country houses. But, scrubbed and white-painted as these quarters may have been, cramped they certainly were and often situated behind and adjacent to the state rooms and grand corridors where the ceremonial life of the court was led. Access to these back parts is through doors flush with the panelling or covered in camouflaging wallpaper; when Greville, say, comes on duty it's as if he's threading his way through a complicated backstage before coming out on to the set.

There should be a sense too that what happens to the King in the course of his illness is reflected in the topography of the castle. His behaviour, previously geared to the public and state rooms, gradually becomes inappropriate for such settings; when he periodically escapes into the back parts of the castle (as when he is looking for the Queen, for instance), it's comparable to his escape into the back parts of his personality, the contrast between what he seems and what he is echoed by that between the state rooms and the attics.

The notion of courts as overcrowded places I took from Nancy Mitford's *The Sun King*, with its vivid account of conditions at Versailles. Not to be at court in France was social death, and the aristocracy were prepared to put up with almost any inconvenience to avoid having to reside on their estates. In order to cope with the demand, rooms in the palace were divided and divided again, the elegant state apartments of the palace backing on to a labyrinth of poky lodgings and what were, in effect, bedsitters.

While the social set-up was different in England – the court never quite the same magnet – nevertheless here too conditions must have been pretty cheek by jowl, particularly in unreconstructed Windsor. Formality there was (too much of it, the courtiers complained), but with a crowd of well-to-do people crammed together in a tight place etiquette was always under strain, and once the door closed on the King and Queen the relief must have been as palpable as it is in the film: the royal brothers sink thankfully on to the vacated thrones and take off their shoes, and poor pregnant Lady Townsend is at last permitted to sit down. In the first version of the script I wanted to emphasize the unbuttoning that occurred once the King and Queen left the room, by having Fitzroy unexpectedly return: the court is suddenly stunned back into silence and immobility, thinking Their Majesties are about to come back; however, Fitzroy is only retrieving a shawl the Queen had left, so the hubbub resumes. Revising the script, I could see that there would be no time for such underlining and it was an early cut.

'No time' is, of course, always the problem. Film is drama at its most impatient, 'What happens next?' the perpetual nag. One can never *hang about*, thinks the writer, pertulantly. There's a bit more leeway on stage, depending on the kind of story one's telling, and more still on television, where the viewers are so close to the characters as not to mind whether they dawdle a bit. But meandering is out of the question with film: it has to be brisk, so most of my atmospheric backstairs stuff never made it to the final version – so little, in fact, that I wonder now how I could ever have thought it would, and was that preamble to the script just a sales pitch?

Not really, as the odd glimpses of life behind the scenes that did make it to the screen do pay off. There is the cupboard in the wall opened by the distraught King to reveal his three pages sleeping stacked on shelves one above the other (like the Fettiplaces on their monument in Swinbrook church in Oxfordshire). The King dashes along a vaulted corridor (Broughton Castle), bursts in upon a sleeping lady-in-waiting, and demands her chamber-pot. 'Do it, England,' he adjures himself, 'do it.'

But time and the budget put paid to much of the rest – no back corridors thronged with courtiers, still primping and titivating themselves as they hurry down to the opening concert; no shot of the same corridors silent in the small hours as one by one the doors open and sleepy courtiers stumble out *en déshabille* to listen to the distant howling of the King. The loss of such scenes was a sacrifice, but they were cut with resignation and general agreement, the telling of the King's story always taking priority and so edging out some of these nice vignettes.

Besides, the screenwriter's hopes for his film must always be a little fanciful. I'd have liked (who wouldn't?) the scene (later cut) where the King, gone suddenly mad, is followed at a discreet distance by the wondering court to have had some of the suspense and trepidation of a similar scene in Eisenstein's *Ivan the Terrible*. I may even have put that daunting note in the stage directions. It can't have helped; I might as well have said, 'If it can be arranged, I'd like this film to be masterpiece.'

Earlier in life I used to revel in the break from my routine that filming provided, while feeling myself as scriptwriter to have as necessary a role as the Make-Up department or Costumes. The scene often needed tweaking, for instance, to adapt it to the chosen location; the dialogue might have needed tweaking too, particularly if it was a Northern piece. So I used to take my place in that ritual dance that unfolds before the shot: the production assistant calls for 'final checks' and, as the camera assistant runs out the tape to determine the focus, Make-Up and Costumes dart in to powder a nose or straighten a tie, while the author (director, of course, permitting) has an earnest word with the actor about some emphasis or other.

That this hands-on authorship has loosened is partly due to age. Happy enough to sit around on the set all day if I'm acting, when I'm in attendance as scriptwriter I feel it's not a proper investment of time. Besides, many of the cast knew this piece better than I did, having played it on the stage off and on for two and a half years. So, whereas once upon a time I'd have been able to give a day-by-day account of the shooting of the film, my visits during the summer of 1994 to the unit on *The Madness of King George* were quite sporadic. Here are my notes on some of them:

8 July, Thame Park, Oxfordshire. First day of shooting *George III*. Twenty-two years since I first went on location (to Halifax in 1972 for *A Day Out*). Then I was full of jokes and enthusiasm, watching every shot and fussing over how my precious words were spoken. Today it's raining and I'm full of aches and pains and can scarcely bother to trail along the track to the pigsty, which is the first set-up of the film – and Nicholas Hytner's first set-up ever. As always, even on a modest film like ours, the sheer size of the operation depresses: a dozen vans, two or three buses, half-a-dozen caravans, rows of cars, and dozens and dozens of people, all of whom have good reason for being there except me, who started it all.

I watch the first shot – Nigel Hawthorne as George III on the brink of madness, talking to a pig – marvelling between takes at some wonderful run-down eighteenth-century barns with intricate grey-beamed roofs and sagging tiles. Nick H. seems happy enough and has at least got round the obstacle which always stopped me directing films – namely, having to say, 'Action!' My instinct would be to say, 'Er, I think if everybody's agreeable we might as well sort of start now – that is, if you're ready.' Today Mary Soan, the first assistant, says the dread word, Nick simply Making Decisions about the Shot.

28 July, Thame Park. From the outside the house looks pleasantly dilapidated, with a handsome eighteenth-century front, behind that a Tudor house which in its turn incorporates the quite substantial remains of a medieval priory. It's a country house out of a novel, in its lost park scattered with ancient oaks an easy metaphor for England.

And maybe it still is, because until ten years or so ago it was lived in by the descendants of the original owners; then at the height of the Thatcherite boom it was bought by a Japanese consortium to be turned into a country club. So step inside and one finds all the period features intact – a magnificent staircase, fine fireplaces, the original doors – but all so spick and span and *squared off* they might have been designed by Quinlan Terry. And (the metaphor still holding) work is at a standstill: having done a radical conversion job, the consortium ran out of money and now the house is empty, just rented out from time to time for films such as ours or as a setting for commercials.

In yesterday's morning mist, when we started shooting, it must have looked like the park and mansion in *Le Grand Meaulnes*, but Ken Adam, our designer, has had a hard job taking the new look off the interior. The house is standing in for Kew Palace, where George III was briefly confined during his illness. The requirements of the script mean that it should look cold and uncared-for, so the air of dereliction the Japanese so ruthlessly banished is being just as ruthlessly reintroduced, our painters still hard at work distressing the walls and pasting on peeling wallpaper. Incurious, careless, mildly destructive, the crew isn't much concerned about the house; and, though Thame Park isn't Brideshead, film units nowadays are not unlike the units of a different sort that were billeted in such places fifty years ago.

5 August, Oxford. Most of the cast of the stage play are taking part in the film, though some of them in much smaller roles just for old times' sake. I have been given the part of a loquacious MP who happens to be addressing the Commons when news arrives that the King, whom everyone believes still to be mad, is actually outside in Palace Yard. The House rapidly empties, leaving the MP (MP 2, as he's known in the script) addressing the empty benches with only the Speaker left. Eventually the Speaker tiptoes out too.

The House of Commons has been set up in Convocation, with the adjoining Divinity School representing the Lobby. Coming on to the set, with Pitt and Co. on the front bench and the place crammed with two hundred extras, I am struck, as one often was in the stage production, by how like an eighteenth-century illustration it looks.

'Do you do much extra work?' says my neighbour on the back benches. 'Not really,' I say, and am thankful for it, as it's swelteringly hot and more humid inside than out because of the vapour machine pumping out steam to make the scene more photogenic and blur its edges a bit. The extras – some of them undergraduates, others local amateurs – are far more tolerant and unprotesting than their professional London counterparts. Despite the heat, they seem actually to be enjoying themselves, strolling about between takes in the Sheldonian quad, showing off their costumes and being photographed by Japanese coach parties, who maybe think that this is all a normal part of university life.

Between shots I sit around chatting with the actors, John Wood, Geoffrey Palmer, Jim Carter and Barry Stanton, whiling away the day in a fashion I still find powerfully seductive.

6 August, Oxford. Today is cool and grey ('Shakespeare in the park weather,' someone says), which is perhaps fortunate as we have to get through eighteen or so set-ups in the day (the normal quota for a feature film being some five or six). Still, everybody is greatly encouraged from having seen last night a rough assembly of what has been shot so far, the snow scenes at Thame looking particularly good, with no hint that these were filmed on the hottest day of the year. Nor had I expected the change-over to much more muted colours as the King's madness takes hold, Kew (Thame Park) almost in black and white, with the bearded King in his black cloak looking especially dramatic. At the moment, though, we don't have enough money to finish the shooting at Thame, where we needed an extra day, just as we really need an extra half-day in Oxford.

The unit base is in the grounds of the Dragon School, and

after lunch I walk across the playing-fields to look at the war memorial, a cross by the cricket pavilion on the bank of the river. Names of boys virtually cover the cross, and not listed in an impersonal fashion, with surname and initials, but with the boy's first name (and sometimes his nickname) written out in full, with no indication of the rank he attained or the service in which he died. After the rain there are mushrooms dotted about the field, and two of the ground staff are marking out the football pitch for next season. I have a pee behind the sight-screen, as the school lavatories have no locks on the doors (though at least they have doors), the bleak dressing-rooms and showers making me thankful it's not a childhood I had to go through.

10 August, Eton. Eton is standing in for the Palace of Westminster and the exteriors of the State Opening of Parliament at the start of the film. We film first in the cloisters, the walls of which are studded with memorial plaques to the dead of two world wars – the First War particularly. There are bronze plaques so dark as to be indecipherable, ceramic panels that look quite festive, a memorial to all the Etonians who died in the Grenadier Guards, and umpteen tablets besides, some in self-conscious Latin to masters as well as boys, the conclusion of many of them '*Floreat Etona.*'

A dolly mounted with a ramshackle light-screen trundles the camera round the cloisters with the actors rushing along behind as the King argues with the Prince of Wales and the courtiers scurry after them, trying to keep up. What I hope we capture is how wanting in proper ceremony the eighteenth-century monarchy was, how slipshod and unmanaged were its public appearances, with, whatever the flummery, not much dignity about it at all. Then we shift to School Yard, where the MPs mass on the staircase by the chapel, watching the departure of the royal party. I sit by the statue of Henry VI (a pigeon feather caught on his nose) as the coaches wheel about the yard and Janine Duvitski as Margaret Nicholson rather shyly tries to assassinate the King.

Afterwards I wander down the immaculately preserved High Street. Here are Coutts Bank and some smart tailor's, established in the eighteenth century; there's a grand photographer's that looks as if it was established not long after, and other smart and elegant shops are hangers-on and camp-followers of the school. The message is plain: these boys are rich. And I hate it, and feel the worse for hating it because the school has been so helpful and cooperative over the film. I can see, though, that to be educated here isn't an unmixed blessing and that afterwards it could, as in Cyril Connolly's case, be downhill all the way, even the most lustrous Oxford or Cambridge college something of a comedown after all this.

I go back to the filming to find Greville on camera, knocking at a door covered, as is most Eton woodwork, in ancient graffiti. Some of it, though, is not quite so ancient (or not ancient enough for us), and it's only when we view the rushes that we see the date 1862 large and plain on this door at which he is knocking in 1788.

3 September, Broughton. Drive in grey drizzle to Banbury. Feel, even just passing through the town, the rootless anonymity that has swamped the place, the centre still intact and even handsome, but ringed by superstores and huge drive-in centres that service the acres of fuck-hutch estates that house its expanded population. 'Thriving' as I suppose it's called.

Broughton, a mile or two away, could not be in sharper contrast: the most beautiful of houses, medieval in a sixteenth-century or seventeenth-century shell with Gothick additions, entered across a moat and through a gatehouse – almost a standard kit for an idyll. There are a formal garden, great plush borders along the old ramparts, and cows and sheep grazing in the water meadows beyond, and overlooking it all this rambling honey-coloured house.

On to this rural paradise the film unit has descended like an invading army. Twenty or so vans have ploughed up one of the meadows, thirty cars are parked under the trees; there are half a dozen caravans and two marquees, and the sodden ground is rapidly turning into a quagmire. Churning up the edges of the perfect lawns, company cars ferry the actors to and from the location in the house, where the sparks, who have seen it all before, lug their lights and tripods down the superb vaulted corridors.

Seemingly unaffected by all this is the lady of the house, Mariette Saye – really Lady Saye and Sele (only nobody is quite sure whether one says Saye and Sele or just says Saye; say nothing the simplest). She's tall, cheerful and wonderfully welcoming, happy to show anybody round the house, which is as magical inside as out, handsome rooms lined with linenfold panelling, and a splendid drawing-room overlooking the moat. My wonder at the place makes me foolish, and I'm sure I gush – though it's partly to offset the unimpressed one-location-very-much-like-another behaviour inseparable from film crews, who congregate at the door, having coffee and a cig and trampling on yet another bit of lawn.

As always I find I'm pretty surplus to requirements, my only contribution a muttered suggestion to Nick Hytner that Rupert Graves's ad lib 'I'm fine, I'm fine' would be more in period if he said, 'It is no matter, no matter.' I watch Nigel H. rehearse the pisspot scene, then walk round the garden with Mark Thompson before buying some plants on sale in the potting-shed and coming away. Except then I call in at the church, which is full of the sound of hoovering – a friendly grey-haired man,

Welsh, who may be the vicar, though I don't like to ask, seemingly vacuuming the altar. It's the bats, he explains, the church being disputed territory between English Heritage, who want them expelled, and English Nature, who don't. In the meantime he hoovers.

Unnoted in my diary were locations even more spectacular. The opening concert was shot in the Double Cube room at Wilton, where the handbell ringers give their somnolent rendering of 'Greensleeves' ('Fascinating stuff!' says the King) in front of the sumptuous backcloth of Van Dyck's portrait of the Earl of Pembroke and his family. The Prince of Wales's lodging were at Wilton and the Royal Naval College at Greenwich, where Wren's Painted Hall was the setting for the second concert, when the King runs amok. The long gallery in which George III sees Pitt at the start of the film and its close, and down which Pitt bows himself endlessly out, is at Syon House, as was the Prince of Wales's breakfast room. Arundel Castle doubled for Windsor. Medievalized around the same time, Arundel shares many of the features of its more familiar counterpart, though catch either of them on a wet day and they look like long-stay institutions for the criminally insane.

The title of the stage play is *The Madness of George III* and of the film *The Madness of King George*. This was a marketing decision: the American backers somewhat shamefacedly explained that the audience might think, seeing *The Madness of George III*, that they had missed out on *The Madness of George* and *The Madness of George II*, a survey having apparently shown that there were many moviegoers who came away from

Kenneth Branagh's film of *Henry V* wishing they had seen its four predecessors. Where this leaves *The Third Man* (or *The Second Mrs Tanqueray*) I'm not sure.

Many of the actors and actresses in the stage play took part in the film, though not always in the same roles. Nigel Hawthorne remained George III, and Julian Wadham Pitt, and two of the King's doctors and two of his pages were the same on stage and on film. Even when this continuity wasn't possible there was often a niche in the film for actors who had been displaced: Iain Mitchell, who played Sheridan on the stage, is the pig farmer (with terrible teeth) at the start of the film. Helen Mirren played Queen Charlotte, but Selina Cadell, who had played the Queen in the second National Theatre production, became Mrs Cordwell, a patient in Dr Willis's Lincolnshire asylum who lost her wits when her sea-captain husband was drowned off the Goodwin Sands. The scene in the asylum was originally much longer, with the patients due to be played by some of our leading stage directors, including Richard Eyre, Sam Mendes and Declan Donnellan. The directors proved, of course, much more temperamental and hard to please than actors and one by one got cold feet, leaving only Stephen Daldry gamely plying a lonely sickle. Alas for his loyalty, his scene was one of the earliest cuts.

The marriage of the Prince of Wales to Mrs Maria Fitzherbert comes into the film as it didn't into the play. The Prince had married her secretly (in her own drawing-room) in 1785, really in order to satisfy Mrs Fitzherbert's Catholic conscience, as she refused to sleep with him otherwise. Valid in the eyes of her Church, the marriage was always invalid in legal and constitutional terms, as the Prince could not marry without his father's permission and if he married a Catholic he forfeited his right to the throne. Not that this mattered to Mrs Fitzherbert, who –

sensible woman that she was – had no interest in the throne anyway. No one has a wrong word for her: sweet-natured, amiable and no great beauty, she was received at court and was on good terms with the King and Queen, both of them seemingly in no doubt about her relation to the Prince. However, when, early in 1787, the existence of the marriage was raised in Parliament, the Prince of Wales denied it even to his friend Fox, who, believing him, stood up in the Commons and denied it too. Not surprisingly, Mrs Fitzherbert was very cross and, though she forgave the Prince, she never forgave Fox, who in turn found it hard to forgive the Prince.

All this had blown over by the time George III became ill late in 1788, and the marriage played no part in what came to be called the Regency Crisis. In my script it does, partly because the plot needed thickening and also because I wanted Mrs Fitzherbert to have her own story and not just be sitting around as the companion of the Prince. At the end of the film the Prince is seen to have rejected Mrs Fitzherbert, but in fact they lived together openly for another fourteen years, even after the Prince's marriage (legal but disastrous) to Princess Caroline of Brunswick. Rejection, when it did come in 1803, was as crude and brutal as royal behaviour often is, recalling the unfeeling-ness with which a later Prince of Wales, having met Mrs Simpson, briskly put aside his long-time mistress, Mrs Dudley-Ward. Sometimes it's as if royalty know about good behaviour by hearsay and can give only a faulty imitation of it, or, as Willis remarks before meeting the King, 'Deferred to, agreed with, acquiesced in. Who can flourish on such a daily diet of compliance? To be curbed, stood up to, in a word thwarted, exercises the character, elasticates the spirit, makes it more pliant. It is the want of such exercise that makes rulers rigid.' Or spoiled, as Nanny would say.

In general the Prince of Wales is more forceful and more of a villain in the film than he was on the stage or in life. There's no doubt that he was anxious to be made Regent, but he was more careful of appearances than I have made him and was more governed too by that fellow-feeling all royals have for each other. The Prince of Wales, for instance, was understandably sensitive to any suggestions, particularly in the press, that his father was mad. For a subject to remark on the King's state of mind seemed to the Prince insolent and intolerable. Or *sometimes* seemed to him insolent and intolerable. For the Prince himself to make such a suggestion (and to make jokes on the subject) was permissible, and permissible for his cronies too, a lot of the time. But suddenly they would find they had gone too far, the Prince would get on his high royal horse again, and his friends would have to mind their p's and q's for a bit. It's a characteristic of royalty that one minute they are happy to masquerade as ordinary persons and the next they demand to be treated as a race apart. Like the rest of us, I suppose, they just want things both ways, but this 'Now you "Sir" me, now you don't' must make intimacy with royalty a little wearing, and friendship with them must always involve an element of Grandmother's Footsteps. Like Fitzroy, courtiers must learn to be pretty sure-footed, with little hope of ever being 'natural', the ideal being somewhere between those who can't forget the royals' highness (and so are stilted) and those who forget it altogether (and so are cheeky).

These reservations apart, I found I was less sceptical about the monarchy as an institution than my colleagues on the production team, partly because (and slightly to my surprise) I was older than most of them and more set in my ways. Certainly I'm no republican and find nothing particularly extraordinary in the difficulties and embarrassments of the present Prince of Wales. It's a role, after all, which has seldom been satisfactorily filled; I suppose George V was good enough at it, but he was a dull man who was heir-apparent for a relatively short time, acceding to the position on the unexpected death of his much less suitable elder brother for whom no one had a good word, some even identifying him with Jack the Ripper. (Even the *Sun* hasn't managed to insinuate that Prince Charles is a serial killer.) But when the Prince of Wales in the film says that to be heir to the throne is not a position, it is a predicament, it's meant to be both a cry from the heart and a statement of an obvious truth.

Given my royalist inclinations, I haven't followed the goings-on over the break-up of the marriage of the Prince and Princess of Wales, or read any of the literature it has occasioned. I don't say this prissily. In my own circle of friends divorce dismays me for entirely selfish reasons: it alters the social landscape in unpredictable ways, curtailing friendships, shutting down havens, and generally making life less comfortable. The Prince of Wales's marriage, I need hardly add, does not impinge in quite this way, but like everything to do with the monarchy I'd just like to be able to take it for granted as one used to do. I don't want to have to think about it. I just want it to be *there*.

However, I would like to tiptoe into a royal bedroom if only to see how far, when one party is royal and the other not, the game of Grandmother's Footsteps still goes on between the sheets. At what point is rank suspended and royalty discontinued, and is the subject, even when forgetting him/herself utterly, still obliged to remember his/her place? Toiling over that regal eminence, I can imagine Edward VII's mistresses still feeling constrained to call him 'Sir', and without their 'Sir' or 'Ma'am' royals may feel too naked altogether. Though maybe the discarding of this last rag of distinction gives them a thrill denied to the rest of us who, when we have no clothes on, have nothing left to take off. More reports please.

The parallels with today's monarchy were largely unsought, but they became more obvious as the film proceeds, the final shot of St Paul's consciously recalling the television coverage of the marriage of the Prince and Princess of Wales. (On the other hand, if one is going to film the entry into St Paul's, there is only one place from which to do it; television chose it and so did we.)

Still, the conversation as the royal family pauses at the top of the steps to acknowledge the crowds has acquired a resonance it did not quite have when the play was written in 1991.

'We must try to be more of a family,' says the King. 'There are model farms now, model villages, even model factories. Well, we must be a model family for the nation to look to.'

'But, Pa,' complains the Prince of Wales, 'I want something to *do*.'

'Follow in my footsteps,' says his unfeeling father. 'That is what you should do. Smile at the people. Wave to them. Let them see we are happy! That is why we are here.'

George III has a bad reputation in the United States, because he is thought of as the king who caused the War of Independence. Were this true (which it isn't), then he could be said to have earned America's gratitude: if without him there would have been no war, there would also have been no United States (or they would at least have been postponed). By the same token I always feel Judas deserves some sort of slap on the back, because without him Christianity would never have got off the ground.

By 1788, as Pitt says in one version of the stage play, 'America is over', meaning not merely the war but the relevance of America as a factor in English politics. In the shake-up of parliamentary allegiances brought about by the war Pitt had sided with Fox against the King and Lord North. This so rankled with George III that he would not leave the subject alone, to the extent that when at the King's request Pitt formed a ministry in 1782 he made it a condition the King would not mention America. So when at the outset of his illness the King starts to 'harp on about America' it is a sign that the royal self-control is beginning to break down.

Fox was temperamentally drawn to the colonists, Pitt less so, but neither was in sympathy with the King's view that the colonies were an inalienable estate and part of his royal patrimony. The King's attitude has echoes today, with the monarch much more wedded to the idea of the Commonwealth than is the Prime Minister: it was one of the points of difference between the Queen and Mrs Thatcher, who probably found Her Majesty every bit as intractable on the subject as Pitt did George III. In the language of the higher Civil Service, George III was 'a bit of a loose cannon'; one never knew what he would be up to (and into) next. At the end of the eighteenth century the monarch was, of course, less circumscribed than today, and constitutional practice still permitted the crown a good deal of freedom, and it wasn't a freedom George III was prepared to share.

KING: When people in Parliament oppose, go against my wishes, I still find it very vexing. Try as I can, it seems to me disloyalty.

PITT: Your Majesty should not take it so personally.

KING: Not take it personally? But I'm King. This is my Government. How else should I take it but personally?

PITT: The Whigs believe it is their duty to oppose you, sir.

KING: Duty? Duty? What sort of duty is that?

It was a duty to the future, in fact, as the idea of an Opposition that was legitimate and not simply bloody-minded was only just beginning to emerge. I have made Pitt say, 'The King will do as he's told.' That's a bit in the future too, as it was quite hard, until his health began to fail, to tell George III anything – he was far too conscientious and well-informed for that. Certainly had he been less dutiful, less *busy*, he would have been less trouble to the politicians and perhaps to himself, as some at least of his mental torment can be put down to the frustration of a conscientious nature. 'Cork too tight in the bottle,' says Dundas. 'The man has to break out somehow.'

Whether America played any part in causing his 'breaking out', it would be hard to say. He never wanted to be opposed, and to be contradicted as ordinary mortals were was, as Willis says, one of the lessons he had to learn. Certainly after his illness he was able to swallow America as he could not before, and he learned to be more sly – neatly reversing Pitt's embargo on mentioning America by making Pitt promise that he in his turn would not mention, still less propose, Catholic emancipation.

KING: As for the future, Mr Pitt, you are not to disagree with me on anything, what? My mind is not strong enough to stand it.
PITT: (*Drily*) I will do my duty, sir.

Whether or not George III was suffering from the metabolic disease porphyria remains an open question. In their book *George III and the Mad Business* (1969), Ida Macalpine and Richard Hunter argue convincingly for this retrospective diagnosis on the strength of the purple tinge the King's urine took on while he was ill. Less convincingly, they trace the supposed incidence of the disease in other royals, nipping up and down George III's family tree, attributing no end of assorted ailments to the same cause. So Mary Queen of Scots was said to have had the condition, and her son James I, Queen Anne, George IV and even Frederick the Great. Although Hunter and Macalpine suggest that George IV's brother, the Duke of Kent, was similarly affected, the condition does not seem to have been passed on to his daughter, Queen Victoria, so the (rather heartless) joke of the final caption probably has no substance.

The condition presents problems that are as much metaphysical as medical. If porphyria is a metabolic disease, the symptoms of which are similar to, and which even today can be mistaken for, those of mental illness, in what sense is a sufferer from porphyria different from someone who is more routinely deranged? In what sense is all mental illness physical in origin? These are large questions, and I didn't want to venture into what is both a swamp and a battlefield but felt that I needed at least to show that I was aware of the problem. Hence this exchange between Greville and Dr Willis:

GREVILLE: Do you think His Majesty is mad? Sometimes he
    seems . . . just . . . ill.

    [*The dots indicate my opacities as much as Greville's.*]

WILLIS: Perhaps. But he has all the symptoms of madness.

GREVILLE: So what is the difference?

WILLIS: I am a doctor, Mr Greville, not a philosopher.

'And this is a film,' he might have added. 'And I've not been got up in a bob wig and black silk stockings just to safeguard the intellectual credentials of the author.' So the exchange was, of course, cut.

There had to be some sort of explanation, though, if only because of the scenes involving the urine. But since it was only identified in the 1930s porphyria could not be acknowledged in the film or the play without anachronism. When the play was first put on at the Royal National Theatre, there was a penultimate scene which catapulted the pages and equerries into the twentieth century where Mrs Macalpine explained about the blue piss. This didn't entirely work, and when the play was revived the following season the scene was omitted. Trying to work out how to get across this information in the film, I sometimes wished I'd been writing for Hollywood thirty years ago, because then there would have been no problem.

EXT. RIVER BANK DAY

As BRAUN *and* PAPANDIEK *pour the contents of their chamber-*

pots into the river a sudden shaft of sunlight catches
PAPANDIEK*'s face and he looks up, dreamily.*

PAPANDIEK: There will one day come a time when our
master's disease will be recognized for what it is . . . not
madness   (*cue Heavenly Choir*) but *porphyria*!
(*He raises the crystal chamber-pot to heaven and we see
looking down on him the faces of Mary Queen of Scots,
James I, Queen Anne, George IV and Frederick the Great.
And they are all* smiling!)

Except, of course, that they wouldn't be smiling, because, even
though the condition is more often (though not always)
diagnosed today, there is still no cure, just improved alleviation.

Monarchy is a performance, and part of the King's illness
consists in his growing inability to sustain that performance.
When the King is on the road to recovery, Chancellor Thurlow
discovers him reading *King Lear* and congratulates him on
seeming more himself.

'Yes', says the King, 'I have always been myself . . . Only now
I seem myself . . . I have remembered how to seem.'

The King is then rushed off to Westminster to be shown to
the MPs, who, still under the impression that he is mad, are
busy passing the Regency Bill. They rush out to greet him, and
he addresses them – haltingly at first, but with increasing
confidence, muttering to the pages at the finish, 'How's that,
lads? Not bad, eh?' i.e. the performance has gone well; he has
remembered how to seem.

Finally, as the royal family go up the steps of St Paul's for the
Thanksgiving Service, at the close of the film, the King urges
his family to smile and wave and pretend to be happy, because
that is their job. These scenes would, I hope, have rung a bell
with the late Erving Goffman, the American sociologist, whose
analysis of the presentation of self and its breakdown in the

twentieth century seems just as appropriate to this deranged monarch from the eighteenth century.

The Thanksgiving Service at St Paul's did not have to be invented: it's a nice conclusion to the King's illness and needed no departure from historical truth. Beginning my career as an historian, I find it harder to take liberties with the truth than someone whose upbringing has been less factually inhibited. I have to be forced into departures from history by the exigencies of the drama, the insistence of the director and sheer desperation. Had Nicholas Hytner at the outset suggested bringing the King from Kew to Westminster to confront the MPs, I would have been outraged at this adjustment to what had actually happened. By the time I was plodding through the third draft I would have taken the King to Blackpool if I thought it would have helped.

Filming and Rehearsing

Forty Years On

===

Forty Years On was my first play. It is set in Albion House, a run-down public school on the South Downs, where the Headmaster is about to retire. To mark the occasion, staff and boys devise an entertainment, 'Speak for England, Arthur', which is set during the Second World War and looks back over the period 1900–1940. I had put the play together in 1967 and sent it to the National Theatre. It came back pretty promptly, with a note from Ken Tynan saying that it wasn't their cup of tea but might have commercial possibilities. With a cast of nearly thirty it seemed unlikely. I showed it next to Frith Banbury, who suggested to Toby Rowland, a director of Stoll Theatres, that they should present it. I wrote a second draft, and the play eventually went into pre-production in March 1968. The director was to be Patrick Garland, the designer Julia Trevelyan Oman, and with what at that time seemed to me great presumption, Toby Rowland sent the script to Sir John Gielgud. Would he like to play the Headmaster?

These are some extracts from my diary of the months that followed.

===

24 May. Patrick and I have supper at Toby Rowland's house in Smith Street to meet Gielgud. He is taller, squarer than he seems on stage. I am very nervous, knowing that if it comes to 'selling' the play I won't be able to say much. Not to worry, as Gielgud talks all the time, telling story after story, head back on the sofa, famous nose in profile. He recalls a tour of India during the war, remembers Oxford, unspoiled in the 1920s as Waugh describes it in *Brideshead*, and the OUDS production of *Richard II* he directed at the Playhouse with Florence Kahn, Beerbohm's wife, playing the Duchess of Gloucester, while Max sat shrinking with embarrassment in the stalls.

He is currently appearing at the National in Peter Brook's production of *Oedipus*, which I don't let on having seen. Stories are rife of the indignities to which the actors have been subjected – some, representing plague-stricken Thebans, being tethered to pillars in the auditorium, where latecomers regularly take them for programme-sellers. The cast are dressed in matching sweaters and slacks in a tasteful shade of tan, and look like a Bulgarian table-tennis team. Gielgud is very loyal to Brook over all this, saying simply that, while it has been hard going, he is sure the difficulty and embarrassment of it have done him good.

I am beginning to be conscious that nothing is being said about the play when suddenly, disconcertingly, Gielgud starts straight in on what is wrong with it. His first target is the twenty-five boys we have decided would be the minimum requirement for the school. He would prefer none at all: they will fidget, they will distract, surely cardboard cut-outs would be better? He is not put out when one opposes such suggestions, but he does not abandon them easily. (A few months later, when the play is happily running in the West End, this suggestion of cardboard boys will become a huge joke, but this evening it seems to augur a very rough ride.)

At eleven we break off to watch a trailer for Patrick's

television programme on Dr Johnson. The sound doesn't work and the aerial is faulty. We sat gazing at this grey, silent pantomime, with Gielgud getting steadily more bored and irritated. Patrick is seemingly unaware of this, and we are stuck there until luckily the set breaks down altogether and we get back to the play.

A quarter of an hour before he leaves, Gielgud announces that he does not intend to commit himself until the final draft of the script is finished, and at 12.30 he strides off into Chelsea as fresh as when he arrived. 'Don't be shy,' he says as he shakes hands. 'It is very funny.' I take this to mean he has decided against it.

20 June. A second meeting with Gielgud, lunch at The Ivy. He is now reconciled to the boys, but, having seen John Lennon's *In His Own Write* at the National, he is worried about the back-projections. More stories. Of Emerald Cunard, who summoned him to dine at the Dorchester during the Blitz. 'And a very dull meal it was – chicken and ice-cream. Emerald surveyed the table and rang for the butler. "And where is the butter?" "There is no butter, ma'am." "No butter? But what is the Merchant Navy doing?"' He returns to the play. 'I am not sure about singing "Forty Years On". After all, it was Churchill's favourite song. And he is dead. And everyone knows that. I think it's terribly dangerous.'

'Oh no, it isn't.'

'Isn't it? No, I suppose not.'

And off he goes again on his ever-rolling stream of anecdote.

Many of the figures featured in the play he has met – Nijinsky, Diaghilev, T. E. Lawrence, Ottoline Morrell. There is a parody of a lantern lecture on Lawrence which I had earmarked for myself. Gielgud makes no bones about wanting to do it. I point out primly that it wouldn't fit in with the character of the

Headmaster to deliver it. He pooh-poohs this. I'm in no position to disagree, and besides he will do it far better than I could, but I'm thankful, as I see a large chunk of my part disappear, that I'm the author of the piece, not simply an actor in it.

Once this is settled he gives his final approval to the script and we get down to casting.

9 July. Yesterday and today are spent auditioning boys at Her Majesty's. When I first arrive at the stage door I am put at the end of the line. Since we had advertised for boys of fifteen to eighteen this flatters me, until I see that many are considerably older – and seem increasingly so as the day draws on: by the time five o'clock comes round I would not have been surprised to see Lewis Casson walk out on to the stage.

We are looking for public schoolboys, and find very few. They have regional accents, which they do not attempt to disguise. Had one advertised for public schoolboys, fifteen or twenty years ago they would have come in neat flannel suits with plastered-down hair. They wouldn't have been any better as actors, but at least they would have looked the part. Nowadays the fashion in looks and the fashion in actors has changed. They turn up in matador pants, turtle-neck shirts, a few rings on each hand. We ask them to read a passage from Leonard Woolf's autobiography *Beginning Again*. 'Who am I supposed to be, then?' asks one kid with golliwog hair and velveteen pants. 'Leonard Woolf?'

Many belong to a species of stage boy, only related to childhood by their small size. All the other attributes of boyhood – youth, gaiety, innocence – have long since gone. Squat creatures, seemingly weaned on Woodbines, they are the boys who have been in *Oliver!* Lionel Bart has cut a swathe through the nation's youth like the 1914–18 war. They are the new Lost Generation.

Often I am aching with silent laughter, which I hide by writing endless notes on my list. 'Too old.' 'Too common.' 'Sly face. Fat arse. Possible.'

'I was at drama school,' says one, 'near Doncaster.'

We need not only actors, but also musicians. 'Do you play any musical instrument?' 'Not quite.'

One is called Lionel Barrymore.

Another, explaining the fact that he has not been working, says cryptically, 'You see, I damaged my leg.' 'Perhaps somebody pulled it,' murmurs Toby.

In the afternoon, when we have been going for about an hour, there is a quavering voice from the upper circle: 'Could you tell me when you're going to start, please?' It is an old lady who has come for the matinée of *Fiddler on the Roof* on the wrong day.

We see over a hundred boys in two days. Sixteen are possible. We find a horn-player, a trumpeter and a flautist and a boy whose voice has broken but who has retained a lovely high treble voice besides.

At the start I had wondered how one would ever tell whether they were suitable or not. But it is just like marking scholarship papers at Oxford: the boys with vitality and enthusiasm walk in; the painstaking ones are put straightaway on one side.

We arrange to advertise in *The Times* in an effort to tap new non-showbiz sources. It's a thin bag, but the agents say that all the likeliest boys have already been snapped up for the musical of *Mr Chips*.

26 August, Stoll Theatres. A reading of the play this evening in Prince Littler's boardroom. It had been set for the previous Friday, but the management felt that Gielgud would be so upset by the bad reviews of *Don Giovanni*, his production at the Coliseum, that they had put it off. In fact he is quite perky. 'Bloody but unbowed,' he murmurs, 'bloody but unbowed.' I meet three of the players – Dorothy Reynolds, Nora Nicholson and Robert Swann – for the first time.

Patrick is nervous and makes a fatuous opening. 'We're just going to read the play and I think the best thing for us to do would be to . . . read it . . . starting at the beginning.'

Gielgud starts in on his opening speech at a furious speed, occasionally breaking off to say, 'That's wrong, isn't it? You can cut that. That's too long.' We come to the end of the play. Gielgud reads the last speech superbly, and there is a long silence. It is broken by the Stoll company manager, Rupert Marsh. 'You'll have to do it quicker than that. We can't be late closing the bar.'

In the subsequent discussion Gielgud sits silent and detached while everyone talks round him. He doesn't like the beginning of the play within the play. It is a parody of Oscar Wilde set in 1900. 'They weren't playing Wilde in 1900,' he says. 'They didn't revive *The Importance* until 1911.' I don't think this matters. 'But the audience won't understand. It's too sudden. Couldn't you do something about the Wilde case? I remember my mother saying she wasn't allowed to read the papers during the trial.' This doesn't seem to me to be particularly useful, and I don't want to get involved in all the tiresome Wilde business. But in the end Gielgud proves to be right, and not until Wilde's name is actually introduced before the parody does it really take off.

27 August, Gstaad. Fly to Switzerland for five days' holiday before we start rehearsals. It is only the fourth time I have flown and the first time by jet. I am scared but, as usual, more of making a fool of myself than of actual disaster. Will I be able to fasten my seat belt or will I have to ask the air hostess? Where do I hand in my baggage?

I wander about the terminal waiting to be called, and only at the last minute realize I have to go into the departure lounge. Denis Healey sits alone in the first-class section, returning to Switzerland after the Czechoslovakia debate. 'Whenever I can I fly Air India,' says the young executive on my right. 'People think it's a wog airline, but it's actually first-rate.' I try to discern the ratio of condescension to compliment in this remark and hope that the handsome Persian on my left hasn't heard. But he has. I keep an idiot smile of universal benevolence on my face for the rest of the flight in order to indicate my dissociation from such sentiments.

At Geneva I get on the wrong train, which stops every five yards at stations all along the lake. I change to a faster train at Nyon, and as it draws into Lausanne I see that the manuscript of the play, with all my pencilled-in alterations, has gone from my grip. The train from Montreux potters up the mountains through back gardens and farmyards to Gstaad, while the passengers rush from side to side, gazing at the peaks and pinnacles and the view over Lac Leman. I think only of my precious folder, peered at and pawed over by some foul porter at London Airport and thrown into an Uxbridge dustbin.

2 September, Drury Lane. Bank Holiday Monday and the first rehearsal on stage at Drury Lane, in the shadow of Sean Kenny's enormous Four Musketeers set. The principals rehearse upstairs and the boys below stage in the Ballet Room. Paul Eddington, who plays the Housemaster, is a man after my own heart, brooking no interference with physical comfort: he is greatly put out that due to the holiday there is no coffee. Eventually tea is procured in the cracked cups belonging to the stage-hands. Gielgud doesn't want it, nor Nora Nicholson, the old nanny in the play. They don't like interruptions.

In the morning the plotting goes ahead slowly, with Gielgud sitting apart doing his eternal crossword. I have heard stories that he is apt to fill in any old word that is the right length. I sneak a look and am disappointed to find this a myth. He learns his script by writing it out in a neat hand on the page opposite the text. 'I am a very bad study. After fifty, one gets much worse.'

He is full of ideas for his own part and for the play, many of them good, some cock-eyed. The cock-eyed ones take a lot of getting rid of. He is quite frank about this, saying that when he directs he always warns the actors he will come up with a dozen ideas, only one of which will be of any help. At the close of the afternoon he wants to scrap the whole of the ceremonial opening we have spent hours blocking, in which the boys enter singing round him. Why not make it just a quiet chat on stage?

'I think I should speak to the audience,' he had said at the first reading. 'I am very good at that. I like singling people out.'

'I can't bear speaking to the audience,' he says this afternoon. 'And it's so old hat, singling people out. I can't bear that.' (The job of persuading him to address the audience will turn out to be the biggest problem Patrick has to face. But when, in the nick of time, Gielgud is persuaded and begins to do so it transforms the whole production.)

Patrick and I go down to the Ballet Room to listen to the singing. Carl Davis, who has arranged the music and is to play the organ on stage, has already got the boys looking and sounding like a group. A lot of them smoke furiously, as if afraid of being caught. The singing sounds well – solid and moving and better in this echoing room than it will sound on stage.

In the evening I go through the cuts, taking out a parody of Dorothy L. Sayers's *Man Born to be King*, lest it should be thought simply a revue sketch, which it is. We lose some good jokes.

5 September. The text of *Forty Years On* includes several short extracts from the works of Osbert Sitwell, Leonard Woolf and Harold Nicolson which are used in a documentary way. So far I have had no difficulty in getting permission for the use of these. But there is also one extract from Sapper, and today there comes a letter from the literary agents who act for Sapper's executors, A. P. Watt Ltd, saying that they will not grant permission while the offensive references to Sapper, Buchan and Dornford Yates remain in the script. This refers to my collective description of these novelists as 'the school of snobbery with violence'. They add that they are also agents for the Tweedsmuir estate and that any parody of Buchan's characters might well be pursued in the courts.

It is the ignorance rather than the arrogance of this last remark which annoys me: as well say that a parody of Shakespeare is open to action by the Society of Authors. I swallow my irritation and write back pointing out that parody springs ultimately from affection and offer to remove the offending phrase. (This did not satisfy them, and they demanded much more extensive cuts in the script. I was therefore forced to substitute a cod extract from Sapper.) In the month that sees the final abolition of the Lord Chamberlain's licence, this form of censorship seems especially dubious. If a book has been published it has been launched into the public domain. Whatever happens to that book, short of piracy, is no concern of literary agents or literary executors. [The Buchan family, whom I met subsequently, were delighted by the play and appalled at the agent's officiousness.]

We have other difficulties with the Sapper–Buchan parody because Dorothy [Reynolds] has great difficulty in capturing the idiom of it. She is Sandy Clanroyden, who appears in the parody disguised as a maid. She is a woman playing a man playing a woman. Not surprisingly she is uncertain how to do it. I am scant help. 'Just find the voice,' I say, 'and don't bother about the rest.' But that is the short cut of a revue performer and actors don't work like that.

6 September, Her Majesty's. The papers are full of a fat contract landed by Millicent Martin. During a lull in rehearsal I come across John G. at the back of the stage, dancing round by himself, singing, 'Who cares about Millicent Martin? Oh, who cares about Millicent Martin?'

14 September, Her Majesty's. Nora Nicholson, who is nearing eighty, refers to death in a most unmorbid way. 'I will do it', she says, when offered a film part, 'if I am still here. I've just moved into a flat with a three-and-a-half-year lease. That should just about see me out.' She first appeared with John G. when he acted a butterfly in *The Insect Play*, and was herself in Benson's company. When she auditioned for Benson he inquired what parts she had played; she couldn't think of any and went home disconcerted, only to remember that she'd played Juliet. She is the nanny in the play, and had a nanny herself, who, when anyone laid an uninvited hand on her arm, would say, 'Don't touch me there; something might form.' Today the management takes us out to lunch at Rules. Speculating on what might be under a monster dish cover, Nora says, 'I hope it's not boiled baby. Still, I'd rather have boiled baby than boiled mouse.' As I leave her in the King's Road, she shouts after me, 'And remember to buy me a very big wreath.'

18 September. Patrick telephones tonight asking whether he can come over, refusing to talk on the telephone. I thought it was over a fit of temper I threw at the end of the rehearsal over the obstacles being put in the way of the designer, Julia Oman. It is much worse. Mrs Vinogradoff, the daughter of Lady Ottoline Morrell, has got wind of the sketch about her mother and wants it removed. Patrick recalls the conversation – the pain she has suffered from the portraits of her mother in the memoirs of the period, in the novels of Huxley and Lawrence, the autobiographies of Spender and Bertrand Russell, all those accounts, in fact, that I have read and through which I know her. Can we find it in our hearts, she asks, to give her more pain? Patrick is sympathetic. I am not. If the section dealing with her is cut it will destroy the end of the first act. We decide to change the name to Lady Sibylline Quarrell and hope that the storm will pass over. Those who know of her will realize it is Ottoline Morrell. Those who don't will be mystified anyway. It adds another ten cigarettes to the day's quota.

23 September, Donmar Studios. A good day today, the first on the set, which has been put up in a studio near Seven Dials so that we have a week to get used to it before we open in Manchester. The boys adapt themselves to it splendidly and play with a new freshness and spontaneity which pulls the whole thing together.

They will find it hard to retain this freshness in the five weeks left before the London opening. They will lose it, then gradually regain it, or the semblance, the practice of it. That is why first readings are often so much better than what comes after, until gradually one regains through technique what one first did spontaneously.

25 September, Donmar Studios. Gielgud telephones at 9.30 to say he has flu. We rehearse without him. It is a bloody day. The boys are restless and thunder about the set, drowning the dialogue and irritating the principals. George Fenton, the biggest and gentlest of the boys, is sick. He lies down on the child's bed we use in the nanny scene, and as we go off to lunch he is fast asleep with a gollywog cradled in his arms. It is the one nice thing about the day.

At lunch Patrick and I argue with Toby about publicity. Stoll are worried because the advance booking in Manchester is only £500, despite large adverts in the papers. They believe it is because there is no national publicity, no gossip, no tittle-tattle. They want articles about the show before it opens in London – gossipy, taste-whetting pieces, all the silly paraphernalia of showbiz which I loathe.

We stand firm on this. I am gambling on the show being a success and think it more likely to be so if it is a surprise. The management want to hedge their bets, get some advance booking through extensive pre-publicity so that, whatever the reviews, they will have some cash in hand. It is an understandable point of view commercially, but artistically it is wrong.

We have a bad run-through in the afternoon in which I several times lose my temper and nearly clout some of the kids. It is getting too like school. One realizes how important John G.'s presence is: he is always impeccably polite, and any slight flurry of temper is followed by an instant apology. His modesty and good behaviour infect everyone else.

26 *September, Dress Rehearsal.* Prince Littler comes in the afternoon to see a run-through, the last before the dress rehearsal in Manchester, where we open. He is the Chairman of Stoll, who own all the theatres on Shaftesbury Avenue. 'I see we've got the bricks and mortar in,' mutters Dorothy Reynolds as we make our first entrance.

Littler is a round, innocent-looking man who sits bland and expressionless throughout. He laughs once, at a joke about Edward VII. All too soon the boys realize he is not laughing, and they begin to giggle. This is what always used to happen on a bad night of *Beyond the Fringe*: the laughter on stage was inversely proportional to that from the audience. John G. struggles under a heavy cold, his eyes swollen and racked by sneezes, while the assistant stage manager follows him round with a box of Kleenex. It worries me that we open in Manchester in three days and he is still a long way from knowing his words.

30 September, Press Conference, Manchester. 'How many boys did you audition?'

'About a hundred and seventy.'

'I've got seven hundred.'

'No, it was nearer two hundred.'

'I'll put down seven hundred – it sounds better.'

No it doesn't, I long to say. Facts are what you want.

I talk to another reporter, who is anxious to make me say that writing is an agony. 'No, it's not really. I quite enjoy it. More sometimes than others. It's like anything else.' In the paper that night my few jokes are made to sound like Pascal's *Pensées*, wrung from aeons of nameless suffering. He was also surprised by how young I look. But since he gives my age that night as forty-three it is not so surprising.

The Palace turns out to be a cavernous theatre, far bigger than my worst imaginings. It has been closed all summer and we are to reopen it. 'You won't fill this place,' the stage doorman says to Gielgud. '*Ken Dodd* doesn't fill this place.' In the afternoon we have a disastrous technical rehearsal with a few actors from Michael Elliott's 69 Theatre in the audience. They laugh a lot in the first half, then fall silent. I presume they have left, and it is only when the house lights go up that I see they are still there: it's just that they have stopped laughing. I go out before the first performance and find George Fenton and Roger Brain, the horn-player, elbow-deep in muck, rubbing their rugger boots up and down the streaming gutter in the pouring rain. Julia Oman had thought they looked too new. Waiting for the curtain, I talk to Mac, John G.'s dresser. He is in his eighties and was dresser to another Sir John (Martin-Harvey) and before that to Fred Terry.

Gielgud rises splendidly to the presence of our first audience, but we all feel lost in this barn of a theatre. The doorman had been right: even on a first night it's less than a third full. And again the same thing happens: halfway through the second act we lose the audience.

1 October, Manchester. The *Guardian*, albeit only a second-string critic, is very sour: my intention has been simply to write a fat part for myself. It also deduces some message about the barrenness of English public and literary life, which is precisely the opposite of my intention. Others are complimentary, but with phrases of dubious value like 'a bellyful of laughs', 'all the makings of a very big hit indeed'. As always with criticism, I discount the praise and remember only the slights. I sit writing this on the dressing-table in front of the mirror and see I look older . . .

There follow three days of cumulative disappointment. A succession of thin and unappreciative audiences erodes our confidence. On Thursday evening it is a particularly bad performance. Michael Elliott sees it that night. He is very helpful and says it will be all right. Jonathan Miller also sees it and doesn't like the back-projections.

After the performance, Jonathan, Peter Cook and I go to speak at a symposium at the 69 Theatre. The subject is 'This England' and revolves around nostalgia. I say little and observe how the seven years since *Beyond the Fringe* have hardly altered the relationship between us. We still retain much the same characteristics we had when we first worked together, only in an intensified form, Jonathan is voluble and lucid, Peter seizes opportunities for laughs and delivers good cracking insults, while I make occasional heartfelt but dull remarks. The difference between 1961 and 1968 is that all feeling of competition between us has gone. In 1961 I cared very much more. I longed to be witty, to keep my end up, make impromptu jokes like Peter and stunning comparisons like Jonathan. Now I know I can't and am content not to.

2 October, Manchester. I go at six o'clock to do a live interview for Granada. Mr Budd, the company manager, goes with me, hopefully to ensure that I stress what a comic show it is. The management are always terrified that a serious discussion will lead the public to suppose that the show is serious. The producer of the programme is just coming out as we arrive and an assistant whispers my name.

'Who?'

'Alan Bennett.'

He seizes Mr Budd's hand warmly. 'Hello, Alan, I'm so glad you could be with us.'

It is straight out of *A Face in the Crowd*.

The interview is a boring and pointless exercise. The interviewer hasn't seen the show, and nothing of value emerges. The studio is unaccountably full of triplets, and the atmosphere subtly different from the BBC – more fraught, less confident, nastier.

4 October, Manchester. John G. is still far from knowing his words. The opening speech is full of names. He often confuses these and the boys are called by masters' names, masters by boys'. Though he never actually stops, and audible prompts are rare, it must leave the audience with a peculiar impression of the play. I *think*. The truth is an audience accepts whatever it sees on the stage as meant. Though an audible prompt embarrasses and withers any laughs in the immediate vicinity, provided one can just keep going an audience will assume everything is as it should be. What is surprising about John G. is that, even when it is plain to the audience that he has forgotten his words, the last person to be embarrassed is him. He treats this fortnight in Manchester like an open rehearsal to which the audience are admitted by courtesy. If the show isn't all it should be, that is their look-out. I don't agree with this, but when the curtain goes up night after night on only thirty or forty people I begin to think he's right. And even with such sparse audiences it's noticeable that if they like him and laugh at his jokes then his confidence grows and his memory improves. But this first week has been very rough, and on one evening he so far loses his nerve that he begins the play addressing the boys with his back to the audience.

Tonight my parents come. They have obviously been a bit mystified by the play, and sit in my dressing-room in awkward silence as my dresser, a veteran of the music halls, puts away my stuff. After he's gone, it transpires they thought *he* was Sir John Gielgud and was ignoring them deliberately because he was unhappy with the play.

8 October, Manchester. Gradually the show is being carved into a slimmer, simpler shape. Gielgud is a very humble man. He can be wayward, obstinate and maddeningly changeable, but one can forgive all these because he sets so little store by his own reputation. He is entirely without malice or *amour propre*, and in a succession of gruelling rehearsals he never once loses his composure. Today I find myself telling him how to deliver a line in order to get a laugh, and I begin to apologize. But he pooh-poohs the apology and begs me to go on. He will not be shielded by his own reputation or allow it to intrude between him and his fellow actors.

9 October, Manchester. The boys are gradually emerging as the best thing in the show, and as a result we bring them more and more into it, and even when they have nothing particular to do Patrick ranges them round the gallery to look on. They are quick on the uptake and add business of their own, though rarely so as to distract. They disprove all the stock maxims about children on the stage. They are imaginative and articulate – more so perhaps now than they will ever be again in their lives – and yet they don't have a couple of 'O' levels to rub together.

I find this very heartening. Moreover, they have great kindness and consideration and are quick to notice if one is glum or out of sorts and go out of their way to cheer one up. I am far more shy than they are; they come up and ask about the play and talk sensibly about it. I could not have done that at fifteen.

Supper with Sidney Bernstein in his penthouse on top of Granada TV. J. G., Patrick, Denis Forman and Gordon McDougall. A nice Mark Gertler, some silver in a bureau, and lots of what look like steakhouse Turners but I'm sure aren't. A lovely Gielgud remark: he asks me whether I couldn't write a Noël Coward parody for the second act: 'You know the sort of thing – lots of little epigrams, smart witty remarks. It wouldn't be at all difficult.'

'I couldn't possibly.'

'Why not? It's terribly easy. Noël does it all the time.'

It is after midnight when they begin to talk seriously about What Must Be Done With The Play. To start with they have seen it on a depressing night, and Sidney Bernstein, though kind and charming, is slightly deaf and hasn't caught all the dialogue. He also has the defect, peculiar to high television executives and editors of popular newspapers, of thinking the public stupider than it is. He doesn't think the Bloomsbury parody will work, for instance, because nobody will have heard of Virginia Woolf. Denis Forman, however, makes one valuable suggestion, which we later adopt, namely that the Headmaster should formally take his leave at the end.

John G. is still anxious about the opening. 'All that terrible organ music, the slow march and the hymns. Oh, those hymns,' he wails. 'It's just like school.'

'But it *is* school.'

'Oh yes. I suppose it is.'

They talk on until three in the morning, but by half past two I can stand it no longer and walk out. The cardinal rule in such circumstances is to be sure beforehand that one's exit is clear. Mine isn't, as I don't have a key to the executive lift. I hang about in the lobby feeling foolish until Denis stumps out after me and we go awkwardly down through the dark and empty building, and I walk back to the Midland through the wet streets of Manchester.

11 October, Manchester. A group of the boys have written a pop song on themes arising out of the play, and in gaps of rehearsal they orchestrate it with the help of Carl Davis. This afternoon they sing it over to me. George Fenton and Anthony Andrews singing in high altos above the guitar and organ accompaniment: 'In a boater, in a bowler, in a boat, We were drifting away, Never expecting the day, When we wouldn't have our tailors, our servants and our sailors, And our old boys playing cricket on the green.' I sit in the Tea Centre in Manchester's Oxford Road, working on the lyrics with George Fenton and Keith McNally, and I see suddenly how I shall look back on this time as very happy.

15 October, Theatre Royal, Brighton. All the time we were in Manchester the management would encourage us by holding out the prospect of Brighton – glittering, sophisticated, metropolitan audiences in a bandbox of a theatre, an ideal setting for a play like ours. I was sceptical. I had been here before in 1961 with *Beyond the Fringe*. It was the week before we went to London, and we played to a handful of old ladies, most of whom had left by the interval: the seats were going up like pistol shots throughout the performance. Brighton is a difficult place to play and can make or mar a production, infested as it is with theatricals who offer advice and scent disaster. 'We loved it, darlings,' they told us in 1961, 'but don't, whatever you do, take it in.' However, the first night is good, the audience solid and responsive, and the next day we have a perceptive notice from the Brighton critic, Jack Tinker. After the performance Diana Cooper, Enid Bagnold and T. C. Worsley come round, with Worsley being especially helpful.

It is odd to see Diana Cooper standing in my dressing-room, friend and contemporary of figures who are legends to me. She had apparently been in tears during Gielgud's memoir of the Lost Generation, an imaginary visit to a country house on the eve of the First World War. 'How did you know to choose all those names?' she asks vaguely, eyeing herself in the glass. 'They were all my lovers.'

At last we seem to be coming out of the wood and producing the sort of reaction we have been after, the transition from nostalgia and genuine regret to laughter and back again, without the one destroying the other.

19 October, Brighton. The boys are a problem. If they are too rigidly disciplined then they lose the spontaneity that is part of the charm of the play. More experienced actors would counterfeit spontaneity, but these can't. So every night they whisper, fight and fart – behave, in fact, like a classful of kids. To an actor with a speech to make this is a nightmare, as the attention of the audience is subject to constant distraction. Few leading actors would risk this, let alone put up with it, but it never bothers Gielgud. He is completely confident of his ability to hold the stage and the attention. What is going on behind him he treats as an irrelevance. The result is we get the best of both worlds. As for talking directly to the audience there is now no stopping him. He leans far out over the footlights, shading his eyes with his mortarboard, ostensibly searching for his straitlaced sister Nancy, but in reality seeing whether there's anyone in that he knows. Audiences who have grown accustomed to him as a somewhat remote and awesome presence obviously find the change delightful. He even starts waving.

He completely lacks pretension. The most moving and magical part of the play is the visit to the country house at the end of the first act. John G. is off-stage at the start of this scene, and as like as not in the middle of a story. He tears himself away from the joke, steps out on to the stage, and within seconds he is wreathed in tears and the audience is in the palm of his hand. The curtain comes down and he turns round and finishes the story. He is not a sentimental man.

After the Saturday matinée I bump into Cyril Connolly coming in at the stage door. I have never met him before and assume he is going to see John. 'No. It is you I want to see. I want to show you how tall I am.' He is referring to a passage in the memoir of Virginia Woolf. 'She was one of the tallest writers I have ever known. Which is not to say that her stories were tall. They were not; they were short. But she did stand head and shoulders above her contemporaries, and sometimes of course much more so. Cyril Connolly, for instance, a man of great literary stature, only came up to her waist. And sometimes not even there.' It is Connolly's own descriptions of himself in *The Unquiet Grave* that have led me into error. I promise to change it (to Dylan Thomas), but I think he's slightly disappointed. He'd rather have me keep his name and change the joke.

29 October, Apollo Theatre, Shaftesbury Avenue. Two days in

London and already the close-knit feeling of the cast is beginning to dissolve. Friends reappear, one slips back into old routines, and the sense of being part of a group fades. From now on it will just be work, and we will come together for a couple of hours each night and then go our separate ways and lead our separate lives. The best part of the play is over, over before it has even started. I go home after the first preview and have some baked beans on toast.

30 October. Noël Coward comes to the final preview. After the performance I hear his party announced at the stage door and they disappear into John G.'s dressing-room. It has been a charity show, the audience very quiet as they invariably are when they have paid too much for their seats. (Curiously, if they pay nothing at all the effect is the same.) I sit in my room hoping Coward has liked it and that if he hasn't he'll have the tact not to show it. Any criticism or even advice at this late date is destructive. And I remember the story of Gielgud rehearsing a speech in an empty theatre, the only other person there a charwoman mopping the stage. At the finish she is reputed to have leaned on her mop and said, 'I don't think you should do it like that, dear.' 'Really? Oh God, how do you think I should do it?' John G. sends Mac to fetch me in to meet Coward, who is brimming with enthusiasm and saying all the right things. John is standing there in his shirt tails with Mac waiting to slip on the knightly trousers, a ritual I am sure John indulges him in out of the kindness of his heart: to be helped into one's trousers is no help at all. Meanwhile Coward is recalling his favourite moments and John is glowing with pleasure. Though I don't know it at the time, this is going to be the pattern for this moment in the day for the next twelve months. Manchester seems a long way away.

1 November. I open *The Times* first. It is a niggling notice. But the rest are solid in praise, with the *Financial Times* particularly perceptive. But how sick I am of being told how wicked and irreverent it all is: critics should be searched for certain adjectives at the door of the theatre – 'irreverent', 'probing' and (above all) 'satirical'. I would have all such adjectives left with their coats in the foyer, only to be redeemed when their notices are written.

10 November. In the first week the play has broken all box-office records, and is an assured success. Gielgud is very happy and in wonderful form. I listen to the BBC Critics. They all say it is very funny, but what is it about, what am I trying to do, is there a message? Nobody knows, and I certainly don't. If one could answer these questions in any other way than by writing what one has written, then there would be no point in writing at all.

The boys got the play right. One of its themes is memory, the dull, distorting effects of time, in phrases which sound right, but aren't: 'Patience is mine, I will delay saith the Lord.' 'They are rolling up the maps all over Europe. We shall not see them lit again in our lifetime.' 'One always forgets the most important things, it's the things one can't remember that stay with you.' The Headmaster remembers and reveres the Lost Generation of 1914. His successor, Franklin, shrugs them off, but in his turn recalls with passion and conviction the Second War. But in the eyes of the boys this war too is ancient history and its causes mere catchwords. While Churchill is announcing victory in Europe, the boys step out of the play to have a scuffle on their own account. On the first night I heard one of the boys shout 'Fascist' at his attacker. It wasn't my line – he had thrown it in off his own bat – but it summed up more neatly than I could have done one of the main themes of the play.

Certain specific points I could set straight. The upper-class

couple in the basement of Claridge's was suggested by, though
not modelled on, Harold Nicolson and Vita Sackville-West. All
the literary and other memoirs of the period 1900–1940 were
within the compass of their lives and the scope of their
background. The MP's attitude to the war, his hatred of the
Munichers, his love of Churchill, coupled with a dread of the
outcome of the war for himself and his class, all echo Harold
Nicolson's attitudes and his fear of the post-war 'Woolworth's
world'. I sympathize with this attitude, and my heart is very
much in Gielgud's final speech in which he bids farewell to
Albion House and this old England. And yet the world we have
lost wasn't one in which I would have been happy, though I look
back on it and read about it with affection. And from this
affection stem both the parody and the nostalgia; they are very
close together.

Today is Armistice Day and the fiftieth anniversary of the
end of the First World War. I listen to the ceremony on the
radio, and as I type this I hear the guns rumbling across the park
for the start of the Two Minutes' Silence. I find the ceremony
ridiculous and hypocritical, and yet it brings a lump to my
throat. Why? I suppose that is what the play is trying to resolve.

A Day Out

I wrote *A Day Out* in 1969. Then called *There and Back to See How Far It Is*, it's an account of a Halifax cycling club on a day's outing in 1911 – an idea I'd got from an old photograph. I sent the script in to the producer of 'The Wednesday Play' and had it back a month or two later: it wouldn't fit into their seventy-five-minute slot. Besides, it wasn't really about anything: it didn't go anywhere, did it? The script then drifted round the BBC, eventually being washed up on the shores of BBC2. 'It's not quite our slot,' I remember them saying ruefully, 'though we occasionally do forty-five-minute plays on "Thirty-Minute Theatre".' I mention this delay because by the time the film came to be made, in May 1972, I had very little sense of the script as being my own. I talked to Stephen Frears, who was to direct it, and found I had forgotten the impulse that made me write it or whether I had had any other intention than to tell a story.

Looking back, I think this remoteness partly explains why I found the filming process so enjoyable. Tactfully, I was never cast in the role of The Author and everyone did their best to make the process of filming comprehensible to me, but much was and remains a mystery. Invited to examine the shot, I peer through the viewfinder with what I hope looks like assurance. But too often it's like a seaside telescope before you put the sixpence in: total darkness. Maybe this is because I wear glasses.

I nod enthusiastically and express myself satisfied – the first priority, as always, being not to make a fool of oneself.

════════

1 May, Halifax. The first ten days of filming are in and around Halifax. Ten years ago, when I was last here, this area looked pretty much as the nineteenth century had left it: villages huddled round the mill in the valley bottom, rambling seventeenth-century farms on the tops. A line of gas-lamps ran out into the country, stopping in the middle of the moors at the council boundary. There were cobbled streets between green fields, boarded-up chapels and black, leaning cemeteries. Now many of the mills are pulled down, the chapel is a carpet warehouse, the solid, sensible dwellings have been tarted up with bow-windows to fetch them into line with a Christmas-card view of the past. Flush doors, leaded lights, 'Monk's House' on a glazed slice of log, and not a gas-lamp to be seen except as salvaged to grace the drive of 'Four Winds' and its tastefully converted frontage.

But if you're looking for locations it's more than a matter of taste, and it very early becomes clear that to shoot a period film in urban surroundings involves frequent and costly shifts of location. You may find a nineteenth-century ginnel intact, but pan fifteen degrees and there's a cooling-tower. Here's a good row of mill cottages, but pull out and there's a car-port. In colour, anachronistic details are hard to lose, and the BBC is persuaded to settle for black and white. Everyone is slightly surprised when it agrees. Even so, the production assistants and props boys spend the first part of the morning shinning up walls, swathing concrete lamp-standards in blackout material, draping 'a spot of dingle' (greenery) over the intrusive bus-stop.

And always a nagging feeling that somewhere in shot is something so obviously wrong that no one has noticed it. At the first rushes, all I was looking for were lamp-standards.

2 May, Ackroyden Square, Halifax. A good start. The day dull and cold, but since we're not shooting in colour this is a possible light for early morning, when the club meets before setting off for the day. Because of traffic we don't shoot sound, so filming bowls along. Once in costume and on their bikes, the individual character of the actors takes over and they become fully fleshed versions of characters only sketched in the script. In Hebden Bridge we do one shot when they all come down a steep hill on their bikes: Philip Locke as Wilkins, a shy, chapel-ridden man, very sedate; Jimmy Cossins playing a pompous fool, nervously running with his bike; David Hill, as Gibson, a lout stood up on his pedals; and David Waller as Mr Shuttleworth, the father of the club, bringing up the rear. Most of the cast know each other already. Several are from the RSC, some from the Royal Court, where they were together in David Storey's *The Changing Room*. Bernard Wrigley, who plays a retarded boy, is a folk-singer from Bolton, Paul Shane a club comedian from Rotherham.

We are sitting in the hotel this evening and a football crowd is braying up and down the street. 'Oh God,' sighs John Normington, 'I knew Patience Collier would tell all her friends we were here.'

4 May, Oats Royds, Luddenden. In between takes, while shots are being set up, we sit in the coach, drink coffee, and eat bacon sandwiches. The actors do the *Times* crossword, tell stories, play the cinema game: 'In what film did Cedric Hardwicke star with Arthur Lucan and Bela Lugosi?' '*Old Mother Riley Meets the Vampire.*' Sitting around like this is the most characteristic part

of an actor's life. They swap anecdotes about the awfulness of
the shows they have been in, the sadism of directors and the
terrible things that have happened to them on the stage.

My function here is not defined. I am called in if there's a
problem about the script, and I watch any scene that involves
dialogue, but my main job seems to be to help jolly things
along. If I want to make a suggestion about the acting of a scene
I'll generally ask the director first, though relations are so easy
it wouldn't be remarked on if I didn't. Since the film has been
carefully cast, the actors are encouraged to fill out the
characters themselves. It's the best way. Most of my suggestions are to do with pronunciation. I think anyone not brought
up in the North finds it hard to get dialect pronunciation
exactly right. If you say 'up at t'mill' as it's written, it comes
over like a parody. The 't' shouldn't be sounded at all: it's a
syncopation, not a sound. If you're not careful the whole thing
sounds like the *Take It From Here* take-off of *The Crowthers of
Bankdam*:

'There's trouble at t'mill. T'workers are upset. They say they've too
far to come to t'mill.'
'Too far to come? Nay, but they've only three fields to cross.'
'Ay, but they're Huddersfield, Macclesfield and Sheffield.'

Electricians' slang. 'An elephant': a small box to stand on. 'A
pancake': a smaller box. 'Horse': electrician's assistant. 'Make it
Chinese': give me just a slit of light. 'A pup with a snoot on it': a
small light, shaded. 'Baby legs': small tripod for the camera.
'Follow the money': make sure the lights are on the star.
'Running all the way, Guvnor': I'll walk over to that light and
switch it on.

Sequence of calls before a shot. Production assistant: 'Quiet.
Going for a take. Standing by.' Director: 'Right.' Sound: 'Sound
running.' Director: 'Turn over.' First assistant: '245, Take 5.'

Director: 'And remember it's tight on you, Paul. Action.' Then the take. Director: 'Very good. Now let's go once more.'

10 May, Mytholm Steps. After three days in London I come back to Leeds, arriving in City Square just as Leeds United begin their triumphal progress to Elland Road. At Halifax they are shooting the country-pub scene. It ought to be an idyllic country place, a lush pub garden with an earth-closet set in a bower of honeysuckle. Instead it's a grim, dark spot, with a few thin privet bushes and a tussocky garden set with sooty plants. It looks dismal and is bitter cold. The bad weather, which we've had consistently since we started, has altered the character of the film. We'd decided to film in May because you can generally bank on a spell of fine, prematurely hot weather. But not this year, and each day is worse than the last. However, this natural disaster puts everybody on their mettle, and the atmosphere of the slightly crisis-ridden unit is very good. Stephen Frears realizes that the slow, dreamy piece I'd written won't work in this sort of weather: you can't film an idyll in temperatures of forty-five degrees. So he shoots the script much more off the individual characters of the actors, and the story becomes brisker and, I think, stronger than I had imagined. Not figures in a landscape, but characters in relation to one another.

This is the last sequence in Halifax, and we move to Ripon. At the hotel there is chaos, partly endemic but also because of improvements being made against a visit by the Queen Mother. The manageress, a genteel Scotswoman, regards the BBC as a subversive organization. 'No one has ever complained about the bed before,' she says to Philip Locke. 'No one of normal size, that is.' It is a hotel straight out of Feydeau, with residents to match. On television in the lounge, the Duke of Edinburgh remarks on the unemployment among young people on

Teeside. 'Rubbish,' comes a voice from an armchair. 'They can work. They just don't want to.'

11 May, Fountains Abbey. The abbey is set in a deep wooded valley, so that you come upon it from above. What at first sight looks a plain, squat tower – like a Norman keep – turns out to be only the last stage of the bell tower soaring above the valley-top to the level of the surrounding fields. Now it's encased in shining stainless-steel scaffolding, so it's useless for our purposes. 'How long will it take, all this?' someone asks the foreman. 'I don't know. It'll last me out.'

As I am writing, we are waiting for silence. These days there is nowhere in the world where there is still continuous natural silence. Six years ago, on Jonathan Miller's *Alice in Wonderland*, I can remember occasional delays. But not like this. Now, when there is silence, there is no sun. When sun, sound. High up above Fountains, a young man leading a man's life in the regular Air Force idly loops the loop hour after hour. Stuart, the boom operator, who has seen it all before, explains that the offending plane is practising stall turns. Innes Lloyd, the producer, phones the BBC. The BBC phones the nearest RAF base, Leeming, but they say it's not one of theirs. He could be from Leuchars or St Mawgan. At his speed here is only ten minutes from anywhere. But there he is, two miles up with all England spread out below him.

Kay Fraser, the director's assistant, is putting a daffodil into her hat before writing up her continuity notes. Anne Ailes, the make-up girl, is cutting Laurie, the second assistant's, hair. James Cossins is doing the *Times* crossword. Stephen does the odd clue, then goes over the next shot. Bob, one of the grips, keeps an eye on the sky through a glass. Jimmy and Alf, the prop boys, are changing a wheel on one of the bikes. Joan Hamilton, the production assistant, sits by the refectory wall ready to warn sightseers who might wander into shot. John Normington is doing an imitation of Bette Davis in *Mrs Skeffington*. Philip Locke is doing Marlene Dietrich going round to a friend's dressing-room to congratulate her after a terrible performance. Bernard Wrigley, Paul Rosebury and Don McKillop are playing football. Ray Henman, the cameraman, is handing round a pattern-book of shirt samples he can get cheap from Hong Kong. David Hill is making a daisy chain.

12 May, Sawley Hall. The shot is down an avenue of Wellingtonias at Sawley Hall. ('Used this last year for *Jane Eyre*,' Judy Moorcroft says drily.) The sun casts long shadows across the path, trees are alive with birds, midges flickering in the sun. 'Oh dear. This is what the film was supposed to be about,' says Stephen.

Next day it is bitter cold again. On the lawn in front of the house, the tea-party scene is set up. There is a fierce east wind cutting across from the wolds. Dorothy Reynolds in a thin cotton frock pours tea, with the tablecloth weighted down against the gale. As soon as one shot is in the can, make-up and wardrobe rush out from behind a wall and swathe the cast in rugs and coats. On the lawn, Virginia Bell plays croquet. She is a great-niece of Virginia Woolf, to whom she bears an extra-ordinary resemblance. A fragile, transparently beautiful face, with sad downcast eyes, but underneath, I suspect, as strong and direct as her great-aunt. I sit in on this scene as an extra in blazer and straw hat, eating chilly little fancies at Dorothy's frozen elbow.

19 May, Laver Banks. The sex scene takes place by a stream in Winksley Woods above Fountains Abbey. A sex scene it is too: not a love scene. Connie, the girl, lies passive and silent while Edgar unbuttons her blouse, searching her face for some reaction. When eventually he has her blouse open, he puts his hand quickly on her breast in a very odd way. It looks almost as though if he weren't quick the breast would take to its heels. We wait half an hour for a patch of sun, and I wander off into the woods and find a duck's nest full of cold blue eggs.

Bad day for planes. There is an air display at Biggin Hill. At one point we wait ten minutes for an ancient Wellington droning its slow way from horizon to horizon.

23 May, Galphay. Watched this afternoon by a long line of village children sat on a wall, including, on this May afternoon in the middle of Yorkshire, two little girls who are the great-grandchildren of Tolstoy. We film late-sunset shots. The actors are fed up of their heavy black bikes, bumping over fields, humping them over stiles, and always the chains coming off. Brian Glover, who plays Boothroyd, an early socialist, is a wrestler as well as an actor, and at the end of these long days he drives off to Newcastle or Leicester to wrestle.

24 May, Ripon. Some of us talk over supper about fees. No one mentions any figures. I have been paid £700. The leading performers, when expenses have been calculated, will get about two-thirds of that. Stephen, since he's a freelance and his work editing and dubbing goes on until July, quite a bit more. I feel slightly aggrieved, I think, but fortunately our waitress, Maggie, joins in the conversation. She has come on duty at seven that morning. It is now 8.30 at night and she has had one hour off. She works six, sometimes seven, days a week. She is paid £9 plus her keep. 'And there's folks queueing up in Ripon to do the job if I didn't.'

25 May, Halifax. The last day of filming. I drive to Halifax and shop in the covered market. Cheese cut from the block, bacon from the roll, flowers and good bread, all served with interest and friendliness and with none of the aggression you get in London street markets with all their Cockney cockiness and Bow Bells rubbish.

We film the last scene at the memorial in Ackroyden Square, where we started four weeks ago. Here, where the club forgathered at the start of the day out in 1911, the survivors meet at an Armistice Day service in 1919. It's an afterthought on my part, and doesn't quite work in the film because of that. The filming ends with the whole unit and a few interested housewives standing on a street corner in the rain, singing 'O Valiant Hearts' for a wild track of the sound. And still bitterly cold.

The Writer in Disguise

These five television plays were part of a series of six produced for London Weekend Television in 1978–9. Reading them now, five years after they were produced and six years after they were written, I can see that three of them (*Me, I'm Afraid of Virginia Woolf*, *Afternoon Off* and *One Fine Day*) are not dissimilar and that Hopkins, the polytechnic lecturer, Lee, the Chinese waiter, and Phillips, the estate agent, share the same character, indeed *are* the same character. Passive, dejected, at odds with themselves, they are that old friend, the Writer in Disguise. A doleful presence, whatever his get-up, he slips apologetically in and out of scenes being heartfelt, while the rest of the cast, who are invariably more fun (and more fun to write, too), get on with the business of living. They are not heartfelt at all; one doesn't have to be fair to them, nor are they around long enough to elicit understanding. And, unlike the sorry hero, they *talk*. But it's hard to find words to put into the mouth of the central character when 'Gr-rr-rr' or 'Oh dear' seems to say it all. Lee, the Chinese waiter, who scarcely speaks but only smiles, is the ineffectual hero taken to a logical conclusion and the natural condition of all three is what Lee ends up doing – namely, lying in his underpants staring at the ceiling.

What distinguishes a television play from a stage play I find hard to say. It's plain that of these plays only *The Old Crowd* could conceivably have been presented on the stage because it's the only one not set in a variety of locations, besides being written in a deliberately theatrical way. The empty house in *The Old Crowd* is a kind of stage, and whereas the other plays are in varying degrees naturalistic *The Old Crowd* is not naturalistic at all (which may explain why it annoyed so many viewers and was generally disliked). The difference between writing for stage and for television is almost an optical one. Language on the stage has to be slightly larger than life because it is being heard in a much larger space. Plot counts for less on the television screen because one is seeing the characters at closer quarters than in the theatre. The shape and plot of a stage play count for more in consequence of the distance between the audience and the action. A theatre audience has a perspective on a play as a television audience does not. The audience in a theatre is an entity as a television audience is not. On television the playwright is conversing. In the theatre he is (even when conversing) addressing a meeting. The stage aspires to the condition of art as television seldom does (which is not to say that it shouldn't). The most that can be said for these plays in that respect is that occasionally they stray into literature.

Of the five scripts printed here three were shot wholly on film (*Afternoon Off*, *One Fine Day* and *All Day on the Sands*); one in the studio wholly on tape (*The Old Crowd*), with the other (*Me, I'm Afraid of Virginia Woolf*) a mixture of both. If I prefer working on film to working in the studio it is for entirely frivolous reasons. Being on location with a unit, like being on tour with a play, concentrates the experience; one is beleaguered, often enjoyably so, and for a short while the film becomes the framework of one's life. I am more gregarious than I like to think and to be working on a film with congenial people in an unfamiliar place seems to me the best sort of holiday. In the studio this camaraderie and shared concern is more circumscribed. There are homes to go to, lives to be lived and the recording process is altogether more routine. For the studio staff it may be a play for today, but tomorrow it's *The South Bank Show* and the day after *Game for a Laugh*. It's work in a way that filming on location, however arduous, never quite is.

Not that it is often arduous. To an onlooker, which for much of the time I am, it's like war: long periods of boredom punctuated by bouts of frenzied activity. The scene in Tony Richardson's *The Charge of the Light Brigade* in which Lord Raglan and his party view the charge from a nearby hilltop is (perhaps deliberately) very like watching the making of a film. The terminology of film (cut, shoot, action, reload) is the terminology of battle and it is a battle in which the director is the general and the actors are infantry, never told what is happening, left hanging about for hours at a time, then suddenly, because 'the light is right', on standby, ready to go. Troops in the trenches used to stand to when the light was right; actors share their pessimism and the sense that, though seldom consulted, they are the ones who must get up and do it. The director is staff; he is behind the gun. The actors face it. And it isn't simply a metaphor. There is a lot of playing soldiers about it. Forget film – there would be many directors just as happy conducting a small war.

How well these scripts *read* I'm not sure. Strictly speaking there is no such thing as a good script, only a good film, a good play. But though a script is only a partial document, a guide to what ends up on the screen, I'm old-fashioned enough to have more faith in the permanence of print than of any other medium: tapes can be wiped, films lost. Television has been going full blast now for more than thirty years without the BBC or ITV working out a foolproof archive system. Besides, these plays went out once only and on a Saturday night opposite *Match of the Day*, which is virtually a recipe for oblivion, so I'm happy to see them rescued and printed.

I owe a good deal to Stephen Frears, who produced all five plays and directed three of them, to Lindsay Anderson and Giles Foster who directed the others, and also to George Fenton who scored them all. Writing incidental music for films is a thankless task precisely because most of the time it has to be incidental. But occasionally it's crucial and then the writer or the director as like as not get the credit for the effect of scenes the composer has brought off or (more likely) has had to rescue: the entry of each character in *The Old Crowd* on the page seems quite flat and would have done so in the film without the lilting tune, both sad and silly, that comes in with them. Lindsay Anderson has written his own account of directing *The Old Crowd* and the extracts from my diary that follow give some flavour of what working on that and the other plays was like.

⸻

11 January 1978, London (*The Old Crowd*). Lindsay Anderson lives in a flat in one of the redbrick turn-of-the-century blocks behind John Barnes in Swiss Cottage. With its solid turreted houses, backing on gardens, Canfield, Compayne, Aberdare, Broadhurst, it's the haunt of refugees and Jewish old ladies, and perhaps (Lindsay would strike out that 'perhaps') the most European bit of London.

Lindsay comes to the door in a plastic apron in the middle of preparing leeks or parsnips. He makes me some coffee, then we sit at the kitchen table and work on the script. He looks at me enquiringly, then puts a straight line through half a page. 'Boring, don't you think? Too tentative.' He invariably crosses out all my 'possiblys' and 'perhapses'. To be epic is, if nothing else, to be positive. He agreed to do the *The Old Crowd* in the first place because he detected 'epic' qualities in it. I think this is to do with the house being completely bare and with George and Betty, the middle-class couple, not letting anything interfere with their intention to have a party. Lindsay wants the script to be more epic, but I am still not sure what epic means. 'The doors all open downstairs when everybody has gone. That is epic.' I think it means things do not have to be explained, but am not sure of the difference between this and mystification. I don't say this. Sometimes I resent seeing a day's work crossed out at a stroke (except that I can generally salvage it for something else). It is like having one's homework marked, and there is a lot of the schoolmaster about Lindsay, and some of wanting to please the teacher about me. Every few minutes work stops and gossip takes over. 'You didn't like that?' (Incredulously, mouth set in a long firm line.) The eyes close in despair and he shakes his head. 'And I can't stand *him*. So *English*.' 'English' is invariably a word of abuse, representing smallness of mind, intimacy, gossip, charm. All the things Auden fled from. Yet Lindsay is himself very English. Sometimes he routs out his scrapbook to illustrate a point. There is a picture of the Archbishop of Canterbury gingerly touching the bone threaded through the nose of some Zulu warrior. Peter Hall's Sanderson advert. Many telephone calls. Alan Bates. William Douglas-Home. Michael Medwin. Actors wanting advice about their lives (which he gives) accompanied by an elaborate pantomime of despair for my benefit.

The flat is airy and comfortable. A corridor lined with photographs, but not, as in my house, picked up at junk shops. His own school. His own life. Lindsay as a child in India astride an enormous gun. Pre-war gym displays at Cheltenham College. Awards for films and for commercials. A pinboard on which is a picture of Brecht, a photo of the cast of *What the*

Butler Saw. Lindsay directing Ralph Richardson. A group photo of some critics. 'Look at them, Alan. I mean, is it surprising?' He shakes his head. 'England.' In the lavatory a jokey warning notice. (He is not afraid of conforming to type even when the type is a bit of a joke.) He has no pretensions to taste and would presumably despise the word. Dozens of bottles of slivovitz and vodka in the kitchen, souvenirs of visits to Eastern Europe. Odd bits of peasant art. A poster of a Polish film festival. Solid, plumpish, with his long nose and wide mouth, Lindsay looks quite Polish himself. Coffee over he starts preparing my lunch. He is a hospitable man, though the odd thing is he prepares my lunch separately from his and serves it first, though his consists of the same ingredients.

We have finished the script now. He has suggested only small sections of dialogue, but dealt more positively with the characters than I would dare to: had Totty, the uninvited guest, die in the drawing room; sent the waiters mysteriously into the night. At the moment we are hung up on the music. I wanted the entertainers who come to the house to sing, very formally, the song from *High Noon* ('Do not forsake me, O my darling'). Lindsay wants something much straighter, more 'cultural'.

At another point he wants all the guests to sing a song round the body of Totty, who collapses and dies in the middle of a slide show. He suggests 'The Sun Shines Bright' from the John Ford film, a song that has happy associations for him. It has none for me. Or not quite none. It brings back a terrible film about Stephen Foster that I saw as a child at the Crown down Tong Road in Leeds. We joke about these songs and no decision is reached, except that Lindsay goes round softly crooning 'The Sun Shines Bright' in the hope I will get to like it.

He doesn't understand jokes. Or why people make them. 'No, I don't like jokes,' he admits. 'Wisecracks, yes. Jokes, no. Have you heard there's a new punk rock group. They perform in

Brady and Hindley masks and call themselves "The Moors Murderers". That's why we can't have satire in England.'

'Never mind,' he says as I go. 'This will just be thought of as a small hiccup in your career.'

I'm enjoying it.

11 February, London (*The Old Crowd*). A run-through of *The Old Crowd* in the Territorial Army Drill Hall in Handel Street, Bloomsbury. Whereas I had thought it bitty and formless and without point or humour I see now much of it works, particularly when the actors have the courage to declaim the lines and not invest them with too much heart or meaning. John Moffatt is particularly good and Jill Bennett very stylish. The play's greatest virtue is that it does not seem like mine.

Rachel Roberts and Jill Bennett go off to lunch together to compare notes on their various husbands. They are like old-fashioned stars, both in expensive fur coats, and when together sly and mischievous and in league against men.

Lindsay has no false pride. He will consider suggestions from anybody. 'Grateful for them. I mean, come on. One has few enough ideas of one's own.' He is often accused of cribbing from Buñuel, but has actually seen very few Buñuel films. People have told him about them, though. 'That gives you a much more vivid picture. I don't think I want to see them in case I'm disappointed.' He believes in the creative power of mischief. At one point I suggest that Jill Bennett should say a line in a different way. 'Oh yes. Tell her that. I've just told her to do the opposite. Now she won't know what to do.' He turns the rehearsals into school. He is the schoolmaster by turns praising, sarcastic or self-revealing. The actors vie with each other to please him. He makes them children again so they do not mind being childish and showing their uncertainty. Stood in his cap and old windcheater he listens to them with a long-suffering air, wide mouth set in a slightly mocking smile. 'Aren't they stupid? Don't you just want to shoot them all? I do. I just want to machine-gun them all.' He suddenly shouts at them. 'Fucking actors.'

'Oh, don't start that,' Jill Bennett shouts back.

'Fucking actors!'

22 February, London (*The Old Crowd*). Lindsay says he doesn't like jokes but it's not true. He's not keen on wordplay or the nuances of class as reflected in dialogue but some of the nicest jokes in the script are his.

As Frank Grimes, the disreputable young butler, relieves Jill Bennett of her fur coat, his hand rests momentarily on her breast. She doesn't turn a hair but just murmurs, 'Oh, thank you very much.'

The party stand round the body of Totty. 'I've never seen anybody dead before,' says Sue brightly. 'Have you?'

'Only at school,' says Peter. A remark that is funny, shocking but truthful. School is exactly where he might have seen someone dead. And again it's Lindsay's line and Lindsay's life.

The only disagreement we have had has been about publicity. Lindsay believes in talking to the press at length about what he does, preparing the public for it. I've always thought that a recipe for disaster. He wins and there's a good deal in the papers. Though no one has had a chance to read the play and though it hasn't even been shot yet, he is already quite combative about it.

28 February, Hartlepool (*Afternoon Off*). Stephen Frears shows me Seaton Carew, the seedy holiday resort near Hartlepool he thinks he may use for *Afternoon Off*. A green art-deco marina, a stretch of prom, then cranes, cooling towers and a skyline filled with factories and derricks. On the shore thin Lowry figures fill sacks with sea-coal and wheel them dripping across the prom to the gates of the power station where they sell for a few shillings. Hartlepool itself has been largely flattened and a new centre built. A few of the larger buildings survive, including Baltic Chambers, a huge redbrick building with a steep pitched roof looking in the middle of the acres of rubble like the town hall at Ypres after the First World War. We wander past miles of palings and upended sleepers lining recreation grounds and allotments. The word 'television' opening all doors, we are taken round the Athenaeum, a men's club. The ceiling of the pool room, where tiny old men play snooker, is cone-shaped, like the inside of a hive. The walls are lined with cues in locked tin boxes, a name painted on each. Stephen is excited, thinks I should write a new scene for the room. The young man who shows us round apologizes for it. 'Although', he says happily, 'it's all going to be altered soon.'

6 March, London (All Day on the Sands). What nobody ever says about writing is that one can spend a whole morning, like this one, just trying to think of a name . . . the name of a character, the name of a place, or, as in this case, the name of a boarding house. The boarding house has been jazzed up, made into a 'private hotel', rooms give the names of Mediterranean resorts: the Portofino Room, the Marbella Lounge. What should the establishment as a whole be called?

Somerset Maugham set himself to write 2,000 words a day.

Did you ever have this problem, Somerset?

I eventually settle on the Miramar.

14 March, Leeds (Me, I'm Afraid of Virginia Woolf). A night shoot near Malvern Ground, a vast demolition site at Beeston overlooking the lights of Leeds. This is the frontier of devastation where demolition laps at the neat front doors and scoured doorsteps of solid redbrick back-to-backs. Neville Smith as Hopkins, the polytechnic lecturer, stands at a bus stop by a street lamp, the arc-lights trained on him, to say his one line at this location. It is 'O my pale life!'

In Barton Grove people come to their doors, oldish mostly, couples who have lived here all their lives, lives now narrowed and attenuated by this approaching tide of destruction. I suspect that Hopkins's 'O my pale life' is me presenting an edited version of my own. Located in this desperate place, observed by these bewildered people, the line insults them. I insult them.

The shot is soon done and we pack up. I imagine a similar scene, technicians coming to the bottom of a street, setting up lights as other groups arrive and stand about. A girl with a clipboard, a man with a loud hailer, waiting. Then the chief actor arrives and he is positioned under the lights, stood against a lamp standard. And shot. And not on film either. Or also on film. The technicians pack up, the cars drive away, leaving the body slumped under the lamp as the doors begin to edge open down the street.

15 March, Leeds (*Me, I'm Afraid of Virginia Woolf*). Thora Hird arrives to film the main scene of the play, in which she meets her son, Trevor, and questions him about his private life (or lack of it). We are due to film in the Civic Restaurant below the Town Hall, but shooting cannot start until it closes, so we sit in the Wharfedale Room at the Queen's Hotel having a long lunch. Thora was brought up in Morecambe, the daughter of the manager of the Winter Gardens, and she keeps up an unending flow of reminiscence; her early days in rep, her screen test at Ealing, her time with the Crazy Gang. While we chat Don Revie comes in and hangs about the entrance to the kitchen. A waiter appears and gives him a parcel. He uses the Queen's Hotel as a takeaway.

The Civic Restaurant is in the basement of the Town Hall, which also houses the Crown Court. All through the long evening's filming the corridors upstairs are thronged with lawyers and policemen, awaiting the verdict in a murder trial. A twenty-year-old man is accused of battering a baby to death; there are also cigarette burns on its body. To the police and the lawyers it seems an open and shut case, but the jury has surprised everyone (and ruined all social arrangements) by staying out for seven hours. The police attribute this to the fact that the foreman of the jury is a member of the Howard League of Penal Reform and herself an unmarried mother. The judge had been hoping to go out to dinner and his Bentley waits in Victoria Street. The court caterers have gone home and eventually the judge's chamberlain lines up at Kennedy's, the film's caterers, and gets some dinner there for the judge and the high sheriff. Meanwhile the lawyers and bored policemen drift down into the basement to watch the filming and we chat.

One of the good things about being in a group, engaged in what to other people seems a glamorous activity is that I can chat to these lawyers about their job and to the policemen about theirs, behave in fact in the way writers are generally supposed to behave, but which I seldom do. I'd normally sidestep policemen and would want to keep out of the way of their prejudices lest they expect one to corroborate them, but established as part of another scene, with a setting and frame of my own, I find I am set free, enfranchised in the way people of a more outgoing temperament are all the time.

Suddenly there is a flurry of activity: the jury is being called back and the lawyers and policemen scurry back upstairs into the court. The judge's chamberlain takes me and some of the crew and puts us in the well of the court. It is like a theatrical matinée, the cast of one show going to see another. Indeed, when he follows the judge on to the bench the chamberlain gives us a little showbiz wave. The jury now file in, surprisingly informal and at ease, the men in shirtsleeves, one woman with her knitting. The judge is kind and courteous, emphasizing they must feel under no pressure to bring in a verdict. What he wants to know is whether there is any likelihood of them coming to an agreement. The foreman must answer yes or no. She asks when. 'Ah,' says the judge, 'I mustn't answer that. That would be to put pressure on you. Obviously there will come a time when you are too tired to go on, but the very fact that you have asked that question seems to indicate to me that point has not yet been reached.' It is like Oxford philosophy. The jury files out to deliberate further and out we file to do reverses on shots already filmed. I am in the corridor two hours later when the verdict comes through. A man walks through the policemen shaking his head in disgust, saying, 'Manslaughter. Seven years.' The prisoner was a good-looking boy. Naïvely I expected to see some depravity in his face.

We finish at 11.30 with the customary call, 'Right, that's a wrap.' The judge could have said the same. 'Manslaughter. Seven years. And that's a wrap.'

16 March, Leeds (*Me, I'm Afraid of Virginia Woolf*). More filming in the Town Hall, this time in a corridor which leads from the cells. Two men are led by in handcuffs, the father and uncle of a family, both deaf and dumb. The father had been sleeping with his children and allowed the uncle to do the same. Mother, father, uncle, all were deaf and dumb, but the children could speak and speech was the father's downfall. 'Would this be any more Life,' says Hopkins in the play, 'would this be any more Life than a middle-aged lady sitting reading in a garden?' Yes, I'm afraid it would.

18 March, London. When I come back from filming – emerge, as

438

Goffman would say, from an intense and prolonged period of social interaction – I feel raw, as if I have in some unspecified way made a fool of myself.

11 April, Morecambe (*All Day on the Sands*). A bright, bitter cold morning. Over the sand the low tumbled hills of the Lake District and one white mountain. Blue council buses ferry schoolchildren along the empty promenade. Old couples take the air. Why do people find the seaside out of season sad? I never do. It's much sadder when the streets are filled with tired families, cross because they're not happy. Which is what the film is about.

Two women pass. 'I said to him, "If you've brought me here to mix with a lot of old people, you're mistaken. You've got the bowling green to go to. Well, I'm not spending the rest of my life on bowling greens."'

An old gentleman watches the filming on the front. Apparently he made boots for Field Marshal Earl Haig. Another front. This information he volunteers readily to anyone who comes near him, so I keep out of his way, suspecting he is a bore. This is foolish, since to be a bore about making boots for Earl Haig constitutes interest. A life flying this small flag. Had he met the Field Marshal?

'Oh, yes.'

'What was he like?'

A long pause. 'Very smart.'

14 April, Morecambe (*All Day on the Sands*). Alun Armstrong, who plays the father in the film, is full of jokes and stories and on the go the whole day. This morning he sits apart, silent and withdrawn. I ask him what's the matter.

'I woke up in the night and I'd nothing to read, so picked up my Gideon's, opened it at a page, the way you do, thinking there might be some sort of revelation, change my way of life and so on. And it's Ecclesiastes, "the joker is a foolish man", "empty pots make most noise"; all that stuff. I mean *my story*. So I'm piping down a bit this morning.'

On a wall on one of the roads off the promenade in clear large letters written without haste and correctly spelled: 'Mark Lambert is a Paedophiliac (Ask Tracy)'.

30 April, Hartlepool (Afternoon Off). In my mind's eye I had seen this play taking place in Scarborough or Harrogate. It is the story of a Chinese waiter on his afternoon off, searching the town for a girl called Iris, whom he has been told fancies him. I'd got the idea from a Chinese waiter I glimpsed from a car, wandering about a small town on early closing day. That had been in Lewes in 1972. Now it is six years later and it's not Lewes, it's not Harrogate but somewhere that couldn't be more different, Hartlepool.

It was this main street that gave Stephen the idea of setting the film here. The buildings all date from the same period, around when the town was founded in the 1880s. The date gives it the look of a town in a western, the main street lined with saloons, shipping offices, tackle shops and behind it, like in a western, the desert. Only it's a desert of rubble where all the symmetrical side streets have been demolished, leaving only occasional outcrops of bright, boiled brick, where the grander buildings await a more elaborate and accomplished destruction. A sense too of the proximity of Germany and the Baltic coast. The dullness and loutishness of a rundown port; pubs, prostitutes. Sailors returning.

Sunday morning and the street is closed off, emptied of cars as rails are laid down for the camera. It's Meccano time, a big tracking shot, 'real filming'. Along the pavement a wavering trail of blood leads the length of the street. Last night a man was stabbed and wandered along, holding his arms, looking for a taxi. Blood is sticky. It smears the pavement and members of the unit examine it curiously. It does seem indelible, more so than paint. Seagulls yelp over the empty street and mount each other on chimneystacks this grey Sunday while boys in baggy trousers phone possible girls from shattered phone boxes.

1 May, Hartlepool (Afternoon Off). We film in the sluice room of the cottage hospital. Racks of stainless-steel bottles and bedpans, a sink that flushes and a hideously stained drum on which the bedpans are sluiced out. This room would be my mother's nightmare. Conditions are cramped and I crouch behind the camera tripod in order to see the action. I am kneeling on the floor under the bedpan sluice. If my Mam saw this she would want to throw away trousers, raincoat, every particle of clothing that might have been touched and polluted. This has got into the film. Thora Hird plays a patient in the hospital being visited by her husband. 'I bet the house is upside down,' she says to him.

'It never is,' says her husband. 'I did the kitchen floor this morning.'

'Which bucket did you use?'

'The red one.'

She is outraged. 'That's the outside bucket. I shall have it all to do again.'

I am assuming this is common ground and that the tortuous boundary between the clean and the dirty is a frontier most households share. It was very marked in ours. My mother maintained an intricate hierarchy of cloths, buckets and dusters, to the Byzantine differentiations of which she alone was privy. Some cloths were dish cloths but not sink cloths; some were for the sink but not for the floor. There were dirty buckets and clean buckets, brushes for indoors, brushes for the flags. One mop

441

had a universal application while another had a unique and terrible purpose and had to be kept outside, hung on the wall. And however rinsed and clean these utensils were they remained tainted by their awful function. Left to himself my Dad would violate these taboos, using the first thing that came to hand to clean the hearth or wash the floor. 'It's all nowt,' he'd mutter, but if Mam was around he knew it saved time and temper to observe her order of things. Latterly, disposable cloths and kitchen rolls tended to blur these ancient distinctions but the basic structure remained, perhaps the firmest part of the framework of her world. When she was ill with depression the order broke down: the house became dirty. Spotless though Dad kept it, she saw it as 'upside down', dust an unstemmable tide and the house's (imagined) squalor a talking point for the neighbours. So that when she came home from the hospital, bright and better, her first comment was always how clean the house looked. And not merely the house. It was as if the whole world and her existence in it had been rinsed clean.

Grand Hotel, Hartlepool. Breakfast. The waitresses are two local girls who are marshalled, instructed and generally ordered about by an elderly waitress with jet–black hair and glasses. This morning she is off. A man behind me raises his voice to ask whether anyone is serving his table. The two young waitresses whisper briefly, then one goes across. The man studies the menu.

'I would like fresh grapefruit.'

'Are you suffering from diabetes?'

A hush has fallen on the room.

'I beg your pardon?'

The waitress smiles helpfully. 'Fresh grapefruit. Are you diabetic?'

The man is now in a towering rage. 'No, I am not diabetic.

Furthermore I am not suffering from Bell's palsy, tuberculosis, cancer or Parkinson's disease.'

Everyone buries themselves in their cornflakes as the waitress, scarlet, rushes from the room to tell the kitchen of this madman.

2 May, Hartlepool (*Afternoon Off*). I take photographs in the old cemetery by the sea on the north side of the headland. The graveyard is flanked by two huge factories, where the pier of Steetley Magnesite runs out into the sea. The graves are of dead mariners, a Norwegian from a shipwreck, a man killed by a shell in the bombardment of Hartlepool in 1914 and many men and children killed 'in the course of their employment'.

Filming gives one an oblique perspective on English life, taking one into places one would not otherwise go, bringing one up against people one would never normally meet. This morning busmen in the depot on Church Street, yesterday the chef and waiters in the hotel kitchens. I have very little knowledge of 'ordinary life'. I imagine it in a script and come up against the reality only when the script gets filmed. So the process can be a bit of an eye-opener, a kind of education. Cameramen in particular are educated like this, men of the world who have odd pockets of understanding and experience gleaned from the films they have worked on. I imagine someone could be educated in the same way by promiscuity.

Sunderland. An old-fashioned shoe shop. High ladders and shelves piled with shoeboxes. Feeling this is what a genuine writer would do I make a note of the labels:

    Alabaster Softee Leather
    Clover Trilobel Fur Bound Bootees
    Buffalo Grain Softee Chukkas
    Malt Gibsons

Fawn Suede Apron Casuals
Burnished Brown Concealed Gusset Casuals
Red Derby Nocap
Tan Gibson Bruised Look
Mahogany Lear Peep Toe

3 May, Hartlepool (*Afternoon Off*). We are filming an OAP concert at St Hilda's Church Hall. The Chinese waiter wanders on to the stage while two entertainers are giving a rendition of 'Pedro the Fisherman' to the whistled accompaniment of an audience of old ladies. They arrive in a coach, smart and warm in fur hats, check coats and little bootees with one solitary man. I see my father in him, going with my Mam on the WI trip from the village. 'Well, your Mam and me always do things together. We don't want splitting up to go with lots of different folks.' And he was not embarrassed by it.
My mother's description of her clothes:

My other shoes
My warm boots
My tweedy coat
That greeny coat of mine
That fuzzy blue coat I have
My coat with the round buttons

Like the inventory of a medieval will.

Casual onlookers find it difficult to detect the hierarchy of a film unit. Who is in charge? It seems to be the cameraman. He is making them move all the lights anyway. Or is it one of those two young men who keep changing their minds about where everybody in the audience is meant to sit? Perhaps it's the man with the long microphone. Certainly, now that he's shaken his head they're changing it all again. The proper actors haven't even appeared yet, you'd think they'd have some say. Suddenly everything settles down and somebody shouts out (quite rudely), 'Settle, everybody, settle', and the boss turns out to be the scruffy young man who has been sat on the window-sill doing the crossword. He scarcely looks old enough.

And so it was in the days when Mam and Dad used to come and watch the filming. Dad would think he was talking to a key figure on the film, when in fact he was talking to one of the props boys or the animal handler, members of the unit I'd scarcely come across and whose names I didn't know. Once when they visited me at Oxford they took my scout for a don, and in the theatre my dresser for John Gielgud. And it's happened to me. When we were on Broadway with *Beyond the Fringe* the Kennedys came backstage after the show. Having been introduced I spent most of my time talking to a distinguished but rather abstracted young man who, though (and perhaps because) he kept looking over my shoulder, I took to be an important section of the New Frontier. He was a secret serviceman.

13 May, Hartlepool (Afternoon Off). The final sequences with Peter Postlethwaite and Stan Richards, in the Municipal Art Gallery and Museum, which combines art, archaeology, natural and local history. Downstairs is an exhibition of flower arrangements, 'Britain in Bloom', with the comments of the adjudicators affixed: 'It speaks to me'; 'Lovely arrangement, but a bit delicate flowerwise'. Upstairs a case of stuffed birds and in another case, 'Hartlepool in Palaeolithic Times'. There is an old bicycle, a Japanese suit of armour and a dismal collection of pictures, scarcely above the highland-cattle level. Kids wander through, bored out of their heads, mystified by a culture that can comprehend a Japanese suit of armour, a stuffed otter and a calcified Roman waterpipe.

The filming finishes as filming usually does, with a wild track.

In the midst of clearing up everybody suddenly freezes into silence and immobility as on sound only the actors record their lines.

The Insurance Man

The Insurance Man is set in Prague. It begins in 1945 with the city on the eve of liberation by the Russians, though the main events of the story, told in flashback, take place before the First World War. The film was shot in Bradford, where every other script I've written seems to have been shot, and also in Liverpool, a city I didn't know and had never worked in. Bradford was chosen because among the few buildings the city has elected to preserve are some nineteenth-century warehouses behind the Cathedral. From the nationality of the merchants originally trading there, this neighbourhood is known locally as Little Germany. The trade has gone but the buildings remain, the exteriors now washed and sandblasted but the interiors much as they were when the last bolt of cloth was dispatched in the 1960s. Liverpool likewise has many empty buildings, and for the same reason, and there we had an even wider choice. I found both places depressing – Liverpool in particular. Work though it is, a play, however serious, is play, and play seems tactless where there is no work.

9 July 1985, Connaught Rooms, Bradford. These masonic chambers on what's left of Manningham Lane serve as part of the Workers Accident Insurance Institute, the office in Prague where Kafka was a conscientious and well-thought-of executive. It is only the first day of shooting, and already I feel somewhat

447

spare. We are filming scenes in the lift, which is just large enough to contain the actors and the camera crew. There's no hope of hearing the dialogue, so I sit on a window-sill and read, wishing, after writing nearly a score of films, that I didn't still feel it necessary to be in attendance at the birth. Just below where we are filming is Valley Parade, Bradford City's football ground, where two months ago dozens of fans perished in a fire. Glance down a back street and there is the blackened gateway.

10 July, Holcroft Castings and Forgings, Thornbury. Periodically between 1911 and 1917 Kafka helped to manage an asbestos factory set up by his brother-in-law. The hero of *The Insurance Man* is Franz, a young man who contracts a mysterious skin disease, seemingly from his job in a dyeworks. As a result he is sacked and comes to the Workers Accident Insurance Institute to claim compensation. He fails, but Kafka, anxious to do him a good turn, offers him a job in his brother-in-law's asbestos factory. The story is told in flashback thirty years later when Franz, now an old man, comes to his doctor to be told that Kafka's good turn has sealed his death warrant. Kafka describes in his diary the dust in the original asbestos factory and how, when they came off shift, the girls would dash it from their overalls in clouds. Even so I feel the design department has overdone it: dust coats every surface and lies in drifts against the machinery. I mention this to Richard Eyre, wondering if it's a little too much. It turns out we have had nothing to do with it: the forge, shut down six months ago, is just as it was.

The offices too have not been touched, a ledger open on a desk, records and files still on the shelves. In a locker are a cardigan and three polystyrene plates, remnants of a last takeaway, and taped to the door a yellowing cyclostyled letter dated 12 June 1977. It is from a Mr Goff, evidently an executive of the firm, living at The Langdales, Kings Grove, Bingley. Mr

Goff has been awarded the OBE in the Jubilee Honours, and in the letter he expresses the hope 'that the People, who are the Main Prop in any endeavour, many with great skill and ability, will take Justification and Pride in it and will', he earnestly hopes, 'feel that they will be sharing in the Honour conferred on me.'

11 July, Downs, Coulter & Co., Currer Street, Bradford. Another empty factory, which we fit out as the office and medical room of a dyeworks. The firm has moved to new premises in Thornton but still on the wall is a list of internal telephone numbers: Mr Jack, Mr Ben, Mr Jim, Mr Luke. It is evidently a family firm, and sounds straight out of *The Crowthers of Bankdam.* Also on the wall is an advertising calendar sent out by Chas Walker & Sons, Beta Works, Leeds, and headed *Textile Town Holidays 1974.* From big cities like Leeds and Manchester down to the smallest woollen and cotton towns like Tottingham and Clayton-le-Moors, the calendar lists the different fortnights in the summer the mills would close down. If they hadn't closed down for good already, that is. The artwork is a fanciful drawing of a toreador watched by elegant couples under Martini umbrellas but the obstinate echoes are of men in braces sat in deck-chairs, fat ladies paddling at Bridlington and Flamborough and Whitley Bay. For most of them now one long holiday.

16 July, Bradford. A boy of sixteen, hair streaked and dressed in the fashion, leads an old lady down Bridge Street. In this town of the unemployed he is probably her home help or on some community-care scheme so it's not just the spectacle of youthful goodness that makes it touching. But, not yet of an age to go arm in arm, he is leading her by the hand. He little more than a child, she a little less, they go hand in hand along Hall Ings in the morning sunshine.

Night Shoot, Little Germany. In the original script the first scene was set in the doctor's surgery in Prague at the end of the war. Old Franz is let in and mentions there is a body hanging from the lamp-post outside. Richard Eyre thought that a more arresting opening would be of Franz picking his way down the bombed street and the man's body hanging in the foreground.

The corpse is played by an extra, who is perhaps sixty. It is a complicated shot, done at night, and involves water flooding down the street, the camera on a crane, and high above it another much taller crane, a 'cherry-picker', from which (since the lamp-post is false) the 'corpse' has to be suspended. There is no dialogue and nothing for me to do. It's too dark to read and too cold to be standing about. We have done the first shot when I notice that a placard has been hung round the corpse's neck saying TRAITOR. I think this is too specific and ask Richard if we can do a shot without it. There are other technical problems to be sorted out before we do a second take, and those not involved hang around chatting and drinking coffee. As so often on a film, the atmosphere is one of boredom and resignation, troops waiting for the action. Or the 'Action'.

Suddenly there is a commotion at the lamp-post. The hanging man has been sick, is unconscious. There is a rush to get him down, many hands reaching up, the scene, in our carefully contrived light and shade, like a Descent from the Cross. Thankful at last to have something to do, the duty policeman briskly calls up an ambulance while the make-up girls (odd that this is part of their function) chafe the man's feet. At first it is feared that he has had a heart attack, but soon he is sitting up. We abandon the shot, and Mervyn, the production manager, calls a wrap. The water is turned off, props begin to clear the rubble from the street as an ambulance arrives and the patient gets in under his own steam. There is some discussion whether anyone from the unit should go with him, as someone undoubtedly should. But it is 3.30 a.m. and he goes off in the ambulance alone. I note my own reluctance to assume this responsibility. I could have gone, though there is no reason why I should. Except that it's my play. I'm to blame for him hanging there in the first place.

(Though it seems fairly obvious to me, in the finished film the meaning of this hanged man puzzles some people. The doctor had heard the man running down the street the previous night, trying to find a refuge from his pursuers. He bangs on a door and it is opened – by his pursuers. His refuge turns out to be his doom. This kind of paradox is one associated with Kafka, and it's also the paradox at the heart of the play: Kafka does Franz a favour by giving him a job in his factory, but since the factory turns out to make asbestos this good turn leads in the end to Franz's death.)

17 July, Peckover Street, Little Germany. Dan Day-Lewis, who plays Kafka, has a stooping, stiff-necked walk which I take to be part of his characterization. It's certainly suited to the role, and may be derived from the exact physical description of Kafka given by Gustav Janouch. Even so, I'm not sure if the walk is Kafka or Dan, since he's so conscientious he seldom comes out of character between takes and I never see him walking otherwise.

We film the scenes between Kafka and his father (Dave King), the Kafka family home set up on another floor of the same empty warehouse. When I first worked on the script with Richard Eyre he wondered whether these scenes of the Kafka household were necessary, feeling that the film is really the story of Franz, to which Kafka is only incidental. I pressed for them then, the producer Innes Lloyd agreed, so here we are in the Kafka apartment. Any doubts are resolved by a scene in which Hermann Kafka gets into his son's bed, then stands on it (an image taken from one of Kafka's stories) and begins to bounce up and down, the sound that of the sexual intercourse Kafka could often hear from his parents' bedroom when he was struggling to write.

(Richard's instinct proves right, nevertheless: in the editing the scene is cut, as it seems to hold up the story.)

The Bradford sequences over, we now have three days off before moving to Liverpool.

23 July, Fruit Exchange, Victoria Street, Liverpool. This is a great rarity: a location that exactly matches the scene as I imagined it. A small, steeply raked auditorium with a gallery done in light oak and lit by five leaded windows. It was built in 1900 and is as pleasing and nicely proportioned as a Renaissance theatre. Each seat is numbered, the numbers carved in a wood that matches the pews, and facing them a podium on which is the hydraulic lift that brought up the produce to be auctioned. Ben Whitrow stands on the podium now as we wait to rehearse a scene in which, as a professor of medicine, he uses Franz in a clinical demonstration for his students. The students are played by fifty Liverpool boys, some of whom are given lines to speak. ('What is this word?' asks one. 'Origin.' 'What does that mean?')

One is tempted to think that this auditorium and another that adjoins it should be rehabilitated and used as theatres. For revues possibly. Seeing it for the first time Vivian Pickles remarks, 'Look out! I feel a song coming on.' Yet if it was a theatre it would straightaway lose its charm, part of which lies in its being unwanted, a find. We do our little bit to hasten its decline by cutting out one section of the pews to accommodate a gallery. Pledged to restore it to its original state, our carpenters will patch it up but it will never be quite the same.

In the scene, Robert Hines, who plays Franz, has to stand naked on the podium under the bored eyes of fifty medical students. As the day wears on the extras have no problem simulating boredom, often having to be woken for the take. I never fail to be impressed by the bravery of actors. Robert is a striking and elegant figure, seemingly unselfconscious about his nakedness. Did I have to display myself in front of a total stranger, let alone fifty of them, my part would shrink to the size of an acorn. Robert's remains unaffected. I mention this to John Pritchard, the sound supervisor. 'I see,' he says drily. 'You subscribe to the theory of the penis as seaweed.' It later transpires that Robert's seeming equanimity has been achieved only after drinking a whole bottle of wine.

24 July, St George's Hall, Liverpool. We film a long and complicated shot that introduces the Workers Accident Insurance Institute, the office where Kafka worked for most of his life. I had written this shot in several scenes, but Richard Eyre combines them into one five-minute tracking shot. An office girl is making her rounds, collecting on behalf of the retiring head of department. The camera goes with her as she moves from office to office, calling in turn on the three clerks who figure in the story, finally ending up in Kafka's office, where he is dictating to his secretary.

The WAII office has been built in the St George's Hall, the massive municipal temple on the Plateau at the heart of Liverpool. Ranged round the vast hall are statues of worthies from the great days of the city, and on the floor a rich and elaborate mosaic, set with biblical homilies. 'By thee kings reign and princes decree justice,' say the roundels on the floor. 'Save the NHS. Keep Contractors Out,' say other roundels, badges stuck there at a recent People's Festival. 'He hath given me skill that He might be honoured,' says the floor. 'Save the pits,' say the stickers. It is a palimpsest of our industrial history. Peel and George Stephenson look down.

Most of the unit are staying in the Adelphi, a once grand hotel and the setting of the thirties comedy *Grand National Night*. More recently the vast lounge figured in the television version of *Brideshead Revisited* as the interior of a transatlantic liner. One gets a hint of its former grandeur in the size of the towels, but the service is not what it was. At breakfast I ask for some brown toast. The waiter, a boy of about sixteen and thin as a Cruikshank cartoon, hesitates for a moment then slopes over to the breakfast bar and riffles through a basket of toast. Eventually he returns with two darkish pieces of white toast. 'Are these brown enough?' It is not a joke.

26 July, St George's Hall. At the centre of the gilded grilles on the huge doors of the St George's Hall is the motto SPQL – the senate and people of Liverpool. There isn't a senate now and the building serves no civic function, the courts, which once it housed, transferred to less noble concrete premises down the hill. As for the people, they occasionally figure at rallies and suchlike, and marches seem to begin here, but the portico stinks of urine and grass grows on the steps.

In front of the St George's Hall is a war memorial, a stone of remembrance inlaid with bronze reliefs. The inscription read: OUT THE NORTH PARTS A GREAT COMPANY AND A MIGHTY ARMY. The panels, soldiers on one side, civilians on the other, are vaguely Vorticist in inspiration, the figures formal and angular and all inclined at the same slant. It was designed by Professor Lionel Budden of Liverpool University, and the bronze reliefs done by H. Tyson Smith. These aren't notable names but it is a noble thing, far more so than Lutyens's Whitehall Cenotaph.

Behind the war memorial one looks across the Plateau to the Waterloo Monument and a perfect group of nineteenth-century buildings: the Library, the Walker Art Gallery and the Court of

Sessions. Turn a little further and the vista is ruined by the new TGWU building, which looks like a G-Plan chest of drawers. A blow from the left. Look the other way and there's a slap from the right – the even more awful St John's Centre. Capitalism and ideology combine to ruin a majestic city.

Tony Haygarth plays Pohlmann, the kindly clerk in Kafka's office. In his period suit he is hanging about the steps at lunchtime, wanting company. 'I'd like to go over to the pub, you see, but in this outfit I'd feel a bit *left-handed*.'

28 July, Cunard Building. Kafka was once standing outside the Workers Accident Insurance Institute watching the claimants going in. 'How modest these people are,' he remarked to Max Brod. 'Instead of storming the building and smashing everything to bits they come to us and plead.' We film that scene today, with the injured workers thronging up the steps. Most of them are made up to look disabled, but a couple of them genuinely are – a fair young man with one arm who plays one of the commissionaires and a boy with one leg and a squashed ear who, like the lame boy in the Pied Piper, comes limping along at the tail of the crowd. Without regarding the disabled as a joke, I have put jokes on the subject into the script. 'Just because you've got one leg', shouts an official, 'doesn't mean you can behave like a wild beast.' Though the intention is to emphasize the heartlessness of the officials and the desperation of the injured workpeople, the presence of these genuine cripples shows one up as equally heartless. I can't imagine, have not tried to imagine, what it is like to have a limb torn off or have half an ear. 'You say you understand,' says Franz in the film, 'But if you do and you do nothing about it then you're worse than the others. You're evil.' This is an echo of Kafka's own remark that to write is to do the devil's work. And to say that it is the devil's work does not excuse it. One glibly despises the photographer who zooms in on the starving child or the dying soldier without offering help. Writing is not different.

28 July. It is nine o'clock and still light, and I go looking for a restaurant to have my supper. I walk through the terrible St John's Centre. It has a restaurant, set on a concrete pole (may the architect rot); now empty, it boasts a tattered notice three hundred feet up advertising to passing seagulls that it is TO LET. I pass three children, the eldest about twelve. They are working on a shop window which has CLOSING DOWN painted on it. Spelling obviously not their strong point, they are standing back from it puzzling how they can turn it into an obscenity when I pass with my book. The book takes their eye and there's a bit of 'Look at him. He's got a book.' 'What's your book?' I walk on and find myself in an empty precinct. The children have stopped taunting and seem to have disappeared. I look round and find that the trio are silently keeping pace with me. In an utterly empty square they are no more than three feet away. I am suddenly alarmed, stop, and turn back to where there are more people. I have never done that before in England, and not even in New York.

30 July, St George's Hall. Bob the gaffer is giving one of the sparks directions over a faulty lamp. 'Kill it before you strike it,' he says. It is a remark that could be called Kafkaesque did not the briefest acquaintance with the character of Kafka discourage one from using the word. But he lives, and goes by public transport – at a bus-stop today the graffiti: HOPE IS FUCKING HOPELESS.

31 July, St George's Hall. Happy to be drawing towards the end of the shoot, I have come to dislike Liverpool. Robert Ross said that Dorsetshire rustics, after Hardy, had the insolence of the artist's model, and so it is with Liverpudlians. They have figured in too many plays and have a cockiness that comes from being told too often that they and their city are special. The accent doesn't help. There is a rising inflection in it, particularly at the end of a sentence, that gives even the most formal exchange a built-in air of grievance. They all have the chat, and it laces every casual encounter, everybody wanting to do you their little verbal dance. One such is going on at hotel reception tonight as I wait for my key. 'You don't know me,' says a drunken young man to the receptionist, 'but I'm a penniless millionaire.' You don't know me, but I'm a fifty-one-year-old playwright anxious to get to my bed.

1 August, Examination Schools, University of Liverpool. In St George's Hall we had been insulated against noise. The vastness of the building meant that even a violent thunderstorm did not interrupt filming, the only problem the muffling of its huge echo. This final location is different. Outside three roads meet, and the bus station is nearby, so that traffic makes filming almost impossible. As chairman of the tribunal, Geoffrey Palmer has a long, passionate speech, his only scene in the film. Traffic noise means that we go for take after take before we get one that the sound department thinks is even passable. Then, between buses, we re-record the scene sentence by sentence, sometimes even phrase by phrase. It is an actor's nightmare, as all feeling has to be sacrificed to achieve consistency of tone. Entitled to get cross, Geoffrey remains good-humoured and in complete control, and when the speech is edited there is no hint of the conditions under which it was recorded. A splendid actor with an absolutely deadpan face, he is an English Walter Matthau.

5 August. The guard, an elderly and distinguished-looking West

Indian, announces over the Tannoy that this is the 16.45 from Leeds to Kings Cross, the estimated time of arrival 19.15. He adds, 'May the presence of the Lord Jesus Christ be with you and keep you always if you will let him. Thank you.' Nobody smiles.

9 August, London. Dr Macgregor sends me for an X-ray to University College Hospital, and I go down to Gower Street to make the appointment. I stand at the Enquiry Desk while the plump, unsmiling receptionist elaborately finishes what she is doing before turning her attention to me.

'Yes?' She glances at my form. 'Second floor.'

I long to drag her across the counter and shake her till her dentures drop out. 'Listen,' I want to say, 'you are as essential to the well-being of this hospital as its most exalted consultant. You can do more for the spirits of patients coming to this institution than the most skilful surgeon. Just by being nice. Be *nice*, you cow.'

I sit upstairs waiting for the next receptionist and realize that this is what we have been acting out, playing at, these last two weeks in Liverpool. Here I am with my form, queuing with my docket in UCH in 1985 as we have filmed the claimants queuing with theirs in Prague in 1910. I note that even when we were filming and playing at bureaucracy we fell into its traps. I never had much to do with the extras for instance. I mixed with the actors, who were known to me and who played the officials, the named parts, but kept my distance from the throng of claimants, none of whose names or faces I knew. Indeed I resented them just as the real-life officials must have done, and for the same reasons: they crowded the place out, mobbed the coffee urn, and generally made life difficult. Well, I reflect, now I am punished.

It is a feature of institutions that the permanent staff resent those for whose benefit the institution exists. And so it will go on, even beyond the grave. I have no doubt that in heaven the angels will regard the blessed as a necessary evil.

Books and Writers

Gielgud's Achievements

Sir John Gielgud is seventy-five. To hear him talk or watch him on the stage he seems much younger, whereas his recollections of the lions of the Edwardian theatre ought to put him well past his century. It's an elastic life because baby Gielgud was so quick off the mark, the famous nose soon round the edge of the pram observing the odd behaviour of his Terry uncles and aunts. He had instantaneous success as a young actor and put his popularity with audiences to good effect, bringing Shakespeare and Chekhov to the West End. As an actor manager between the wars he ran what was virtually a national theatre on Shaftesbury Avenue. In the fifties new directions in the theatre led him to flounder for a while, but in the last ten years he has found his place again. Adjectives like 'spry' and 'vigorous', indicating the subject is past it, are here inappropriate. His powers show no sign of diminishing, nor his enterprise. He has come a long way. As a juvenile his 'ambition was to be frightfully smart and West End, wear beautifully cut suits lounging on sofas in French-window comedies'. Fifty years later 'I was asked to put suppositories up my bottom under the bedclothes and play a scene in the lavatory which I confess I found somewhat intimate.' Knighthoods nothing: actors should be decorated for gallantry.

This book has been put together from conversations recorded by John Miller and John Powell for the BBC. They

Review of *John Gielgud: An Actor and His Time*, by John Gielgud with John Miller and John Powell (Sidgwick and Jackson, 1997).

were delightful broadcasts: talking off the cuff, Gielgud rambled backwards and forwards over his life; he rarely paused, and then needed only the gentlest nudge to set him off again, bowling down the years. Put together into a book, the talks come much closer to his tone of voice than previous writings. The only thing one misses is the sound of his laughter: in the broadcasts, a narrative would begin seriously enough, then he would start to snuffle, the snuffle became a giggle and the whole episode would end on a snort of laughter – the object of the joke as often as not himself. It's a winning characteristic, and an artless one; few public figures can be less concerned with the presentation of self, less calculating of the effect produced. Hence the famous gaffes.

The foot went into the mouth quite early. At a first night of *Romeo and Juliet* in 1919, Ellen Terry's last professional appearance, the Terry family was out in force, Gielgud's grandmother, Kate Terry, and her sister Marion were both given a round of applause as they made their separate entrances into the auditorium. 'In the interval I said in a loud voice to Marion, "Grandmother had a wonderful reception," and Marion replied "Yes, dear. I expect they thought it was me."' To compare even implicitly the popularity of two actresses (let alone in a 'loud voice') is to invite disaster, but the joy of the story is that even sixty years afterwards Gielgud doesn't seem to realize that his aunt wasn't just being witty but that he had put his foot in it.

There were still giants to be glimpsed in the streets of Edwardian London. He saw Sir Squire Bancroft walking every morning to his bank, 'where he would demand a slip with the amount of his current balance, which he would diligently examine before proceeding to lunch at the Garrick'. Bancroft was scrupulous about attending funerals and memorial services, 'and was heard to remark on his return from a cremation service, in those days something of a novelty: "A most impressive occasion. And afterwards the relatives were kind enough to ask me to go behind." ' Gielgud's language still retains a flavour of those days. He can talk of 'bounders', of someone being 'out of the picture' or 'caddish' even. 'She was jolly and red-faced,' he says of a costume-designer, 'like an admiral's daughter.'

In his own person he retains a visible characteristic of that less inhibited generation in his 'Terry tears'. He has ready access to his emotions and, like Churchill, he weeps with unaffected ease. On the stage he will produce a wonderfully effective tear seconds after telling some ribald story in the wings, and in full flood his tears are a remarkable phenomenon. I saw him once giving the address at a memorial service – one of those gatherings that seem to occur more frequently in the theatrical profession than in any other, generally in the Covent Garden area. This was a service for the old Bensonian actress Nora Nicholson. Nora had had a happy life and was eighty-one when she died, so the service was by no means a gloomy one. Sybil Thorndike, herself ninety-two and crippled by arthritis, sat enthroned in the front pew, surrounded by a posse of ladies who were scarcely younger. At a given moment, these attendants slid along the pew, got their frail shoulders under Dame Sybil and slowly hunched her into a standing position, remaining massed behind her like an aged rugger scrum while she recited the Twenty-Third Psalm in wonderful ringing tones. The contrast between Dame Sybil's physical incapacity and the undimmed beauty of her voice set Gielgud off crying. By the time he stood up for his memorial address he could scarcely speak, the tears splashing on the chancel steps in a display of grief which, if it was disproportionate, was not inappropriate. It was a sight both moving and funny, and much appreciated by the congregation.

Gielgud is dispassionate about his own talents, and generous about those of others. The publishers are said to have had a hard time preparing this book, with the gentle knight anxious to tone down any remark that might offend. None do, but the anxiety is typical – and so is the hard time, as he's notorious for changing his mind. In fact the only person who does get any stick is young Mr Gielgud. 'I had little idea at that time of playing a part with any originality,' he says, and dismisses many of his youthful efforts as just 'showing off'. There have been many failures, particularly as a director. 'I am feather-headed,' he says, 'not really thorough.' True, but he is also conscientious in hidden and unexpected ways. Like many actors, from time to time he tapes books for the blind. It's a one-off job which most do without much thought. Once in his dressing-room I picked up a book which he was due to record: he had scored and stressed and underlined it as if for a Command Performance.

Methodical, however, he is not, particularly as a director. His production of *Don Giovanni*, which opened the newly restored Coliseum in 1968, was a disaster (though that's not surprising, as opening productions generally are – why anybody ever consents to open a theatre I do not understand). At the last dress rehearsal some members of the chorus had still not been placed. A final dress rehearsal in the theatre is done properly, behind closed doors. Opera dress rehearsals seem slightly busier than the first night – grand and populous, with all the members of the board on view. There are titled patrons and their ladies, and crowds of discreet functionaries discreetly function in an atmosphere of hushed reverence. This is Art with a capital S. The opera was well under way when Gielgud suddenly noticed the hitherto undirected members of the chorus uneasily wandering about the stage. He rose from his seat and rushed down to the front of the stalls to call a halt while he told them what to do. But operas are not so easily stopped as plays, and the orchestra ploughed on relentlessly, with Gielgud trying to make himself heard. Suddenly his voice rose above the din in an anguished wail: 'Oh, do stop that awful *music*.'

His has been a fabled and fabulous life, and the book is a stream of anecdotes and vignettes. 'I am Mrs Sabawala,' an Indian admirer announces. 'My house on Malabar Hill is a sermon in stone. Lunch with me tomorrow.' He takes part in a gala at the Foreign Office to celebrate the visit of the French President in March 1939: 'It was a tremendous affair, the last of its kind before the war and I could not help referring to it afterwards as the Duchess of Richmond's Ball.' Sacha Guitry was to appear with Seymour Hicks in a not very funny sketch they had written, adorned but not improved by Guitry's latest wife, Genevieve Sereville, an extremely pretty girl. 'At rehearsal Mlle Sereville was dressed in a very short skirt and her stockings were rolled below her knees like a footballer's, showing a considerable expanse of thigh.' Sounding unaccountably like Ralph Lynn in an Aldwych farce, Gielgud ventured to remark to Hicks, 'I say, sir, that's a remarkably attractive girl with M. Guitry, don't you think,' and was rewarded with the trenchant comment 'Try acting with her, old boy. It's the cabman's goodbye.'

In one respect, however, this anecdotal style does him less than justice. One would not gather from these pages the nature of the role Gielgud played in the theatre between the wars, nor the extent to which he has been a pioneer. 'It was not until the Thirties,' he writes, 'that by a lucky chance I was able to bring Shakespeare back to the West End as a commercial success.' This 'lucky chance' occurred in a period of theatrical history vividly re-created by Irving Wardle in his biography of George Devine. Devine brought Gielgud to Oxford to direct the OUDS production of *Romeo and Juliet* in 1932. He had never directed before, though he had played Romeo at the Old Vic. Gielgud has always been interested in stage design – he had at one time considered going into the theatre in that capacity – and it was at his suggestion that three unknown designers were brought in to do the costumes. These were Elizabeth Montgomery and her two partners Margaret and Sophia Harris – the Motleys – who specialized in producing stunning effects with the cheapest materials. The OUDS *Romeo and Juliet* entranced all who saw it and was the trial run for the triumphant version Gielgud directed at the New Theatre in 1935, when he and Olivier alternated Romeo and Mercutio. In this and his other productions in the thirties, Gielgud was able to put into practice some of the lessons he had learned from Harcourt Williams at the Old Vic, and through Harcourt Williams from Granville-Barker. These were simple productions with continuity of action and unity of design, and were entirely modern in feeling. Wardle quotes Tyrone Guthrie as saying that Gielgud's production of *The Merchant of Venice* at the Old Vic 'made Maugham and Coward seem like two nonconformist parsons from the Midlands'.

It must have been an exciting time to be in the theatre, and some of Wardle's best pages are about the early days of Motley. They had taken as a studio Chippendale's old workshop behind St Martin's Lane, where a gang of actors, led by Gielgud, could generally be found sitting around, gossiping, discussing productions, and having tea. With a tea bill that sometimes came to £100 per week, it sounds cosy, cliquey and not the stuff of theatrical revolution, and this is the way Gielgud tells it – casually, with lots of anecdotes about Komisarjevsky and Michel Saint-Denis, both of whom he backed. What he does not say is that to design and direct productions in this way brought a gust of fresh air into the English theatre. He made Shakespeare a commercial success twenty years before the Royal Shakespeare Company. Through Komisarjevsky and Saint-Denis he put the English theatre in touch with a European tradition twenty years before the Royal Court. It cannot have been easy to bear that when the Court's day did come his pioneering work had been forgotten. Out of sympathy with Beckett and Brecht, he missed the bus to Sloane Square and it was a long time before another one came along. But when he did begin to take part in modern plays again it should be remembered that it was a return, not a departure.

Gielgud's greatest success in the fifties was his one-man show *The Ages of Man*, adapted from George Rylands' anthology. It was a *tour de force*, a showcase for his talents and also a copy-book exercise in which he could demonstrate as no one else how Shakespeare should be spoken. He did it superlatively well, and he did it everywhere. It was something he could fall back on to earn money and to wipe out the memory of less successful enterprises, of which in the fifties and sixties there were quite a few. But if *Ages of Man* was a *tour de force* it was also a cul-de-sac. It typed him in the eyes of younger theatregoers as grand, solemn and remote. He was the Voice Beautiful. Not to mention the Voice Imitable. And it was not theatre: 'I toured it for so many years I feared I would be out of practice when it came to acting again with other people. Also eight performances a week all by myself and sitting alone in a dressing-room between the acts was a very lonely and depressing business.'

I had always assumed that this fairly bleak period in his life came to an end with his portrayal of Lord Raglan in Tony Richardson's *The Charge of the Light Brigade* in 1967, and then his success in *Forty Years On* the following year. It was certainly clear from Richardson's film that Gielgud was beginning to act in a different way. Indeed, he was hardly acting at all, allowing much more of his own personality to be seen. In many ways he was like Raglan, absent-minded, impulsive, out of touch. The Headmaster in *Forty Years On* was the same sort of man, and I had thought it was the succession of the two parts that broke the mould. But this is to forget Peter Brook's National Theatre production of *Oedipus*, which intervened between the film and my play.

Gielgud had had a glorious season at Stratford in 1950 in which he had done *Measure for Measure* with Brook. But this was Brook 'when he was still young and approachable and jolly', not the legend he had since become. On *Oedipus* he would walk into the rehearsal room and bark, 'No newspapers.' Deprived of his beloved crossword, Sir John was made to do exercises. 'It was rather like being in the army and I dreaded it; but at the same time I knew I wanted to be part of such an experiment.' Brook even tried to alter his voice: 'I had to go into the voice and manner of the blinded Oedipus, trying to produce my voice in a strange, strangled tone which Peter had invented at rehearsal with endless experiment. Technically one of the most difficult things I had ever done in my life . . . very good, I suppose, for my ego.' That 'I suppose' hides the doubts, the sense of humour suspended, the abject subjection and the outlawing of common sense that working with Brook now seems to entail. If the experiment comes off, as it did with his production of *A Midsummer Night's Dream*, the result is magical. If it doesn't (and it didn't with *Oedipus*), it is just embarrassing.

Stories abound. One of the exercises in rehearsal required each member of the cast to come down to the front of the stage and shout out at the top of his voice the worst thing he could think of. 'We open in three days!' bellowed one bold spirit. But such jokes were not encouraged, and Gielgud was systematically battered down to his lowest ebb, shorn of experience and expertise. 'You can't do that,' Brook would tell him. 'It's awfully false and theatrical.' But though Brook might strangle his voice and strip him of his manner, he could not eradicate the iron streak of tinsel that runs through Gielgud's character. This, after all, was a man who first saw his name in lights in 1928, in a farce called *Holding Out the Apple*. He had one immortal line:

470

'You've got a way of holding out the apple that positively gives me the pip.' Dissolve to *Oedipus* forty years later. Irene Worth, playing Jocasta, has to impale herself on a small portable projection that was brought on to the stage. 'I can't find my plinth,' she moaned at one rehearsal. 'Really,' said the veteran of *Holding Out the Apple*: 'Do you mean Plinth Philip or Plinth Charles?'

But I would guess now that it was *Oedipus*, though rated a failure, with Gielgud somewhat out of place in it, that gave him a new lease of life. He has always been a self-conscious man, his shyness masked by a bubbling stream of anecdote. Brook had somehow inoculated him against embarrassment, and in his subsequent career, at a time of life when most men would be standing on their dignity, he threw his away entirely and to splendid effect.

There were plenty of terrible jokes in *Forty Years On*, and maybe it was those which commended it to him. It still surprises me that he agreed to do it, and I'm sure there were times, particularly on tour in Manchester, when he thought he had backed the wrong horse. If so, he never showed it, even though there were nights in Manchester when we played to only thirty people. The performances seemed like rehearsals, the more so since Gielgud still had only a shaky hold on the text and, as always when he is nervous, kept coming up with suggestions for radical alterations, even suggesting at one point that he deliver the opening speech with his back to the auditorium. This was because he was reluctant to address an audience directly, thinking it vulgar and against all his training. When he eventually plucked up courage to do it and found that it worked, there was no stopping him. He has always been a great counter of the house, able to tell you within five minutes of curtain-up exactly who is in the stalls. Now he could do it legitimately: he would lean far out over the footlights, shading his eyes with his

471

mortarboard, supposedly trying to catch the eye of his sister, Nancy, a woman of easily outraged sensibilities. In reality he was spotting friends, sometimes even waving. His dressing-room was always crammed with visitors, including a fair quota of the great and famous. I would be summoned in to meet them while Mac, his eighty-year-old dresser, who had dressed Martin-Harvey and Fred Terry before him, would be struggling to put on the knightly trousers, something old-fashioned dressers take pride in doing. We had been so close to disaster on tour that it took time for him to register that audiences actually loved him: that the ovation he received at every performance was not only respect, which he was used to, but affection.

How narrow an escape we had had with *Forty Years On* I only appreciated when I saw what happened to Charles Wood's play *Veterans* in 1972. This was a play about the making of a film, loosely based on *The Charge of the Light Brigade*, so that Gielgud virtually played himself playing Lord Raglan. It was a very funny piece, with a memorable image of Gielgud hoisted in the air astride a headless wooden horse, doing simulated riding. It was also mildly scatological. Due to go on at the Royal Court after a short provincial tour, it suffered a rough passage. At Nottingham pennies were thrown on to the stage and Gielgud was bombarded with abusive letters saying, 'You have been sold a pup.' When the play reached Brighton the audience left in droves, something audiences in Brighton are very prone to do. Indeed, having toured there several times myself, I am convinced that one of the chief pleasures of going to the theatre in Brighton is leaving it. The sleek Sussex matrons sit poised in the stalls like greyhounds in the slips. The first 'fuck' and they're a mile down the front, streaking for Hove. Once *Veterans* got to the Court, where the occasional oath is part of the house style, it was a great success and would have transferred to the West End. But the reception on tour had so convinced Gielgud of its ultimate failure that he had meanwhile signed to do a Hollywood remake of *Lost Horizon*.

The public is a problem. Actors of Gielgud's generation had a strong sense of what an audience expected and what it should be given. In the fifties and sixties it was this sense of 'my public', as much as shortage of opportunities, that kept him trundling out *Ages of Man*. In the last ten years he has shed his public and found another. But then so has everybody else, though not as painfully. Few actors now have this sense of 'my public'; one or two actresses perhaps, but that's all. It is not hard to see why. There is no such thing in the West End now as 'the public'. It survived until quite recently; it was there as late as five years ago, surviving, even strengthened by, the tidal wave of Americans that swept up Shaftesbury Avenue every summer. The Americans were at any rate English-speaking even if they were not always English-joking. Now they too have been submerged. In season and out of season, audiences are now so polyglot they no longer constitute an entity, and even playing of the highest quality does not weld them into one. The sense does not carry. The actor is a spectacle, and someone from Taiwan goes to see Gielgud or Guinness in the same spirit as he takes in the Changing of the Guard – which he marginally prefers, if only because he is allowed to film it.

The public which goes to the theatre to see Gielgud goes to see great acting. These days what the public calls Great Acting is often not even good acting. It's acting with a line around it, acting in inverted commas, acting which shows. The popular idea of Great Acting is a rhetorical performance (award-winning for choice) at the extremes, preferably the extremes of degradation and despair. Such a performance seems to the public to require all an actor has got. Actors know that this is a false assessment. The limit of an actor's ability is a spacious and fairly comfortable place to be: such parts require energy rather than judgement. Anything goes. Gielgud's farting, swearing role in *Providence*, while it was riveting to watch, was a feat of courage, not great acting. It's much harder in artistic terms to keep a delicate balance, as he did with Spooner in Pinter's *No Man's Land*. And even more so as Harry in David Storey's *Home*, an understated part of immense technical difficulty. Extremes are not edges, and the edge is where he excels: the edge of comedy, the edge of respectability, the edge of despair. If he continues to amaze and delight, his powers not to stale, it is because at his best nowadays he does not seem to be acting at all. The skill lies in letting it seem that there is no skill. He has broken his staff, but he has kept his magic.

Cold Sweat

I am meeting my father at the station. I stand at the barrier as the train draws in and see him get off. As he walks along the platform he catches sight of me and waves. I wave back, and we both smile. However, he still has some considerable distance to cover before reaching the barrier. Do I keep a continuous smile in my face during that period, do I flash him an occasional smile, or do I look away?

I am waiting in an office for an appointment. A secretary sits at the desk. I shift in my seat and the leather upholstery makes a sound that could be mistaken for a fart. I therefore shift in my seat again, two or three times, making the same sound deliberately in order to demonstrate that I have not inadvertently farted. The secretary looks up inquiringly. She may just be thinking I am uncomfortable. She may, on the other hand, be thinking I have farted, and not once but three times.

I am attending a funeral. It is crowded with mourners, many of them friends and acquaintances. I do not greet any of them but put on a grave face and avoid meeting their eyes. I am just taking my seat when a woman in the row behind leans forward to say an effusive hello.

'We were expecting you yesterday, Princess,' Petrov said to Kitty. He staggered as he said this and then repeated the movement, trying to make it seem as if it had been intentional.

Anna Karenina

Review of *Forms of Talk,* by Erving Goffman (Blackwell, 1981)

He pulled down over his eyes a black straw hat the brim of which he extended with his hand held out over it like an eye-shade, as though to see whether someone was coming at last, made the perfunctory gesture of annoyance by which people mean to show that they have waited long enough, although they never make it when they are really waiting, then . . . he emitted the loud panting breath that people exhale not when they are too hot but when they wish to be thought that they are too hot.

Remembrance of Things Past

Common predicaments and awkward moments with a particular appeal to any reader of the works of Erving Goffman. There was a time when I imagined those readers were few. As with all the best books, I took Goffman's work to be somehow a secret between me and the author, and incidents such as I have detailed above our private joke. Individuals knew they behaved this way, but Goffman knew *everybody* behaved like this, and so did I. Only we were both keeping it quiet. I wasn't even sure Tolstoy or Proust quite knew what they were about, though Tolstoy was instancing 'body gloss' and Proust (I think) 'impression management'. These days any first-year student of sociology would know, and the books I once thought so private are piled promiscuously on any campus counter at the start of every term.

Goffman is now Benjamin Franklin Professor of Anthropology and Sociology at the University of Pennsylvania, a far cry from that hotel in the Shetlands where, back in the days of rationing, he did his first fieldwork. Actually, anywhere would be a far cry from *that* hotel, and not just geographically. It still crops up from time to time in Goffman's books, furnishing him with the stuff of sober insights into region behaviour, say, or impression management, but without his ever acknowledging that, as a catering establishment, it was straight out of Will Hay. In the kitchen, mould would sometimes form on the soup; wet socks dried on the steaming kettle; and, while the manager habitually kept his cap on, the women sat with their feet on the table and the scullery boys spat in the coal bucket. Only the passage of a rich pudding galvanized this Dostoevskian crew, all sampling it by the aggressive fingerful before it was borne through the doors and across the great divide into the front area of the hotel. Which side of those contentious doors did the wee student eat, one wonders. And *what*? 'That puir Mr Goffman hasna eaten his trifle. And he didna touch his soup. At this rate he'll niver mak a dominie.' But he did, and a doctoral thesis, 'Communication Conduct in an Island Community', was what he made of *them*. But what can they have made of him, those gobbing scullery boys, that manager with his cap on, who can never have seen a sociology student before in their lives? They weren't that common in 1950. It was a novel beginning. And a novel.

Sociology begins in the dustbin, and sociologists have always been licensed rag-and-bone men trundling their carts round the backyards of the posher academic establishments. The Benjamin Franklin Professor has done the rounds of more backyards than most, scavenging in anthropology, psychology and social administration, besides picking up a lot of useful jumble 'on the knocker': his books are larded with strips of personal experience and enlivened with items from newspapers, the annals of crime and the dustbins of showbiz. It's this (and the look of so many quotations on the page) that makes his work initially inviting and accessible to a general reader like me. He writes with grace and wit and raises the odd eyebrow at those in his profession who don't, though he can't be too censorious of jargon, having invented a lot himself. He coins new usages and retools terms, giving them a fresh thread for the job in hand: 'flooding-out', 'cooling', 'keying', 'face' and 'frame' are all terms he has made his own – it was hearing 'interaction' in common use that woke me up to the fact that the word (about Goffman) had got round.

Having coined a phrase, Goffman doesn't wait to see it debased but tackles a new problem and tools a new terminology to go with it. The vocabulary is custom-made. Those who follow in his footsteps do not do it quite as well. In *Forms of Talk*, he quotes (and not disparagingly) a

'very useful analysis of error correction' by Schegloff et al., which argues 'for a distinction between correction as such and the initiation of reparative segment' . . . And further, that 'other correction' is very rare, 'other-initiation' less so . . . that remedial work overwhelmingly occurs in one of four possible positions: faulted turn, faulted turn's 'transition space', third turn, and (in the case of other-initiation) second turn.

It could be David Coleman warming up for a commentary on slalom surfing. (Coleman, incidentally, puts his foot into a footnote in *Forms of Talk*.)

Systematic Goffman is not. He writes in a vivid, impressionistic way which he concedes is often, as in much of *Forms of Talk*, tentative and exploratory. This (and his charm) makes more orthodox colleagues uneasy, and some attempt has been made to show that, stripped of his style and wit, in his conceptual nakedness, he is but a sociologist like the rest.* Maybe. But no other writer in this field so regularly startles one into self-recognition. We skitter anxiously from cradle to grave like a tart between lamp-posts. 'I won't make you feel bad as long as you don't make me feel bad.' That is the social contract. And there is nothing much to be done about it. Goffman's work, as he admits in *Frame Analysis*, 'does not catch at the differences between the advantaged and the disadvantaged classes' (he loses points there in British common-rooms, I'll bet), adding, 'I can only suggest that he who would combat false consciousness and awaken people to their true interests has much to do, because

* Most recently in *A View from Goffman*, edited by Jason Ditton.

the sleep is very deep. And I do not intend here to provide a lullaby but merely to sneak in and watch the way the people snore.'

I go to sociology not for analysis or explications but for access to experience I do not have and often do not want (prison, mental illness, birthmarks). Goffman treats these closed areas as lying alongside normal experience (or the experience of 'normals') in a way that makes them familiar and accessible. The approach is robust, humane and, despite his disclaimer, moral. 'The normal and the stigmatized are not persons but perspectives,' he writes in *Stigma*, 'and it should come as no surprise that in many cases he who is stigmatized in one regard nicely exhibits all the normal prejudices held toward those who are stigmatized in another regard.' And again:

The most fortunate of normals is likely to have his half-hidden failing, and for every little failing there is a social occasion when it will loom large, creating a shameful gap between virtual and actual social identity. Therefore the occasionally precarious and the constantly precarious form a single continuum, their situation in life analysable by the same framework. Hence persons with only a minor differentness find they understand the structure of the situation in which the fully stigmatized are placed – often attributing this sympathy to the profundity of their human nature instead of to the isomorphism of human situations.

Goffman may claim to be just watching people snore, but now and again they get a good dig in the ribs for it.

Whole novels take place in footnotes. This is a note about the strengths and weaknesses of the lover's position in an adulterous relationship:

Over time, the errant spouse is likely to find reason to goad her husband with what she has done, or, perhaps more commonly, to confess in order to provide evidence that a sincere effort is now being made to give the marital relationship another chance. This betrayal of the betrayal is sometimes not betrayed, in which case it is the lover, not his loved one's spouse, who ends up in the dark, not knowing who knows what. There are two other possibilities. The errant spouse may secretly confess that she has confessed, thus restoring a little of the lover's prior edge. Or the re-established marital couple can agree to inform the lover that the affair has been confessed (and is presumably over) and that the informing has been jointly sanctioned. All in all, then, your seducer often ends up having no say in what is said.

Frame Analysis

A note on the candidness of cameras:

At the state funeral of President Kennedy participants who were away from the immediate bereaved and the centre of ritual did what is quite standard in these circumstances: they got caught up in little conversations or 'aways' . . . they smiled, laughed, became animated, bemused, distracted and the like. The transmission of this behaviour by the roving camera discredited their expression of piety otherwise displayed.

Frame Analysis

Sharper than George V, he spots a button undone:

Young psychiatrists in state mental hospitals who are sympathetic to the plight of the patients sometimes express distance from their administrative medical role by affecting shirts open at the collar, much as do socialists in their legislative offices . . . What we have in these cases is a special kind of status symbol – a disidentifier. . . telling others not what he is but what he isn't quite.

Encounters

Forms of Talk is a collection of papers, the longest of which, 'Radio Talk, a Study of the Ways of Our Errors', takes as its subject 'bloopers', the verbal slips of radio announcers and their routines of recovery. The veteran of mouldy soup and dog-eared trifle is taking it a bit easier these days. He hasn't sat glued to his set gleaning gaffes: the bloopers are taken from records and books produced by Kermit Schafer (another backyard there). It's maybe just as well. To maintain the flow while addressing a vast, unseen audience is terror enough. To suspect that somewhere there is Erving Goffman waiting for one to fall down (if only to see how one picks oneself up) would be to risk multiplying the occasions on which one would be likely to do so – thereby playing into the hands of any passing ethnomethodologist.

Goffman shows that the special pressure upon a radio announcer to maintain the flow furnishes insights into forms of face-to-face talk where no similar pressure exists. I suspect that he already knew what he was out to demonstrate before he embarked on the study, and he doesn't in the end tell us much more than we know already – though what we know is what he has already told us. Still, he manages to have a lot of fun on the way. Words with sexual or scatological double meanings he terms 'leaky'. Example: 'balls', 'can', 'behind', 'big ones', 'parts', 'fanny'; this last footnoted 'Does not leak in Britain.' Actually 'can' does not leak in Britain, but no sweat. An instance of a leaky utterance (in an appropriately watery context) – BBC announcer at the launching of the *Queen Mary*: 'From where I am standing I can see the Queen's bottom sticking out just over her water line.'

One of the pleasures of reading Goffman is in taxonomy: items that one has had lying around in one's mind for ages can be filed neatly away. Like a caption I saw years ago and am delighted now to dignify as a leaky utterance: a newspaper picture of a drama group headed 'Blackburn Amateurs examine each other's parts.' And another (which ought to be in Goffman's book if only because the reasoning behind the remedial work is so complex and ultimately futile): Dorothy Killgallan, an American columnist, began a radio talk, 'Tonight I am going to consider the films of Alfred Hitchcack . . . *cock!*

. . . CACK!' I wouldn't like to see Mr Schegloff et al. let loose on that one.

Goffman remarks that there is often a possibility after a verbal slip 'that hearers will be left with ambiguity as to actual or feigned obliviousness, as I was on hearing an announcer unfalteringly say, "She'll be performing selections from the Bach Well-Tempered Caviar, Book Two, and also from Beethoven, Sonata in G Minor."' There was once a performance of *The Seagull* at the Old Vic in which Dorn, delivering the final line, 'Konstantin has shot himself,' instead came out with 'Konstantin has shat himself.' The audience looked at each other in wild surmise, then, deciding they had better not believe their ears, began to applaud – and more vociferously than if no mistake had been made.

Fruitful are the ways of our errors, and frightful too: we spend our lives in a twitter of anxiety and potential embarrassment, and there is no such thing as idle conversation. In the first essay in *Forms of Talk*, entitled 'Replies and Responses', Goffman analyses this seemingly simple exchange:

A: Do you have the time?

B: Sure. It's five o'clock.

A: Thanks.

B: (*Gesture*) T's okay.

Goffman detects possible offence in 'Do you have the time?' 'Sure' is a promise that no such offence is going to be taken. 'Thanks' is gratitude not merely for the information but that the request for it has not been taken amiss; and 'T's okay' is a final assurance to the questioner that he remains undiminished by the encounter. Thus both parties go on their way with their sense of self intact. 'If you want to know the time ask a policeman' becomes Ivy Compton-Burnett meets Gilbert Ryle.

In philosophy I would find this kind of analysis arid and dispiriting. With Goffman it is different. Funny and perceptive though he is about forms – whether in talk, behaviour or social organization – forms are never his central concern. In philosophy what we do with words is about what we do with words. In Goffman what we do with words (or what we do with our hands and feet) is about what we are. Central is the self, 'that sacred object which must be treated with proper ritual care and in turn must be presented in a proper light to others'.

Two men in a park:

A: Do you have the time?

B: Sorry. I haven't got a watch.

A: Never mind.

B: (*walking away, then stopping and calling back*) But thank you for asking.

Too late, B had become aware that he was being asked not so much for the time as a way to spend it; his lack of a watch was neither here nor there. While he might quite properly wish to turn down A's implied request, the last-minute reassurance of his 'But thank you for asking' showed that, while it might be right to leave someone disappointed, one ought not to leave them crestfallen.

We must love one another or die – of embarrassment. Life is a perilous path across social quicksands, and no effort must be spared to save each other from the ultimate fate, when the swamps of confusion close over our heads leaving that last clutching hand clawing the air to the echo of an apologetic voice: 'Sorry, did I say the wrong thing?'

In the second essay, 'Response Cries', Goffman takes to pieces remarks of the nature of 'Oops', 'Ouch' and 'Ugh.' Under the heading 'The *threat startle*, notably *Eek!* and *Yipe!*', he writes, 'A very high open stairwell, or a walk that leads up to a precipice, can routinely evoke *yipes* from us as we survey what might have been our doom . . . A notion of what a fear response would be is used as a pattern for mimicry.' Goffman notes that these particular response cries may be 'sex-typed for feminine use', but my response would still be 'Uh huh.' I can't offhand recall negotiating any very high open stairwells with a member of the opposite sex, but were I to do so I trust she wouldn't come out with 'Yipe!' I'd prefer the non-sex-typed response 'Shit!' 'Yipe!' might find her five storeys down and the focus of some response cries herself. If I must needs be on top of Blackpool Tower in mixed company I'd prefer less modish ladies who would utter response cries typed for feminine use, like 'Goodness me!', 'Heavens above!' or plain, downright 'Ooh!' Certainly not 'Eek!' And the fact that the Goffman girls may, as he points out, be consciously imitating the language of comics is no excuse: I'd rather they didn't.

I don't think it's simply that 'Eek!' and 'Yipe!' are American terms that haven't caught on here yet: an element of taste enters into the use of response cries, and this Goffman is missing. There is something suspect (and potentially ridiculous) about those in the vanguard of slang. ('Far out!') Goffman doesn't actually discuss the currently fashionable response cry of disgust, 'Yuk!', but even when used as a pattern for mimicry I always find it wince-making. The nightmare would be to find oneself on the edge of Beachy Head with someone who, in the course of looking over, managed also to step in a cowpat and thus had occasion to say all three: 'Eek!', 'Yipe!' and 'Yuk!'

Maybe Goffman's heavy-footed helpers are to blame: Messrs Carey, Draud, Fought, Galman, Grimshaw, Jefferson, Sankoff, Sherzer and Smith, who presumably (though not, I hope, in a body) haunted steep drops and precipitous stairwells logging the necessary shrieks. Of course, the sort of person who visits Niagara Falls or the top of the Empire State Building may be typified precisely by the fact that he or she does say 'Eek!' – as distinct, say, from those who ascend to high points requiring more character and effort. Walkers do not say 'Yipe' on the summit of Great Gable, for instance. Still less (ugh) 'Wow!' I personally associate such exclamations with 'zeebs' – a species I lack space to describe, but one of the characteristics of which is compulsive and inappropriate response cries. Enthusiasts for hi-fi, they frequently lapse into the accents of *The Goon Show*. More often men than women, they can be recognized by the battery of pens on display in their breast pockets. They say 'Hail, friend' instead of 'Hello', not 'Goodbye' but 'Farewell', and depart with an inappropriateness of gesture and a gangling uncoordinated gait that, to adapt Goffman, could be called 'lack of limb discipline'.

Forms of Talk is harder to read and less varied than some of the earlier books. The text is tough-going, and there are fewer truffles in the footnotes, with Goffman dodging up snickets, pressing himself into ever shallower entries, perhaps to evade his admirers.

I have just been reading Robert Byron's *The Road to Oxiana*, recently reissued with a nice introduction by Bruce Chatwin. Byron's book is made rather than marred by his unrepentant snobbery. Chatwin, who travelled the same road thirty years after Byron, in 1962, looks back with a different snobbishness that I found less engaging: he regrets, as travellers are wont to do, those who came after – in this case, the droves of young people who took to the road in the sixties and seventies, headed for Nepal. In 'Where the Action Is', one of his best essays (collected in *Interaction Ritual*), Goffman remarks, 'When persons go to where the action is they go to the place where there is an increase, not in the chances taken, but in the chances that they will be obliged to take chances.' These days it is true the chances are that one will be obliged to take more chances in wilder places than Nepal (Patagonia, say). And maybe the hippies are to be blamed for not perceiving that, or not perceiving it sooner. But Chatwin to Patagonia, a mod to

485

Brighton on Bank Holiday – Goffman makes them kin.

Some must escape his net. Dukes wouldn't find much here to interest them, except some clue as to how the other half live. Or 'die' – which *they* never do, of course, being dukes: indifference to the impression one makes is a constituent of aristocracy and (in a different sense) of royalty. 'There is only one man in the whole world who walks,' said Diderot, 'and that is the sovereign. Everybody else takes up positions.' An actor must not forget his lines (or show distress, should he do so). Royalty must never seem to be embarrassed, because that would embarrass us. Except that democracy, or television, is altering this. Royalty must now be seen to be 'human'. Or (since they are taking part in a performance) be seen to seem 'human'. Still, blushes cannot be performed. Watching the Queen returning from the royal wedding, trying to manage the happy chatting of Earl Spencer on the one hand and acknowledging the frenzy of the crowd with the other, was to detect someone in grave danger of 'flooding out'. And, though it is given to few of us to drive through the streets of London in an open landau to the cheers of a delighted throng, the situation elicited fellow-feeling because it was one we had all at some time or other experienced.

Of Goffman himself I know nothing. I take it, as much from his first name as his second, that he is Jewish, which may be significant, in that so much of his work, like Freud's, is to do with 'passing' or fitting in, and some of it is a gloss on Maurice Samuel's remark that 'the Jews are probably the only people in the world to whom it has ever been proposed that their historic destiny is – to be nice.' About face we are all Jews. His footnotes, his followers and (I am presuming) his Jewishness link Goffman with another founder of a school, Namier. There is a passage in *England in the Age of the American Revolution* that bears on the interests of the Benjamin Franklin Professor: 'A man's status in English society has always depended primarily on his own consciousness . . . whatever is apt to raise a man's self-consciousness – be it birth, rank, wealth, intellect, daring or achievements – will add to his stature; but it has to be translated into the truest expression of his sub-conscious self-valuation: uncontending ease, the unbought grace of life.' Goffman would endorse the phrase 'uncontending ease', while having more to say about it being the '*unbought* grace of life', since so much of his work has been to show how strenuously (and unknowingly) we do try to procure it.

Death is all the rage at the moment, particularly in America, where whole sections are devoted to it in the more life-enhancing bookshops. Coincidentally, or not, capital punishment in America is being patchily resuscitated. Goffman hasn't contributed much to the literature of physical as distinct from social extinction, but in *Frame Analysis* there is a fine passage (again relegated to a footnote) about the hypocrisy implicit in the expectation that a man should die well on the scaffold. It also makes nonsense of Goffman's claim not to be a moralist.

Such ceremonialization of killing is sometimes contrasted to the way in which savages might behave, although I think it would be hard to find a more savage practice than ours – that of bestowing praise upon a man for holding himself to those forms that ensure an orderly, self-contained style to his execution. Thus he (like soldiers in the field) is being asked to approve and uphold the action which takes his life, in effect setting the first above the second. *That* sort of line is fine for those who write or preach or legislate in one or another of the names given to society. But to accept death politely or bravely is to set considerably more weight on moral doctrine than is required of those who formulate it.

It is not often that one gets such a clear moral note from the watcher at the bedside. A corresponding passage in fiction is the final scene of *The Trial*, when Joseph K. is about to die. His executioners pass a knife from one to the other until it dawns on K. that, in order to spare their feelings, he must grasp the knife and execute himself. He doesn't, and feels guilty for failing to do so. It is his final failure, for he is then killed. He has 'died'. Then he dies. Much of Goffman could be a commentary on Kafka. One puts it that way round, the artist before the academic, but the truth one finds in Goffman's work is the truth one goes to fiction for.

A final word, on book-reviewers. Goffman is summarizing (in a footnote in *Frame Analysis*) an article by Walter Gibson from *College English*. (Not quite a backyard but certainly a sub-basement of the stack.) Gibson, he says,

> took up the case in regard to book-reviewing, suggesting how much of that literary form consists in using the works of others as a target of response which will confirm for the reader that he has found a brilliant, many-sided critic who appreciates that the reader is the appropriate recipient for this response. Writing, then, breeds a presumed (Gibson calls him mock) writer who, in fact, is likely to be vastly different from the actual writer, and a presumed reader who on the same grounds is likely to be vastly different from the actual one. The posturing of the writer, Gibson argues, calls out a posturing from the reader – a mutually affirmed affectation.

So there we both were, this presumed reader and me, just having a nice little zizz of mutually affirmed affectation, when in creeps this American guy, sits down, and starts watching. The first click of his ballpoint and, I tell you, we didn't get another wink.

Bad John

———

One of John Osborne's Thoughts for 1954: 'The urge to *please* above all. I don't have it and can't achieve it. A small thing but more or less mine own.' This book does please and has pleased. It is immensely enjoyable, is written with great gusto, and Osborne has had better notices for it than for any of his plays since *Inadmissible Evidence*.

Books are safer than plays, of course, because (unless one is a monk at lunch) reading is a solitary activity. A play is a public event where, all too often these days, for the middle-class playgoer, embarrassment rules, oh dear. Especially where Osborne is concerned. Nor does reading his book carry with it the occupational hazards of seeing his plays, such as finding the redoubtable Lady Redgrave looming over one ready to box one's ears, as she did to a vociferous member of the audience at *A Sense of Detachment*. The book as a form is safe, even cosy, and I suspect that critics, who have given Osborne such a consistently hard time for so long, heaved a sigh of relief at this autobiography, since it was something, to quote another John's spoof of Dorothy L. Sayers, 'to be read behind closed doors'. Though without necessarily taking Orton's other piece of advice – namely to 'have a good shit while reading it'.

Osborne, like Orton, had a bleak childhood (or would like us to think so). Both had weak chests, and both spent a brief period learning shorthand at Clark's Colleges. There the resemblance

Review of *A Better Class of Person: An Autobiography*, 1929–1956, by John Osborne (Faber and Faber, 1978)

ends. At the outset of his career Orton changed his name from John to Joe, lest the public confuse him with Osborne – and tar him with the same brush. For Joe, unlike John, did very much want to please. But do playgoers mind very much if they're *pleased*? I never do. Boredom is my great terror. 'All I hope is that the dog hasn't been sick in the car' is the epitaph on too many a wearisome evening in the theatre. I have never been bored by Osborne – well, by Bill Maitland a little, but that was meant. I often disagree with his plays, but I invariably find his tone of voice, however hectoring, much more sympathetic than the rage or the patronizing 'Oh dear, he's at it again' he still manages to provoke in an audience. (At Brighton, the stage carpenter used to greet him in mock-despair: 'Oh blimey, it's not you again!'). I actually enjoyed the frozen embarrassment of the glittering house that packed the Lyttelton when his *Watch it Come Down* opened the National Theatre, and at *A Sense of Detachment* was told off for laughing too much (or laughing at all) at the catalogue of pornographic films, recited in nun-like tones by the said Lady Redgrave, her title an important ingredient of the audience's resentment, their fury fuelled by a touch of class.

Osborne thinks those days are past: 'Most of my work in the theatre has, at some time, lurched head on into the milling tattoo of clanging seats and often quite beefy booing. The sound of baying from dinner-jacketed patrons in the stalls used to be especially sweet. Nowadays one is merely attacked by a storm cloud of pot and BO.' Another way of saying that the audience is (Gr-rr-r) young.

It's hard to see who made Osborne a writer. In working-class childhoods the Curtis Brown role generally falls to the mother, but not apparently in this case. A colleague of his mother's, Cheffie, cast him as a future 'thousand-a-year man'. This was in Surrey in the forties. In much the same class and period in the

North aspirations were approximately half this. My mother thought £10 a week the salary of a successful man in the profession she had picked out for me, the unlikely one of 'gentleman farmer'. Osborne's mother had no aspirations for him at all: 'My mother always made it clear to me that my place in the world was unlikely ever to differ from her own.' Nellie Beatrice was a barmaid, almost an itinerant one she changed her job (and their accommodation) so often – thirty or forty times during the first seventeen years of the boy's life. Flitting flats, changing schools: Osborne's life was like a rep long before he became an actor.

The name Nellie Beatrice seems odd. It took me some time to get used to the fact that this was his mother, not his aunt. It is an aunt's name, and, according to him, an aunt was pretty much what she was – unsmiling, given to sulks and Black Looks, not at all the jovial lady smiling, if Osborne is to be believed, an almost unique smile to face page 144. Other people's mothers are always easier to swallow than one's own, and Nellie Beatrice is funnier than her son will allow. He conned her into going to see him in *Hamlet*: 'I've seen it before,' she remarked to her companion. 'He dies in the end.' Osborne lovingly records her make-up:

Her lips were a scarlet-black sliver, covered in some sticky slime named Tahiti or Taboo . . . She had a cream base called Crème Simone, always covered up with a face powder called Tokalon . . . topped off by a kind of knickerbocker glory of rouge, which . . . looked like a mixture of blackcurrant juice and brick dust. The final coup was an overgenerous dab of Californian Poppy, known to schoolboys as 'fleur des dustbins'.

She lives on, Mrs Osborne, 'hell-bent' on reaching her century.

Osborne's father, Godfrey, was the more sensitive of the two, living apart from his mother, though Osborne does not remember why ('I have a vague remembrance of them hitting each other'). A copywriter in an advertising agency, he died of consumption when John was about twelve. (I say 'about' because dates are quite hard to come by in this book: nowhere, for instance, is Osborne's date of birth plainly stated.) His father came home to die at Christmas 1939:

I was sitting in the kitchen reading . . . when I heard my mother scream from the foot of the uncarpeted staircase. I ran to see what was happening and stared up to the landing where my father was standing. He was completely naked with his silver hair and grey, black and red beard. He looked like a naked Christ. 'Look at him!' she screamed. 'Oh, my God, he's gone blind.' He stood quite still for a moment and then fell headlong down the stairs on top of us. Between us we carried him upstairs. She was right. He had gone blind.

This gentle wraith had some literary ambitions, writing short stories, two of which his son submitted as his own work when taking a correspondence course at the British Institute of Fiction Writing Science. The stories were extravagantly praised, but when Osborne started his own work the reaction quickly became 'reproachful, impatient and eventually ill-used and sorrowful'. It's a progression he must have got used to since. But if one were to ask (as presumably his multitudinous relatives did and do ask), 'Who is it Osborne "takes after" ' or 'Where does he get his brains from?' then I imagine it is his father who would take the credit. His father was born on 8 May 1900. And it was on 8 May 1956 that *Look Back in Anger* opened at the Royal Court. Osborne notes that it is the one unforgettable feast in his calendar.

I generally assume that childhoods more or less ended with the First World War – halcyon childhoods certainly – and that most of them since have been the 'forgotten boredom' of Larkin's poem 'Coming'. Anyone born after 1940 got the Utility version, childhood according to the Authorized Economy

Standard. But Osborne (unexpectedly) seems to have had a childhood of Dickensian richness and oddity, divided between his mother's relations, 'the Grove Family Repertory', based in Fulham, and his father's, who made up 'the Tottenham Crowd'. There are relatives and relatives of relatives, and Osborne remembers them all, together with their small claims to fame: his grandfather's Uncle Arthur, 'said to be a director of Abdulla' (of 'cigarettes by'); his grandmother's sister, 'Auntie Min', whose life revolved round milk bottles; her husband, Uncle Harry, with his ferocious cockatoo. His great-grandmother, Grandma Ell, was laid out in the front parlour. The undertaker, who doubled as her son, Osborne's great-uncle Lod (the *names*!), lifted up the baby John to see his aged forebear lying in her coffin 'in what seemed unthinkable luxury'. Another uncle threw himself under a tube train *en route* for thé cobblers, and a grandma chucked Marie Lloyd out of the pub she ran, the Duncannon, off St Martin's Lane, with the first lady of the music-hall screaming, 'Don't you fucking well talk to me! I've just left your old man after a weekend in Brighton.' All these, not to mention a strong supporting cast that features a proper quota of nancies and at least one of what in our family used to be referred to as 'them man-women'. 'Oh,' one is tempted to exclaim with the Radlett children, 'the *bliss* of being you!' Or at any rate the bliss of being him now, remembering (and being able to remember) it all. Of course, it wasn't much fun at the time. 'There was no cachet in youth at that time. One was merely a failed adult. I sought the company of people like my grandparents and great aunts and uncles: they were infinitely more interesting. And I was an eager and attentive listener.'

I said his childhood was 'unexpectedly' rich, because to date there's not much hint of it in his work. He quotes examples from *The Entertainer* and *Hotel in Amsterdam* that draw directly on members of his family, but not much of the personnel or atmosphere of his childhood has hitherto found its way into his plays, even on television. Speaking as one who has recycled his only two serviceable aunts so often in dramatic form they've long since lost all feature or flavour, I'm sure his restraint is to be commended.

When he does start drawing on his later experience for the plays, it's nice to find that the relation between Art and Life doesn't unduly exercise him. In this narrative the real become the fictional almost in mid-sentence: characters are dragged struggling out of Life, allowed a quick visit to Wardrobe before being shoved breathless on to the stage. And no *Brideshead* rubbish about 'I am not I: thou art not he or she: they are not they.' His first wife, Pamela Lane, becomes Alison at her ironing-board, and her hapless parents leap on to the stage with her. She is she: they are they: and he himself makes no bones about coming on as Jimmy Porter – in 1956 anyway. Newspapers won't believe he's come on as anything else since.

Much of his childhood was spent in the more run-down bits of suburban Surrey, with spells at umpteen schools where he grew to expect to get beaten up as a matter of course on the first day. He was sent away to school at various times because of his health, the bills being paid by the Benevolent Society that had looked after his father. The account of the cold convalescent home in Dorset where he was sent at the end of 1942 makes grim reading, but for all that he doesn't come over as ever having been desperately unhappy in the way sensitive boys sent away to school are supposed to be (if they have an eye on Art, that is). One has no sense of his looking for affection, though there is a beautiful account of his friendship with a self-assured and decidedly eccentric boy, Mickey Wall. 'When he introduced me to his sister, Edna, a nice but slightly irritable nineteen-year-old, she was bending over the fire grate. "This is my sister, Edna," he said . . . I was prepared to be impressed both by her seniority

494

39 Prunella Scales (HMQ) and A. B. (Anthony Blunt) in *A Question of Attribution*,
Royal National Theatre, December 1988

40 With John Schlesinger on the set of *A Question of Attribution*, BBC Ealing, July 1991

41 With Alan Bates on the set of *102 Boulevard Haussmann*, BBC Elstree, July 1990

42 *Talking Heads*, BBC, 1988: Julie Walters in *Her Big Chance*

43 *Talking Heads*, BBC, 1988: Maggie Smith in *Bed Among the Lentils*

44 *Talking Heads*, BBC, 1988: Patricia Routledge in *A Lady of Letters*

45 *Talking Heads*, BBC, 1988: Stephanie Cole in *Soldiering On*

46 *Talking Heads*, BBC, 1988: Thora Hird in *A Cream Cracker Under the Settee*

47 *The Wind in the Willows*, Royal National Theatre, December 1990

48 Michael Bryant (Badger) and David Bamber (Mole) in *The Wind in the Willows*

49 Nigel Hawthorne in *The Madness of George III*, Royal National Theatre,
December 1991

50 Harold Innocent (Sir George Baker) and Nigel Hawthorne (George III)
in *The Madness of George III*

51 A. B., January 1994

and attractive appearance, but not for his comment. "Hasn't she got a big arse?" he said thoughtfully.'

There is something of Richmal Crompton's William (and his more than slightly irritable sister Ethel) about Mickey Wall, and also of Saki's Bassington – a boy too self-assured and finished ever to turn into an adult. I've no doubt there will be some research student, maybe one of those paid-up, card-carrying members of the London Library that figure on Osborne's hit list, who will one day sift the plays for evidences of Wall. But on to sex.

Convalescing in Cornwall after an operation for appendicitis, he finds himself alone on a beach. 'I took off my bathing suit and began to cauterize my appendicitis wound with a stick, rather like a crayon, which I had been given for this purpose. It was six months since my operation but my scar had refused to heal and was still partially open with patches of wormy flesh protruding from it.' The naked Osborne, poking away at his stomach, is espied by a handsome middle-aged man sunbathing in the next cove. He turns out to be a writer and asks him back to his cottage. They drink china tea out of nice cups, listen to a record of Arthur Bliss's *Miracle in the Gorbals* and the author, J. Wood Palmer (that initial says it all), suggests Osborne stay the night. At the same time, he cheerfully warns our hero that a bit of the other is quite likely to be on the cards. Exit the author of *A Patriot for Me*, hot and confused. But the scar, the writer, the nice cups make it all straight out of the last writer one would ever associate with Osborne – Denton Welch.

Mind you, this sort of thing is always happening to him. He's able to drop his guard temporarily during a brief (and glorious) stint as a reporter on *Gas World* – not, one imagines, the most epicene of periodicals – but no sooner does he give up journalism than the word goes round and the forces of pederasty are on the qui vive. No rep does he join but at the first read-through the resident Mr Roving Hands is giving him the glad eye. One is even observed fumbling him under a café table by a private detective specially hired (in Minehead!) by his fiancée's parents. Nothing ever comes of these approaches, despite the assertions of colleagues like Gerald at Ilfracombe that 'I didn't know what I wanted.' Osborne knew what he wanted all right, and he'd been wanting it for years.

'Sex was the most unobtainable luxury in the winter of our post-war austerity.' What passed for sex in 1947 was 'a few snatched pelvic felicities during the quickstep, what I came later to know as a Dry Fuck on the Floor'. For the boy who, at school, did not know what a twat was, opportunity finally knocked in Llandudno, on tour with an actress called Stella. Knocked and knocked and knocked. He was nineteen, and to read back from Art to Life (*A Sense of Detachment* again), he 'could do it nine times in the morning'. And, what is nice, five wives later he still thinks it a very worthwhile activity. 'If I were to choose a way to die it would be after a drunken, fish-eating day, ending up at the end of the Palace pier . . . To shudder one's last, thrusting, replete gasp between the sheets at four and six o'clock in Brighton would be the most perfect last earthly delight.' Even this last, putative fuck is due for a matinée performance.

Little mothered but much married, Osborne has a complicated relationship to the opposite sex, pointed up by a happy printer's error. For his first performance with Stella he had invested in a pair of yellow poplin pyjamas from Simpson's. Stella, however, jumped the gun and 'began to make love to me with alarming speed, but I was still sober and self-conscious enough to insist on going to my own room to get my pymamas.' Once in his 'pymamas', he came back to bed and Stella, and burst into tears. It was some considerable time before he ceased crying, took off the pymamas and got down to the serious business of sexual intercourse.

This is a lovely book. It has jokes ('Handing over the Hoover to my mother was like distributing highly sophisticated nuclear weapons to an underdeveloped African nation'). It is not mellow. And it constantly brings alive that remotest of periods, the recent past.

Instead of a Present

My first thought was that this whole enterprise is definitely incongruous. A birthday party for Philip Larkin is like treating Simone Weil to a candlelit dinner for two at a restaurant of her choice. Or sending Proust flowers. No. A volume of this sort is simply a sharp nudge in the direction of the grave; and that is a road, God knows, along which he needs no nudging.

And why now in particular? Apparently he is sixty, but when was he anything else? He has made a habit of being sixty; he has made a profession of it. Like Lady Dumbleton, he has been sixty for the last twenty-five years. On his own admission there was never a boy Larkin; no young lad Philip, let alone Phil, ever. And I'm not going to supply the textual references: there'll be enough of that going on elsewhere.

Besides, why a *book*? He must be fed up at the sight of books. It's books, books, books every day of his life, and now here's another of the blighters. Why not something more along the lines of a biscuit barrel? Because that's all this collection is, the literary equivalent of an electric toaster (or a Teasmaid perhaps) presented by the divisional manager at an awkward ceremony in the staff canteen, and in the firm's time too. Still, any form of clock would have been a mistake. Better to have played safe and gone for salad-servers or even a fish-slice. I had an auntie, the manageress of a shoe shop, who every birthday gave me shoe-trees. They were always acceptable.

Written for *Larkin at Sixty*, edited by Anthony Thwaite (Faber and Faber, 1982)

These are some of the reasons why I feel ill at ease in this doleful jamboree. Added to which there is the question of his name. Without knowing Mr Larkin, what do I call him? I feel like the student at a dance, suddenly partnered by the Chancellor of the university, who happened to be Princess Margaret. Swinging petrified into the cha-cha, he stammered, 'I am not sure what to call you.' The strobe was doused in the Windsor glare: 'Why not try Princess Margaret?' A bleak smile from Hull could be just as disconcerting. *Philip* he plainly is not, though *Larkin* is overfamiliar too, suggesting a certain fellow-footing. Being a librarian doesn't help: I've always found them close relatives of the walking dead.

Of course this book is presumably not addressed to the librarian. I imagine all librarians get at sixty is piles. If they're lucky. No, we are addressing the real Larkin, the one who feels shut out when he sees fifteen-year-olds necking at bus-stops. But that's risky too: authors resent the knowledge of themselves they have volunteered to their readers, and one can never address them in the light of it without turning to some extent into a lady in a hat.

Whether as Larkin, Philip Larkin or plain Philip, his name is bound to turn up on every page of this book. Names strike more than they stroke, and I would like to think of him wincing as he reads, staggering under repeated blows from his own name, Larkin buffeted not celebrated. I should be disappointed in him, too, did he not harbour doubts about the whole enterprise, echoing Balfour's remark: 'I am more or less happy when being praised, not very uncomfortable when being abused, but I have moments of uneasiness when being explained.'

It's very gingerly, therefore, that I say my thank you. For what? Often simply because his poems happen to coincide with my own life. And, yes, I know that is what one is supposed to feel, and that is Art. But it's not art that stood me for the Two

Minutes' Silence on the parade ground at Coulsdon one November morning in 1952 when the Comet came looming low out of the fog, as in 'Naturally The Foundation Will Bear Your Expenses'. Or put me in a Saturday train from Leeds on a slow and stopping journey southwards, the only empty seats reserved for a honeymoon couple who got on at Doncaster. One of the first of his poems I read was 'I Remember, I Remember', and it was this sense of coincidence, even collocation, that made me go on to read more. It isn't my favourite among his poems, but it's the one that made me realize that someone who elsewhere admitted his childhood was 'a forgotten boredom' might be talking to me.

I had always had a sneaking feeling my childhood didn't come up to scratch, even at the time; and when I began at the usual age to think there might be some question of becoming 'a writer' (I do not say 'writing') the want of this apparently essential period seemed crucial. In all the books I had read childhoods were either idyllic or deprived. Mine had been neither. In point of memories I was a non-starter. I had not spent hours in the crook of a great tree devouring Alice or Edgar Rice Burroughs. I read (and even then patchily – I never *devoured* anything) *Hotspur*, *Wizard*, *Champion* and *Knock-Out*, not quite the ore of art. It's true that for a long time I too went to bed early, but most children did in those days, with no effect on the percentage turning out to be Proust. I scanned my childhood for eccentrics, and found none. I had an aunt who had played the piano in the silent cinema – her music is still in the piano stool today (snap again) – but there was nothing odd about her, apart from her large, elderly bust; and there was no shortage of those either.

My school was dull too. It wasn't old. It wasn't new. There was not even a kindly schoolmaster who put books into my hands. I think one may have tried to, but it was not until I was sixteen, and a bit late in the day. Another boy had shown me

Stephen Spender's *World Within World*, or at any rate the bits dealing with homosexuality, the references to which (while pretty opaque by today's standards) were thought rather daring in 1951. Spender had been befriended by the music master, Mr Greatorex, who had told young Stephen that, although he was unhappy now, there would come a time when he would begin to be happy and then he would be happier than most. I took great comfort from this, except that I wasn't particularly unhappy (that was the trouble); but the thought that I was about to get the Greatorex treatment, that a master in my dull day-school had divined beneath my awkwardness the forlorn and troubled essence, produced in me a reaction of such extravagant enthusiasm and wanting to be 'brought out' that the master in question (who had merely suggested I might like to read his *New Statesman* from time to time) scuttled straight back into his shell. It was further proof that literature and life (or my life at any rate) were different things. For the time being, anyway. At Oxford I was sure it would be different.

So to Oxford I duly went, changing stations at Sheffield and probably taking for a train-spotter that balding man at the end of the platform eating a pie. That I had still not acquired a past hit me the minute I entered the lodge of my college. It was piled high with trunks: trunks pasted with ancient labels, trunks that had holidayed in Grand Hotels, travelled first-class on liners, trunks painted with four, nay even *five*, initials (that's another sympathetic thing about Larkin, the bare essentials of his name). They were the trunks of fathers that were now the trunks of sons, trunks of generations. These trunks spoke memory. I had two shameful Antler suitcases that I had gone with my mother to buy at Schofields in Leeds – an agonizing process, since it had involved her explaining to the shop assistant, a class my mother always assumed were persons of some refinement, that the cases were for going to Oxford with on a scholarship and were these the kind of thing? They weren't. One foot across the threshold of the college lodge and I saw it, and hurried to hide them beneath my cold bed. By the end of the first term I hadn't acquired much education but I had got myself a decent second-hand trunk.

It didn't stop at the trunk either. Class, background, culture, accent – all that was going to have to be acquired second-hand too. Had I read 'I Remember, I Remember' in 1955, when *The Less Deceived* came out, I might have been spared the trouble. Though I doubt it. Poems tell you what you know already, and I still had it to learn. Besides I didn't read poetry. I thought I read Auden, but to tell the truth – except in the shortest poems – I never got beyond the first dozen or so lines without being completely lost. One of the good things about Larkin is that he still has you firmly by the hand as you cross the finishing-line, whereas reading Auden is like doing a parachute drop: for a while the view is wonderful, but then you end up on your back in the middle of a ploughed field and in the wrong county. I heard Auden give his inaugural lecture as Professor of Poetry at Oxford in 1956. That put the tin hat on any lingering thoughts of Literature (one of my problems was that I still thought of both Literature and Life as having capital letters). Here were 'blinding theologies of flowers and fruits', a monogrammed set of myths and memories carried over from a bulging childhood, and not in Antler suitcases either. Obsessions, landscapes, favourite books, even (one's heart sank) the Icelandic sagas. If writing meant passing this sort of kit inspection, I'd better forget it.

Dissolve to 1966. Life, love and literature were all long since in the lower case and I had drifted into show business. I was looking for ideas to beef up a comedy series. It was practically a clause in the BBC charter at that time that comedy sketches should be linked only with vocal numbers. I was after something that bit classier. My producer, Patrick Garland, suggested filming poems, gave me *The Less Deceived*, and I read 'I Remember, I Remember'. I think I had realized by then that to write one doesn't need credentials, but I must be the only one of his readers who came to Larkin as an alternative to Alma Cogan.

If presents are in order I would like him to have that sound, part sigh, part affirmation, that I heard once in Zion Chapel, Settle, in Yorkshire, after I'd read 'MCMXIV'. And another sound: reading Larkin in public, I've sometimes followed on with Stevie Smith's 'Not Waving But Drowning', which contains the lines 'Poor chap, he's always loved larking/And now he's dead'. Of course, being the sort of person he was the poor chap would have loved Larkin too, and half thinking it a pun – and not inappropriate at that – one or two people in the audience *mew* to themselves.

He would also appreciate something my mother said. My brother had gone to Athens. She was asked where he was but could not remember. 'It begins with an A,' she said. 'Oh, I know. Abroad.' I am abroad writing this in another place beginning with A, America. He would not thank me for New York, I imagine, but if he does not feel at home here he would not feel out of place among streets like Greene and Grand and Great Jones, the cast-iron district which I see from my window. I would give him, too, any work by Edward Hopper, whose paintings could often pass as illustrations to the poems of Larkin, and in particular 'People in the Sun' (1960).

Finally, something I saw scrawled up in the subway. On the wall someone has written 'Pray for me.' Another hand has added 'Sure.'

The Wrong Blond

On a bitter-cold morning in January 1939 Auden and Isherwood sailed into New York harbour on board the SS *Champlain*. After coming through a blizzard off Newfoundland the ship looked like a wedding cake, and the mood of our two heroes was correspondingly festive and expectant. On their first visit to New York the previous year Auden had sometimes been in tears, telling Isherwood no one would ever love him and that he would never have any sexual success. True to form, on this second visit it was Isherwood who already had a date lined up: Vernon, 'a beautiful blond boy, about eighteen, intelligent, with very sexy legs'. From that out-of-the-body vantage point he shares with God and Norman Mailer, Isherwood looks down on himself and his friend:

Yes, my dears, each of you will find the person you came here to look for – the ideal companion to whom you can reveal yourself totally and yet be loved for what you are, not what you pretend to be. You, Wystan, will find him very soon, within three months. You, Christopher, will have to wait much longer for yours . . . At present he is only four years old.

If looking for Mr Right was what it was about, this celebrated voyage that put paid to a decade, it was lucky that Auden's quest so soon found its object. Otherwise the start of the war might have fetched him home still on the same tack, 1 September 1939 finding him not in a dive on Fifty-Second Street but in some

Review of *Auden in Love* by Dorthy Farnan (Faber and Faber, 1985)

bleak provincial drill hall having those famous bunions vetted for service in the Intelligence Corps. Auden might (and some say should) have condemned himself to five years as a slipshod major, sitting in a dripping Nissen hut in Beaconsfield decoding German intelligence, with occasional trips to the fleshpots to indulge in those hectic intimacies hostilities notoriously encourage. In the short view, it would almost certainly have landed him with the MO. In the long view, it would almost certainly have landed him with the OM. It was not to be. True love had walked in on Auden six months earlier. Henceforth it was to be personal relations for ever and ever.

While Isherwood's man of destiny had not yet made it to playgroup, Chester Kallman had turned eighteen and was a junior at Brooklyn College. As Dorothy Farnan describes him, 'he was naturally blond, about five feet 11 in height, slender, weighing about 145 pounds with gray-blue eyes, pale flawless skin, a Norse skull, Latin lips and straight narrow nose' – a description that smacks both of the mortuary slab and (more appropriately) a 'Wanted' poster. In April 1939 Auden, Isherwood and MacNeice gave a reading at the Keynote Club in Manhattan. Kallman and another Brooklyn student, Walter James Miller, were in the audience, with Kallman sitting in the front row giving the two international pederasts the glad eye. Afterwards he and Miller went backstage. Miller was tall, blond, Anglo-Saxon and (a friend who was not a friend) heterosexual. Predictably it was to the unavailable Miller that Auden took a fancy, leaving the more realistic Isherwood to chat up the all-too-available Kallman. Miller had written an article for the college literary magazine, and Auden expressed a desire to read it. (Twenty years later, when he was Professor of Poetry at Oxford, Auden's desires were still being expressed in the same guileless way: undergraduate poets asked round to read him their verse, in the hope that one thing might lead to another.)

However, on the day appointed it was not Miller who turned up but Kallman. Isherwood was in the next room when Auden came through and said, 'It's the wrong blond.' The rest is history. Or literature. Or the history of literature. Or maybe just gossip. And on that score anathema to Auden himself, who, wanting no biography, would have been appalled to read this blow-by-blow account of his sex life.

Whether Kallman *was* the wrong blond is the whole question of it. The right blond, Miller, would also have been the wrong blond, so maybe the wrong blond was the right one, wrong blond(e)s after all having some tradition in literature: Lord Alfred Douglas, Zelda Fitzgerald, Marilyn Monroe, to name but three who were all wrong, all right. This account of the relationship between Auden and Kallman is written by the blond's late-in-the-day stepmother, Dorothy J. Farnan, also blonde, who, if not wrong, is not always right, but very readable for all that. (I don't want to beat this blond business to a bloody pulp, but in his biography of Auden Humphrey Carpenter gives Kallman's fancied companion as the poet Harold Norse. Norse thinks Auden was expecting him. The right blond, and ready to be just as obliging as Kallman, Norse was a better bet all round. This is one of those moments when three, possibly four, lives go rattling over the points. But Norse or Miller? Auden studies are still in their infancy, and it is perhaps too early to say. The fact that Ms Farnan describes Kallman's skull as 'Norse' is neither here nor there. Or is it?)

Auden now wore a wedding ring, bought one for Chester, and moved in on Chester's life. There was a honeymoon at Taos in New Mexico, weekly visits to the opera in rented tuxedos, and dinners in Auden's Brooklyn household, where, among others regularly passing the (obligatory) potatoes, were Benjamin Britten and Peter Pears, Carson McCullers, Lincoln Kirstein and Gipsy Rose Lee.

When love comes to the confirmed bachelor, old friends find it difficult to take. Chums winced to see T. S. Eliot spooning with wife number two, smirked when they brazenly held hands, and there was a bit of that with Auden. Look at it from the friends' point of view. They have to budge up to make room for the new companion, knowing as they do so that they will be seeing less of the great man. Pretty college boy introduced to glamorous world by famous writer in return for services rendered: is he, they telephone each other, on the make? A male lover is judged more harshly than a wife (wives are women, after all), the likelihood of children somehow a safeguard. If the lover comes on too strong in company he is thought to be pushy; if he keeps mum he is put down as just a pretty face. Oh well, the friends shrug, it won't last. Boredom will drive him back to us. But it did, and it didn't. Chester wasn't just a pretty face: he was an amusing companion and better company than Auden because less full of himself. ('Less of himself to be full of,' said the friends.) Still, Chester stayed the course, and thirty-odd years later walks behind the coffin in Kirchstetten as Siegfried's Funeral March gives way to the more comfortable strains of the village band, the medley of the two just about summing it up.

Back in 1939, Auden is typically bold – not to say boastful – about his affair. Even nowadays, with parents the stunned and submissive onlookers at their children's lives, a middle-aged man would think twice about meeting the family of the seventeen-year-old son he's knocking off. Auden had no such scruples, but then he liked families, particularly those belonging to other people. Casting no spell, they always exercised a powerful attraction. Auden was a practised (if not always accomplished) *ami de maison*, homing in on comfortable domestic set-ups and establishing himself as a frequent and not undemanding guest. Several families of academic sparrows were flattered, if slightly startled, to find themselves playing host to this celebrated cuckoo, who scattered his ash as liberally as he did his aperçus. If one wanted to entertain Auden, the first requirement was a good Ewbank.

In this matter of family Chester was well-supplied. He was the son of a Brooklyn dentist, Edward Kallman. His mother, Bertha, was a cultivated woman, who had acted in Yiddish theatre. She died when Chester was small, his father remarried, and the boy was largely brought up by his grandmother. His grandmother's name was Bobby. His stepmother's name was Syd. (In their choice of names the Americans have always been more eclectic than we are: a girl in *Dynasty*, for instance, is called Kirby, a name hitherto confined to a grip). These Kallman names can't have helped. With a grandmother called Bobby and a stepmother called Syd, it's not surprising Chester turned out to be a nancy.

Edward Kallman sounds an engaging character, even allowing for the fact that this book is written by his wife: Ms Farnan succeeded the terrible Syd as the third Mrs Kallman, though more or less a contemporary of her stepson. Syd had been the bane of Chester's life, and tales of her appalling behaviour never failed to fascinate him and (reportedly) Auden too. The tales of Kallman *père*, on the other hand, suggest a cross between Phil Silvers and S. Z. ('Cuddles') Szakall.

Before Auden came on the scene Chester had taken the fancy of a New York financier, Robert King ('not his real name'). King duly enrolled as a patient with Dr Kallman, and, after a little bridgework had broken the ice, invited the dentist to supper at the Astor Roof. There was presumably some routine orthodontic small talk ('How's the bite?') before King levelled with his guest. 'I want to adopt Chester,' said King. 'I can do a great deal for him. Send him to Harvard. Take him to Europe. I just want to be near him. Travel with him. Sleep next to him.' Apart from some poisoned remarks from hissing Syd ('That boy is a hothouse flower'), this urbane proposition was the first hint the dentist had that Chester was not all set to be a model of heterosexuality. Cut to the surgery, where the patient is now a psychiatrist. Dr Kallman puts the problem to him. ('So my son is a faggot. Where did I go wrong? Rinse please.') The psychiatrist recommends another psychiatrist, whom Chester dutifully sees but, finding he has never heard of T. S. Eliot, leaves in disgust. It is at this opportune moment that Auden, who *has* heard of T. S. Eliot, appears on the scene. No more is heard of Mr King.

Both generations were incorrigible lechers, the father as active on one side of the street as the son was on the other. Chester was not without girlfriends, though whether Anything Happened is not clear. At one point he had an apartment above his father's and his female callers sometimes knocked on the wrong door, whereupon Edward Kallman would waltz out on to the landing, clad only in a bath towel, saying 'Won't I do?' Ms Farnan calls him a pragmatist: 'He knew one must make the best of what cannot be changed.'

One comes to like Chester's father, whose adult education must have come from coping with the vagaries and enthusiasms of his wayward son and the increasingly unsympathetic behaviour of his ex-officio son-in-law. He and Auden seem to have quarrelled finally over a kitten which Auden was trying to entice into his house at Kirchstetten. Old Kallman, now deaf, banged a door during the wooing process and the not-so-cosy poet blew his top. The old man left the house the next day. 'Forever after he was quick to tell all who would listen that W. H. Auden had lost his temper because of a cat. What kind of cat? "One hundred per cent alley."' Presumably he is still telling whoever will listen, for, twenty years later and in his nineties, he seems to be still around.

It was two happy years after he had met Chester (and, back in the world of telegrams and anger, a month after the Germans invaded Russia) that Auden discovered he was not the only one laying his head human on Chester's faithless arm. The first (or at any rate the first known to biography) was Jack Lansing ('not his real name'), who, 'despite his Latin eyes', was 'as English as cricket. He could trace his ancestors back to the Saxons in the Domesday Book while his father claimed a distant kinship to William the Conqueror.' Ancestry soon got confused with dentistry, as Chester would meet Lansing on the quiet at his father's surgery ('Wider please'), and on one occasion their antics kept Edward waiting over an hour outside the locked door. When Auden found out about the affair his rage and jealousy were murderous. These were emotions he seems not to have experienced before, and the effect on him was profound. It's not just the confusion of heartache and toothache that makes Auden's grief less than tragic. It's hard to understand how Auden could have lived with Kallman for two years without cottoning on to the younger man's character, or how he had reached the age of thirty-four without finding himself in this situation before. Here was one of the most acknowledged of unacknowledged legislators who had laid down the law about love with seemingly no experience whatever of its pains and penalties. There is a powerful impulse to say, 'Well, serve you right.'

That the friendship survived is taken by Ms Farnan to be somewhat unusual, and a tribute to Auden's strength of character: a lesser man, she implies, would have packed his bags. But a period of exclusive physical attachment followed by a close friendship in which each party goes his own (sometimes promiscuous) way is not uncommon. Or wasn't – these days homosexuals are having to do what the people the other side of the fence call 'working at the marriage'. Auden had the sense to realize that sharing a joke is rarer than sharing a bed, which, according to Chester, they ceased to do. Whatever it was they did together (and Ms Farnan is not unspecific on the point), they didn't any more. This does seem unusual. Ms Farnan puts it down, if not to principle on Chester's part, at least to his romantic temperament. There seems to be a streak of wanton cruelty in it – or the cruelty of a wanton. Chester found nothing so easy as attracting company to his bed – a quality, once he had come to terms with it, in which Auden took pride. With the world's fighting men lining up eagerly for Chester's favours, did Auden *never* get a look in, even if not on quite the one-to-one basis with Chester that he wanted? Well, maybe. Ms Farnan chooses to see Auden's love-life from here on as tragic, the short-lived affair a lifelong heartache. It doesn't seem to have been too bad, particularly when one remembers that for some people sexual intercourse only began in 1963. He certainly didn't want for consolation. Unhappy but not unhappy about it just about sums it up.

The cast of the sex lives of Auden and Kallman is large. It is also coy. Since this is the love that dares not speak its name, the sex, when it is not anonymous, is pseudonymous, with over a score of the participants footnoted 'not his real name'. Nor are the names under which they do appear of a noble simplicity. Here is no Chuck, no Rick, no Lance. Ms Farnan has lavished much art on these fellatious appellations: they include Royce Wagoner, Dutch Martell, Peter Komadina, Mr Schuyler Bash and (a real ball of fire) Lieutenant Horace Stepole. Francis Peabody Magoun, on the other hand, *is* a real name, as is Giorgione, who is footnoted as 'famous Venetian painter' – presumably to distinguish him from all those other Italian boys who went down on posterity but not to it.

The reluctance of Auden's partners to be named is worth lingering over. The Baring family coined the phrase 'Shelley plain' to mean a personal glimpse of a great man – from

Browning's 'Ah, did you once see Shelley plain,/And did he stop and speak to you . . .?' In Philip Roth's superb novel *The Professor of Desire* the professor visits Prague and is taken to meet the aged whore once fucked by Kafka. She had had a 'Shelley plain', and would for a consideration reveal to visiting scholars its central location. To have gone down on W. H. Auden is a lesser 'Shelley plain', not so exclusive perhaps, but it's interesting that so many of those who had the experience are still reluctant to acknowledge it. It's a narrow niche, one must admit, but still fame of a sort.

In the early days Auden was proud of Chester, and this is still touchingly obvious in the photograph of them taken in Venice in 1950. To begin with Auden had shown the boy off to his friends but had shut him up when he tried to join in the grown-ups' conversation. But, as Auden came to acknowledge, Chester was funny and clever in a way Auden was not. A visiting New York publisher was telling them that he was bringing out an autobiography of Klaus Mann, and thinking of calling it *The Invisible Mann*. No, said Chester (and it's a joke such as Nabokov would have made), you should call it *The Subordinate Klaus*. Nobody believed Auden when he said Chester had the quicker mind, but he would not have come to opera without Kallman, or written libretti – a debt Auden always acknowledged, and where the ascription of credit was concerned he was scrupulous. At the second performance of *The Rake's Progress* at La Fenice he left early because Chester was not there to take the curtain-call with him. In other reviews of this book that I have read Kallman has got some stick because he couldn't hold down a job or wasn't a better poet, never made a success of his life. Wives – which is to say female wives – don't get told off in quite this way, aren't weighed in the same scale. The first Mrs Eliot has been taken to task, but not because her verse wasn't better or because she didn't make her own way in the world. She was a woman, so that was only to be expected. Even a literary wife as talented as her husband, like the second Mrs Lowell, Elizabeth Hardwick, finds her work calibrated on the scale of accomplishment not achievement, and the sincerest recognition still hints at the escape from the washing-up or stolen hours while children sleep. Whether you call this condescension or consideration, men who marry men don't get it: they're expected to be career girls besides.

To his credit, Auden never tried to make Chester his housekeeper. Chester answered the telephone and, when he was around, produced meals with digital accuracy, but the households on Ischia and at Kirchstetten were a far cry from I Tatti. Chester never played the role of the great man's wife or the guardian of his talent, rationing visits, anticipating needs, turning away friends, still less hiding the bottle. He was too interested in himself for that. Wives of the proper gender play this role without comment, or without comment in biography: 'To my wife, without whom etc.' is reckoned to make up for everything. Chester was more fun to have around than Auden – less likely to go into a huff for a start – and if he was always hell-bent on bed, at least it didn't have to be on the stroke of nine o'clock like his lover. With Auden in bed and Chester still in shrieks with his chums next door, there must often have been something of 'We're having a whale of a time below stairs' to the ménage. Auden made touching attempts to be more light-hearted, swapping genders ('Who shook *her* cage?') and trying to come on as a bit of a queen himself. But it didn't really work, and he always seemed to get it slightly wrong: his famous 'Miss God', for instance, doesn't exactly pinpoint the deity. Camp is no substitute for wit, and Auden wasn't especially good at either.

Luckily for the peace of their various households, they were both sluts. If Auden had been as big as stickler for tidiness as he was for punctuality he would never have had his pinny off.

Chester was an inspired cook, though wasted on Auden, who preferred good nursery food and lashings of it. A toilet innocent of Harpic, a sideboard barren of Pledge, the New York set-up on St Mark's Place was not an apartment for the fastidious. Those who are not as other men often like a place just so, and the wonder is that none of the visiting bits of fluff didn't nip round and do a spot of post-coital dusting. One who did lend a hand, though very much not a bit of fluff, was Vera Stravinsky. Chester's working surfaces included the bathroom floor, and, paying a call of nature, Mrs Stravinsky spotted what she took to be a bowl of dirty water standing there. In a forlorn attempt to give the place a woman's touch, Mrs Stravinsky emptied the contents into the washbasin, only to discover later on that this had been the *pièce de résistance* of the meal, a chocolate pudding. The basin was incidentally the same basin in which Auden routinely pissed. Where, one wonders, did one wash one's hands after one washed one's hands?

Auden was wise to want no biography written. The more one reads about him, the harder it is to see round him to the poetry beyond, and he grows increasingly hard to like – just as it grows hard for one's thinks to be all thanks. In the tribute that came out the year after his death, edited by Stephen Spender, much was made of how cosy he was. He grows less cosy by the memoir, even if one like Ms Farnan's is less than fair. Particularly hard to take is the 'All do as I do' side of him that early on bullied off Britten. It's a masculine characteristic, and it stands out so painfully because he happily lacked other masculine characteristics that often cluster round it. He didn't care much for fame, for instance, or go in for self-advertisement, was careless about his reputation, and was unmoved by criticism. So much about him is mature and admirable, he seems a bigger baby for what is not. It was Kallman who found Auden dead in 1973, lying in his hotel bed in Vienna after a poetry recital the night before.

Kallman knew Auden was dead because he was lying on his left side, and he never lay on that side. It is just this side of him that's hard to take, the rules he made for himself but which others were expected to know and observe. If he hadn't in his later work made such a point of domestic virtue and the practice of loving kindness it might not matter so much. 'You're not the only pebble on the beach,' one wants to say. 'Grow up.' Grow up, or don't grow old.

There will be other memoirs. There are currently at least three published in America that haven't yet appeared here. In one of them, *Auden: An American Friendship*, by Charles Miller, the peculiar gouging of his face is put down to 'a medical condition known as the Touraine-Solente-Golé syndrome, which also affected Racine'.* The skin seemed to divide up into clints, like the limestone Auden praised – the best remark about that coming, I think, from David Hockney. Auden sat to Hockney, who, after tracing those innumerable lines, remarked, 'I kept thinking, if his face looks like this, what must his balls look like?' At this rate it can only be a matter of time before we are told that too.

---

* It was a condition Auden could be thought to have called down by some lines in his 'Letter to Lord Byron':

> 'However proud,
> And mighty, of his trade, he [the artist]'s not allowed
> To etch his face with his professional creases,
> Or die from occupational diseases.'

Kafka at Las Vegas

I have written two plays around if not altogether about Kafka, and in the process have accumulated a good deal of material about and around the Prague insurance man. Some of this is fanciful – sketches and speculations that never had a hope of being included in either piece. Some of it is the kind of stuff that's always left over after writing a play – the speeches one has not managed to get in, or the jokes that have had to be cut out and which are invariably the jokes and the speeches of which the playwright is most fond. Indeed he often thinks them the heart of the play, whereas the director (who never had to sweat over them) can see they're diversions, distractions or ornament: not wanted on voyage. There is a word for this kind of thing which I have just come across (and, having come across it, can't think how I've managed so long without it); it is *paralipomena* – the things omitted but which appertain and are put in later as afterthoughts. It describes half my life as well as the notes that follow.

There are many perils in writing about Kafka. His work has been garrisoned by armies of critics, with some fifteen thousand books about him at the last count. As there is a Fortress Freud so is there a Fortress Kafka, Kafka his own castle. For admission a certain high seriousness must be deemed essential, and I am not sure I have it. One is nervous about presuming even to write his name, wanting to beg pardon for doing so, if only because Kafka was so reluctant to write his name himself. Like the Hebrew name of God, it is a name that should not be spoken, particularly by an Englishman. In his dreams Kafka once met an English-man. He was in a good grey-flannel suit, the flannel also covering his face. Short of indicating a prudent change of tailor, the incident (if dreams have incidents) serves to point up the temptation to English Kafka and joke him down to size. The Channel is a slipper bath of irony through which we pass these serious Continentals in order not to be infected by their gloom. This propensity I am sure I have not escaped, or tried to; but then there is something that *is* English about Kafka, and it is not only this self-deprecation. A vegetarian and fond of the sun, he seems a familiar crank; if he'd been living in England at the turn of the century and not in Prague one can imagine him going out hiking and spending evenings with like-minded friends in Letchworth. He is the young man in a Shaw play who strolls past the garden fence in too large shorts to be accosted by some brisk Shavian young woman who, perceiving his charm, takes him in hand, puts paid to his morbid thoughts, and makes him pull his socks up.

Charm he certainly had, but not at home. Chewing every mouthful umpteen times so that at meals his father cowered behind the newspaper, Kafka saved his charm for work and for his friends. Home is not the place for charm anyway. We do not look for it around the fireside, so it's not so surprising Kafka had no charm for his father. His father, it seems, had none for anybody. There is something called Home Charm though. In the forties it was a kind of distemper, and nowadays it's a chain of DIY shops. In that department certainly Kafka did not excel. He was not someone you would ask to help put up a shelf, for instance, though one component of his charm was an exaggerated appreciation of people who could, and of commonplace accomplishments generally. Far from being clumsy himself (he had something of the dancer about him), he would marvel (or profess to marvel) at the ease with which other people managed to negotiate the world. This kind of professed incompetence ('Silly me!') often leads to offers of help, and carried to extremes it encourages the formation of unofficial protection societies. Thus Kafka was much cosseted by the ladies in his office, and in the same way the pupils of another candidate for secular sainthood, the French philosopher Simone Weil, saw to it that their adored teacher did not suffer the consequences of a practical unwisdom even more hopeless than Kafka's.

One cannot say that Kafka's marvelling at mundane accomplishments was not genuine, was a ploy. The snag is that when the person doing the marvelling goes on to do great things this can leave those with the commonplace accomplishments feeling a little flat. Say such a person goes on to win the Nobel Prize: it is scant consolation to know that one can change a three-pin plug.

Gorky said that in Chekhov's presence everyone felt a desire to be simpler, more truthful and more oneself. Kafka too had this effect. 'On his entrance into a room', wrote a contemporary, 'it seemed as though some unseen attendant had whispered to the lecturer, "Be careful about everything you say from now on. Franz Kafka has just arrived."' To have this effect on people is a not unmixed blessing. When we are on our best behaviour we are not always at our best.

This is not to say that Kafka did not make jokes in life and in art. *The Trial*, for instance, is a funnier book than it has got credit for, and Kafka's jokes about himself are better for the desperate circumstances in which they were often made. He never did win the Nobel Prize, of course, but he contemplated the possibility once in fun and in pain, and in a fairly restricted category (though one he could have shared with several contemporaries – Proust, Katherine Mansfield and D. H. Lawrence among them). When he was dying of TB of the larynx he was fetching up a good deal of phlegm. 'I think,' he said (and the joke is more poignant for being so physically painful to make), 'I think I deserve the Nobel Prize for sputum.' Nothing if not sick, it is a joke that could have been made yesterday.

Dead sixty-odd years, Kafka is still modern and there is much in the present-day world to interest him. These days Kafka would be intrigued by the battery farm and specifically, with an interest both morbid and lively, by the device that de-beaks the still-living chickens; by waste-disposal trucks that chew the rubbish before swallowing it; and by those dubious restaurants that install for your dining pleasure a tank of doomed trout. As the *maître d'* assists the discerning diner in the ceremony of choice, be aware of the waiter who wields the net: both mourner and executioner, he is Kafka. He notes old people in Zimmer frames stood in their portable dock on perambulatory trial for their lives. He is interested in the feelings of the squash ball, and of the champagne bottle that launches the ship. In a football match his sympathy is not with either of the teams but with the ball, or, in a match ending nil-nil, with the hunger of the goalmouth. He would be unable to endorse the words of the song by Simon and Garfunkel, 'I'd rather be a hammer than a nail', feeling himself (as he confessed to one of his girlfriends) simultaneously both. And in a different context he would be concerned with the current debate on the disposal of nuclear waste. To be placed in a lead canister which is then encased in concrete and sunk fathoms deep to the floor of the ocean was the degree of circulation he thought appropriate for most of his writing. Or not, of course.

Kafka was fond of the cinema, and there are short stories, like *Tales of a Red Indian*, that have a feeling of the early movies. He died before the talkies came in and so before the Marx Brothers, but there is an exchange in *Horse Feathers* that sums up Kafka's relations with his father:

BEPPO: Dad, I'm proud to be your son.

GROUCHO: Son, you took the words out of my mouth. I'm ashamed to be your father.

The Kafka household could have been the setting for many Jewish jokes:

FATHER: Son, you hate me.

SON: Father, I love you.

MOTHER: Don't contradict your father.

Had Kafka the father emigrated to America, as so many of his contemporaries did, things might have turned out differently for Kafka the son. He was always stage-struck. Happily lugubrious, he might have turned out a stand-up Jewish comic. Kafka at Las Vegas.

Why didn't Kafka stutter? The bullying father, the nervous son – life in the Kafka household seems a blueprint for a speech impediment. In a sense, of course, he did stutter. Jerky, extruded with great force, and the product of tremendous effort, everything Kafka wrote is a kind of stutter. Stutterers devise elaborate routines to avoid or to ambush and take by surprise troublesome consonants, of which K is one of the most difficult. It's a good job Kafka didn't stutter. With two Ks he might have got started on his name and never seen the end of it. As it is he docks it, curtails it, leaves its end behind much as lizards do when something gets hold of their tail.

In thus de-nominating himself Kafka was to make his name and his letter memorable. Diminishing it he augmented it, and not merely for posterity. K was a significant letter in his own time. There were Ks on every banner, palace and official form. Kafka had two Ks, and so, in the *Kaiserlich* and *Königlich* of the Habsburg Emperors, did the Austro-Hungarian Empire. The Emperor at the time was Franz Joseph, and that comes into it too, for here is Franz K. writing about Joseph K. in the time of Franz Joseph K.

There was another emperor nearer at hand, the emperor in the armchair, Kafka's phrase for his father. Hermann Kafka has had such a consistently bad press that it's hard not to feel a sneaking sympathy for him, as for all the Parents of Art. They never get it right. They bring up a child badly and he turns out a writer, posterity never forgives them – though without that unfortunate upbringing the writer might never have written a word. They bring up a child well and he never *does* write a word. Do it right and posterity never hears about the parents; do it wrong and posterity never hears about anything else.

'They fuck you up, your mum and dad', and if you're planning on writing that's probably a good thing. But if you are planning on writing and they haven't fucked you up, well, you've got nothing to go on, so then they've fucked you up good and proper.

Many parents, one imagines, would echo the words of Madame Weil, the mother of Simone Weil, a child every bit as trying as Kafka must have been. Questioned about her pride in the posthumous fame of her ascetic daughter, Madame Weil said, 'Oh! How much I would have preferred her to have been happy.' Like Kafka, Simone Weil is often nominated for secular sainthood. I'm not sure. Talk of a saint in the family and there's generally one around, if not quite where one's looking. One thinks of Mrs Muggeridge, and in the Weil family it is not Simone so much as her mother who consistently behaves well and elicits sympathy. In the Kafka household the halo goes to Kafka's sister Ottla, who has to mediate between father and son, a role in weaker planetary systems than that revolving round Hermann Kafka which is more often played by the mother.

Kafka may have been frightened that he was more like his father than he cared to admit. In a letter to Felice Bauer, Kafka indulged in the fantasy of being a large piece of wood, pressed against the body of a cook 'who is holding the knife along the side of this stiff log (somewhere in the region of my hip) slicing off shavings to light the fire'. Many conclusions could be drawn from this image, some glibber than others. One of them is that Kafka would have liked to have been a chip off the old block.

Daily at his office in the Workers Accident Insurance Institute Kafka was confronted by those unfortunates who had been maimed and injured at work. Kafka was crippled not at work but at home. It's hardly surprising. If a family is a factory for turning out children then it is lacking in the most elementary safety precautions. There are no guard rails round that dangerous engine the father. There are no safeguards against being scalded by the burning affection of the mother. No mask is proof against the suffocating atmosphere. One should not be surprised that so many lose their balance and are mangled in the machinery of love. Take the Wittgensteins. With three of their five children committing suicide, they make the Kafkas seem like a model family. One in Prague, the other in Vienna, Kafka and Wittgenstein often get mentioned in the same breath. Socially they were poles apart, but both figure in and are ingredients of the intellectual ferment of the last years of the Austro-Hungarian Empire. Not at all similar in character, Kafka and

Wittgenstein sometimes sound alike, as in Wittgenstein's Preface to his *Philosophical Investigations*:

I make [these remarks] public with doubtful feelings. It is not impossible that it should fall to the lot of this work, in its poverty and in the darkness of this time, to bring light into one brain or another – but, of course, it is not likely. I should not like my writing to spare other people the trouble of thinking. But, if possible, to stimulate someone to thoughts of his own, I should have liked to produce a good book. This has not come about, but the time is past in which I could improve it.

Though Nabokov was sure he had travelled regularly on the same train as Kafka when they were both in Berlin in 1922, Kafka and Wittgenstein could meet, I suppose, only in the pages of a novel like *Ragtime* or in one of those imaginary encounters (Freud and Kafka is an obvious one) that used to be devised by Maurice Cranston in the days of the BBC Third Programme. But if Wittgenstein had never heard of Kafka, Kafka would certainly have heard of Wittgenstein. It was a noted name in Bohemia, where the family owned many steelworks. A steelworks is a dangerous place, and the Wittgenstein companies must have contributed their quota to those unfortunates crowding up the steps of the Workers Accident Insurance Institute in Poříč Street. So when Kafka did come across the name Wittgenstein it just meant more paperwork.

It must have been a strange place, the Workers Accident Insurance Institute, a kingdom of the absurd where it did not pay to be well and loss determined gain; limbs became commodities, and to be given a clean bill of health was to be sent away empty-handed. There every man carried a price on his head, or on his arm or his leg, like the tariffs of ancient law. It was a world where to be deprived was to be endowed, to be disfigured was to be marked out for reward, and to trip was to jump every hurdle. In

Kafka's place of work only the whole man had something to hide, the real handicap to have no handicap at all, whereas a genuine limp genuinely acquired cleared every obstacle and a helping hand was one that had first been severed from the body. The world as hospital: it is Nietzsche's nightmare.

Kafka's career in insurance coincided with the period when compensation for injury at work was beginning to be accepted as a necessary condition of employment. Workers' compensation was and is a pretty unmixed blessing, but it did spawn a new disease – or at any rate a new neurosis. Did one want a neurosis, the turn of the century in Austro-Hungary was the time and place to have it, except that this condition was a product of the factory, not the drawing-room, not so richly upholstered or so literate or capable of literature as those articulate fantasies teased out at 19 Berggasse. Compensation neurosis is a condition that affected and affects those (they tend to be women more than men) who have suffered a slight accident at work, and in particular an accident to the head: a slight bump, say, a mild concussion, nothing significant. Before the introduction of compensation such a minor mishap was likely to be ignored or forgotten. With no chance of compensation there was no incidence of neurosis; grin and bear it the order of the day. But once there is the possibility of compensation (and if the – scarcely – injured party does not know this there will be well-wishers who will tell him or her) then the idea is planted that he or she might be owed something. One does not need to be a conscious malingerer to feel that some recompense is perhaps called for, and from this feeling is bred dissatisfaction, head-aches, wakefulness, the whole cabinet of neurotic symptoms.

With Lily in *The Insurance Man* I have assumed that such a case did occasionally get as far as the Workers Accident Insurance Institute. If so then here was one more hopeless quest going on round the corridors of that unhappy building. This kind of quest, where what is wanted is the name of the illness as well as compensation for it, has something in common with Joseph K.'s quest in *The Trial*. He wants his offence identified, but no one will give it a name; this is his complaint. Until his offence is named, he cannot find a tribunal to acquit him of it.

Kafka and Proust both begin on the frontiers of dreams. It is in the gap between sleeping and waking where Marcel is trying to place his surroundings that Gregor Samsa finds himself transformed into a beetle and Joseph K. finds himself under arrest. *Metamorphis* and *The Trial* are the two works of Kafka that are best known, are, if you like, classics. Classics – and in particular modern classics – are the books one thinks one ought to read, thinks one has read. In this category particularly for readers who were young in the fifties come Proust, Sartre, Orwell, Camus and Kafka. It isn't simply a matter of pretension. As a young man I genuinely felt I ought to read Proust and Eliot (though it did no harm to be seen reading them). However, a few pages convinced me that I had got the gist, and so they went on to the still uncluttered bookshelf beside Kafka, Camus, Orwell and the rest.

The theory (or one of them) these days is that the reader brings as much to the book as the author. So how much more do readers bring who have never managed to get through the book at all? It follows that the books one remembers best are the books one has never read. To be remembered but not read has been the fate of *The Trial*, despite it being the most readable of Kafka's books. Kafka on the whole is not very readable. But then to be readable does not help a classic. Great books are taken as read, or taken as having been read. If they are read, or read too often and too easily by too many, the likelihood is they are not great books, or won't remain so for long. Read too much they crumble away as, nowadays, popular mountains are prone to do.

The readers or non-readers of *The Trial* remember it wrong. Its reputation is as a tale about man and bureaucracy, a fable appropriate to the office block. One recalls the office in Orson Welles's film – a vast hangar in which hundreds of clerks toil at identical desks to an identical routine. In fact *The Trial* is set in small rooms in dark houses in surroundings that are picturesque, romantic and downright quaint. For the setting of *The Trial* there is no blaming the planners. It is all on an impeccably human scale.

The topography that oppressed Kafka does not oppress us. Kafka's fearful universe is constructed out of burrows and garrets and cubby-holes on back staircases. It is nearer to Dickens and *Alice* and even to the cosiness of *The Wind in the Willows* than it is to our own particular emptinesses. Our shorthand for desolation is quite different: the assembly line, the fence festooned with polythene rags, the dead land between the legs of the motorway. But it is ours. It isn't Kafka's. Or, to put it another way, the trouble with Kafka is that he didn't know the word Kafkaesque. However, those who see *The Trial* as a trailer for totalitarian bureaucracy might be confirmed in this view on finding that the premises in Dzherzhinsky Square in Moscow now occupied by the Lubyanka Prison formerly housed another institution, the Rossiya Insurance Company.

Joseph K.'s first examination takes place one Sunday morning in Juliusstrasse, a shabby street of poor tenements. The address he had been given was of a gaunt apartment building with a vast entrance that led directly into a courtyard formed by many storeys of tenement flats.

Futile to go looking for that courtyard in Prague today. It

exists, after all, only in the mind of a dead author whom you may not even have read. But say you did go looking for it, as a Proust reader might go looking for Combray, or Brontë fans for Wuthering Heights, and say even that you found the address: it still would not be as Kafka or as Joseph K. describes it. These days the stone would have been scrubbed, the brick pointed, the mouldings given back their old (which is to say their new) sharpness in what the hoarding on the site advertises as a government-assisted programme of restoration and refurbishment. Go where you like in the old quarters of Europe it is the same. Decay has been arrested, the cracks filled; in Padua, Perpignan and Prague urban dentistry has triumphed.

The setting for Joseph K.'s first examination is a small room with a low ceiling, a kind of upstairs basement, a rooftop cellar. It is a location he finds with difficulty, since it can be reached only through the kitchen of one of the apartments. It is this block of apartments, let us imagine, that has now been restored, the architect of which – grey hair, young face, bright tie and liberal up to a point (architects, like dentists, being the same the world over) – here shows off his latest piece of conservation:

What we had here originally was a pretty run-down apartment building. The tenants, many of whom had lived here literally for generations, were mainly in the lower-income bracket – joiners, cleaners, factory workers and so on, plus some single ladies who were probably no better than they should be. I believe the whole district was rather famous for that, actually. My problem was how to do justice to the building and improve the accommodation while (single ladies apart) hanging on to some sort of social mix.

Stage 1 involved getting possession of the building itself, which, since it's situated in the heart of the conservation area, we were able to do by means of a government grant. Stage 2 was to empty the apartments. Happily many of the tenants were elderly, so we could leave this largely to a process of natural wastage. When the overall population of the building had come down to a manageable number, Stage 3 involved locating this remnant in local-authority housing on the outskirts. Which brings us to Stage 4, the restoration and refurbishment of the building itself.

Initially what we did was to divide it up into a number of two- and three-bedroom units, targeted, I suppose, at lawyers, architects, communications people – the kind of tenant who still finds the demands of urban living quite stimulating. We've got one or two studios on the top floor for artists of one kind and another – photographers and so on – and a similar number of old people on the ground floor. Actually we were obliged to include those under the terms of the government grant, but, though they do take up some very desirable space, I actually welcome them. A building of this kind is after all a community: old, young – variety is of the essence.

The particular unit associated with the gentleman in the novel is on the fifth floor. Trudge, trudge, trudge. I'm afraid the lifts are still unconnected. Bureaucracy, the workings of.

And so they go upstairs to the fifth floor as Joseph K. went up that Sunday morning in the novel, looking for the room where his examination was set to take place.

'Actually I remember this particular apartment,' says the architect, 'because it was a bit of an odd one out. Whereas most of the other flats amalgamated quite nicely into two- and three-bedroomed units, this particular one wouldn't fit into any of our categories. Here we are. You come into a small room, you see, which has obviously served as a kitchen . . .'

'Yes,' says the visitor. 'That's described in the book.'

'Never read it, alas,' says the architect. 'Work, pressure of. Come in, have supper, slump in front of the old telly-box, and that's it for the night. However, this kitchen rather unexpectedly opens into this much larger room. Two windows, rather nicely proportioned, and I think once upon a time there must have been a platform at the far end.'

'Yes,' says the visitor. 'That's in the book too.'

'And does he mention this?' asks the architect. 'This rather attractive feature, the gallery running round under the ceiling?'

'Yes,' says the visitor. 'People sat up there during his examination. They were rather cramped. In fact they were so cramped they had to bend double with cushions between their backs and the ceiling.'

'Is that in the book?' asks the architect.

'Yes. It's all in the book,' says the visitor.

'Really,' says the architect. 'It sounds jollier than I thought. I thought it was some frightful political thing. Anyway, we had a site conference, and all of us – architects, rental agents and prospective tenants – agreed it would be a great pity to lose the gallery. Someone suggested converting the place into a studio, with the gallery as a kind of sleeping-area, but that smacked a little bit of alternative lifestyles, which we were quite anxious to avoid, so in the end we've given it a lick of paint and just left it, the upshot being that the management are probably going to donate the room to the tenants. If it has some connection with this fellow in the novel perhaps we could call it after him.'

'The Joseph K. Room,' says the visitor. 'But what would you use it for?'

'Well, what will we use it for?' says the architect. 'I don't want to use the dread words "community centre", with all the overtones of bingo and the Saturday-night hop. But it could be used for all sorts. As soon as you say the word "crèche", for instance, you've got the ladies on your side. Encounter groups and suchlike; keep-fit classes. And then, of course, we have the Residents' Association. What we are hoping, you see, is that the residents will *join in*. After all, this is a co-operative. Everybody needs to pull their weight, and to that end all the tenants have been carefully – I was going to say screened, but let's say we've made a few preliminary inquiries in terms of background,

outlook and so on. Nothing so vulgar as vetting, you understand, but if we are all going to be neighbours it makes for less
trouble in the long run.

'And supposing anybody does step out of line – stereo going
full blast in the wee small hours, ladies coming up and down a
little too often (or indeed gentlemen in this day and age), kiddies
making a mess on the stairs – then in that event I think this room
would be the ideal place for the culprit to be interviewed by the
Residents' Association, asked to be a little more considerate and
even see the error of their ways. After all, I think a line has to be
drawn somewhere. And the Joseph K. Memorial Room would
be just the place to do it.'

In our cosy little island, novel readers must seldom be accused
of crimes they did not commit, or crimes of any sort for that
matter: PROUST READER ON BURGLARY RAP is not a headline
that carries conviction. Few of us are likely to be arrested
without charge or expect to wake up and find the police in the
room, and our experience of bureaucracy comes not from the
Gestapo so much as from the Gas Board. So *The Trial* does not
at first sight seem like a book to be read with dawning
recognition, the kind of book one looks up from and says, 'But
it's my story!'

Nor is it a book for the sick room, and seldom to be found on
those trolleys of literary jumble trundled round the wards of
local hospitals every Wednesday afternoon by Miss Venables,
the voluntary worker. The book trolley and the food trolley are
not dissimilar, hospital reading and hospital food both lacking
taste and substance and neither having much in the way of
roughage. The guardian and conductress of the book trolley,
Miss Venables, seldom reads herself and would have been
happier taking round the tea, for which the patients are more
grateful and less choosy than they are over the books. But in the

absence of a Mr Venables, and because she has no figure to speak of, Miss Venables is generally taken to be rather refined and thus has got landed with literature. The real life sentences come from judgements on our personal appearance, and good behaviour, far from remitting the sentence, simply confirms it and makes it lifelong. Kafka was always delicate, and his father therefore assumed he was a bookworm – an assumption his son felt was unwarranted and which he vigorously denied.

Miss Venables is not a bookworm either, seldom venturing inside the books she purveys, which she judges solely by their titles. Most patients, she thinks, want to be taken out of themselves, particularly so in Surgical. In Surgical, novels are a form of homeopathy: having had something taken out of themselves, the patients now want something else to take them out of themselves. So coming out of Surgical Miss Venables finds her stock of novels running pretty low as she pauses now at the bedside of a patient who been admitted, as he has been told, 'just for observation'. Presumptuous to call him Mr Kay, let us call him Mr Jay.

'Fiction or non-fiction?' asks Miss Venables.

'Fiction,' says Mr Jay, and hopes he is going to do better than last week. Last week he had wanted a copy of *Jake's Thing*, but could not remember the title and had finished up with *Howards End*.

'Fiction,' says Miss Venables (who would have come in handy in the Trinitarian controversy), 'Fiction is divided into Fiction, Mystery and Romance. Which would you like?'

Truthfully Mr Jay wants a tale of sun and lust, but, daunted by Miss Venables's unprepossessing appearance, he lamely opts for Mystery. She gives him a copy of *The Trial*.

How *The Trial* comes to be classified under Mystery is less of a mystery than how it comes to be on the trolley at all. In fact it had originally formed part of the contents of the locker of a deceased lecturer in modern languages and had been donated to the hospital library by his grateful widow, along with his copy of Thomas Mann's *Magic Mountain*. This Miss Venables has classified under Children and Fairy Stories. So, leaving Mr Jay leafing listlessly through Kafka, she passes on with her trolley to other wards and other disappointments.

It does not take Mr Jay long to realize that he has picked another dud, and one even harder to read than *Howards End*. What is to be made of such sentences as 'The verdict doesn't come all at once; the proceedings gradually merge into the verdict'? Mr Jay has a headache. He puts *The Trial* on his locker beside the bottle of Lucozade and the Get Well cards and tries to sleep, but can't. Instead he settles back and thinks about his body. These days he thinks about little else. The surgeon, Mr McIver, has told him he is a mystery. Matron says he has baffled the doctors. So Mr Jay feels like somebody special. Now they come for him, and he is carefully manoeuvred under vast machines by aproned figures, who then discreetly retire. Later, returned to his bed, he tries again to read but feels so sick he cannot read his book even if he really wanted to. And that is a pity. Because Mr Jay might now begin to perceive that *The Trial* is not a mystery story and that it is not particularly about the law or bureaucracy or any of the things the editor's note says it is about. It is about something nearer home, and had he come once again upon the sentence 'The verdict doesn't come all at once; the proceedings gradually merge into the verdict' Mr Jay might have realized that Kafka is talking to him. It *is* his story.

In the short story *Metamorphosis*, Gregor Samsa wakes up as a beetle. Nabokov, who knew about beetles, poured scorn on those who translated or depicted the insectified hero as a cockroach. Kafka did not want the beetle depicted at all, but for the error of classification he is largely to blame. It was Kafka who first brought up the subject of cockroaches, though in a different story, *Wedding Preparations in the Country*. 'I have, as I lie in bed,' he writes, 'the form of a large beetle, a stag beetle or a cockchafer, I believe.' Cockroach or not, Gregor Samsa has become so famous waking up as a beetle I am surprised he has not been taken up and metamorphosed again, this time by the advertising industry. Since he wakes up as a beetle, why should he not wake up as a Volkswagen? Only this time he's not miserable but happy. And so of course is his family. Why not? They've got themselves a nice little car. The only problem is how to get it out of the bedroom.

The first biography of Kafka was written by his friend and editor Max Brod. It was Brod who rescued Kafka's works from oblivion, preserved them, and, despite Kafka's instructions to the contrary, published them after his death. Brod, who was a year younger than Kafka (though one somehow thinks of him as older), lived on until 1968. The author of innumerable essays and articles, he published some eighty-three books, one for every year of his life. Described in the *Times* obituary as 'himself an author of uncommonly versatile stamp', he turned out novels at regular intervals until the end of his life, the last one being set during the Arab–Israeli war. These novels fared poorly with the critics, and were one able to collect the reviews of his books one would find few, I imagine, that do not somewhere invoke the name of Kafka, with the comparison inevitably to Brod's disadvantage. This cannot have been easy to take. He who had not only erected Kafka's monument but created his reputation never managed to struggle out of its shadow. He could be forgiven if he came to be as dubious of Kafka's name as Kafka was himself.

Never quite Kafka's wife, after Kafka's death Brod's role was that of the devoted widow, standing guard over the reputation,

authorizing the editions, editing the diaries, and driving tres-
passers from the grave. However, living in Tel Aviv, he was
spared the fate of equivalent figures in English culture, an
endless round of arts programmes where those who have known
the famous are publicly debriefed of their memories, knowing as
their own dusk falls that they will be remembered only for
remembering someone else.

Kafka was a minor executive in an insurance company in
Prague. In *Kafka's Dick* this fact is picked up by another minor
executive in another insurance firm, but in Leeds seventy-odd
years later. Sydney, as the insurance man, decides to do a piece
on Kafka for an insurance periodical. (I imagine there are such,
though I've never verified the fact.) As he works on his piece,
Sydney comes to resent his subject, as biographers must often
do. Biographers are only fans, after all, and fans have been
known to shoot their idols.

'Why biography?' asks his wife.

Sydney's answer is less of a speech than an aria, which is
probably why it was cut from the play:

I want to hear about the shortcomings of great men, their fears and
their failings. I've had enough of their vision, how they altered the
landscape (we stand on their shoulders to survey our lives). So. Let's
talk about the vanity. Read how this one, the century's seer, increases
his stature by lifts in his shoes. That one, the connoisseur of emptiness,
is tipped for the Nobel Prize yet still needs to win at Monopoly. This
playwright's skin is so thin he can feel pain on the other side of the
world. So why is he deaf to the suffering next door; signs letters to the
newspapers but holds his own wife a prisoner of conscience? The
slipshod poet keeps immaculate time and expects it of everyone else,
but never wears underwear and frequently smells. That's not
important, of course, but what is? The gentle novelist's frightful
temper, the Christian poet's mad, unvisited wife, the hush in their

households where the dog goes on tiptoe, meals on the dot at their ironclad whim? Note with these great men the flight and not infrequent suicide of their children, their brisk remarriage on the deaths of irreplaceable wives. Proud of his modesty one gives frequent, rare interviews in which he aggregates praise and denudes others of credit. Indifferent to the lives about him, he considers his day ruined on finding a slighting reference to himself in a periodical published three years ago in New Zealand. And demands sympathy from his family on that account. And gets it. Our father the novelist; my husband the poet. He belongs to the ages – just don't catch him at breakfast. Artists, celebrated for their humanity, they turn out to be scarcely human at all.

Death took no chances with Kafka and laid three traps for his life. Parched and voiceless from TB of the larynx, he was forty, the victim, as he himself said, of a conspiracy by his own body. But had his lungs not ganged up on on him there was a second trap, twenty years down the line, when the agents of death would have shunted him, as they did his three sisters, into the gas chambers. That fate, though it was not to be his, is evident in his last photograph. It is a face that prefigures the concentration camp.

But say that in 1924 he cheats death and a spell in the sanatorium restores him to health. In 1938 he sees what is coming – Kafka, after all, was more canny than he is given credit for, not least by Kafka himself – and so he slips away from Prague in time. J. P. Stern imagines him fighting with the partisans; Philip Roth finds him a poor teacher of Hebrew in Newark, New Jersey. Whatever his future when he leaves Prague, he becomes what he has always been, a refugee. Maybe (for there is no harm in dreams) he even lives long enough to find himself the great man he never knew he was. Maybe (the most impossible dream of all) he actually succeeds in putting on weight. So where is death now? Waiting for Kafka in some Park

Avenue consulting-room where he goes with what he takes to be a recurrence of his old chest complaint.

'Quite curable now, of course, TB. No problem. However, regarding your chest, you say you managed a factory once?'

'Yes. For my brother-in-law. For three or four years.'

'When was that?'

'A long time ago. It closed in 1917. In Prague.'

'What kind of factory was it?'

'Building materials. Asbestos.'

This is just a dream of Kafka's death. He is famous, the owner of the best-known initial in literature, and we know he did not die like this. Others probably did. In Prague the consulting-rooms are bleaker but the disease is the same and the treatment as futile. These patients have no names, though Kafka would have known them, those girls (old ladies now) whom he described brushing the thick asbestos dust from their overalls, the casualties of his brother-in-law's ill-starred business in which Hermann, his father, had invested. A good job his father isn't alive, the past master of 'I told you so.'

In the last weeks of his life Kafka was taken to a sanatorium in the Wienerwald, and here, where the secret of dreams had been revealed to Freud, Kafka's dreams ended.

On the window-sill the night before he died Dora Dymant found an owl waiting. The owl has a complex imagery in art. Just as in Freudian psychology an emotion can stand for itself and its opposite, so is the owl a symbol of both darkness and light. As a creature of the night the owl was seen as a symbol of the Jews, who, turning away from the light of Christ, were guilty of wilful blindness. On the other hand the owl was, as it remains, a symbol of wisdom. It is fitting that this bird of ambiguity should come to witness the departure of a man who by belief was neither Christian nor Jew, and had never wholeheartedly felt himself a member of the human race. He had written of himself as a bug and a mouse, both the natural prey of the bird now waiting outside the window.

Comfortable Words

When Canon Williams asked me to address this meeting I thought it would be a relatively easy task. He had sent me some of the contributions of my distinguished predecessors in this place, and what seemed to be required was a celebration of the merits and qualities of the Book of Common Prayer as opposed to such versions as have succeeded (though not superseded) it, plus some personal thoughts or reminiscences along the lines of 'The Prayer Book and Me'.

I take it that these occasions are in some sense rallies, and, since like most people here I am convinced of the superiority of the BCP, the only difficulty in demonstrating its abiding virtues would be to select from so much abundance. As easy, or as hard, to enumerate the virtues of Shakespeare.

That the style of the Prayer Book has permeated English prose for five centuries hardly needs saying again, except to point out that this is not just confined to the serious stuff. Frivolity owes Cranmer a debt too.

Cranmer and P. G. Wodehouse would seem a peculiar twosome, but I'm sure there is a paper to be written on the evidence of the Prayer Book in the world of Bertie Wooster, and another on the influence of the Prayer Book on English detective fiction. Phrases from the Prayer Book turn up in the silliest places. I was once in a Ben Travers farce, *Cuckoo in the Nest*, which is set in a village pub. As she locks up for the night,

An Address to the Prayer Book Society, Blackburn Cathedral, 12 May 1990 the landlady, Mrs Spoker, interrogates the potboy: 'Alfred. Have you done all the things you ought to have done?' 'Yes, mum.' 'And have you left undone those things you ought not to have done?' 'Yes, mum.' It's not actually a joke, and it didn't do very well back in 1964. Twenty-six years later the exchange would probably be cut, and if the director is under thirty-five he or she wouldn't recognize the quotation anyway. Jokes depend on shared reference, and anyone like myself who thinks making jokes is a serious matter must regret the eclipse of the Book of Common Prayer because it has diminished the common stock of shared reference on which jokes – and of course it's not only jokes – depend.

But I have already strayed into reminiscence, and the second requirement of your speakers – notes under the heading of 'The Prayer Book and Me.' I didn't anticipate any difficulty here either, as I had a religious upbringing and one of the two books of which I have large sections by heart is the Book of Common Prayer (the other being Hymns Ancient and Modern). Knowing we would all be of one mind, my concern was simply not to be dull; a playwright likes, perhaps ought, to take his audience on a journey, even if it's only from A to B, and this I thought might be a problem as I knew I would be preaching to the converted. That apart, though, talking about the Prayer Book would be a pushover.

How wrong I was. No sooner did I try to write this address than I began to struggle. I thought I knew what I wanted to say, only to find doubts beginning to creep in and other, less comfortable, words demanding to be spoken. For a writer, of course, this is not a novel experience. One seldom sits down knowing exactly what one wants to say, the knowing very often coming out of the saying. 'One draws', says Lichtenberg, 'from the well of language many a thought one does not have.' A writer does not always know what he or she knows, and writing is a way of finding out. The surprise to me in this matter of the Prayer Book was that I thought I did know, and writing has shown me that I didn't. I began in one mind and ended up in two.

I begin with a poem by Stevie Smith. I won't attempt to sing or intone the piece, as Stevie Smith often did with her poems, and it may not sound much like a poem at all but more like a letter to the *Telegraph*. It's called 'Why are the Clergy . . .?'

Why are the clergy of the Church of England
Always changing the words of the prayers in the Prayer Book?
Cranmer's touch was surer than theirs, do they not respect
    him?
For instance last night in church I heard
(I italicize the interpolation)
'The Lord bless you and keep you *and all who are dear unto*
    you'
As the blessing is a congregational blessing and meant to be
This is questionable on theological grounds
But is it not offensive to the ear and also ludicrous?
That 'unto' is a particularly ripe piece of idiocy
Oh how offensive it is. I suppose we shall have next
'Lighten our darkness we beseech thee O Lord *and the darkness*
    of all who are dear unto us'
It seems a pity. Does Charity object to the objection?
Then I cry, and not for the first time to that smooth face
Charity, have pity.

The poem is pretty self-explanatory apart from the last two lines: 'Does Charity object to the objection? / Then I cry, and not for the first time to that smooth face / Charity, have pity.' I think what Stevie Smith means is that living in fellowship with other believers might seem to require her to be silent. Don't rock the boat, in other words. Whereas she begs to be allowed, as you in this Society beg to be allowed, to differ.

Stevie Smith brings me to the first of my difficulties: God, put bluntly. Stevie Smith regarded God much as she regarded producers with whom she worked at the BBC: He had to be kept in His place, not allowed to go too far, and on occasion needed to be taken down a peg or two. But, though she and God didn't always get on, she undoubtedly believed in Him and so was entitled to weigh in with her opinions and objections, including her opinions about the Prayer Book. I'm not sure that I do believe in God. If I don't, it could reasonably be objected that I shouldn't be talking about the Prayer Book at all. Those who rewrote the Prayer Book complained very much at the time – and understandably – that many of the protests came from those, such as myself, whose connection with the Church was tenuous, the argument implicit in this being that the clergy know what is best for their congregations. This is the same argument that is advanced by farmers in answer to protests about the grubbing-up of hedges and the destruction of field patterns. The land is the farmer's bread and butter, the argument goes, and so he must therefore have its welfare more at heart than the occasional visitor. So in their own field the liturgical reformers grub up the awkward thickets of language that make the harvest of souls more difficult, plough in the sixteenth-century hedges that are hard to penetrate but for that reason shelter all manner of rare creatures: poetry, mystery, transcendence. All must be flat, dull, accessible and rational. Fields and worship.

The folly in the reform of institutions is to fix on an essential or a primary function. The land is there to produce food. The Prayer Book is there to net souls. Once one function has been given priority, all other considerations go by the board. But there is an ecology of belief as well as of nature. Poetry, mystery, the beauty of language – these may be incidental to the primary purpose of the Church, which is to bring people to God, but one doesn't have to be Archbishop Laud to see that these incidental virtues of the Prayer Book are not irrelevant or dispensable. If they were, architecture would be irrelevant too; the logical end of rewriting the Prayer Book being that serious-minded congregations would worship in Nissen huts. And a small voice says, 'Well, perhaps that is what they do.'

Of course in the Anglican Church whether or not one believes in God tends to get sidestepped. It's not quite in good taste. Someone said that the Church of England is so constituted that its members can really believe anything, but of course almost none of them do.

One of the aims of the liturgical reformers was to make God more accessible; but that didn't mean that they weren't also a little embarrassed by Him, and I think it's this embarrassment that has got into their language. God is like an aged father taken in by his well-intentioned children. They want to keep him presentable and a useful member of society, so they scrap his old three-piece suit, in which he looked a little old-fashioned (though rather distinguished), and kit him out instead in pastel-coloured leisurewear in which he looks like everybody else. The trouble is, though, they can't change the habits of a lifetime. It's not so much that he spits in the fire or takes his teeth out at the table but that, given the chance, he is so forthright. He's always laying down the law and seems to think nobody else exists, and his family might be servants the way he treats them. It's a bit embarrassing – particularly when those warm, friendly people from the religion next door come round. Still, it's only a matter of time. Father's old. He may die soon.

But before we adherents (I almost said fans) of the old Prayer Book congratulate ourselves on not being so silly, or trendy or however else the reformers are characterized, it's worth remembering that we have a corresponding dilemma. They are dodging God in one way, we in another. The majesty of the

Prayer Book, the resonance of its language and the grandeur of its architecture, might seem to echo the qualities we attribute to the deity. But centuries of use have made it an accommodating majesty, a familiar grandeur; the sonority does not intimidate. W. H. Auden made the same point:

Those of us who are Anglicans know well that the language of the Book of Common Prayer, its extraordinary beauties of sound and rhythm, can all too easily tempt us to delight in the sheer sound without thinking what the words mean or whether we mean them. In the General Confession, for example, what a delight to the tongue and ear it is to recite 'We do earnestly repent and are heartily sorry for these our misdoings; the remembrance of them is grievous unto us; the burden of them is intolerable.' Is it really intolerable? Not very often.
(*Secondary Worlds*)

Moreover, the Prayer Book is so bound up, as P. D. James said here a couple of years ago, with memories – memories of childhood, of marriages and baptisms, births and deaths. And that is as it should be; but its very familiarity enables congregations to domesticate God. So when we hear what comfortable words Cranmer wrote, should we (and I am saying 'we' I suppose out of politeness, lest I seem to be lecturing you), should we not consider whether these well-worn liturgical paths down which we tread, the aisles and cloisters in this great cathedral of a book, while they are a way of praising God might also be a way of evading Him?

I suppose what I'm saying is that the Prayer Book gives pleasure, is enjoyable, satisfies, in a way that the Alternative Service Book doesn't. But whether that's anything to do with true religion I'm not sure. But it does give pleasure. Even at a funeral it's hard not to feel a quickening of the heart as the coffin passes into the churchyard and the great tolling words of 'I am the resurrection and the life' begin the stately ritual progress that will end in the grave. I think too of services caught by chance, sitting on winter afternoons in the nave of Ely or Lincoln and hearing from the (so-called) loudspeaker a dry, reedy, unfleshed voice taking evensong. And one was grateful that the voice was without feeling – no more emotion than from an announcer giving the times of the departure of trains: the words themselves so powerful that they do not need feeling injected into them, any more than poetry does. Or, as T. S. Eliot said, who had that style of delivery himself, 'Speak the word, speak the word only.'

Talk of long-gone winter afternoons in Ely and Lincoln seems to associate the Prayer Book with Ancient Monuments, or, as we must now call it, the Heritage. I think it was Prince Charles who referred to the Prayer Book under this heading, and with no disrespect I have to say that makes me very nervous. The monarchy is part of the Heritage too, but that is not why we maintain it, but because it works. Start thinking of the Prayer Book as part of the Heritage and the next thing you know they will be putting up those ubiquitous brown signs pointing the visitor to heritage-conscious churches that still use the old forms; tourists will be coming in to watch congregations that still go through these quaint but outmoded rituals, much as they watch corn ground at the original mill or members of the Sealed Knot re-enact the Battle of Naseby. I was going to suggest as a joke that there might even be a Good Service Guide – Real Prayer, like Real Ale, something to be sought out – but I've an awful feeling there already is one. No, the word 'heritage' should be avoided at all costs.

I fear I've already trod on a great many toes, which I did not expect to do when I agreed to talk but which is the result, as I said, of being in two minds. I'd worry, if I were a member of this Society, about some of my fellow-travellers. I'd worry that I was somehow associated with the 'Don't let's mess about with

Shakespeare' brigade, and, going down the scale a bit, with those devotees who believe that shortly after God handed down the tablets to Moses the proper way of producing Gilbert and Sullivan was vouchsafed to the D'Oyly Carte. More seriously I'd worry about the *Spectator*, which sponsors the Thomas Cranmer prize, because on social issues its elegant common sense often seems to me to mask a brutal indifference. I'd worry about the *Daily Telegraph*, another champion of the Prayer Book, but which is always the first to jeer if the clergy undertake a role the paper feels should be properly confined to social workers (not that they don't get jeered at too), and which will always weigh in with some ponderous 'Render to Caesar' stuff if the clergy, individually or on commissions, dare to suggest that this government is not entirely perfect.

I'd ask you too to consider whether you are lately as beleaguered as you imagine, or whether your championship of the unrevised Prayer Book has not now become, or is becoming, the new orthodoxy. I don't know if the number of churches using the BCP is increasing or decreasing, and it may be that the Alternative Service Book is gaining ground, but it seems to me that you have time and enlightened opinion on your side. Nothing looks so tatty as a building that is twenty or thirty years old. It's shoddy, it's old-fashioned, while still a long way from acquiring the dignity or the patina of age. That seems to me increasingly true of the Alternative Service Book. Its absurdities are patent, its language is shoddy, and my guess (and hope) is that it will suffer the same fate as the tower blocks with which it is contemporary. I know that the aim of this Society is not to extirpate the Alternative Service Book, but just to make sure that the Book of Common Prayer survives, is used, and is the ultimate directive for worship in the Church of England. How much better it would have been to leave the BCP as the official service book, with the Alternative Service Book as an option; or, having devised an alternative and done all the consumer testing, put it on the shelf for ten years before taking it down and seeing how it had stood the test of time. It was, I think, the director Peter Brook who said have a revolution by all means, but then, having had it, change nothing for twenty years.

Sometimes, though, the prayer book doesn't matter. About this time last year I had to go to the funeral of an old lady who had been living for fifteen years in a van in my garden. She had been a fervent Catholic, and the service was in the church round the corner from my home in Camden Town. The form of service was flatter and more prosaic than any reform has made the Anglican one, and seemed to have been ruthlessly pruned of any echo of the mass. There were (and this did take me by surprise) cards on the coffin, and not I imagine Get Well cards either. Perhaps 'Have a Good Funeral'. The server did all the preliminary arrangements in his shirtsleeves, one old lady was eating sweets throughout, and the hymns were all like unsuccessful entries for the Eurovision Song Contest. Then we came to that point in the service, the affirmation of fellowship, which I dread and which always puts me in mind of the warm-ups Ned Sherrin used to inflict on the audience of his late-night ITV shows when total strangers had to shake hands with one another. The old man in front, who was my neighbour, turned round and shook hands and with such an expression of unselfconscious goodness that I was straight away put to shame and saw how in these circumstances my liturgical fastidiousness was sheer snobbery.

This doesn't mean that I think the Prayer Book Society is mistaken or its efforts misdirected. One half of me is wholeheartedly with you. But there are circumstances which make controversy irrelevant. A different (or an indifferent) view of the liturgy might be taken by a hard-pressed curate in a slum parish. Taking the sacrament to someone sick on the fourteenth floor of a tower block, he goes up in the lift and as he tries not to look at the graffiti or breathe in the stench of urine I do not think that the beauty of Cranmer's English is very high on his list of priorities. Now of course that is not the whole story, but it seems to me, as an outsider, that in a Society like this that curate is someone you have to take into account and be aware of. Cranmer did not die for English prose.

Alas! Deceived

'My mother is such a bloody rambling fool', wrote Philip Larkin in 1965, 'that half the time I doubt her sanity. Two things she said today, for instance, were that she had "thought of getting a job in Woolworth's" and that she wanted to win the football pools so that she could "give cocktail parties".' Eva Larkin was seventy-nine at the time, so to see herself presiding over the Pick'n'Mix counter was a little unrealistic, and her chances of winning the football pools were remote as she didn't go in for them. Still, mothers do get ideas about cocktail parties, or mine did anyway, who'd never had a cocktail in her life and couldn't even pronounce the word, always laying the emphasis (maybe out of prudery) on the tail rather than the cock. I always assumed she got these longings from women's magazines or off the television, and maybe Mrs Larkin did too, though 'she never got used to the television' – which in view of her son's distrust of it is hardly surprising.

Mrs Larkin went into a home in 1971, a few months after her son had finished his most notorious poem, 'They fuck you up, your mum and dad'. She never read it (Larkin didn't want to 'confuse her with information about books'), but, bloody rambling fool or not, she shared more of her son's life and thoughts than do most mothers, or at any rate the version he gave her of them in his regular letters, still writing to her daily when she was in her eighties. By turns guilty and grumbling ('a

Review of *Philip Larkin: A Writer's Life* by Andrew Motion
(Faber and Faber, 1993)

perpetual burning bush of fury in my chest'), Larkin's attitude towards her doesn't seem particularly unusual, though his dutifulness does. Even so, Woolworth's would hardly have been her cup of tea. The other long-standing lady in Larkin's life (and who stood for a good deal), Monica Jones, remarks that to the Larkins the least expenditure of effort was 'something heroic': 'Mrs Larkin's home was one in which if you'd cooked lunch you had to lie down afterwards to recover.' Monica, one feels, was more of a Woolworth's supervisor than a counter assistant. 'I suppose', wrote Larkin, 'I shall become free [of mother] at 60, three years before the cancer starts. What a bloody, sodding awful life.' His of course, not hers. Eva died in 1977 aged ninety-one, after which the poems more or less stopped coming. Andrew Motion thinks this is no coincidence.

Larkin pinpointed sixty-three as his probable departure date because that was when his father went, turned by his mother into 'the sort of closed, reserved man who would die of something internal'. Sydney Larkin was the City Treasurer of Coventry. He was also a veteran of several Nuremberg rallies, a pen-pal of Schacht's, and had a statue of Hitler on the mantelpiece that gave the Nazi salute. Sydney made no secret of his sympathies down at the office: 'I see that Mr Larkin's got one of them swastika things up on his wall now. Whatever next?' Next was a snip in the shape of some cardboard coffins that Sydney had cannily invested in and which came in handy when Coventry got blitzed, the Nazi insignia down from the wall by this time (a quiet word from the Town Clerk). But he didn't change his tune, still less swap the swastika for a snap of Churchill, who had, he thought, 'the face of a criminal in the dock'.

To describe a childhood with this grotesque figure at the centre of it as 'a forgotten boredom' seems ungrateful of Larkin, if not untypical, even though the phrase comes from a poem

('Coming') not an interview, so Larkin is telling the truth rather than the facts. Besides, it would have been difficult to accommodate Sydney in a standard Larkin poem, giving an account of his peculiar personality before rolling it up into a general statement in the way Larkin liked to do. Sylvia Plath had a stab at that kind of thing with her 'Daddy', though she had to pretend he was a Nazi, while Larkin's dad was the real thing. Still, to anyone (I mean me) whose childhood was more sparsely accoutred with characters, Larkin's insistence on its dullness is galling, if only on the 'I should be so lucky' principle.

As a script, the City Treasurer and his family feels already half-written by J. B. Priestley; were it a film, Sydney (played by Raymond Huntley) would be a domestic tyrant, making the life of his liberal and sensitive son a misery, thereby driving him to Art. Not a bit of it. For a start the son was never liberal ('true blue' all his life, Monica says), and had a soft spot for Hitler himself. Nor was the father a tyrant; he introduced his son to the works of Hardy and, more surprisingly, Joyce, did not regard jazz as the work of the devil, bought him a subscription to the magazine *Downbeat* (a signpost here), and also helped him invest in a drum-kit. What if anything he bought his daughter Kitty and what Mrs Larkin thought of it all is not recorded. Perhaps she was lying down. The women in the Larkin household always took second place, which, in Motion's view, is half the trouble. Kitty, Larkin's older sister ('the one person in the world I am confident I am superior to'), scarcely figures at all. Hers would, I imagine, be a dissenting voice, more brunt-bearing than her brother where Mrs Larkin was concerned and as undeceived about the poet as were most of the women in his life.

Whatever reservations Larkin had about his parents ('days spent in black, twitching, boiling HATE!!!'), by Oxford and adulthood they had modulated, says Motion, into 'controlled but bitter resentment'. This doesn't stop Larkin sending poems to his father ('I crave/The gift of your courage and indifference') and sharing his thoughts with his mother ('that obsessive snivelling pest') on all manner of things; in a word, treating them as people rather than parents. It's nothing if not 'civilized' but still slightly creepy, and it might have come as a surprise to Kingsley Amis, in view of their intimate oath-larded letters to one another, that Larkin, disappointed of a visit, should promptly have complained about him ('He is a wretched type') to his *mother*.

'Fearsome and hard-driving', Larkin senior is said never to have missed the chance of slipping an arm round a secretary, and though Larkin junior took a little longer about it (twenty-odd years in one case), it is just one of the ways he comes to resemble his father as he grows older, in the process getting to look less like Raymond Huntley and more like Francis L. Sullivan and 'the sort of person that democracy doesn't suit'.

Larkin's choice of profession is unsurprising, because from an early age libraries had been irresistible:

I was an especially irritating kind of borrower, who brought back in the evening the books he had borrowed in the morning and read in the afternoon. This was the old Coventry Central Library, nestling at the foot of the unbombed cathedral, filled with tall antiquated bookcases (blindstamped Coventry Central Libraries after the fashion of the time) with my ex-schoolfellow Ginger Thompson . . . This was my first experience of the addictive excitement a large open-access public library generates.

When he jumped over the counter, as it were, things were rather different, though father's footsteps come into this too: if you can't be a gauleiter, being a librarian's the next best thing. When called upon to explain his success as a librarian, Larkin said, 'A librarian can be one of a number of things . . . a pure scholar, a technician . . . an administrator or he . . . can be just a nice chap to have around, which is the role I vaguely thought I filled.' Motion calls this a 'typically self-effacing judgement', but it's also a bit of a self-deluding one. It's a short step from the jackboot to the book-jacket, and by all accounts Larkin the librarian could be a pretty daunting figure. Neville Smith remembers him at Hull stood at the entrance to the Brynmor Jones, scanning the faces of the incoming hordes, the face heavy and expressionless, the glasses gleaming and the hands, after the manner of a soccer player awaiting a free-kick on the edge of the penalty area, clasped over what is rumoured to have been a substantial package. 'FUCK OFF, LARKIN, YOU CUNT' might have been the cheery signing-off in a letter from Kingsley Amis: it was actually written up on the wall of the library lifts, presumably by one of those 'devious, lazy and stupid' students who persisted in infesting the librarian's proper domain and reading the books.

It hadn't always been like that, though, and Larkin's first stint, at Wellington in Shropshire, where in 1943 he was put in charge of the municipal library, was a kind of idyll. Bitterly cold, gas-lit and with a boiler Larkin himself had to stoke, the library had an eccentric collection of books and a readership to match. Here he does seem to have been the type of librarian who was 'a nice chap to have around', one who quietly got on with improving the stock while beginning to study for his professional qualifications by correspondence course. Expecting 'not to give a zebra's turd' for the job, he had hit upon his vocation.

Posts at Leicester and Belfast followed, until in 1955 he was appointed Librarian at the University of Hull with the job of reorganizing the library and transferring it to new premises. Moan as Larkin inevitably did about his job, it was one he enjoyed and which he did exceptionally well. The students may have been intimidated by him but he was popular with his staff, and particularly with the women. Mary Judd, the librarian at the issue desk at Hull, thought that 'most women liked him more than most men because he could talk to a woman and make her feel unique and valuable.' In last year's *Selected Letters* there is a photo of him with the staff of the Brynmor Jones and, Larkin apart, there is not a man in sight. Surrounded by his beaming middle-aged assistants – with two at least he was having or would have an affair – he looks like a walrus with his herd of contented cows. There was contentment here for him, too, and one of his last poems, written when deeply depressed, is about a library.

> New eyes each year
> Find old books here,
> And new books, too,
> Old eyes renew;
> So youth and age
> Like ink and page
> In this house join,
> Minting new coin.

Much of Motion's story is about sex: not getting it, not getting enough of it, or getting it wrong. For a time it seemed Larkin could go either way, and there are a few messy homosexual encounters at Oxford – though not *Brideshead* by a long chalk, lungings more than longings, and not the stuff of poetry except as the tail-end of 'these incidents last night'. After Oxford, Larkin's homosexual feelings 'evaporated' (Motion's word) and were henceforth seemingly confined to his choice of socks.

At Wellington he started walking out with Ruth Bowman, 'a 16-year-old schoolgirl and regular borrower from the library'. This period of Larkin's life is quite touching and reads like a fifties novel of provincial life, though not one written by him so much as by John Wain or Keith Waterhouse. Indeed Ruth sounds (or Larkin makes her sound) like Billy Liar's unsatisfactory girlfriend, whose snog-inhibiting Jaffa Billy hurls to the other end of the cemetery. Having laid out a grand total of 15s. 7d. on an evening with Ruth, Larkin writes to Amis:

Don't you think it's ABSOLUTELY SHAMEFUL that men have to pay for women without BEING ALLOWED TO SHAG the women afterwards AS A MATTER OF COURSE? I do: simply DISGUSTING. It makes me ANGRY. Everything about the ree-lay-shun-ship between men and women makes me angry. It's all a fucking balls-up. It might have been planned by the army or the Ministry of Food.

To be fair, Larkin's foreplay could be on the funereal side. In the middle of one date with Ruth, Larkin (twenty-two) lapsed into silence. Was it something she'd said? 'No, I have just thought what it would be like to be old and have no one to look after you.' This was what Larkin would later refer to as 'his startling youth'. 'He could', says Ruth, 'be a draining companion.'

In the end one's sympathies, as always in Larkin's affairs, go to the woman, and one is glad when Ruth finally has him sized up and decides that he's no hubby-to-be. And he's glad too, of course. Ruth has Amis well sussed besides. 'He wanted', she says, 'to turn Larkin into a "love 'em and lose 'em type",' and for a moment we see these two leading lights of literature as what they once were: the Likely Lads – Larkin as Bob, Amis as Terry, and Ruth at this juncture the terrible Thelma.

Looking back on it now Ruth says, 'I was his first love and there's something special about a first love, isn't there?' Except that 'love' is never quite the right word with Larkin, 'getting involved' for once not a euphemism for the tortuous process it always turns out to be. 'My relations with women', he wrote, 'are governed by a shrinking sensitivity, a morbid sense of sin, a furtive lechery. Women don't just sit still and back you up. They want children; they like scenes; they want a chance of parading all the empty haberdashery they are stocked with. Above all they like feeling they own you – or that you own them – a thing I hate.' A.C. Benson, whose medal Larkin was later to receive from the Royal Society of Literature, put it more succinctly, quoting (I think) Aristophanes: 'Don't make your house in my mind.' Though with Larkin it was 'Don't make your house in my house either,' his constant fear being that he will be moved in on, first by his mother and then, when she's safely in a home, by some other scheming woman. When towards the finish Monica Jones does manage to move in it's because she's ill and can't look after herself, and so the cause of a great deal more grumbling. With hindsight (Larkin's favourite vantage point) it would have been wiser to have persisted with the messy homosexual fumblings, one of the advantages of boys being that they're more anxious to move on than in. Not, of course, that one has a choice, 'something hidden from us' seeing to that.

Larkin's earliest poems were published by R. A. Caton of the Fortune Press. Caton's list might have been entitled 'Poetic Justice', as besides the poetry it included such titles as *Chastisement Across the Ages* and an account of corporal punishment as meted out to women in South German prisons; since Larkin's tastes ran to both poetry and porn there is poetic justice in that too. He found that he shared his interest in dirty books with 'the sensitive and worldly-wise' Robert Conquest, and together they went on expeditions, trawling the specialist shops for their respective bag in a partnership that seems both carefree and innocent. Unusual, too, as I had always thought that porn, looking for it and looking at it, was something solo. Conquest would also send him juicy material through the post, and on one occasion conned the fearful Larkin into thinking the law was on his tracks and ruin imminent; he made him sweat for two or three days before letting him off the hook. That Larkin forgave him and bore no ill-will seems to me one of the few occasions outside his poetry when he comes close to real generosity of spirit.

Timorous though Larkin was, he was not shamefaced and made no secret of his predilections. Just as Elsie, secretary to his father, took her bottom-pinching Führer-friendly boss in her stride, so Betty, the secretary to the son, never turned a hair when she came across his lunch-time reading in the shape of the splayed buttocks of some gym-slipped tot, just covering it briskly with a copy of the *Library Association Record* and carrying on cataloguing. One of the many virtues of Motion's book is that it celebrates the understanding and tolerance of the average British secretary and the forbearance of women generally. As, for instance, the friend to whom Larkin showed a large cupboard in his office, full of both literary and photographic porn. 'What is it for?' she asked. 'To wank to, or with, or at' was Larkin's reply, which Motion calls embarrassed, though it doesn't sound so, the question, or at any rate the answer, presumably giving him a bit of a thrill. Like the other documents of his life and his half-life, the magazines were carefully kept, if not catalogued, in his desolate attic, though after twenty-odd years' perusal they must have been about as stimulating as *Beowulf*.

One unremarked oddity in the *Selected Letters* is a note from Larkin to Conquest in 1976 mentioning a visit to Cardiff, where he had 'found a newsagent with a good line in Yank homo porn, in quite a classy district too. Didn't dare touch it.' I had assumed that in the matter of dirty magazines, be it nurses, nuns or louts in leather, you found whatever knocked on your particular box and stuck to it. So what did Larkin want with 'this nice line in homo porn'? Swaps? Or hadn't all that messy homosexuality really evaporated? Certainly pictured holidaying on Sark in

1955 he looks anything but butch. One here for Jake Balokowsky.

I am writing this before the book is published, but Larkin's taste for pornography is already being touted by the newspapers as something shocking. It isn't, but, deluded liberal that I am, I persist in thinking that those with a streak of sexual unorthodoxy ought to be more tolerant of their fellows than those who lead an entirely godly, righteous and sober life. Illogically I tend to assume that if you dream of caning schoolgirls' bottoms it disqualifies you from dismissing half the nation as work-shy. It doesn't, of course – more often it's the other way round – but when Larkin and Conquest rant about the country going to the dogs there's a touch of hypocrisy about it. As an undergraduate Larkin had written two facetious novels set in a girls' school, under the pseudonym of Brunette Coleman. It's tempting to think that his much advertised adoration of Mrs Thatcher ('What a superb creature she is, right and beautiful!') owes something to the sadistic head-mistress of St Bride's, Miss Holden.

As Pam finally pulled Marie's tunic down over her black-stockinged legs Miss Holden, pausing only to snatch a cane from the cupboard in the wall, gripped Marie by her hair and, with strength lent by anger, forced down her head till she was bent nearly double. Then she began thrashing her unmercifully, her face a mask of ferocity, caring little where the blows fell, as long as they found a mark somewhere on Marie's squirming body. At last a cry was wrung from her bloodless lips and Marie collapsed on the floor, twisting in agony, her face hidden by a flood of amber hair.

Whether Mr Heseltine is ever known as Marie is a detail; that apart it could be a verbatim extract from A History of Cabinet Government 1979–90.

Meeting Larkin at Downing Street in 1980, Mrs Thatcher gushed that she liked his wonderful poem about a girl. 'You know,' she said, ' "Her mind was full of knives." ' The line is actually 'All the unhurried day/Your mind lay open like a drawer of knives,' but Larkin liked to think that Madam knew the poem or she would not have been able to misquote it. Inadequate briefing seems a likelier explanation and, anyway, since the line is about an open mind it's not surprising the superb creature got it wrong.

Mrs Thatcher's great virtue, Larkin told a journalist, 'is saying that two and two makes four, which is as unpopular nowadays as it always has been.' What Larkin did not see was that it was only by banking on two and two making five that institutions like the Brynmor Jones Library could survive. He lived long enough to see much of his work at the library dismantled; one of the meetings he was putting off before his death was with the Vice-Chancellor designate, who was seeking ways of saving a quarter of a million pounds and wanted to shrink the library by hiving off some of its rooms. That was two and two making four.

Andrew Motion makes most of these points himself, but without rancour or the impatience this reader certainly felt. Honest but not prurient, critical but also compassionate, Motion's book could not be bettered. It is above all patient, and with no trace of the condescension or irritation that are the hazards of biography. He is a sure guide when he relates the poetry to the life, even though the mystery of where the poetry came from, and why, and when, sometimes defeats him. But then it defeated Larkin, or his writing would not have petered out when it did. For all that, it's a sad read, and Motion's patience with his subject is often hard to match. Larkin being Larkin, though, there are lots of laughs and jokes never far away. Before he became a celebrity (and, wriggle though he did, that was what he became) and one heard gossip about Larkin it was generally his jokes and his crabbiness that were quoted. 'More creaking from an old gate', was his dedication in Patrick Garland's volume of *High Windows*, and there were the PCs (which were not PC at all) he used to send to Charles Monteith, including one not quoted here or in the *Selected Letters*. Along with other Faber authors, Larkin had been circularized asking what events, if any, he was prepared to take part in to mark National Libraries Week. Larkin wrote back saying that the letter reminded him of the story of Sir George Sitwell being stopped by someone selling flags in aid of National Self-Denial Week: 'For some of us', said Sir George, 'every week is self-denial week.' 'I feel', wrote Larkin, 'exactly the same about National Libraries Week.' The letters are full of jokes. 'I fully expect,' he says of 'They fuck you up, your mum and dad', 'to hear it recited by 1000 Girl Guides before I die'; he gets 'a letter from a whole form of Welsh schoolgirls, seemingly inviting mass coition. Where were they when I wanted them?' And in the cause of jokes he was prepared to dramatize himself, heighten his circumstances, darken his despair, claim to have been a bastard in situations where he had actually been all charm. What one wants to go on feeling was that, the poems apart, the jokes were the man, and the saddest thing about this book and the *Selected Letters* is to find that they weren't, that beyond the jokes was a sphere of gloom, fear and self-pity that nothing and no one touched. And, so far from feeling compassion for him on this score, as Motion always manages to do, I just felt impatient and somehow conned.

Trying to locate why takes one back to Auden:

A writer, or at least a poet, is always being asked by people who should know better: 'Whom do you write for?' The question is, of course, a silly one, but I can give it a silly answer. Occasionally I come across a book which I feel has been written especially for me and for me only. Like a jealous lover I don't want anybody else to hear of it. To have a million such readers, unaware of each other's existence, to be read with passion and never talked about, is the daydream, surely, of every author.

Larkin was like that, certainly after the publication of *The Less Deceived* and even for a few years after *The Whitsun Weddings* came out. Because his poems spoke in an ordinary voice and boasted his quiescence and self-deprecation, one felt that here was someone to like, to take to, and whose voice echoed one's inner thoughts, and that he was, as he is here engagingly indexed (under his initials), a PAL. So that in those days, certainly until the mid-seventies, Larkin seemed always a shared secret. The great and unexpected outpouring of regret when he died showed this sentiment to have been widespread and that through the public intimacy of his poetry he had acquired a constituency as Betjeman, partly through being less introspective and more available, never entirely did. And while we did not quite learn his language or make him our pattern to live and to die, what one is left with now is a sense of betrayal which is quite difficult to locate and no less palpable for the fact that he never sought to mislead the public about his character, particularly as he got older.

They were deceived, though. When Anthony Thwaite published the *Selected Letters* last year, the balance of critical opinion was disposed to overlook – or at any rate excuse – his racist and reactionary sentiments as partly a joke, racism more pardonable these days in the backlash against political correctness. Besides, it was plain that in his letters Larkin exaggerated; he wasn't really like that. Motion's book closes down this escape route. 'You'll be pleased to see the black folk go from the house over the way,' he says in a 1970 letter, and were it written to Amis or Conquest it might get by as irony, wit even, a voice put on.

But he is writing to his mother, for whom he did not put on a voice – or not that voice anyway. Did it come with the flimsiest of apologies it would help ('I'm sorry,' as I once heard someone say, 'but I have a blind spot with black people'). How were the blacks across the way different from 'those antique negroes' who blew their 'flock of notes' out of 'Chicago air into/A huge remembering pre-electric horn/The year after I was born'? Well, they were in Loughborough for a start, not Chicago. Wanting so much for him to be other, one is forced against every inclination to conclude that, in trading bigotries with an eighty-year-old, Larkin was sincere; he was being really himself:

> I want to see them starving
> The so-called working class
> Their weekly wages halving
> Their women stewing grass.

The man who penned that might have been pleased to come up with the slogan of the 1968 Smethwick by-election: 'If you want a nigger neighbour, Vote Labour.' Larkin refused the Laureate-ship because he couldn't turn out poetry to order. But if he could churn out this stuff for his letters and postcards he could have turned an honest penny on the *Sun* any day of the week.

Then there is Larkin the Hermit of Hull. Schweitzer in the Congo did not derive more moral credit than Larkin did for living in Hull. No matter that of the four places he spent most of his life – Hull, Coventry, Leicester and Belfast – Hull is probably the most pleasant; or that poets are not and never have been creatures of the capital: to the newspapers, as Motion says, remoteness is synonymous with integrity. But Hull isn't even particularly remote. Ted Hughes, living in Devon, is further from London (as the crow flies, of course) than Larkin ever was, but that he gets no credit for it is partly the place's fault, Devon to the metropolitan crowd having nothing on the horrors of

Hull. Hughes, incidentally, gets much the same treatment here as he did in the *Selected Letters*, more pissed on than the back wall of the Batley Working Men's club before a Dusty Springfield concert.

Peter Cook once did a sketch in which, dressed as Garbo, he was filmed touring the streets in an open-topped limousine shouting through a megaphone 'I want to be alone'. Larkin wasn't quite as obvious as that, but poetry is a public-address system too and that his remoteness was so well publicized came about less from his interviews or personal pronouncements than from the popularity of poems like 'Here' and 'The Whitsun Weddings' which located Larkin, put him on (and off) the map, and advertised his distance from the centre of things.

That Hull was the back of beyond in the fifties wasn't simply a London opinion: it prevailed in Hull itself. In 1959 I tentatively applied there for a lectureship in medieval history, and the professor kicked off the interview by emphasizing that train services were now so good that Hull was scarcely four hours from King's Cross. It wasn't that he'd sensed in me someone who'd feel cut off from the vivifying currents of capital chic, rather that my field of study was the medieval exchequer, the records of which were then at Chancery Lane. Still, there was a definite sense that a slow and stopping train southwards was some kind of lifeline and that come a free moment, there one was going to be aimed. Even Larkin himself was aimed there from time to time, and though his social life was hardly a hectic round, he put himself about more than he liked to think.

Until I read Motion's book I had imagined that Larkin was someone who had largely opted out of the rituals of literary and academic life, that he didn't subscribe to them and wasn't taken in by them. Not a bit of it. There are umpteen formal functions, the poet dutifully getting on the train to London for the annual dinner of the Royal Academy, which involves a visit to Moss Bros ('and untold expense'); there's at least one party at Buckingham Palace, a Foyle's Literary Luncheon at which he has to give a speech, there are dinners at his old college and at All Souls, and while he does not quite go to a dinner up a yak's arse he does trundle along to the annual festivities of the Hull Magic Circle. Well, the chairman of the library committee was an enthusiastic conjuror, Larkin lamely explains. When Motion says that Larkin had reluctantly to accept that his emergence as a public man would involve more public duties it's the 'reluctantly' one quibbles with. Of course there's no harm in any of these occasions if you're going to enjoy yourself. But Larkin seemingly never does, or never admits that he does. But if he didn't, why did he go? Because they are not difficult to duck. Amis has recorded how much pleasanter life became when he realized he could refuse invitations simply by saying 'don't do dinners' – a revelation comparable to Larkin's at Oxford when it dawned on him he could walk out of a play at the interval and not come back. But Larkin did do dinners, and not just dinners. He did the Booker Prize, he did the Royal Society of Literature, he did the Shakespeare Prize; he even did a dinner for the Coventry Award of Merit. Hermit of Hull or not, he dutifully turns up to collect whatever is offered to him, including a sackful of honours and seven honorary degrees. He was going to call a halt at six only Oxford then came through with 'the big one', the letter getting him seriously over-excited. 'He actually ran upstairs,' says Monica. And this is a recluse. Fame-seeking, reputation-hugging, he's about as big a recluse as the late Bubbles Rothermere.

Motion says that institutional rewards for his work annoyed him, but there's not much evidence of it. Still, to parade in a silly hat, then stand on a platform to hear your virtues recited followed by at least one formal dinner is no fun at all, as Larkin is at pains to point out, particularly when you've got sweaty palms and are frightened you're going to pass out. His account of the Oxford ceremony makes it fun, of course. His new suit looks like 'a walrus maternity garment', and the Public Orator's speech was 'a bit like a review in *Poetry Tyneside*', so he gets by, as ever, on jokes. But if to be celebrated is such a burden why does he bother with it while still managing to suggest that his life is a kind of Grand Refusal? Because he's a public figure is Motion's kindly explanation. Because he's a man is nearer the point.

A crucial text here is 'The Life with a Hole in it' (1974):

> When I throw back my head and howl
> People (women mostly) say
> *But you've always done what you want,*
> *You always get your own way*
> – A perfectly vile and foul
> Inversion of all that's been.
> What the old ratbags mean
> Is that I've never done what I don't.

It's a set-up, though, that repeats itself so regularly in Larkin's life – Larkin wanting his cake but not wanting it to be thought he enjoys eating it – that it's hard to go on sympathizing as Monica and Maeve (and indeed Motion) are expected to do, as well as any woman who would listen. Not the men, of course. Larkin knows that kind of stuff just bores the chaps, so they are fed the jokes, the good ladies his dizziness and sweaty palms, thus endearing him to them because it counts as 'opening up'.

About the only thing Larkin consistently didn't do were poetry readings ('I don't like going about pretending to be myself') and television. On the 1982 *South Bank Show* he allowed his voice to be recorded but refused to appear in person, and it's to Patrick Garland's credit that he managed to persuade the then virtually unknown Larkin to take part in a 1965

Monitor film, which happily survives. He was interviewed, or at any rate was talked at, by Betjeman, and typically, of course, it's Larkin who comes out of it as the better performer. Like other figures on the right – Paul Johnson, Michael Wharton and the *Spectator* crowd – Larkin regarded television as the work of the devil, or at any rate the Labour Party, and was as reluctant to be pictured as any primitive tribesman. Silly, I suppose I think this is, and also self-regarding. Hughes has done as little TV as Larkin and not made such a song and dance about it. There is always the danger for a writer of becoming a pundit, or turning into a character, putting on a performance of oneself as Betjeman did. But there was little danger of that with Larkin. He claimed he was nervous of TV because he didn't want to be recognized, but one appearance on the *South Bank Show* doesn't start a stampede in Safeways, as other authors could regretfully have told him.

If sticking in Hull seemed a deprivation but wasn't quite, so were the circumstances in which Larkin chose to live, a top-floor flat in Pearson Park rented from the university and then an 'utterly undistinguished modern house' he bought in 1974, 'not quite the bungalow on the by-pass' but 'not the kind of dwelling that is eloquent of the nobility of the human spirit'. It's tempting to think Larkin sought out these uninspiring places because for him they weren't uninspiring but settings appropriate to the kind of poems he wrote. But he seems never to have taken much pleasure in the look of things – furniture, pictures and so on. His quarters weren't particularly spartan or even Wittgenstein-minimalist (deck-chairs and porridge), just dull. The implication of living like this is that a choice has been made, another of life's pleasures foregone in the cause of Art, part of Larkin's strategy for a stripped-down sort of life, a traveller without luggage.

'I do believe', he wrote to Maeve Brennan, 'that the happiest way to get through life is to want things and get them; now I don't believe I've ever wanted anything in the sense of a . . . Jaguar Mark IX . . . I mean, although there's always plenty of things I couldn't do with, there's never been anything I couldn't do without and in consequence I "have" very little.' But the truth is, surely, he wasn't all that interested, and if he kept his flat like a dentist's waiting-room it was because he preferred it that way. He wanted his jazz records, after all, and he 'had' those. In one's own choosier circumstances it may be that reading of a life like this one feels by implication criticized and got at. And there is with Larkin an air of virtue about it, a sense that a sacrifice has been made. After all, Auden's idea of the cosy was other people's idea of the squalid but he never implied that living in a shit-heap was a precondition of his writing poetry; it just happened to be the way he liked it.

Still, Larkin never wanted to be one of those people with 'specially-chosen junk,/The good books, the good bed,/And my life, in perfect order' or indeed to live, as he said practically everyone he knew did, in something called The Old Mill or The Old Forge or The Old Rectory. All of them, I imagine, with prams in the hall. Cyril Connolly's strictures on this point may have been one of the reasons Larkin claimed *The Condemned Playground* as his sacred book and which led him, meeting Connolly, uncharacteristically to blurt out, 'You formed me.' But if his definition of possessions seems a narrow one (hard to see how he could feel encumbered by a house, say, but not by half a dozen honorary degrees), his version of his life, which is to some extent Motion's also, was that if he had lived a more cluttered life then Art, 'that lifted rough tongued bell', would cease to chime. When it did cease to chime, rather earlier than he'd thought, ten years or so before he died, he went on living as he'd always lived, saying it was all he knew.

Striding down the library in the *Monitor* film Larkin thought he looked like a rapist. Garland reassured him, but walking by the canal in the same film there is no reassurance; he definitely does. Clad in his doleful raincoat with pebble glasses, cycle-clips and oceanic feet, he bears more than a passing resemblance to Reginald Halliday Christie. Haunting his cemeteries and churchyards he could be on the verge of exposing himself, and whether it's to a grim, head-scarved wife from Hessle or in a slim volume from Faber and Faber seems a bit of a toss-up. Had his diary survived, that 'sexual log-book', one might have learned whether this shy, tormented man ever came close to the dock, the poetry even a safety valve. As it was, lovers on the grass in Pearson Park would catch among the threshing chestnut trees the dull glint of binoculars, and on campus errant borrowers, interviewed by the Librarian, found them-selves eyed up as well as dressed down.

> Day by day your estimation clocks up
> Who deserves a smile and who a frown,
> And girls you have to tell to pull their socks up
> Are those whose pants you'd most like to pull down

Motion's hardest task undoubtedly has been to cover, to understand and somehow enlist sympathy for Larkin and his women. Chief among them were his mother, whose joyless marriage put him off the institution long before poetry provided him with the excuse; Monica Jones, lecturer in English at Leicester, whom he first met in 1946 and who was living with him when he died: Maeve Brennan, an assistant librarian at Hull with whom he had a seventeen-year fling which overlapped with another, begun in 1975, with his long-time secretary at the library, Betty Mackereth. All of them (mother excepted) he clubbed with sex, though Maeve was for a long time reluctant to join the clubbed and Betty escaped his notice until, after seventeen years as his secretary, there was presumably one of those 'When-you-take-off-your-glasses-you're-actually-quite-pretty' moments. Though the library was the setting for so much of this heavy breathing, propriety seems to have been maintained and there was no slipping down to the stack for a spot of beef jerky.

Of the three, Monica, one feels, could look after herself, and though Larkin gave her the runaround over many years she was never in any doubt about the score. 'He cared', she told Motion, 'a tenth as much about what happened around him as what was happening inside him.' Betty, too, had him taped and besides had several other strings to her bow, including some spot-welding which she'd picked up in Leeds. It's only Maeve Brennan, among his later ladies anyway, for whom one feels sorry. Maeve knew nothing of the darker side of his nature – the porn, for instance, coming as a posthumous revelation, as did his affair with Betty. If only for her sake one should be thankful the diaries did not survive. A simpler woman than the other two, she was Larkin's sweetheart, her love for him romantic and innocent, his for her companionable and protective. Dull you might even say,

> If that is what a skilled,
> Vigilant, flexible,
> Unemphasised, enthralled
> Catching of happiness is called.

A fervent Catholic (trust his luck), Maeve took a long time before she would sleep with him, keeping the poet-librarian at arm's length. Her arms were actually quite hairy – this, Motion says, adding to her attraction. Quite what she will feel when reading this is hard to figure, and she's perhaps even now belting down to Hull's Tao Clinic. While Maeve held him off the romance flourished, but as soon as she does start to sleep with him on a regular basis her days are numbered. Larkin, having made sure of his options with Betty, drops Maeve, who is desolate, and though he sees her every day in the library and they evolve 'a distant but friendly relationship' no proper explanation is ever offered.

There is, though, a lot of other explanation on the way – far too much for this reader – with Monica being pacified about Maeve, Maeve reassured about Monica, and Mother given edited versions of them both. And so much of it in letters. When the *Selected Letters* came out there was general gratitude that Larkin was old-fashioned enough still to write letters, but there's not much to be thankful for in his correspondence with Maeve and Monica. 'One could say', wrote Kafka, 'that all the misfortunes in my life stem from letters . . . I have hardly ever been deceived by people, but letters have deceived me without fail . . . not other people's letters, but my own.' So it is with Larkin, who as a young man took the piss out of all the twaddle he now in middle age writes about ree-lay-shun-ships.

The pity is that these three women never got together to compare notes on their lover, preferably in one of those siderooms in the library Mrs T.'s cuts meant had to be hived off. But then women never do get together, except in French comedies. Besides, the conference would have had to include the now senile Eva Larkin, whose spectre Larkin detected in all the women he had anything to do with, or had sex to do with. Motion identifies Larkin's mother as his muse, which I suppose one must take on trust if only out of gratitude to Motion for ploughing through all their correspondence.

What makes one impatient with a lot of the stuff Larkin writes to Monica and Maeve is that it's plain that what he really wants is just to get his end away on a regular basis and without obligation. 'Sex is so difficult,' he complained to Jean Hartley.

'You ought to be able to get it and pay for it monthly like a laundry bill.' The impression the public had from the poems was that Larkin had missed out on sex, and this was corroborated by occasional interviews ('Sexual recreation was a socially remote thing, like baccarat or clog-dancing'). But though Motion calls him 'a sexually disappointed Eeyore', in fact he seems to have had a pretty average time, comparing lives with Amis ('staggering skirmishes/in train, tutorial and telephone booth') the cause of much of his dissatisfaction. He needed someone to plug him into the fleshpots of Hull, the 'sensitive and worldly-wise Conquest' the likeliest candidate, except that Larkin didn't want Conquest coming to Hull, partly because he was conscious of the homeliness of Maeve. On the other hand, there must have been plenty of ladies who would have been willing to oblige, even in Hull; ready to drop everything and pop up to Pearson Park, sucking off the great poet at least a change from gutting herrings.

I imagine women will be less shocked by the Larkin story, find it less different from the norm than will men, who don't care to see their stratagems mapped out as sedulously as Motion has done with Larkin's. To will his own discomfort then complain about it, as Larkin persistently does, makes infuriating reading, but women see it every day. And if I have a criticism of this book it is that Motion attributes to Larkin the poet faults I would have said were to do with Larkin the man. It's true Larkin wanted to keep women at a distance, fend off family life, because he felt that writing poetry depended on it. But most men regard their life as a poem that women threaten. They may not have two spondees to rub together but they still want to pen their saga untrammelled by life-threatening activities like trailing round Sainsbury's, emptying the dishwasher or going to the nativity play. Larkin complains to Judy Egerton about Christmas and having to buy six simple inexpensive presents when there are rather more people about than usual . . . No doubt in yours it means seeing your house given over to hordes of mannerless middle-class brats and your good food and drink vanishing into the quacking tooth-equipped jaws of their alleged parents. Yours is the harder course, I can see. On the other hand, mine is happening to me.

'And' (though he doesn't say this) 'I'm the poet.' Motion comments, 'As in "Self's the Man", Larkin here angrily acknowledges his selfishness hoping that by admitting it he will be forgiven.' 'Not that old trick!' wives will say, though sometimes they have to be grateful just for that, and few ordinary husbands would get away with it. But Larkin wasn't a husband, and that he did get away with it was partly because of that and because he had this fall-back position as Great Poet. Monica, Maeve and even Betty took more from him, gave him more rope, because this was someone with a line to posterity.

In all this the writer he most resembles – though, 'falling over backwards to be thought philistine' (as was said at All Souls), he would hardly relish the comparison – is Kafka. Here is the same looming father and timid, unprotesting mother, a day job meticulously performed with the writing done at night, and the same dithering on the brink of marriage with art the likely casualty. Larkin's letters analysing these difficulties with girls are as wearisome to read as Kafka's and as inconclusive. Both played games with death – Larkin hiding, Kafka seeking – and when they were called in it got them both by the throat.

Like Kafka, it was only as a failure that Larkin could be a success. 'Striving to succeed he had failed; accepting failure he had begun to triumph.' Not that this dispersed the gloom then, or ever. Motion calls him a Parnassian Ron Glum, and A. L. Rowse (not usually a fount of common sense) remarks, 'What the hell was the matter with him? He hadn't much to complain about. He was *tall*!'

The publication of the *Selected Letters* and now the biography is not, I fear, the end of it. This is early days for Larkin plc as there's a hoard of material still unpublished, the correspondence already printed just a drop in the bucket, and with no widow standing guard packs of postgraduates must already be converging on the grave. May I toss them a bone?

In 1962 Monica Jones bought a holiday cottage at Haydon Bridge, near Hexham in Northumberland. Two up, two down, it's in a bleakish spot with the Tyne at the back and the main Newcastle–Carlisle road at the front, and in Motion's account of his visit there to rescue Larkin's letters it sounds particularly desolate. However, Jones and Larkin spent many happy holidays at the cottage, and on their first visit in 1962 they

lazed, drank, read, pottered round the village and amused themselves with private games. Soon after the move, for instance, they began systematically defacing a copy of Iris Murdoch's novel *The Flight from the Enchanter*, taking it in turns to interpolate salacious remarks and corrupt the text. Many apparently innocent sentences are merely underlined ('Today it seemed likely to be especially hard'). Many more are altered ('her lips were parted and he had never seen her eyes so wide open' becomes 'her legs were parted and he had never seen her cunt so wide open'). Many of the numbered chapter-headings are changed ('Ten' is assimilated into I Fuck my STENographer). Even the list of books by the same author is changed to include UNDER THE NETher Garments.

Something to look forward to after a breezy day on Hadrian's Wall or striding across the sands at Lindisfarne, this 'childishly naughty game' was continued over many years.

As a librarian, Larkin must have derived a special pleasure from the defacement of the text, but he and Miss Jones were not the first. Two other lovers had been at the same game a year or so earlier, only, more daring than our two pranksters, they had borrowed the books they planned to deface from a public library and then, despite the scrutiny of the staff, had managed to smuggle them back on to the shelves. But in 1962 their luck ran out and Joe Orton and Kenneth Halliwell were prosecuted for defacing the property of Islington Borough Council. Was it this case, plentifully written up in the national press, that gave Philip and Monica their wicked idea? Or did he take his cue from the more detailed account of the case published the following year in the *Library Association Record*, that delightful periodical which was his constant study? It's another one for Jake Balokowsky.

At forty-five Larkin had felt himself 'periodically washed over by waves of sadness, remorse, fear and all the rest of it, like the automatic flushing of a urinal'. By sixty the slide towards extinction is unremitting, made helpless by the dead weight of his own self. His life becomes so dark that it takes on a quality of inevitability: when a hedgehog turns up in the garden you know, as you would know in a film, that the creature is doomed. Sure enough he runs over it with the lawnmower, and comes running into the house wailing. He had always predicted he would die at sixty-three, as his father did, and when he falls ill at sixty-two it is of the cancer he is most afraid of. He goes into the Nuffield to be operated on, the surgeon telling him he will be a new man 'when I was quite fond of the old one'. One of the nurses is called Thatcher, another Scargill ('They wear labels'). A privilege of private medicine is that patients have ready access to drink, and it was a bottle of whisky from an unknown friend that is thought to have led him to swallow his own vomit and go into a coma. In a crisis in a private hospital the patient is generally transferred to a National Health unit, in this case the Hull Royal Infirmary, for them to clear up the mess. 'As usual' I was piously preparing to write, but then I read how Louis MacNeice died. He caught a chill down a pothole in Yorkshire while producing a documentary for the BBC and was taken into University College

Hospital. He was accustomed at this time to drinking a bottle of whisky a day but, being an NHS patient, was not allowed even a sip; whereupon the chill turned to pneumonia and he died, his case almost the exact converse of Larkin's. Larkin came out of the coma, went home but not to work, and returned to hospital a few months later, dying on 2 December 1985.

Fear of death had been the subject of his last major poem, 'Aubade', finished in 1977, and when he died it was much quoted and by implication his views endorsed, particularly perhaps the lines

> . . . Courage is no good:
> It means not scaring others. Being brave
> Lets no one off the grave.
> Death is no different whined at than withstood.

The poem was read by Harold Pinter at a memorial meeting at Riverside Studios in the following March, which I wrote up in my diary:

3 March 1986. A commemorative programme for Larkin at Riverside Studios, arranged by Blake Morrison. Arrive late as there is heavy rain and the traffic solid, nearly two hours to get from Camden Town to Hammersmith. I am to read with Pinter, who has the beginnings of a moustache he is growing in order to play Goldberg in a TV production of *The Birthday Party*. My lateness and the state of the traffic occasions some disjointed conversation between us very much in the manner of his plays. I am told this often happens.

Patrick Garland, who is due to compère the programme, is also late so we kick off without him, George Hartley talking about Larkin and the Marvell Press and his early days in Hull. Ordering *The Less Deceived* no one ever got the title right, asking for 'Alas! Deceived', 'The Lass Deceived' or 'The Less Received' and calling the author Carkin, Lartin, Lackin, Laikin or Lock. I sit in the front row with Blake

Morrison, Julian Barnes and Andrew Motion. There are more poems and reminiscences, but it's all a bit thin and jerky.

Now Patrick G. arrives, bringing the video of the film he made of Larkin in 1965, but there is further delay because while the machine works there is no sound. Eventually we sit and watch it like a silent film, with Patrick giving a commentary and saying how Larkinesque this situation is (which it isn't particularly) and how when he was stuck in the unending traffic jam he had felt that was Larkinesque too and how often the word Larkinesque is used and now it's part of the language. Pinter, whose own adjective is much more often used, remains impassive. Patrick, as always, tells some good stories, including one I hadn't heard of how Larkin used to cheer himself up by looking in the mirror and saying the line from *Rebecca*, 'I am Mrs de Winter now!'

Then Andrew Motion, who is tall, elegant and fair, a kind of verse Heseltine, reads his poem on the death of Larkin, which ends with his last glimpse of the great man, staring out of the hospital window, his fingers splayed out on the glass, watching as Motion drives away.

In the second half Pinter and I are to read, with an interlude about the novels by Julian Barnes. Riverside had earlier telephoned to ask what furniture we needed, and I had suggested a couple of reading-desks. These have been provided but absurdly with only one microphone so both desks are positioned centre stage, an inch or so apart with the mike between them. This means that when I read Pinter stands silently by and when he reads I do the same. Except that there is a loose board on my side and every time I shift my feet while Pinter is reading there is an audible creak. Were it Stoppard reading or Simon Gray I wouldn't care a toss: it's only because it's Pinter the creak acquires significance and seems somehow *meant*.

We finish at half-past ten and I go straight to Great Ormond Street, where Sam is in Intensive Care. See sick children (and in particular one baby almost hidden under wires and apparatus) and Larkin's fear of death seems self-indulgent. Sitting there I find myself wondering what would have happened had he worked in a hospital once a week like (dare one say it?) Jimmy Savile.

Apropos Pinter, I thought it odd that in the *Selected Letters* almost alone of Larkin's contemporaries he escaped whipping – given that neither his political views nor his poetry seemed likely to commend him to Larkin. But Pinter is passionate about cricket and, as Motion reveals, sponsored Larkin for the MCC, so it's just a case of the chaps sticking together.

This must have been a hard book to write, and I read it with growing admiration for the author and, until his pitiful death, mounting impatience with the subject. Motion, who was a friend of Larkin's, must have been attended throughout by the thought, by the sound even, of his subject's sepulchral disclaimers. Without ever having known Larkin, I feel, as I think many readers will, that I have lost a friend. I found myself and still find myself not wanting to believe that Larkin was really like this, the unpacking of that 'really', which Motion has done, what so much of the poetry is about. The publication of the *Selected Letters* before the biography was criticized, but as a marketing strategy, which is what publishing is about these days, it can't be faulted. The Letters may sell the Life; the Life, splendid though it is, is unlikely to sell the Letters: few readers coming to the end of this book would want to know more. Different, yes, but not more.

There remain the poems, without which there would be no biography. Reading it I could not see how they would emerge unscathed. But I have read them again and they do, just as with Auden and Hardy, who have taken a similar biographical battering. Auden's epitaph on Yeats explains why:

> Time that is intolerant
> Of the brave and innocent
> And indifferent in a week
> To a beautiful physique
>
> Worships language and forgives
> Everyone by whom it lives;

Pardons cowardice, conceit,
Lays its honours at their feet

Time that with this strange excuse
Pardoned Kipling and his views,
And will pardon Paul Claudel,
Pardons him for writing well.

The black-sailed unfamiliar ship has sailed on, leaving in its wake not a huge and birdless silence but an armada both sparkling and intact. Looking at this bright fleet, you see there is a man on the jetty, who might be anybody.

A. E. Housman, 1859–1936

FOR MY FUNERAL

O thou that from thy mansion,
 Through time and place to roam,
Dost send abroad thy children,
 And then dost call them home,

That men and tribes and nations
 And all thy hand hath made
May shelter them from sunshine
 In thine eternal shade:

We now to peace and darkness
 And earth and thee restore
Thy creature that thou madest
 And wilt cast forth no more.

One thinks of buttons: the buttons on his boots; the buttons on his waistcoat; the four or five buttons on his Norfolk jacket. And in the middle of that funny little round cap, which A. C. Benson likened to a teacake, there was another button. And of course, Housman's heart was buttoned too, and it's an irony – though in the sepulchral congestion of this church hardly a unique one – that Housman's window will look across to the pillar with Epstein's bust of Blake, who was his very opposite and didn't have much use for buttons and who said, 'Damn braces. Bless

An Address given at the dedication of a memorial to A. E. Housman, Westminster Abbey, 17 September 1996 relaxes.' But both were very English – one poet of England's mountains green; the other of those blue remembered hills – and both are now comprehended in this commodious place.

> Into my heart an air that kills
>> From you far country blows.
> What are those blue remembered hills,
>> What spires, what farms are those?
>
> This is the land of lost content,
>> I see it shining plain,
> The happy highways where I went
>> And cannot come again.
>
> *(A Shropshire Lad)*

I'm not sure how comfortable Housman would be, finding himself here. While its popular image is of a cosy place, there is an element of ferrets in the sack about Poets Corner, literary folks not always being the nicest of bedfellows. There are very few classicists here – which would not displease him – one of the few being Gilbert Murray, with whom Housman used to go to music-halls. Hardy he admired, and he was one of the pallbearers at his funeral, but what he would make of Auden, not to mention Dylan Thomas, one doesn't like to think.

Some facts about him:

It was said of him that he looked as if he came from a long line of maiden aunts, and yet this mildness was deceptive. Insults and cutting remarks that occurred to him he stored away, only later allocating them a target – generally one of his academic colleagues.

Were he sitting here now he would be scanning the order of service for misprints and errors of punctuation – a misplaced comma all that would be needed to render the commemoration hollow and offensive.

At Cambridge, where he was Professor of Latin, he took a daily walk and after it would change all his underwear – a habit he shared with Swinburne.

For all his austere appearance he had a liking for rich food, and introduced *crème brûlée* to the menu of Trinity College high table.

He was a pioneer of air travel, flying often and fearlessly to France, where he went on lone gastronomic tours, seeking out in provincial cellars the relics of great vintages.

He shared the same staircase in Whewell's Court in Trinity with the philosopher Ludwig Wittgenstein. Housman had a lavatory in his set, which Wittgenstein didn't. Taken short one day, the philosopher knocked at the poet's door and asked permission to use it. On the grounds that he disagreed with Wittgenstein's philosophical theories, Housman refused. In many respects, though, the two were not unalike – particularly in the austerity of their intellect. Wittgenstein's most famous aphorism is 'Whereof one cannot speak, thereof one must be silent.' And that might well serve as an epigraph for the poetry of Housman, for he is the poet of the awkward silence.

> Shake hands, we shall never be friends, all's over;
> I only vex you the more I try.
> All's wrong that ever I've done or said,
> And nought to help it in this dull head:
> Shake hands, here's luck, good-bye.
>
> But if you come to a road where danger
> Or guilt or anguish or shame's to share,
> Be good to the lad that loves you true
> And the soul that was born to die for you,
> And whistle and I'll be there.
>
> (*More Poems*)

Girls in Housman's poems are really only there as an excuse for the deaths of boys. Women didn't seem to register with him in any department; when he was lecturing at University College, London, his elaborate sarcasm would sometimes reduce his women students to tears, but what really upset them was that the following week Housman couldn't remember whom he had offended or even tell them apart.

Still, the poems are not a masculine preserve, nor should they be, for, though many of them are about love between men, they are all, gender aside, poems about the ineluctable inequity of loving: how there is no symmetry in affection – that one loves more, or differently, truer or longer than the other. They are poems about the difficulty of speaking, about stammering and how hard it is to avow affection; about shyness, which, God knows, is not gender-specific. With their awkward partings and their burden of love undeclared, Housman's characters are not far from Chekhov's, aching to reveal themselves but just a handshake having to say it all. It's what Keats, another of Housman's companions here, called 'my awkward bow'.

> He would not stay for me; and who can wonder?
> He would not stay for me to stand and gaze.
> I shook his hand and tore my heart in sunder
> And went with half my life about my ways.
>
> (*Additional Poems*)

It's fitting that Housman's fenestral neighbour should be Oscar Wilde, from whom he could scarcely have been more different but whose predicament he shared. As a critic has said, from Wenlock Edge one can see as far as Reading Gaol. Wilde was in prison when *A Shropshire Lad* was published, but his friend Robert Ross learned some of the poems by heart and recited them to him there. Housman's boldest poem, though not his best, was occasioned by Wilde's imprisonment, though it

only makes explicit what is implicit in so much of his other
writing:

Oh who is that young sinner with the handcuffs on his wrists?
And what has he been after that they groan and shake their fists?
And wherefore is he wearing such a conscience-stricken air?
Oh they're taking him to prison for the colour of his hair.

'Tis a shame to human nature, such a head of hair as his;
In the good old time 'twas hanging for the colour that it is;
Though hanging isn't bad enough and flaying would be fair
For the nameless and abominable colour of his hair.

Oh a deal of pains he's taken and a pretty price he's paid
To hide his poll or dye it of a mentionable shade;
But they've pulled the beggar's hat off for the world to see and
    stare,
And they're haling him to justice for the colour of his hair.

Now 'tis oakum for his fingers and the treadmill for his feet
And the quarry-gang on Portland in the cold and in the heat,
And between his spells of labour in the time he has to spare
He can curse the God that made him for the colour of his hair.

                                        (*Additional Poems*)

To end, though, Housman as the poet of the English
countryside:

> When summer's end is nighing
>   And skies at evening cloud,
> I muse on change and fortune
>   And all the feats I vowed
> When I was young and proud.
>
> The weathercock at sunset
>   Would lose the slanted ray,

And I would climb the beacon
   That looked to Wales away
   And saw the last of day.

From hill and cloud and heaven
   The hues of evening died;
Night welled through lane and hollow
   And hushed the countryside,
   But I had youth and pride.

And I with earth and nightfall
   In converse high would stand,
Late, till the west was ashen
   And darkness hard at hand,
   And the eye lost the land.

The year might age, and cloudy
   The lessening day might close,
But air of other summers
   Breathed from beyond the snows,
   And I had hope of those.

They came and were and are not
   And come no more anew;
And all the years and seasons
   That ever can ensue
   Must now be worse and few.

So here's an end of roaming
   On eves when autumn nighs:
The ear too fondly listens
   For summer's parting sighs,
   And then the heart replies.

(Last Poems)

Stocking Fillers

Tit for Tatti

We were a small (but distinguished) party that climbed out of Florence that summer morning to call upon Berenson at I Tatti. Logan was there, who was of course Mary Berenson's brother, Bertrand Russell, the mathematical philosopher and brother-in-law of Mary Berenson, Alys, his first wife, her sister, together with Karin Costello, who had married Adrian Stephen and was, of course, the stepdaughter of Berenson. Queen Helen of Romania excepted, we were just another family party.

News of our arrival had preceded us and Berenson was immediately on the defensive and had to be coaxed out from under a large (Renaissance) bed, whither he had retired at our onset. It was twenty years since I had last been at I Tatti, and B.B. looked much older than when I had last seen him. But perhaps that was only to be expected. He must have been eighty at the time of our visit, yet in many not uncharacteristic ways his habits were those of a much younger man. As my wife sat beside him on the couch his hand brushed lightly against her thighs. 'Tactile values,' I heard him murmur. 'How very life-enhancing.' But then, he had such beautiful hands.

We talked for a while about Art, a subject in which he had evinced some interest. But he was not an easy conversationalist as his mind dwelt very much in the past. 'Just fancy,' he said, 'Goethe would have been 190 today, had he lived.' I asked him about people he had known. Did he remember Proust? Or

Wilde? Of Proust he retained a vivid memory, for he had once seen him running down the Boulevard Haussmann, cramming cake into his mouth and shouting at the top of his voice Thomas Hood's poem 'I remember, I remember the house where I was born'.

I wanted to know more. Had he known Queen Victoria? Or Prince Albert? Not well, he said shortly. Or Pitt the Younger, or even Fox? But alas, he could not remember, and seemed weary of such questions. By now the room was beginning to fill up. Hemingway had come in with a trophy of his visit, a tortoise he had shot in the grounds. The Windsors were there, the Duff-Coopers, Kenneth Clark as he then was, and the Berlins, Irving and Isaiah. And there, right at the back, was Toscanini, perched like an organ-grinder's monkey upon the shoulders of the King of Sweden (an eminent archaeologist).

I saw B.B. get hold of C.C. (Cyril Connolly) together with M.M. (Marianne Moore) and M.M. (Margaret Mead) and begin to conduct them upstairs in order to show them his little P.P. (Pablo Picasso). I realized it was time to go. I kissed B.B.'s shaking hand as it reached unerringly into my wife's blouse. 'Ah, B.B.,' I murmured, '*où sont les amitiés amoureuses de ta jeunesse dorée*?' But he was already fumbling with Nancy Cunard.

I remember pausing that sultry summer evening in 1939 as the storm clouds gathered, to look back to the white villa on the hillside. 'Ta ta, I Tatti,' I called, 'Last Bastion of a Vanished World.'

The Pith and its Pitfalls

═══════

Ten years ago, I had some thoughts, first aired on television, about a fairly well-ventilated topic – the writer and his roots.

WRITER: For me, at any rate, speaking personally, writing is a
  kind of love-affair. One is wooing words, isn't one?
  Seducing them on to the page. But it's absolute hell.
  Sheer total hell, like nothing else on earth. Yet I must do
  it.

INTERVIEWER: This is a writer. In mid-career. This is his
  world. He sometimes goes back to the Doncaster he knew
  as a boy, and where his first novel was written.

WRITER: I don't know why I go back. Why did Joyce go back to
  Dublin? Or Brenda to Colchester? I suppose it's a
  question of belonging, really. I love this landscape, the
  hills spreading wide their great thighs, and the pits
  thrusting their gaunt, black fingers into the sky.
    When I die, I don't want to be buried in Ibiza; I shall
  want to be buried here beside my Auntie Cissie Turner,
  who kept us all out of six bob a week. Mind you, six bob
  was six bob in them days. You could buy three
  pennyworth of chips and still have change from sixpence.
    We were all miners in our family. My father was a
  miner. My mother is a miner. These are miner's hands.
  But we were all artists, I suppose, really. But I was the first
  one who had this urge to express myself on paper rather

than at the coalface. But, under the skin, I suppose I'm still a miner. I suppose, in a very real sense, I'm a miner writer. Miners are very strong, very tough, but, in a way, very gentle creatures. But because they're very strong and very tough, they can afford to be very gentle. Just as, being very gentle, they can also be very tough. It's a vicious circle, really, but with all the viciousness taken out of it. I don't know whether you've ever looked into a miner's eyes – for any length of time, that is. Because it is the loveliest blue you've ever seen. I think perhaps that's why I live in Ibiza, because the blue of the Mediterranean, you see, reminds me of the blue of the eyes of those Doncaster miners.

INTERVIEWER: I asked him how success had changed his life.

WRITER: Hardly at all, really. Whereas, before, I would have been sweating away at the coalface in Doncaster, now I'm sweating away in London talking to Peter Hall.

At the moment, I'm working on a novel set entirely in the mind of a cinema usherette during a festival of Anna Neagle films in Fleetwood. This girl is at the crossroads, desperately trying to come to terms with herself and the demands of her career. We explore her reverie, which is broken in on occasionally by the film and by patrons wanting to be shown to their seats. We see how deeply she has identified herself with the personality of Anna Neagle and how tragic the inevitable outcome. It takes in, *en passant*, the eternal themes – love, death, birth – and some of the less eternal ones – her love-hate relationship with the ice-cream girl, for instance. If I can sum up, it's everything Virginia Woolf failed to do, plus the best of Naomi Jacob.

INTERVIEWER: So this is the writer in mid-career, in the mid-sixties – lonely, dedicated, determined.

WRITER: What, above all, I'm primarily concerned with is the substance of life, the pith of reality. If I had to sum up my work, that's it, really. I'm taking the pith out of reality.

I wrote that parody of a television arts documentary ten years ago, and, in the naïvety of what I now realize was my youth (a season that eluded me while it was actually going on), I imagined that, at one stroke, I had disposed of the form. Nobody would dare do it quite like *that* any more. But, of course, they would. And they have. And what is more, they do.

Can there be a slag-heap north of the Trent up which ardent young directors from *Omnibus, Aquarius* or *2nd House* have not flogged their disgruntled camera-crews, in pursuit of that forward-retreating figure, the artist? One half expects to see Ivy Compton-Burnett herself stumbling up the slurry with her reticule between her teeth, on the strength of having spent a fortnight in Halifax when she was five. They would have filmed Proust down a cork-lined coalmine, had he lived. And always, of course, it is art as struggle, art as pain, art as redemption and transcendence. Not art as a relatively easy way of keeping the wolf from the door. Or art as actually quite a nice thing to be doing. Always it must be torture: 'Can you zoom in on the eyes, Brian love? I want to get the pain behind the eyes, if I possibly can.'

Even L. S. Lowry must needs be described as a sad and embittered man because he happened to say, at eighty, that he was not sure there was much point in doing paintings any more. A fairly mild and understandable doubt to creep in at the end of a lifetime of intense production, but wolfishly seized on and brought up at the time of his death to indicate how, such is the tyranny of art, this mild, lovable and industrious man should think his life-work without point. No matter, of course, that a similar doubt might occasionally creep into the mind of someone working for the Leeds Permanent Building Society.

Or that an employee of the Midlands Water Board might occasionally ask himself whether he was doing anybody any good. Or that even the traveller in Skefko ball-bearings goes through an occasional dark night of the soul. No. It is this demon art, demanding so much from its practitioners that they are destroyed. And if one says it is like many another job, that it helps to pass the time and brings home the bacon, you are being shy and self-effacing. Art is pain. It must be. Otherwise it is not fair.

'Look, we have come through' is the stock version of the northern artist's life, though why a childhood in the industrial North or any other outlandish place should be thought to handicap anyone writing novels, poems or plays seems to me to be odd. Rather see it as a stroke of luck. True, if you find yourself born in Barnsley and then set your sights on being Virginia Woolf it is not going to be roses all the way. Or think of Dame Ivy, wrestling with a novel called *A Pit and Its Pitfalls*. But what if one was born in Hendon? How do you wrench life in Basingstoke into the stuff of art? Or Canberra?

The fact is, northern writers like to have it both ways. They set their achievements against the squalor of their origins and gain points for transcendence, while at the same time asserting that northern life is richer and, in some undefined way, truer and more honest than a life of southern comfort.

I suppose, though, I should declare an interest, or maybe confess a lack of one. I was born and brought up in Leeds, in what I suppose must have been a working-class family. When I say 'I suppose', I do not mean that I did not actually notice, but simply that it all seemed perfectly satisfactory to me at the time. I had, after all, nothing to compare it with. My friends lived similar lives in similar houses and talked in a similar way. I was educated at elementary school, then secondary school and, eventually, university, but never with any great sacrifice on anyone's part. If I was deprived, it was only in point of deprivation. Nor did it ever seem that great hopes were set upon me.

What I do recall of my childhood was that it was boring. I have no nostalgia for it. I do not long for the world as it was when I was a child. I do not long for the person I was in that world. I do not want to be the person I am now in that world then. None of the forms nostalgia can take fits. I found childhood boring. I was glad it was over.

There are fashions in childhood as in anything else. A nice, middle-class background was no longer in vogue by the time I started to write. No longer in *Vogue*, either. Early in 1960, when my colleagues and I were writing the revue that was to end up as *Beyond the Fringe*, we were photographed for that magazine. We sped in a large Daimler to North Acton, where the photographer spent some time finding a setting appropriately stark and gritty for the enterprise on which we were to embark. We ended up gloomy and purposeful against a background of cooling-towers and derelict factories.

I have never done one of those filmed portraits I started off by parodying, though the urge is strong. It is always gratifying to be asked to explain yourself, if only because it makes you feel there is, perhaps, something to explain. I admit, too, that from time to time I catch myself slightly overstating my working-class origins, taking my background down the social scale a peg or two. It is a mild form of inverted snobbery, which Richard Hoggart might dignify by calling it 'groping for the remnants of a tradition'. As the man says in the sketch, it is a question of belonging. You would like to think you belong somewhere distinctive, whether it is a place or a class, but you know you are kidding yourself. However, I see that opens up another vast area of humbug and self-indulgence, namely, the writer as rootless man, so I think I had better stop and go home – wherever that is.

Say Cheese, Virginia!

'Dilys!' I called to my wife, who was in an adjacent room, 'You'll never guess what's just plopped through our letter-box!'

'Oh, Duggie!' she cried, with a hint of annoyance, 'I'm in the middle of the cat's tea. What is it, precious?'

'Only Lady Ottoline Morrell's Photograph Album,' I rejoindered. 'Snapshots and photographs of her famous contemporaries photographed by Lady Ottoline herself.' Then I played my trump card. 'With an introduction by Lord David Cecil.'

'Ottoline Morrell,' cried Dilys. 'Teamed with Lord David Cecil! Bugger the cat!' And before you could say Saxon Sydney Turner we were leafing through these magic pages.

Dilys and I have been dedicated fans of Bloomsbury ever since Dilys's dandruff and my appliance finally put paid to the ballroom dancing. Together we travel the length and breadth of the country, spending a fortune on fares simply for the thrill of meeting other Bloomsbury groupies.

Billingham, Prestatyn, Loughborough – scarcely a town of any size but does not boast one, sometimes two, Woolf Clubs. This last Tuesday, for instance, saw us both at Garstang, a fork supper prior to Kevin Glusburn's thought-provoking paper 'Lytton Strachey: An Hitherto Unrecorded Incident in the Slipper Baths at Poulton-le-Fylde'. Need I add that Carrington fans were out in force?

Review of *Lady Ottoline's Album: Snapshots of Her Famous Contemporaries*, with an Introduction by Lord David Cecil (Michael Joseph, 1976).

However, to our text, *le livre des photographies*. Aficionados of Bloomsbury, that much abused postal area, will need no reminding that Ottoline Morrell was the chatelaine of Oxford's Garsington Manor, famed rendezvous of artists, intellectuals and anybody who was anybody who happened to be passing. No Nobel Prize-winner was ever turned away.

Well-to-do and six foot two, Ottoline was never a beauty, but no one can deny she was possessed of a certain dignity. On page 52 is a picture of the painter Henry Lamb. Ottoline was very smitten with Henry, and one afternoon they were in the front room at Garsington and Ottoline was giving Henry a very French kiss when who should walk in but hubby Philip! Ottoline never turns a hair. She just wipes her mouth on her stole and says, 'Henry has a temperature. I was just giving him an aspirin.' As Dilys says, I think quite rightly, 'What Bloomsbury had, Duggie, which we've lost subsequently, was style.'

Here, on page 53, is Katherine Mansfield. This was before she had the shoe shop. Bertrand Russell and Dora on page 60, Dora wearing a lovely frock which Dilys swears is by Adèle of Romford only the index doesn't say; Lord David doesn't seem to have done his homework there. Augustine Birrell, on page 59, is pictured with the economist Maynard 'Sugar' Keynes.

Dilys and I are so genned up on Bloomsbury that Leonard and Virginia Woolf are just like friends of the family to us.

'I don't think Virginia would like that,' says Dilys – 'sitting in front of the fire cutting your toenails.'

'Toenails nothing,' I retort. 'If we had Morgan Forster coming round to his tea, you might invest in a new brassière.'

And so the battle is joined.

Of course it's all fun. That's the good thing about Bloomsbury – no hard feelings.

The young man on page 59 is Frank 'Toronto' Prewitt. Now he is not hard-core Bloomsbury. In fact neither Dilys nor I had any gen on him at all, but we got on to the grapevine (in the person of the indefatigable Pauline Lucas of Huddersfield) and came up with a few facts. Turns out Frank was Canadian, and half Red Indian. Thanks, Pauline, for that valuable info. Aught you want to know about Maynard Keynes's undies, just give us a tinkle.

The other gentleman in the photograph is fellow of King's College, Cambridge, Goldsworthy Lowes Dickinson. Now I don't think I'm treading on anybody's corns when I tell you that what he used to like was his friends to stand on him in their highly polished boots. This used to disturb Goldsworthy Lowes Dickinson's mother, Lois Lowes Dickinson: 'Give over, Goldsworthy' she used to shout. 'Don't let your friends wipe their feet on you. Is that what they teach you at King's College?'

And on page 65 we've got E. M. Forster. What a sweet person. But look at those trousers. Talk about half-mast! I said to Dilys, 'Only connect? The person who measured his inside leg wants his head examining.'

Of course, as you might expect, Ottoline's album is full of pictures of the uncrowned queen of Bloomsbury, our own Virginia Woolf. And you know Virginia, she always seemed to have a cig in her mouth. It's smoke, smoke, smoke. No wonder hubby Leonard called his autobiography *Dunhill All the Way*.

I hope I've told you enough about this book to make you want to rush rush rush to your nearest bookseller. You may be too late. It's already unobtainable in Barnsley, and in Huddersfield they're fighting over copies.

Something, though, bothered me about this book. As Dilys and I scoured its pages I was tormented by a resemblance I couldn't pin down. 'It's Ottoline, Dilys,' I said. 'Who does she take after? She's got a look of somebody.'

And then I remembered.

'Dilys,' I said. 'Cast your mind back. Batley. The Ace of

Clubs. Summer of '67, was it?

'Oh Duggie,' she said. 'Those were the locust years.'

'Yes,' I said, 'Batley. Dusty Springfield live on the stage of the Ace of Clubs. That's who Ottoline is. She's the spitting image of Our Dusty!'

So if Ken Russell's got any ideas about giving Ottoline the treatment then think on, Ken – this is Dusty to a T.

It isn't one for Glenda.

Christmas in NW1

In 1966, after eighteen months' sketch-writing for Ned Sherrin's *Not So Much A Programme* and *The Late Show*, I put together a television comedy series of my own, *On The Margin*, for BBC2. A regular spot in these programmes was *Life and Times in NW1*, a saga of the dilemmas – moral and aesthetic – encountered by a young media couple, the Stringalongs. ('But darling,' I hear Joanna breathe – 'aren't a moral and aesthetic really the same thing?')

Like me, the Stringalongs had taken up residence in Victorian Camden Town and, along with so many other buyers of the still relatively cheap former rooming-houses, had 'knocked through' their basements to make a commodious kitchen/dining-room, shoved the au pair in the attic, and crammed the house with collectable items gleaned from the many junk stalls of the neighbourhood.

Rather sooner in life than they had expected, and not altogether in accordance with their liberal principles, the Stringalongs suddenly found themselves property-owners. These days the process is called gentrification and involves no soul-searching (few troubled consciences in Docklands, I imagine) but we were genuinely uneasy about it – or there would have been no need for jokes – and, though our unease could be handily recycled into resentment of those who bought into the area later than we had, there was a definite sense that we

598

were shoving the indigenous population out.

A nice instance of this came one evening in 1965 when a dinner party in one of our newly knocked-through kitchens was interrupted by an old man, not quite a tramp, who rang at the door asking for the landlady. The last time he had been in London he had rented a room in this house, and was there one available now? It was hard to explain how things had changed, and it was again bad conscience that made us put him in a car and tour round Camden Town looking for a rooming-house that had retained its integrity and was still a going concern.

Later I wrote a sketch based on the incident which we filmed for one of the Sherrin programmes, coarsening it in the process, with the old man becoming quite definitely a tramp and my Mini a Rolls Royce (partly, though, to accommodate the camera-crew) and the social implications nowhere. Still, it was this that gave me the idea for *Life and Times in NW1*, no episodes of which now survive (nor any from *On the Margin* either), as in those days programmes were wiped as easily as dishes, and scarcely had the series been transmitted before it was obliterated.

The Stringalongs, though, did have a continuing life thanks to the late Mark Boxer, who in 1967 was trying out a cartoon strip for the *Listener* and asked if he might develop my characters. The Stringalongs became so associated with Marc's cartoons that I would be reluctant to mention it, feeling as if I'm stealing flowers from his grave, had not he himself always been careful and gracious enough to acknowledge their origins. I only wish I could have invested them with as much life and wit as he did.

This sketch did not appear in the original *On The Margin* but was written for *Tatler*.

Scene: the North London home of Simon and Joanna Stringalong.
Simon is on the telephone. Joanna is on the gin. Neither is happy.

SIMON: She must be out.

JOANNA: A schoolteacher? Where? Stoned, more likely. Let it
    ring.

SIMON: Rock concert, wholefood restaurant . . . she could be
    anywhere – oh *hello*. Is that Jessica's teacher? This is
    Simon, Jessica's father. I'm sorry if I'm ringing at an
    impossibly late hour . . .

JOANNA: It's only half past eight!

SIMON: . . . I just hope I'm not interrupting a candlelit dinner
    à deux. But what I'm ringing about, Miss . . . Pru. (*To*
    Joanna.) She says I've to call her Pru.

JOANNA: Pru!

SIMON: What I'm ringing about, Pru, is that we've just put
    little Jessica to bed in what quite honestly was a very
    distressed condition. She came home from school with
    this letter . . .

JOANNA: Letter!

SIMON: . . . about the nativity play. All pretty straightforward.
    I probably wouldn't even have read it . . .

JOANNA: No.

SIMON: . . . only Joanna, my wife, gave it to me so I idly
    glanced through it to see what part Jessica was playing.
    But I couldn't seem to find her. I couldn't find her *at all*.
    It was only when I got right to the very end, the bottom of
    the bill as it were, that I came across her name: 'Pauline
    Greenwood, Kevin Strutt, Charlotte Hindle and Jessica
    Stringalong – *Icicles*'. Now Joanna, my wife, and I may be
    getting hold of the wrong end of the stick, Pru, and it may
    be these icicles have a sizeable part to play in the action,
    but just judging from the billing it doesn't look like it.

JOANNA: (*snatching the phone*) What the hell do these icicles do,

Pru?

(SIMON *snatches it back*.)

SIMON: Sorry. That was my wife. The icicles do what? They drip. I see. (*To* JOANNA.) They drip.

JOANNA: Oh God.

SIMON: Do they drip verbally? No? Ah.

What is worrying Mrs Stringalong and myself, Pru, is that in last year's show Jessica had quite an interesting part as . . .

JOANNA: A Bethlehem housewife.

SIMON: A Bethlehem housewife.

We hear a great deal about falling educational standards and, as you probably know, Pru, my wife and I only decided to put Jessica into the state system after a great deal of heart-searching and now we find that last year she played a housewife and this year she just drips. What kind of progress is that?

JOANNA: Jessica had a long speech last year. *Tell her.*

SIMON: Last year she had quite a bit to say. What was it, Joanna?

JOANNA: 'You can't move in the middle of Bethlehem. I understand there's not a bed to be had.'

SIMON: 'You can't move in the middle of Bethlehem. I understand there's not a bed to be had.' And there was a bit more (and I'm not sure this didn't come off the top of Jessica's little head): 'Next thing you know they'll be sleeping in the stables.' That was about the gist of it, 'You can't move in the middle of Bethlehem. I understand there's not a bed to be had. Next thing you know they'll be sleeping in the stables.' Quite an interesting part, with a significant piece of plot-laying. Which Jessica did superbly. Very clear. Very sharp. 'You can't move in the middle of Bethlehem. I understand there's not a bed to be had. Next thing you know they'll be sleeping in the stables.'

And this year she just drips.

It's so disappointing.

We, who so much enjoyed her performance last Christmas, were looking forward to this Yuletide to see what she made of a more taxing role. I'm sure she'll make a good icicle . . . a superb icicle. Knowing Jessica she'll throw herself heart and soul into the part.

JOANNA: But why the hell isn't there more of a part for her to throw herself heart and soul into? *Pru.*

SIMON: My wife, again, I'm afraid. She is a bit upset, yes. I imagine from the cast list that you're filling out the gospel story a little. Icicles hanging by the wall, Dick the Shepherd blowing his nail and so on? What about Dick the Shepherd – has that part gone? She'd probably do that rather well. There is a distinction between sucking her thumb and blowing her nail, but only a purist would know the difference.

Dick's gone? Pity.

It probably wouldn't have been a good idea anyway. If she had a part in which she had to suck her thumb and was applauded for it, which knowing Jessica she would be – her Bethlehem housewife stopped the show, I remember – it might undo all the good work done by her remedial teacher. Now who else is there in the gospel story?

JOANNA: (*seizing the phone again*) Who the hell's playing Mary?

SIMON: Sorry. Who is playing Mary as a matter of interest? Tracy Broadbent!

JOANNA: *Tracy Broadbent?* Jesus!

SIMON: Yes, we do know Tracy as a matter of fact. Her mother used to clean for us, after a fashion. I have a vivid memory of Tracy as Herod in last year's offering. The performance was obviously modelled on Wolfit and it was not good, Pru. Tracy Broadbent was not good at all. Way over the top. I frankly couldn't believe in her. No. Tracy's Herod didn't work for either of us.

You also must remember Tracy comes from a one-parent family and that one parent, her mother, goes out to work and therefore won't be able to attend the performance. So, let's face it, from a box-office point of view Tracy Broadbent is a no-no. She is a Big Nothing, Pru. You aren't going to get a line round the block with little Tracy. Whereas with Jessica in the role you'd sell half a dozen tickets on her name alone. Her granny would come with one or two of her more mobile friends, Ulla, our au pair, Ignaz, Ulla's Turkish boyfriend – I mean it's house-full notices practically before the box office opens.

JOANNA: (*bitterly*) Besides, Tracy Broadbent was the one who bit Jessica in the bottom.

SIMON: My wife has just reminded me that Tracy bit little Jessica in the bottom. That's hardly my idea of the Virgin Mary. The Mother of God didn't go round biting people in the bottom, or if she did the gospels are silent on the point. Well I agree, Pru: Tracy probably is disturbed, but do you want a disturbed child in the role of the Blessed Mother? You do? I should have thought calm was the keynote. Oh, I see. Mary is being played as a battered wife. And baby Jesus as a battered baby. So what does that make Joseph?

Gay. I was a fool to ask.

JOANNA: Is he cast?

SIMON: My wife inquires if Joseph is cast. Jessica can play gay, I'm sure. No. She wouldn't object to dragging up. Oh, I see. He's going to be black. Well she could black up. You don't seem to *understand*, Pru: this is an adaptable little girl.

JOANNA: Skip it. Ask her about the Three Wise Men.

SIMON: What about the Three Wise Men? There are no Three Wise Men? Not as such. So what are they? Three Social Workers of Camden. I see.

So as I understand it the story-line is this: Herod is the Chancellor of the Exchequer making swingeing cuts in the social services. This puts battered baby Jesus at risk, but he is rescued by the Three Social Workers of Camden. It's uncanny how it all fits in. The potency of myth, I suppose.

But no role for little Jessica.

Let's get back to this icicle, the part for which you've got her pencilled in. Where is it hanging from? I see.

The bloated body of capitalism.

(JOANNA *shakes her head vigorously*.)

I'm not sure that we are wholly in agreement with that, Pru. Mrs Stringalong's father is quite prominent in wholesale floor coverings and I think we would feel that if little Jessica was going to be involved in making a direct political statement, even if it's only by dripping in silence, then we might well have to keep her at home. No, Pru. We are not just talking about a nativity play. We are talking about the most precious thing in the world, a child's mind.

JOANNA: Scrub it.

SIMON: No, I'm sorry. That is final.

Pickets? What sort of pickets?

(*To Joanna*.) There's a part as a picket.

JOANNA: Are they speaking pickets?

SIMON: Speaking pickets and flying pickets. Like flying ballet, you mean. That sounds wonderful!

What's the scene?

A hotel in Bethlehem. Trust House. Yes, yes. Go on.

604

Catering staff on strike, yes, yes. I get the picture. An
enraged guest, played by Rhoda Allnatt, comes out of the
hotel and says 'What's happened to Peace on Earth,
Goodwill to All Men?' And Jessica shouts out 'Scab!'
That sounds marvellous. What do you say, Joanna?

JOANNA: Does she get billing?

SIMON: Would she get billing at all? I don't think we'd want
anything special . . . 'And Jessica Stringalong as The
Picket' would be ideal.

I don't think you'll regret it, Pru. I mean, all those
exciting things happening and Jessica just stood there,
dripping her little heart out. No, 'Scab!' is better. And if I
know Jessica she'll really throw herself into it. I'll see she
gets down to learning it at the earliest opportunity.
Goodbye.

Going Round

I seldom go to the theatre nowadays. I used to go quite often, but these days I hardly go at all. Plays are very much as they were, so I generally pretend it's the cost. 'Six pounds for a stall. It's highway robbery. I just won't pay it.'

There's a handy Yorkshire expression 'to thoil', a tight little parcel of a verb meaning to be able to afford an object, but to feel guilty spending the money on it. 'I don't dislike that candlewick bedspread,' a Leeds woman might say, 'but I couldn't thoil to pay that price.' I feel the same way about a theatre ticket. And yet, if I'm honest, I know that that isn't what keeps me away.

Is it then the box office, that Checkpoint Charlie one has to negotiate to pass from the cold world of reality into the free world of art? Getting out of Czechoslovakia is a cinch compared with getting into see Penelope Keith. Maybe it's because it's an opening like a kennel, but certainly the staff tend to model themselves on the Dobermann Pinscher, and even those box-office ladies who don't take your arm off at the elbow still have that air of 'We have far better things to do than sell tickets.' Why aren't they gutting haddock for a living, or de-beaking chickens? How come they have missed their way? For these, after all, are the doorkeepers to the halls of art.

I am speaking now of the West End, but things are exactly the same on the fringe – though, of course, different. On my last visit to a fringe theatre the child selling tickets had quite plainly

606

drowned several days before, displaying so little animation she made the corpse of Emily Brontë seem like something out of *No, No, Nanette*.

But 'twas ever thus, and hardened playgoers take all this in their stride. It is part of the magic of theatre. So what else is it that keeps me away? I will tell you.

As one grows (imperceptibly) older, the list of actors and actresses with whom one has worked naturally lengthens: a playwright builds up an acquaintance among actors much as a villain does among fences. So it is seldom nowadays that I settle in my seat, dispose my Dairy Box and consult the cast list without finding that there is at least one member of the company personally known to me. Not that finding the cast list is the falling off a log it used to be. Theatre programmes haven't yet got into two volumes but they're well on the way, and it can't be long before they come with an index. As it is, one searches among advertisements for low-level bathroom suites and clinics anxious to remove one's unwanted hair, and nowhere is there a list of who's in the play. Instead there is a lengthy essay on the issues purportedly touched on in the production. If it's a revival of an unpretentious domestic comedy from the thirties there is likely to be a photomontage of the dole queues to emphasize The Other Side of the Picture, and any play that uses words (and some of them still do) is as like as not accompanied by a thumbnail sketch of the life and loves of Wittgenstein, just to put the critics in the proper frame of mind. And, worst of all, the actors themselves are nowadays encouraged to set down their thoughts not only about their roles but also about Life in General. I love the company of actors, but reading these effusions it's hard not to feel that when they are not required on the stage actors should be kept in their place – namely a locked wardrobe, and ideally with adhesive tape over their mouths.

However, the cast list once located, there one finds, as I say, at least one actor or actress with whom one has worked.

'Oh, *she*'s in it. I filmed with her once. In Hartlepool. Everybody else had gone home for the weekend and we had a curry together on Sunday afternoon.' Memories are made of this. 'And *him*. He was in a play I did in Morecambe. But was he Boring Man at Bus-Stop or Man with New False Teeth in Café?' The precise circumstances are unimportant. What is important is that you know each other. Slightly. Which could be quite pleasant. One ought to be able to sit there, smug in the knowledge that the acquaintance concerned was rather better in your piece than he is being in whatever it is you have just laid out a small fortune to see. You could spend the evening bathed in complacency and self-congratulation – a real tonic in fact – but for one thing, one thought, a thought that haunts you every minute of the play and makes the evening torture.

You will have to Go Round.

To Go Round means to visit an actor or actress in the dressing-room after the performance, and I am not sure whether it is a ceremony peculiar to the theatre. Do clergymen, worshipping in alien churches, feel it incumbent upon them to go round to the vestry afterwards to congratulate the vicar on his conduct of the service? 'The litany had me on the edge of my seat! And that canticle! I was on my knees.'

Are judges in their underpants surprised by colleagues who rush into the robing-room in ecstasies over the summing-up or the severity of the sentence? Do dons go round after lectures? Or footballers after a match? I think not. It only happens in the theatre. And it is one of the great advantages television has over the theatre that with television you never have to go round. Or if you do all you find is dust, an old copy of *Gardeners Weekly* and the vertical hold.

Which is actually slightly more rewarding than what you find at the back of a theatre. If, that is, you can find it. In the West

End stage doors are obscurely situated, often in streets so distant and unrelated to the front of house it almost pays to take a bus.

Like the box-office staff, the stage doorman is seldom a lover of the performing arts. Persons wishing to see an actor or actress are invariably regarded with hostility or regaled with the doorman's memories of Dan Leno. Of the two, the first is preferable.

Once past the stage doorman you start to look for the dressing-room of the actor or actress, and at this point I think I must stop saying actor or actress every time and for conciseness's sake just stick to actor. The gender of actors is in any case a fairly murky area, and they are often pretty vague about the matter themselves. But as you scour the bare stone corridors for the right dressing-room you very soon realize that backstage of most theatres is a hell-hole. It is cold. It smells. And it is a labyrinth. In this labyrinth the situation of a dressing-room varies inversely with the status of the actor. The grander the actor, the lower and therefore nearer the stage his dressing-room will be.

Suppose you are lucky enough to be going round to see one of the principals. You knock on the door and are told to come in. You do so and find someone extremely famous in a state of Considerable Undress. It is a fact that very few leading actors are in the least bit self-conscious. Speaking as one who can scarcely remove his tie without first having a police cordon thrown round the building I find this unselfconsciousness very disconcerting. An actor can conduct a conversation heedless of the fact that he is removing not only make-up and costume but also elastic stockings, corset, even his false teeth. He is standing without a stitch on and you do not know where to look. All in the public view. There will be people who will tell you that since an actor leaves the real person on the stage he regards the rest as so much scaffolding. This is fanciful. It may be that he is just brass-faced. Which is probably why he is an actor.

However, do not be so stricken by the sight of the actor in his smalls that you fail to embark on your compliments as soon as you have thrown open his door. Or, better still, before. Begin your enthusiasm coming down the stairs. Feel unable to control it. Let it bear you bubbling into the room. Because this is what you are here for. You have Come Round. He has performed. It is now your turn.

For that is what it is, Going Round: a performance. A performance which, if it is to convince, has to equal and indeed surpass the one you have just seen on the stage. And whatever you thought, even if you slept through the whole of the second act, you have to go in there saying it was all marvellous. Marvellous. It was *marvellous*.

The actor is properly gratified. But he is also suspicious. Other friends have been round on other nights who have not performed as well as you are doing. So he has his doubts. Actors are very uncertain creatures. And he is particularly uncertain because some well-wishers have gone round and told him he was terrible. Whereas here you are saying he was marvellous. And going on saying it. Which you *must*. Marvellous, marvellous, marvellous.

He stops you. 'But tell me,' he says, 'what did you really think?'

Take *no* notice. And, above all, don't tell him.

'Marvellous, marvellous, marvellous.'

So far, so good: he thinks you thought he was marvellous. But wanting (you fool) to introduce a note of reality into the proceedings and, by implying a criticism of someone else, to enhance how truly marvellous he has been, you add, 'But, I'm curious: what made you choose *this* play. I mean, who persuaded you?' And has the person concerned (though you do not say this), has he been forthwith committed to an institution for the criminally insane?

He is on to you like a rat.

'Why, didn't you like it?'

You instantly realize your mistake and recover.

'*Like* it? I thought it was marvellous. *Marvellous*. You were marvellous. The play was marvellous. I've had a marvellous evening.'

He probes.

'What did you think of her?'

'Her? Well I thought she was marvellous too. She was marvellous.'

This is a mistake. Actors never like praise to go to anyone but themselves. Unless, of course, they are saints. And if they are saints they are in a damp vault below the south aisle after a life of exemplary devotion. If they are actors they are in a damp vault below Shaftesbury Avenue after a not so exemplary performance of *Private Lives*. The damp vault is about all they have in common. But now his face has fallen. You thought she was marvellous. This must mean you did not think he was as marvellous as she was. Or as marvellous as you have been saying he was. It is, after all, well known that there is a limited quantity of marvellousness in the world. And someone else is getting a share. It is tragic.

Some visitors, thinking they have given the actor his due, now make the mistake of switching the conversation to topics other than the play: the furnishings of the dressing-room, for instance; the whereabouts of the loo; the air-conditioning in the theatre or absence of same; the other members of the audience or absence of same. This is fatal. 'They came round', he will go home and say, 'and never said a single word about the play.'

Whereas the single word you have to say is 'marvellous'.

Never stray too far from that.

But I have no room to talk. For on those occasions when I find I have actually enjoyed a play and *want* to go round and make my feelings known, then I invariably say the wrong thing. Or say the right thing, but in such a diffident way (wanting to be thought honest and not one of those frightful people who go round and just say 'Marvellous') that I end up convincing the actor I hated him. Honesty is not easy to perform. Iago's is the longest part, but Othello's is the hardest.

And make no mistake about it: the actor knows. He knows you didn't like him, even if you did. He heard you not laughing. He saw you not crying. He knows, and in his heart of hearts he knows too that nothing you can say will help. The only thing that will help will be doing it again tomorrow night.

But when you have closed the door and thankfully departed he is left. And if he has given a bad performance he knows, and there is nothing one can say. So often Going Round is like trying to comfort the bereaved. Except, when an actor thinks he has died a death, deceased and bereaved are one.

Acknowledgements

The original text of 'The Lady in the Van' was first printed in the *London Review of Books* in 1989, and was published in book form by LRB Ltd in 1990. 'Uncle Clarence' (1986), 'Kafka at Las Vegas' (1987), a number of book reviews ('Gielgud's Achievements', 'Forms of Talk', 'Bad John', 'The Wrong Blond', 'Alas! Deceived') and extracts from the Diaries also first appeared in the *London Review of Books*.

Other articles were first printed in the *Independent on Sunday* ('The Treachery of Books', 1990), the *Listener* ('Tit for Tatti', 1971; 'The Pith and its Pitfalls', 1981) and the *Tatler* ('Christmas in NW1', 1979). 'Leeds Trams' appeared as the Foreword to *Leeds Trams since 1950* (Silver Link Publishing, 1991). 'Say Cheese, Virginia!' (1977) was written for BBC2's *The Book Programme*, and 'Going Round' (1981) for Radio 4.

The Prefaces to Plays were written for the Faber editions. The production diaries (in the section entitled Filming and Rehearsing) for *The Insurance Man* (1985) and for the television plays broadcast by LWT in 1978–9 ('The Writer in Disguise': *Me, I'm Afraid of Virginia Woolf*; *All Day in the Sands*; *One Fine Day*; *The Old Crowd*; *Afternoon Off*) were also included in the Faber editions of the plays.

Index

Norse, Harold 506
North, Lord 362, 387
Norton, Kevin 119
Norwich 286
Not So Much a Programme More a Way of Life (television programme) 119, 598
'Not Waving But Drowning' (Smith) 503
Notes Towards a Definition of Culture (Eliot) xii
Novikov (Russian writer) 237
Novodevichnaya Cemetery, Moscow 234–5
Novy Mir 239
Nuffield College, Oxford 20n
Nunn, Trevor 136

Observer 257, 335
Odeon, the, New York 151, 162, 190
Oedipus (Brook production) 396, 469–70, 471
Old Country, The (Bennett) xiii, 303, 329–30
Old Crowd, The (Bennett) 427–8, 430–34
Old Vic, The, London 467, 468, 482
Oliver! (musical) 398
Olivier, Lord 148, 169–70, 246, 256, 289, 319, 468
Olivier stage, National Theatre, London 341, 342–3
Oman, Julia Trevelyan 317, 395, 405, 407
On the Margin (Bennett) 598, 599
One Fine Day (Bennett) 427, 428
102 Boulevard Haussmann (Bennett) xiv, 74, 262–3
One Over the Eight (Cook) 77
O'Neill, Jamie 68
Ono, Yoko 152, 293
Ophuls, Marcel 251
Orel 236–7, 238
Orton, Joe 12–13, 159, 204, 205, 206, 366, 489–90, 573
Orwell, George 10, 196, 340, 367, 525
Osborne, Charles 260
Osborne, Godfrey 491–2
Osborne, John 320, 489–97
Osborne, Nellie Beatrice 491, 497
Oscar ceremony 174–5
Othello (Shakespeare) 289
Our Lady of Hal church, Camden Town 118

Oxford 227, 299
Oxford Playhouse 396
Oxford Theatre Group 25–6
Oxford University: AB at xii, 20–28, 63, 295, 354–6, 399, 445, 501–2; AB votes for Chancellor 217; flowering of talent in theatre at 20; funding 264; and Hungarian uprising 260; Larkin at 550, 553, 563–4; and *Wind in the Willows* 337; Wykehamists at 249
Oxford University Dramatic Society (OUDS) 23, 396, 467, 468

Pagan Papers (Grahame) 344
Palace Theatre, Manchester 407
Palach, Jan 266
Palin, Michael 76, 180
Palladino, Don 299, 307
Palm Court Orchestra 16
Palmer, Geoffrey 378, 457
Palmer, J. Wood 495
Palmer, Tony 246
Pares, Richard 354, 355–6, 365
Park Prewett Hospital, Basingstoke 327
Parker-Bowles, Camilla 269
Parkinson, Lord (Cecil) 179
Pascoe, Richard 136
Passchendaele 35
Paxman, Jeremy 298
Pears, Peter 506
Peck, Gregory 293
Peel, Clarence (AB's uncle) 29–30, 31, 33–5, 200
Peel, Evelyn (AB's great aunt) 30
Peel, Kathleen (AB's aunt) x, 30, 34
Peel, Lemira (Myra; AB's aunt) x, 30, 34
Peel, Mary Ann (AB's maternal grandmother) 15, 29, 30, 32, 252
Penshurst Place, Kent 189–90
'People in the Sun' (Hopper) 503
Perfume (Suskind) 227–8
Perkins, Anthony 281
Philby, Kim 239, 329, 332–3
Philip, Prince, Duke of Edinburgh 422–3
Philip Larkin: A Writer's Life (Motion) 548–76
Philosophical Investigations (Wittgenstein) 523
Pickles, Vivian 209, 452

628

INDEX